SPECIAL EDUCATIONAL NEEDS

Praise for the first edition

This book is timely. I hope that it will be very widely read.
Baroness Mary Warnock

An excellent book which gives comprehensive information on a wide range of issues. I think that it will prove very useful for students.
Sian Howie, Department of Education, Chichester University

This is a very comprehensive and well written book which provides an excellent backdrop to the dilemmas facing practitioners working with children identified as having special needs. In addition to providing perspectives from practice, it raises contentious issues for discussion about the social model of disability and inclusion.
Patricia Shaw, Institute for Learning, Hull University

It truly is a multidisciplinary publication, which addresses the complexities and vagaries that exist within the educational system.
British Journal of Occupational Therapy

Edited by two experts in the field of special educational needs, Lindsay Peer and Gavin Reid, this book makes an immediate impact as being worth reading.
REACH: Journal of Special Needs Education in Ireland

This book brings together a wealth of information and guidance from professionals in the field of Special Educational Needs ... ideal for anyone wanting to become a specialist teacher.
Shobha Coutinho, *Dyslexia Review*

Essential reading for all teachers in mainstream and special schools.
Alison Silby, School of Sport and Education, Brunel University

This is an essential resource for anyone working in education at all levels. I have used information from this to apply to learners along with using the information to guide and support fellow colleagues.
Karen Gray, Teacher Education, Simply-Training

An absolutely fabulous book, absolutely essential for all SEN teaching.
Georgina Spry, Education, Chester University

This book brings together a wealth of information and guidance from professionals in the field of Special Educational Needs. The emphasis is on linking together the broad area of special educational needs. This is achieved through fascinating contributions from experts in a range of fields including, amongst others, Sheena Bell and Bernadette McLean discussing key issues pertaining to teacher training best practice and Steve Chinn on dyscalculia. This book is ideal for anyone wanting to become a specialist teacher.
Jan Seabourne, Training and Educational Development, Dyslexia Action

SPECIAL EDUCATIONAL NEEDS

A Guide for Inclusive Practice

2ND EDITION

Edited by

LINDSAY PEER AND GAVIN REID

Los Angeles | London | New Delhi
Singapore | Washington DC

Los Angeles | London | New Delhi
Singapore | Washington DC

SAGE Publications Ltd
1 Oliver's Yard
55 City Road
London EC1Y 1SP

SAGE Publications Inc.
2455 Teller Road
Thousand Oaks, California 91320

SAGE Publications India Pvt Ltd
B 1/I 1 Mohan Cooperative Industrial Area
Mathura Road
New Delhi 110 044

SAGE Publications Asia-Pacific Pte Ltd
3 Church Street
#10-04 Samsung Hub
Singapore 049483

Editor: Jude Bowen
Assistant editor: George Knowles
Production editor: Tom Bedford
Marketing manager: Lorna Patkai
Cover design: Wendy Scott
Typeset by: C&M Digitals (P) Ltd, Chennai, India
Printed and bound in Great Britain by Ashford
Colour Press Ltd

Library of Congress Control Number: 2015943585

British Library Cataloguing in Publication data

A catalogue record for this book is available from the British Library

ISBN 978-1-4739-0453-8
ISBN 978-1-4739-0454-5 (pbk)

At SAGE we take sustainability seriously. Most of our products are printed in the UK using FSC papers and boards. When we print overseas we ensure sustainable papers are used as measured by the PREPS grading system. We undertake an annual audit to monitor our sustainability.

Contents

About the Editors

Dr Lindsay Peer CBE, Educational and chartered psychologist, international speaker, author and expert witness, Lindsay is widely recognised as an expert in the range of specific learning difficulties, Special Educational Needs (SEN) and mainstream education. In 2002, she was appointed CBE for services to education and dyslexia. In 2011, she was awarded the Outstanding Lifetime Academic Achievement Award by the British Dyslexia Association (BDA). She is Patron of GroOops, a charity dedicated to creating an emotionally healthy dyslexia-aware world. She has lectured extensively as a keynote speaker internationally since the late 1980s and advises governments, trade unions, policy makers, lawyers, adults, schools, psychologists, therapists and parents.

She is an Associate Fellow and chartered scientist of the British Psychological Society and a Fellow of both the International Academy of Research in Learning Disabilities and the Royal Society of Arts. She is a member of the Association of Child Psychologists in Private Practice and of the Association for Child and Adolescent Mental Health (ACAMH). She is registered to practise with the Health and Care Professions Council (HCPC). She has been a keynote speaker in the UK, the USA, India, Sweden, Belgium, Finland, Israel, Iceland, Norway, Italy, Spain, Majorca, Greece, South Africa, Botswana, Swaziland, Cyprus, the Czech Republic and the Netherlands.

She held the posts of Education Director and Deputy CEO of the BDA until 2003. She has many years' experience as a teacher, teacher trainer and Special Educational Needs Coordinator. She has published a considerable body of material both theoretical and practical, and published the first ground-breaking book linking 'glue ear' with dyslexia. She assesses children, students and adults facing challenges in learning.

Her email is lindsay@peergordonassociates.co.uk and her website is www.peergordon associates.co.uk.

Dr Gavin Reid is an international consultant and psychologist with consultancies in Canada, the UK, Europe, the Middle East, Asia and Australasia. He was Visiting Professor at the University of British Columbia in Vancouver, Canada, in the Department of Education and Counseling Psychology and Special Education in 2007 and 2010.

He is an ambassador for the Helen Arkell Dyslexia Centre in the UK and is also a consultant for the Child Enrichment Medical Centre in Dubai, the Centre for Child Evaluation and Teaching (CCET) in Kuwait and for the Institute of Child Education and Psychology Europe (ICEPE).

He is also currently a consultant to the Open University in the UK and co-founder and director of the Red Rose School for children with specific learning difficulties in St Annes on Sea, Lancashire, UK. He is a visiting educational psychologist to organisations and schools in Switzerland, the UK, the Middle East, Asia and Egypt.

He was formerly senior lecturer in the Department of Educational Studies (formally Department of Special Education), Moray House School of Education, University of Edinburgh, from 1991 to 2007. He has written 28 books on learning, motivation and dyslexia and lectured to thousands of professionals and parents in 75 countries. He has also had books published in Polish, Italian, Arabic, Hebrew, French, Chinese and Slovak. He is an experienced teacher with over ten years' experience in the classroom and has held external examiner appointments at 18 universities worldwide for PhD and masters' courses.

His email is gavinreid66@gmail.com and his is website www.drgavinreid.com

About the Contributors

Jane Abdullah is an occupational therapist and qualified in 1984. She worked in adult neurology, before specialising in paediatrics, first in Manchester, UK, before moving to South Hertfordshire as Head of Paediatric Occupational Therapy Services. In 1998, she left the NHS to work as an independent therapist. Currently she provides occupational therapy interventions within both special and mainstream schools. She is experienced in preparing independent reports for Special Educational Needs and Disability Tribunals (SENDIST) and is currently involved in establishing a new occupational service within a specialist independent school in Hertfordshire.

Elias Avramidis is a Senior Lecturer at the Department of Special Education, University of Thessaly, Greece, and Honorary Research Fellow at the Graduate School of Education, University of Exeter, UK. His research (covering primary, secondary and tertiary settings) mainly focuses on examining the theory and practice of inclusive education. He has published on topics such as teachers' attitudes towards inclusive education, the social impacts of inclusive education, and the methodological issues surrounding research in the field of special and inclusive education.

Judy Barrow qualified in 1995 in the specialties of community development, education and person centred counselling, and has worked on overseas projects as a researcher in special needs. She has been a member of Tourette Scotland's support and research team since 2000. She works as an advocate and advisor for special education needs families. She has written articles on spectrum disorders and devised support packages for specific issues such as dealing with court cases connected with Tourette syndrome.

Sheena Bell is a Senior Lecturer in SEN and Inclusion at the University of Northampton, UK. She is a member of the CeSNER team (Centre for Special Needs Education and Research) and leads courses for specialist teachers and assessors of dyslexia/specific learning difficulty (SpLD). She has taught in a range of settings in the UK and abroad, from prisons to primary schools.

Steve Chinn, Fellow of the Royal Society of Arts, received a PhD in applied physics in 1967. In 1986, he founded a school for dyslexics. It received Beacon School status and the Independent Schools Association's 'Award for Excellence'. Steve's many research papers, articles and books include the award-winning *The Trouble with Maths*. He was editor of *The International Handbook of Dyscalculia and Mathematical Learning Difficulties* (2015) and has an on-line series of teaching videos. He chairs the BDA's dyscalculia group and is a member of the Economic and Social Research Council Peer Review College. He has lectured in 30 countries and is Visiting Professor at the University of Derby.

Margaret Crombie has many years' experience as a teacher, specialist, author, lecturer and manager. She has lectured in the national and international contexts, being a keynote speaker at many events. She currently works part-time as a member of the Open University's Associate Membership of the BDA panel and is a member of the BDA's Accreditation Board. She has researched into language learning and dyslexia, and has investigated dyslexia in the early years. She chaired the working group which developed the Addressing Dyslexia Toolkit (www.addressingdyslexia.org).

Jill Duncan is the Director of the Victorian Deaf Education Institute of the Department of Education and Early Childhood Development, Victoria, Australia. She has held academic and senior leadership positions in Australia and the USA. Her research focuses on the social capital of adolescents who are deaf or hard of hearing and the pedagogical practices of teachers of the deaf. She has received many national and international awards for her services to children with a disability.

David Evans is Associate Professor of Special Education at the Faculty of Education and Social Work, University of Sydney, Australia. He is convenor of the special and inclusive education designation at the faculty. He teaches postgraduate classes in the area of curriculum design and evidence-based practices; he supervises research students across a range of topics. His research interests include designing curriculum to include all students, and promoting early numeracy to meet the needs of students with additional learning needs.

Janet Farrugia has worked as a Speech and Language Therapist since 1980 and has an MSc in Human Communication. She worked for the NHS for seven years and then independently. From 1996–2012 she was the director of a paediatric speech and language therapy clinic. Since 1996 she has carried out numerous assessments for special educational needs tribunals. In 2011 she contributed to the book *Towards a Positive Future: Stories, Ideas and Inspiration from Children with Special Educational Needs, their Families and Professionals* (O'Keefe, 2011).

John Friel is a leading barrister, dealing with issues arising out of education and special educational needs. This includes disability rights and Equality Act practice and procedure. John has been involved in many leading cases and has worked with a number of politicians on changing the law. The original 1993 Act leading to independent tribunals arose from a Private Member's Bill drafted by John. He has been responsible for some of the amendments in the 2014 Children and Families Act which help those with special needs and disabilities. He has won leading cases in the House of Lords, Court of Appeal, High Court and the Upper Tribunal. A number of the cases are landmark cases. He regularly lectures and has published numerous articles. He is in the relevant directories of specialist barristers, such as Legal 500 and Chambers. He is also a trustee of education charities. He himself is dyslexic.

Neville Harris is Professor of Law at the University of Manchester, UK. He researches and teaches in areas of public law, including education law. He is the editor of the *Education Law Journal* and an advisor to the Department for Education for its Review of Arrangements for Disagreement Resolution. His books include *Resolving Disputes about Educational Provision* (with Sheila Riddell) (Ashgate, 2011), *Education, Law and Diversity* (Hart, 2007) and *Challenges to School Exclusion* (RoutledgeFalmer, 2000).

Keith Holland was a leading UK optometrist who founded the British Association of Behavioural Optometry. He and his wife **Clare Holland** met whilst studying optometry at City University, London, UK, and the couple went on to have four children. In 1989, Keith and Clare founded the UK's first optical practice specialising in visual factors which affect learning in Gloucestershire, which Clare has continued to run since Keith's death following a brave fight against cancer in 2014.

Colin Lannen is Co-founder (1997), Director, Principal of the Lancashire Centre for Specific Learning Difficulties (Sp.L.D.), including the Red Rose School. He is an international speaker and teacher trainer on Sp.L.D., including ASD and Learning Styles. He was Joint Project Co-ordinator of an EU Lifelong Learning Grundtvig Project: Sp.L.D. Roadmap for Teacher and Adult Learner Training; 2011–13 and is currently Project Co-ordinator EU Erasmus Plus Project: to introduce Sp.L.D. teacher training in Europe, three years 2014–17.

Sionah Lannen is a Chartered Educational Psychologist; is Co-founder, Director and Head Teacher of the Red Rose School (SpLD); has worked in teacher training/educational psychology in Canada, the Middle East and Europe; and is Co-director of a major EU project (2014–17) – introducing and developing SpLD teacher training.

Bernadette McLean is Principal at the Helen Arkell Dyslexia Centre, UK. She serves as an External Verifier for OCR (the Oxford, Cambridge and RSA Examination Board) and is a member of the BDA's Accreditation Board. She regularly contributes to regional, national and international conferences. She has served in the Department for Education and Skills working party, reviewing assessment of dyslexic students in higher education, and has contributed to a dyslexia project for a number of local authorities, and co-authored two books for the Target Series for Teachers, published by Barrington Stoke. She serves as a member of the SpLD Assessment Standards Committee, the national committee which promotes standards in assessment of dyslexia and is a founder member of the Dyslexia SpLD Trust. Bernadette regularly lectures across the world, in the UK, Australia, Norway, Cyprus and South Africa, and has recently edited a handbook for the Learning Differences Convention in Australia.

Brahm Norwich is Professor of Educational Psychology and Special Educational Needs at the Graduate School of Education, University of Exeter, UK. He was previously Professor of Special Needs Education at the Institute of Education, University of London. He has worked as a teacher and a professional educational psychologist, and has researched and published widely in these fields. His recent books have been: *Special Needs: A New Look* (with Mary Warnock) (Continuum Books, 2010), *Addressing Tensions and Dilemmas in Inclusive Education* (Routledge, 2013) and *Lesson Study: Making a Difference to Teaching Pupils with Learning Difficulties* (with Jeff Jones) (Continuum, 2014).

Janet O'Keefe is a speech and language therapist, expert witness and parent to a child with special educational, medical and social needs. Janet supports parents across the UK, giving expert evidence to SENDIST and in the High Court in London, Edinburgh and Belfast. She is also the organiser of an annual conference, Towards a Positive Future: Stories, Ideas and Inspiration from Children with Special Educational Needs, their Families and Professionals – www.senconference.co.uk.

Jo-Ann Page is a clinical supervisor working with children and young adults with autism spectrum disorders throughout the Middle East. She has in excess of 20,000 hours of field experience and a background of working with difficult-to-place teenage foster children in the UK. Jo-Ann has a diagnosis of dyslexia and dyscalculia and two children of her own with similar diagnoses.

John Ravenscroft is the current Editor in Chief of the *British Journal of Visual Impairment* (http://jvi.sagepub.com). He is also Director of the Scottish Sensory Centre (www.ssc.education.ed.ac.uk). John has an international reputation in the education of children with visual impairment, and has published and presented at many international conferences on topics such as the changing profile of childhood visual impairment, haptic language learning, transition and the expanded core curriculum.

Sheila Riddell is Director of the Centre for Research in Education Inclusion and Diversity at the University of Edinburgh, UK. She was previously Director of the Strathclyde Centre for Disability Research at the University of Glasgow, UK.

Artemi Sakellariadis is a teacher who taught in special schools for many years before devoting her time and energy to the development of more inclusive education. She is currently Director of the Centre for Studies on Inclusive Education (CSIE), a national charity that works to promote equality and eliminate discrimination in education, and chairs the Equality, Diversity and Inclusion advisory group which is part of the national expert subject advisory groups (ESAG).

Tony Sirimanna is a senior consultant at Great Ormond Street Hospital for Children, London, UK, and is currently the lead clinician for the Audiology, Audiological Medicine and Cochlear Implant Department, with over 25 years of experience in audiovestibular medicine. His main areas of interest are general paediatric audiology, newborn hearing screening, bone-anchored hearing aids, auditory processing disorder, auditory neuropathy spectrum disorder and aetiology of hearing loss. He is the Founder Chair (currently a member) of the British Society of Audiology Auditory Processing Disorder Interest Group.

Richard Soppitt is a psychiatrist and national expert on attention deficit hyperactivity disorder and autism spectrum disorder. He has lectured nationally and has 15 publications, including two book chapters. He is an expert witness in SEN litigation and also has personal experience of parenting children with special educational needs. He has been a regional Royal College of Psychiatrists Representative and Honorary Senior Lecturer in Birmingham and Kent. He currently works in East Sussex in the NHS with Early Intervention in Psychosis and Youth Mental Health.

Susan Strachan has two teenagers with dyslexia and runs a dyslexia-specific youth club XdysleX through her local Aberdeen branch of Dyslexia Scotland (DyslexiaScotlandNorthEast. org.uk). This youth group has produced a DVD about dyslexia from a youth perspective, with dramatisations of their experiences. Both Susan and the group have also contributed to dyslexia magazines and presented at the national Dyslexia Scotland Education Conference (2013). Susan is a highly experienced additional support needs practitioner, trainer and registered occupational therapist. She co-founded and runs an independent charity SensationALL.org.uk.

Iva Strnadová is Associate Professor of Special Education at the School of Education, Faculty of Arts and Social Sciences, University of New South Wales, Australia. She is also an honorary staff member at the University of Sydney, Faculty of Education and Social Work. Her research interests include lifespan transitions experienced by people with disabilities, well-being of people with developmental disabilities (intellectual disabilities and autism) and their families, women with intellectual disabilities, and mobile learning for people with developmental disabilities.

Charles Weedon taught maths and English before becoming a learning support teacher, and Principal Teacher of Learning Support in Fife, UK, then Tayside, then George Watson's College in Edinburgh, where he is now the school's educational psychologist, as well as practising independently as an educational psychologist. He is an Associate Fellow of the British Psychological Society, and is registered as an educational psychologist with the HCPC. He is an Honorary Fellow of the University of Edinburgh. His research interests are identifying and understanding barriers to learning.

Elisabet Weedon is Deputy Director of the Centre for Research in Education Inclusion and Diversity (CREID) and Senior Research Fellow at the University of Edinburgh, UK. Her main research interests are in the area of education and social justice. She has worked on a range of projects relating to disability and dispute resolution in the area of additional support needs. She was co-author of *Improving Disabled Students' Learning in Higher Education* (RoutledgeFalmer, 2009)

Kevin Woods is Professor of Educational and Child Psychology at the University of Manchester, UK, where he works as the Director of Initial Professional Training in Educational Psychology. He has been a practitioner educational psychologist for 25 years and his research and practitioner interests include the developing role of educational psychologists, student assessment needs, dyslexia and attachment.

Foreword

It is more than 30 years since the 1981 Education Act which introduced the concept of Special Educational Needs (SEN) into legislation, and, as the editors of this volume say, a lot has changed in that time. It is therefore useful to have an updated account of how things stand at the present time. It is useful that the educational provision for children with special needs in Scotland is included in the book, because it is undoubtedly true that the provision in the rest of the UK has been considerably influenced by the Scottish ideal of additional support wherever a need is identified. Indeed, the last government claimed that the abandonment of the 'Statement', and its replacement by a Plan for each individual child for whom an assessment is made, constitutes the radical change of policy, so strongly recommended by the House of Commons Select Committee on Education as long ago as 2005. Whether the change is radical enough, and how it is working in practice for the education of children with identified needs, is what we can discover from the new edition of this book. One of its great merits, shared by the earlier edition, is that the contributors tend to deal with specific difficulties that children experience, and how these are identified, and how the needs they give rise to are met. Too often, policy makers tend to think of children with SEN as one homogeneous group, for whose difficulties there can be one appropriate solution. Any teacher working on the ground knows that this is not the case.

Yet, although the contributors are helpfully specific, there is a common thread running throughout the book. This is the tension between two general philosophical views of educational disability. On the one hand, there is the policy which recognises the reality of the differences between individual children, and seeks by whatever means to meet the needs that arise from these differences; on the other hand, there is the policy which emphasises the sameness of all children as members of one institution, a school or college, and of society outside either, and believes that it is the failure of society or of institutions within it to adapt that exacerbates or even causes the difficulties that some people experience. It is right that this clash of ideologies should make itself felt in a volume such as this, for it is real, and must be recognised. If possible, it must be resolved, not in the lecture hall or the groves of academe, but in the classroom. And the comparative freedom afforded to academies makes this a real possibility. It is salutary to have a chapter devoted to parents, who sometimes, but not always, know what is best for their children, and many of whose battles with their local authority are heroic. For one thing is certain: however much parents may contribute to the assessment of their children, relations between them and local authorities will continue to deteriorate as long as the financial cuts continue. So, although this is in many ways an optimistic book, the scene onto which the new edition is launched is far from cheerful.

Baroness Mary Warnock, 2015

Acknowledgements

It was a privilege for us to be asked to edit a second edition of this book. We would sincerely like to take this opportunity to thank all the authors for their excellent contributions. Each one leads a busy professional life and we recognised this when we invited them to contribute again to this edition. As in the first edition, we have been overwhelmed by the enthusiasm and the quality of responses from each of the contributors. Each one is very well recognised in the field and is held in the highest esteem. We are therefore fortunate that they have been able to collaborate with us in developing the idea and the chapters for this book.

We are also delighted that, in many of the chapters, there has been a great deal of professional collaboration. It is this synthesis of ideas that makes the chapters rich and informative. We are also indebted to those who wrote single-author chapters. Given their professional schedules, this is greatly appreciated.

We have again tried to embrace a breadth of perspectives in this book, with new chapters on Down syndrome and the treatment of autism. But, as readers will appreciate, special educational needs is a large area with a range of views, principles and practices. We recognise that we have not covered every aspect of special educational needs; we have done the best we can in a book this size.

To this end, we are indebted for the advice we received from the editorial team at Sage Publications and, of course, for the quality chapters we received from the authors. We are also grateful to the parents of children with special educational needs who shared their personal stories.

We are sure that the book will be widely appreciated. This will confirm that the efforts of all have been well worthwhile and we hope this second edition will serve as a valued reference and guide for practice for all professionals in a range of fields related to special educational needs. We hope you will benefit from this book as much as we have enjoyed the editing process.

Lindsay Peer and Gavin Reid, 2015

Acronyms and Abbreviations

ABA	applied behaviour analysis
AD	autistic disorder
ADD	attention deficit disorder
ADHD	attention deficit hyperactivity disorder (or hyperkinetic disorder)
APD	auditory processing disorder
AS	Asperger disorder
ASD	autistic spectrum disorder
ASHA	American Speech-Language-Hearing Association
ASL	additional support for learning
ASN	additional support needs
ASNTS	Additional Support Needs Tribunals for Scotland
BDA	British Dyslexia Association
BMI	Body Mass Index
BPS	British Psychological Society
BSA	British Society of Audiology
BSED	behavioural, emotional and social difficulties
CAMHS	Child and Adolescent Mental Health Services

CAPD	central auditory processing disorder
CBT	cognitive behavioural therapy
CDC	(US) Centers for Disease Control
CHSS	Centre for Health Services Studies
CNS	central nervous system
CREID	Centre for Research in Education, Inclusion and Diversity
CSIE	Centre for Studies on Inclusive Education
CSP	coordinated support plan
CVI	cortical visual impairment
CWDC	Children's Workforce Development Council
DCSF	Department for Children, Schools and Families
DCD	developmental coordination disorder
DDA	Disability Discrimination Act 1995
DES	Department of Education and Science
DfES	Department for Education and Skills
DH	Department of Health
DISS	Deployment and Impact of Support Staff project
DSA	Disabled Students' Allowance
DSM	*Diagnostic and Statistical Manual of Mental Disorders*
EBD	emotional and behavioural difficulties
ECG	electrocardiogram
EHRC	Equality and Human Rights Commission
ESRC	Economic and Social Research Council
FM	frequency modulated
FTT	First Tier Tribunal
HCPC	Health and Care Professions Council
HESC	Health Education and Social Care Chamber
ICD	International Classification of Diseases and Related Health Problems
IEP	individualised educational plan/programme
LEA	Local Education Authority
MLD	moderate learning difficulties
NEAT	non-exercise activity thermo-genesis
NIMH	(US) National Institute of Mental Health
NOSI	non-obscene socially inappropriate (behaviour)
NPD	National Pupil Database
NRC	National Research Council
OCB	obsessive–compulsive behaviour
OCD	obsessive–compulsive disorder
ODD	oppositional defiant disorder
Ofsted	Office for Standards in Education

OME	otitis media with effusion
OT	occupational therapy (therapist)
PAIG	Paediatric Audiology Interest Group
PCHI	permanent congenital hearing impairment
PDD	pervasive developmental disorder
PDD–NOS	pervasive developmental disorder – not otherwise specified
PPS	Parent Partnership Service
PTA	pure tone audiometry
QTVI	qualified teacher of the visually impaired
RCSLT	Royal College of Speech and Language Therapists
RCT	randomised controlled trial
RNIB	Royal National Institute for the Blind
SaLT	speech and language therapy
SASC	SpLD Assessment Standards Committee
SEN	special educational needs
SENCo	Special Educational Needs Coordinator
SENDA	Special Educational Needs Disability Act 2001
SENDIST	Special Educational Needs and Disability Tribunal
SENT	Special Educational Needs Tribunal
SIGN	Scottish Intercollegiate Guidelines Network
SLCN	speech, language and communication needs
SLI	specific language impairment
SLT	speech and language therapy (therapist)
SMD	sensory modulation difficulties
SpLD	specific learning difficulty
TA	teaching assistant
TS	Tourette syndrome
UNESCO	United Nations Educational, Scientific and Cultural Organization
VA	value added
VI	visually impaired/visual impairment
VIS	Visual Impairment Scotland
VOCA	voice output communication aid

Introduction

Gavin Reid and Lindsay Peer

The field of Special Educational Needs (SEN) has undergone significant changes in the last quarter of a century and also since we wrote the Introduction for the first edition of this book in 2011. These changes in policy, perception and practice have interwoven with national and international movements in inclusion, equity issues and social equality. It has been a vigorous and dynamic area for research. There is no doubt that the Warnock Report of 1978 and the subsequent legislation that followed the report paved the way for the ensuing developments that have had a considerable impact on policy and practice. As Baroness Warnock indicated in her Foreword for this book, it is more than 30 years since the 1981 Education Act introduced the concept of special educational needs and much, of course, has changed since then. Much has been achieved in the public recognition of children's rights and those of families, with successive legislation – such as the Children and Young People (Scotland) Act 2014 and the *Special Educational Needs and Disability Code of Practice: 0 to 25 Years* (Department for Education and Department of Health, 2014) in England. One of the key breakthroughs in developing student advocacy is integral in the *SEN Code of Practice*, which now covers students aged 0–25 and emphasises the responsibility of schools to assess and support all learners who are not making progress in line with national expectations. This means that schools, colleges, universities and other training providers now need to develop the skills of specialists within their teams. As Bell and McLean point out (Chapter 10), as part of this provision Education and Health and

Care Plans will focus on those children or young people with SEN who need education provision – and that trained specialist teachers are likely to be key players in the process. This places responsibility on the shoulders of the providers and requires that all needs must be catered for by health and education providers.

These factors relating to recent legislation are a key feature in this new edition and it is also the intention of this edition to update the many different strands of SEN from different perspectives – research, policy, practice, parents and the students themselves. It might be argued that one of the features of this field has been the polarisation of perspectives: a continuum of views still exists on best practice for children with SEN. It is not the purpose of this book to become enmeshed in this debate but, rather, to highlight the range of perspectives through the individual chapters included in the book. Some of the chapters strongly promote an inclusive perspective, while others focus on the individual student and their individual needs. For example, there is a new chapter on the treatment of autism which involves a one-on-one specialist intervention (see Chapter 18).

We are also mindful of the needs of parents – parents have been and will continue to be a crucial element in the development of practice and have also influenced policy. Parents are considered throughout and, indeed, the concluding chapter of this book is written from parents' perspectives.

The thrust of this book has therefore been to promote both inclusive provision and to highlight individual needs. Additionally, we have attempted to be as comprehensive as possible and, although we have not been able to include individual chapters on all the existing syndromes, we hope that the general principles and strategies promoted throughout the book will in fact impact on serving the needs of all children, whatever their specific needs.

The scenario of SEN is established in Chapter 2 with Riddell, Harris and Weedon discussing recent changes in England and Scotland, and particularly the issues of categories and resources. The field of SEN has not been without tensions and these are also brought out in this chapter. The authors refer to the tensions as 'dilemmas of difference' – in particular, the tensions between parental expectations and education authority policy and practices. They pinpoint in particular the broader definition encapsulated in the Education (Additional Support for Learning) (Scotland) Act 2004 (the ASL Act) and the tensions that have arisen from this. As they indicate:

> there continues to be a commitment to the over-arching categories of SEN and ASN [additional support needs], with their implicit emphasis on the commonality of all pupils with difficulties in learning, but at the same time there are moves towards the use of fine-grained categories, suggesting a focus on pupil differences.

In many ways, this encompasses the dilemmas that practitioners have to deal with and that parents try to work within. The authors of this chapter support their analyses with several excellent case studies. They also update the debate through reference to recent legislation, for example they note that under the post-September 2014 statutory framework for special educational needs in England, Children and Families Act 2014, mediation has been given a significant push through a requirement that an appeal can only proceed if the parent or the young person him/herself if over compulsory school age, has been notified by the local authority of their right to mediation. They also note that the balance of power in the direction of parents is now more evident, making professionals far more accountable and opening up accessible appeal routes. They suggest that this process is arguably advanced further by the Children and Families Act 2014.

Their chapter is followed by that of Avramidis and Norwich, who discuss the research implications of recent philosophical trends and developments in special education and who present the main research paradigms operating in the field, along with their methodological implications. They also discuss the current trend towards evidence-based practice and the implications of this for policy and the perception of disability in society. They consider the distinction between the medical and social models of disability and the implications of this for research methodology. They also review the trends towards inclusive education and the controversial view that inclusion is a product of social–political arguments, rather than a product of empirical evidence. The agendas that drive research methodology have to be considered. They maintain that:

> more often than not, researchers in the field are firmly attached to particular paradigms or knowledge culture stances, thus reproducing sterile debates about the supremacy of particular methodologies (e.g. the scientific/quantitative vs interpretive/qualitative divide).

They argue that, for research progress to take place, a convergence and consensus about research methodologies and philosophical positioning is necessary.

The theme of inclusion is developed in Chapter 4 by Sakellariadis, who discusses the issues and dilemmas that an individual with SEN experiences. She provides a rationale for inclusion and how it may benefit all people. The chapter questions many of the situations that many take for granted and raises the need to focus more on the support needs of people with SEN. She suggests that inclusion needs to be sufficiently resourced and effectively managed.

The potential impact of the social model of disability is also developed by Weedon in Chapter 5. Weedon, utilising his practical experience, argues that:

> in the early years [of education] there is an almost instinctive inclusivity, and acceptance of a social model of disability. Each child is seen as a unique individual, and it is part of the teacher's craft to find ways for all the individuals in the class to share the learning. In the later years, where subject specialization and formal assessment gain increasing influence, there is an increasing dynamic towards a bio-medical categorization, an allocation of learners to categories in order that they might better fit the demands of the examination system.

This statement questions current thinking in areas of differentiation and in particular the examination system. Weedon argues that:

it can only be helpful to generate a dynamic that seeks continuously and imperceptibly, to shift our perceptions a little further away from a bio-medical model whenever it is possible to do so, towards a socially constructed model; and continuously and imperceptibly away from a view that attributes a deficit to an individual, and to look instead at the barriers we construct within the environment.

This statement has considerable current relevance to the direction of SEN and has implications for all syndromes and support services.

This theme is followed in Part II of the book, which focuses on perspectives from practice. In Chapter 6, O'Keefe and Farrugia highlight the importance of language for all areas of development – educational, social and emotional. They discuss the 'at risk' factors that predispose children to speech and language difficulties and highlight the path for assessment and access to professional services. They also provide pointers for teachers on what signs can reveal the possibility of speech and language difficulties, but they also present detailed analyses of diagnostic criteria and the range and different types of speech and language difficulties, including stammering and stuttering, voice disorders, attention, listening skills, receptive and expressive language and the cognitive factors associated with language learning. This is a practical chapter, well-grounded in current theory, and has a host of useful ideas for teachers and other professionals.

Sirimanna in the following chapter looks at auditory processing difficulties, providing a detailed and comprehensive overview of this area, which is gaining increasing attention from parents and professionals. It is likely this attention will be heightened with the publication of DSM-5 in 2013, which appears to be promoting a co-morbid approach to the field of learning disabilities, with some categories being subsumed under a more general label (www.dsm5.org/ProposedRevisions).

Sirmanna's chapter is followed by a discussion on the role of occupational therapists by Abdullah. In this chapter, Abdullah describes the role of the occupational therapist and focuses in some detail on developmental coordination disorders and dyspraxia. She provides some excellent practical examples and a range of theoretical explanations. She also discusses the very real issues that can be associated with developmental coordination disorder, such as attention difficulties, social difficulties and the challenges in behaviour and in acquiring academic skills.

In Chapter 9, Keith and Clare Holland discuss vision and learning, explain the importance of visual aspects of learning and describe the nature of the visual difficulties that can prevent learning. There is a solid theoretical underpinning to this discussion and they discuss the research from a balanced and insightful perspective. The authors provide in this chapter some excellent suggestions for teachers. They also provide some words of caution when they say that: 'these issues [visual difficulties] may well be misdiagnosed as being part of a specific learning difficulty, and thus treated through additional tuition, when what is really required is an appropriate visual assessment and treatment'.

The theme of dyslexia is tackled by Bell and McLean in Chapter 10, who focus primarily on good practice in training specialist teachers and assessors of people with dyslexia. This chapter is set against the backdrop of increased commitment for the training of dyslexia specialists (e.g. the Rose Report of 2009) and concern about the effectiveness of training in the field of SEN. They quote the comment from the national Lamb Inquiry in England (2009) that:

> we cannot currently be confident that those who are charged with making a judgement about the quality of the education provided for pupils with SEN can do so on the basis of a good understanding of what good progress is or how best to secure it.

Bell and McLean provide an indication of the types of skills needed by specialist teachers in dyslexia, including training in assistive software. They indicate that: 'crucial to any teaching programme for learners with dyslexia is that it should be individualised. Trainees learn how to direct learning programmes towards students' particular strengths and weaknesses [to develop individualised programmes].' In this chapter, the authors remind us of the importance of obtaining first-hand evidence from course participants themselves on their needs and how far the courses meet these needs. On a positive note, the authors conclude by saying that 'this is an optimistic period for training dyslexia specialists', but they also state a concern, indicating that 'as we move into the future it is vital that economic constraints do not prevent us from training the teachers and assessors who can make such a difference to the lives of people with dyslexia at all levels'.

The theme of dyslexia is followed up by Crombie in Chapter 11 on literacy. In this chapter, Crombie looks at the current and future contexts for literacy and literacy difficulties. She highlights the comments from a state-of-the-nation document (Jama and Dugdale for the National Literacy Trust, 2012), which indicates that one in six people in the UK are struggling with 'literacy' and have 'literacy levels below what would be expected of an eleven-year-old'. Crombie discusses different types of literacy and the nature of literacy difficulties and also highlights considerations for identifying literacy difficulties. She refers to both theory and practice and also highlights the importance of school/parent partnerships and the increasingly important role of technology in the digital age and its implications for the future of literacy.

In the following chapter, Chinn focuses on mathematics difficulties and, in particular, dyscalculia. He utilises research in effective learning to highlight the implications of this for students with mathematical difficulties. He explains the key factors that contribute to dyscalculia, the prevalence of dyscalculia, diagnostic criteria and strategies for intervention.

This is followed – in Part III on syndromes and barriers – by a new chapter on Down syndrome by Iva Strnadová and David Evans, both based in Australia and who have an excellent grip on the international field of special educational needs; and then by an updated chapter on attention deficit hyperactivity disorder (ADHD) by Soppitt. There is a great deal of information available on ADHD and much of this can present a confusing picture for professionals and parents. There are a number of entrenched theoretical positions and divergent views on intervention approaches. In this chapter, Soppitt indicates that aetiology is usually multi-factorial, involving interaction between bio-psychosocial factors. He also outlines interventions, including educational, parenting, cognitive behavioural therapy and pharmacological. He suggests that, although multi-agency working in relation to ADHD raises challenges, it must be fully considered as the way forward in order to prevent young people with ADHD from becoming socially excluded.

The theme of visual impairment is addressed in Chapter 15 by Ravenscroft. In this chapter, Ravenscroft presents an insightful overview of the field of visual impairment and discusses current research on the profile and prevalence of children with visual impairment living in the UK. He also discusses strategies to empower the mainstream teacher in relation to addressing the needs of children with visual impairments, and explores the balance between academic attainment and independent daily living skills. As he indicates, it is important for children with visual impairment to fulfil their academic potential but, equally, it is crucial that they can engage with the world around them!

The issue of sensory impairment is continued by Duncan, who summarises the central issues related to students with hearing loss, which include hearing technology, communication modality, literacy and cognition. She also provides practical strategies for supporting classroom teachers with students with a hearing loss. Using a range of case studies, she highlights how important transitional periods can be effectively handled and the struggles and challenges that parents, children and professionals face. As she indicates, students with hearing loss 'have diverse learning needs. They, along with their families and classroom teachers, require specialist practitioner support in order to maximise learning potential.' This is in line with the other areas previously highlighted, such as visual impairment, attention difficulties, dyslexia and dyscalculia, which are, in many ways, priority areas for training agendas.

The current interest in autism and autistic spectrum is vast and diverse. It is challenging to incorporate the range of research and perspectives in this fast-changing and developing field into one succinct chapter. In Chapter 17, Reid, Lannen and Lannen deal with this by focusing on the challenges and the issues. They provide a background to understanding autistic spectrum disorder (ASD), as well as an overview of the criteria for identification and assessment. They also note the main areas of research and provide a range of strategies for intervention. Moreover, they look at the characteristics and identification procedures of ASD, as well as the impact of ASD on classroom learning. They comment on the range of programmes available for young people with ASD and provide pointers for consideration in relation to these programmes, as well as reviewing the issue of co-existence and overlap. In addition, we include a new chapter by Page on applied behavioural analysis (ABA) and how it can be successfully implemented. This is a valuable addition to this book.

This chapter is followed by a chapter on Tourette syndrome by Barrow, who provides a clear explanation of the nature and the impact of Tourette syndrome. Arguably, this is one of the most misunderstood syndromes and there are educational as well as social implications to this. As Barrow points out, in some cases the behaviours of the child with Tourette syndrome can be misunderstood as disruptive, attention seeking and mischievous. They provide a clear explanation of Tourette syndrome and also indicate the range of overlapping disorders. They quote Davidson, who once said that:

> growing up with Tourette syndrome was very difficult. I believed I was different from everyone else due to the involuntary symptoms. I often felt unloved and unwanted by family and friends and felt that I was being a hindrance to the rest of my family.

Reading statements like this can be heart-wrenching and it is this which should persuade educators to pursue educational and training programmes for all those who may have to deal with children and adults with Tourette syndrome. Barrow indicates the range of current issues in relation to supporting people with Tourette syndrome. She writes that:

> the ability to explain and allow for the condition varies from school to school, and particularly at primary school level, where disruptive behaviour has more of an impact. Some schools prefer to leave it to the parents to resolve what they see as 'problems' with Tourette syndrome. Yet, practice shows that the school is the best place to explain the condition for teachers and pupils to resolve a way forward.

This is an important message for educators.

In the final part of the book, the theme is 'working together', which follows on from many of the messages contained in the previous sections. In Chapter 20, Woods focuses on the role of educational psychologists and particularly the wide-ranging and dynamic roles that now need to be adopted by educational psychologists. This is followed by a chapter by Friel on the legal issues which often gain prominence when working together is not possible, positive or effective. It is important to be aware of the legal implications.

The final chapter of the book is on parental perspectives, which have also been considered in many of the individual chapters. In this chapter, Reid, Peer, Strachan and Page indicate that the field of special educational needs can be a confusing one for professionals but can be fraught for parents. All the contributors of this chapter are parents and have experienced the frustration and the anxieties of supporting their child through the educational journey, and have had to deal with a range of circumstances and experiences in education and in society.

As Baroness Warnock indicated in the Foreword, it is fitting to end this book on SEN with parental perspectives. Parents have contributed a great deal to this book and, in fact, have contributed to the direction and impact of provision for SEN in almost every country. They have a key role to play and, together with informed and trained educators, may bring further positive changes in perceptions and working practices in dealing with the range of challenges associated with SEN. This may lead to an enhanced understanding of the needs of children and their families which ultimately will benefit schools, society, families and individuals.

References

Department for Education (DfE) and Department of Health (DH) (2014) *Special Educational Needs and Disability Code of Practice: 0 to 25 Years*. London: DfE.

Jama, D. and Dugdale, G. (2012) *Literacy: State of the Nation: A Picture of Literacy in the UK Today*. London: National Literacy Trust.

Lamb, B (2009) *Report to the Secretary of State on the Lamb Inquiry Review of SEN and Disability Information*. London: Department for Children, Schools and Families (DCSF).

PART I

Policy, Practice and Provision

Special and Additional Support Needs in England and Scotland

2

Current Dilemmas and Solutions

Sheila Riddell, Neville Harris and Elisabet Weedon

Learning objectives

This chapter will help readers to:

- Gain a greater understanding of current SEN and ASN policy in England and Scotland and of recent policy changes
- Problematise SEN and ASN categories, since some may enable children to access additional resources, whilst others have a stigmatising effect
- Understand the tensions between parental power and local authority accountability

Introduction

This chapter will identify a number of current issues stemming from policy and practice in the field of Special Educational Needs (SEN) (England) and Additional Support Needs (ASN) (Scotland). In particular, we focus on dilemmas in two specific spheres: (1) the use of categories and their implications for resourcing, inclusion and the curriculum; and (2) the balance of power between parents and professionals. The chapter is structured around the idea of dilemmas, involving a choice between a number of courses of action, none of which is entirely unproblematic (Norwich, 2008: 3). The first dilemma turns on tensions between a universalist approach, which involves treating everyone the same, and a recognition of difference approach, which may involve positive action for some groups with a view to rectifying existing inequalities. The upside of the universalist approach is that it emphasises common aspirations for all; however, the downside is that it may underplay the disadvantages faced by some children as a result of their impairment combined with their social, political and economic context. Additional resources to fund reasonable adjustments, as well as efforts to bring about attitudinal change, may be necessary in order to level the playing field. Similarly, an approach based on the recognition of difference has upsides and downsides, potentially justifying the allocation of additional resources, but also stigmatising and justifying social marginalisation. These tensions, referred to as dilemmas of difference (Minow, 1985; Phillips, 1999), are not peculiar to education but are common to many social policy arenas and equality strands. Before looking more closely at particular areas where dilemmas of difference arise, we first describe changes within the SEN and ASN policy fields over the past three decades.

The second broad dilemma which we highlight in this chapter concerns the balance of power between parents and professionals. Whilst there has been a move towards the empowerment of parents with a view to delivering personalised services in education and other social policy fields, there are clearly both upsides and downsides to this approach. On the one hand, individual parents may argue that they are in the best position to determine their child's needs and appropriate provision; but on the other hand, local authorities may argue that they should retain the ultimate power in decision-making since they can act as impartial arbiters in the allocation of scare resources. These dilemmas are explored more fully below.

This chapter draws on findings from an ESRC-funded research project entitled *Dispute Resolution and Avoidance in Special and Additional Support Needs* (RES-062–23–0803). The research used a mixture of methods, including: analysis of policy and official statistics; approximately 50 key informant interviews; a questionnaire survey of local authorities in England and Scotland; a survey of parents (Scotland only); a survey of Parent Partnership Services (England only); and case studies of 49 parents in dispute with the local authority in six authorities (three in England and three in Scotland.

Special and additional support needs policy in England and Scotland

For about a decade following the publication of the Warnock Report (DES, 1978), the English and Scottish systems moved along roughly parallel lines, both using the umbrella term 'special educational needs' to define those children having greater difficulty in learning than their peers. In both countries, local authority officers and education professionals retained major decision-making powers with regard to resources and additional support, with a commitment to work 'in partnership' with parents. However, during the 1990s, there was increasing divergence as the Conservative Government's educational reforms were implemented more forcefully in England, promoting managerialism and consumerism. Following the Education Act 1993, all English state schools were obliged to have regard to the *Code of Practice on the Identification and Assessment of Special Educational Needs* (DfE, 1994) and publish information about their policies for children with special educational needs. This legislation also established the Special Educational Needs Tribunal (SENT) to resolve disputes between parents and the local authority. Under the Special Educational Needs and Disability Act (SENDA) 2001, the tribunal's remit was broadened to include disability discrimination complaints against schools. At the same time, local authorities were placed under a duty to make arrangements aimed at the avoidance of, or reduction in, disagreements between authorities or schools and parents. As explained in the *Code of Practice*, dispute resolution mechanisms were to include independent mediation. Under the new post-September 2014 statutory framework for special educational needs in England, in the Children and Families Act 2014, mediation is being given a significant push through a requirement (for many categories of case) that an appeal can only proceed if the parent or the young person him/herself if over compulsory school age, having been notified by the local authority of their right to mediation, participates in it or indicates to the independent person contracted to provide advice on mediation that he or she does not wish to pursue mediation.

Major reform of ASN policy and practice in Scotland took place a decade after the 1990s reforms of the English SEN system described above. The Education (Additional Support for Learning) (Scotland) Act 2004 (the ASL Act) broadened the definition of additional support needs to include children who had difficulty in learning as a result of social problems as well as disabilities, and put in place a raft of measures to increase parental rights and local authority accountability. The legislation also abolished the record of needs and established a new document, the Coordinated Support Plan (CSP), to record the needs of children with multiple, complex and enduring difficulties, requiring significant multi-agency support. However, as we explain below, local authorities have been very reluctant to open CSPs, preferring to use a range of non-statutory plans. Finally, the ASL Act put in place a number of new dispute resolution mechanisms, outlined in a new Code of Practice (Scottish Executive, 2005). The operation of dispute resolution mechanisms in England and Scotland is discussed below in the section on parents and accountability. Public recognition of children's rights in Scotland is set to advance through the Children and Young People (Scotland) Act 2014. This legislation provides the statutory underpinning of the *Getting It Right for Every Child* programme and, among other things, places a duty on Scottish Ministers to promote public understanding and awareness of the rights of children in line with the principles of the United Nations Convention on the Rights of the Child. The new legislation places a duty on local authorities to open a Child's Plan for children and young people whose well-being is compromised, and requires health and social work to cooperate with education in delivering services. The ASL legislation is not being repealed, and the Child's Plan is intended to incorporate existing statutory plans such as the CSP and the Looked After Child's Plan.

The identification and categorisation of children with special and additional support needs: The dilemma of universalism versus difference

In both England and Scotland, about 20% of children are identified as having special or additional support needs (see Figure 2.1).

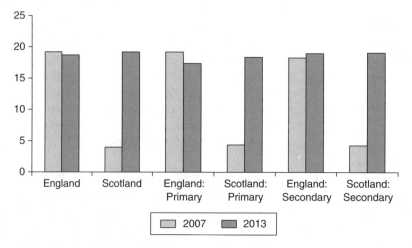

Figure 2.1 Pupils with SEN (England) and ASN (Scotland) in publicly maintained mainstream schools as percentage of all pupils by school type, 2007 and 2013. *Source*: England – Riddell et al. (2012)/DfE (2007/2013); Scotland – Scottish Government (2008/2013).

Over recent years, there has been an apparent significant increase in the proportion of children with additional support needs identified in Scotland, due to the fact that children with a wide range of plans are now counted, whereas previously the label was restricted to children with CSPs and/or IEPs (Individualised Educational Plans/Programmes). In England, there has been a small decline in the proportion of pupils identified as having SEN, due to concerns about over-reporting. The English statistics include children with a statement of special educational needs (replaced, from September 2014, by the 'education, health and care plan' under the 2014 Act) as well as those under 'School Action Plus' (i.e. receiving help from external support sevices) or 'School Action' arrangements (receiving help from school-based practitioners, such as teaching assistants, the class teacher and the learning support teacher) (both categories being replaced under the new Code of Practice (DfE and DoH, 2015) by a single school-based framework of 'SEN support').

As we noted above, whilst efforts have been made to replace individual categories of difficulty with one over-arching category, this has proved very difficult for a variety of reasons. First, parents of children with particular types of difficulty, such as autistic spectrum disorder, and voluntary organisations representing these groups, have campaigned for official recognition of specific categories. The Government has also found it useful to request local authorities to audit the incidence of particular types of difficulty, partly as an accountability mechanism, but also to inform funding decisions. In England, the practice of gathering data by type of difficulty, which was abandoned following the Warnock Report, was re-instated in the 1990s. In Scotland, despite official support for the broad conceptualisation of additional support needs, local authorities have always been required to provide information to the government on numbers of children with particular types of difficulty. Figures 2.2 and 2.3 provide information on the categories of difficulty used in England and Scotland.

In England, about three-quarters of pupils identified with SEN come from 4 of the 12 categories included in the classification. The largest of these 4 categories includes young people with moderate learning difficulties (MLD) and the second largest consists of pupils with behavioural, emotional and social difficulties (BESD). Pupils with speech, language and

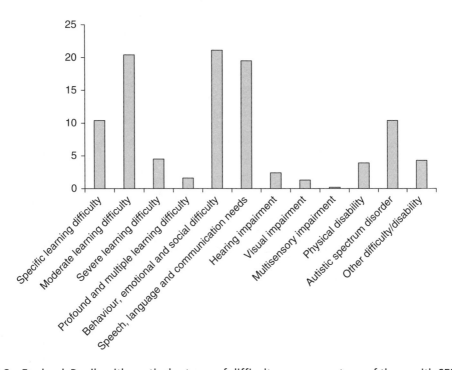

Figure 2.2 England: Pupils with particular types of difficulty as a percentage of those with SEN. *Source*: DfE (2013). *Note*: The category SEN includes pupils on School Action Plus and those with statements. The category will change as education, health and care plans replace statements of need.

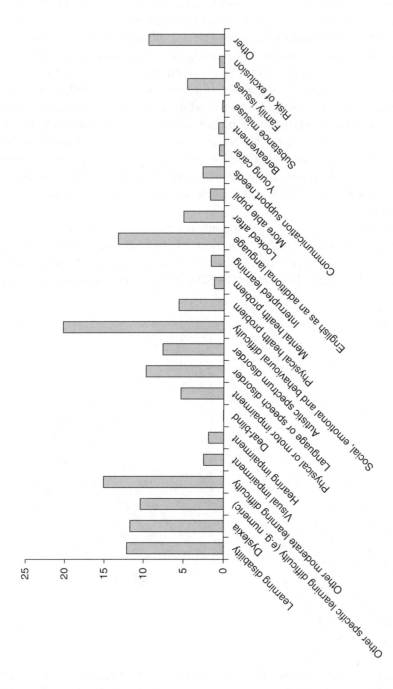

Figure 2.3 Scotland: Pupils with particular types of difficulty as a percentage of all pupils with ASN (pupils with more than one support need are recorded in all relevant categories). *Source:* Scottish Government, 2013.

communication needs (14%) and those with specific learning difficulties (12%) account for just over a quarter of SEN pupils (see Figure 2.2).

A large and growing number of categories of difficulty (24 in total) are used in Scotland (see Figure 2.3). New categories introduced include looked after, interrupted learning, bereavement and more able pupil. As in England, the largest two categories are social, emotional and behavioural difficulties (SEBD) and moderate learning difficulties. About a fifth of all types of difficulty recorded are identified as SEBD, with a greater number of children counted as having SEBD than MLD. There has been more than a fourfold increase in the use of this category since 2007, raising questions about whether social and family trauma is increasing, or whether more children are having needs identified. Dyslexia, other specific learning difficulties and physical and motor impairments each account for 7–9% of recorded difficulties. Visual and hearing impairments continue to be low-incidence disabilities, although even these normative categories appear to be expanding.

However, as noted above, recognition of particular types of difficulty is not necessarily an unalloyed good. As shown in Figures 2.4 and 2.5, there is a strong association between the identification of SEN/ASN and social deprivation (measured by free school meals entitlement), particularly for some types of difficulty such as social, emotional and behavioural difficulties (BESD in England) and moderate learning difficulties. These labels are rarely sought by parents, and are often applied by schools to children whom they find difficult to include. Tomlinson (1985) made a useful distinction between normative difficulties, such as sensory or physical impairments, which can be measured against an agreed norm, and non-normative difficulties, such as social, emotional and behavioural difficulties, whose identification is much more reliant on professional judgement. Non-normative categories, which are also by far the largest, are very strongly associated with social deprivation, whereas lower-incidence normative difficulties are only loosely associated with social deprivation. These patterns of identification raise questions about whether children benefit from being identified as having SEN/ASN, or whether, as argued by Armstrong (2003), this identification is a form of stigmatisation which is used to justify their poor school attainment and exclusion from the labour market. It is worth noting that in both England and Scotland, statutory plans, which provide stronger guarantees of additional resources and greater rights to challenge local authority decisions, are disproportionately allocated to children in more socially advantaged areas, again suggesting that for children in more deprived areas, the dis-benefits of being identified as having certain categories of need may outweigh the benefits (see Riddell and Weedon, 2015).

Overall, the use of categorical systems illustrates tensions between discourses of sameness and difference. There continues to be a commitment to the over-arching categories of SEN and ASN, with their implicit emphasis on the commonality of all pupils with difficulties in learning, but at the same time there are moves towards the use of fine-grained categories, suggesting a focus on pupil differences. Some of these categories have gained currency as a result of pressure from parents and voluntary organisations (e.g. autistic spectrum disorder and dyslexia), whilst others have entered the lexicon as a result of professional pressures (e.g. mental health problems). Whilst normative difficulties are identified across the social

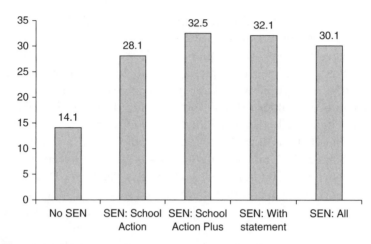

Figure 2.4 Percentage of pupils known to be eligible and claiming free school meals with/without SEN, 2013. *Source*: DfE, 2013.

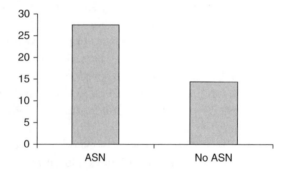

Figure 2.5 Pupils registered for free school meals with/without additional support needs, 2013. *Source*: Scottish Government (2014), requested data.

spectrum, children identified as having non-normative difficulties are concentrated in socially deprived areas. This suggests a dilemma of categorisation, where some labels may have negative educational consequences, whilst others may bring benefits in terms of releasing additional resources without social stigmatisation.

The use of particular categorisation systems has implications for placement of children with special and additional support needs and the type of curriculum provided. The dominance of generic terminology, with its implicit discourse of commonality rather than difference, means that in England and Scotland there has been a presumption of mainstream placement. Around 1% of the total school population in Scotland and England are placed in special schools and units. Similarly, the expectation has been for all children to access a common curriculum with appropriate modifications (Lewis and Norwich, 2005). In England, the statutory requirement in relation to inclusion – in place since 2001 – has required that provision is made in mainstream schools in the case of any child without a statement, unless the local authority is not meeting the cost; and this is to continue under the 2014 Act in the case of a child without an education, health and care (EHC) plan. However, the increasing use of fine-grained categories of details, and the growing influence of voluntary organisations representing particular categories of difficulty, such as autism, has led to growing pressure for more differentiated curricula and teaching methods, potentially increasing the emphasis on children's differences rather than their sameness.

Parents and accountability: The dilemma of participative democracy versus bureaucratic accountability

As noted earlier, a recurring dilemma in the field of special and additional support needs concerns the balance to be struck between local authorities and parents in determining the distribution of scarce resources, particularly in the field of special and additional support needs when particular types of provision may be extremely costly, with consequences for other service users. A theme of the modernising government agenda, which has been developed by successive governments, has been an emphasis on personalised rather than standardised services, in which consumers have a far greater say over the nature of services provided. This has partly been achieved by the growth of a mixed economy of welfare, with the voluntary and private sectors increasingly being funded by government to deliver services which were previously provided by the state, a move deprecated by some social policy critics (e.g. Ball, 2007), but sometimes welcomed by service users, such as the recipients of direct payments (Pearson, 2006). The growth of consumerism through the exercise of voice has been a further element in the personalisation agenda. In the field of special and additional support needs, along with many other spheres of education, parental power has traditionally been limited, with local authority and professionals retaining control over resource allocation decisions (Harris, 2007). The establishment of a number of dispute resolution mechanisms, since 1993 in England and 2004 in Scotland, was intended to increase opportunities for parents to challenge local authority decisions. Our ESRC-funded research project on dispute resolution in special and additional support needs (RES-062–23–0803) explored the use and perceptions of different ways of resolving disagreements (tribunal,[1] mediation and, in Scotland only, adjudication), and questioned whether

---

[1]In England, the separate Special Educational Needs and Disability Tribunal (SENDIST) – which was the former SENT with the disability discrimination jurisdiction added – no longer exists but its jurisdiction is now located within the Health, Education and Social Care Chamber (HESC) of the First-tier Tribunal (FTT). In Scotland, the Additional Support Needs Tribunals for Scotland (ASNTS) deal with references relating to CSPs only, although the Equality Act 2010 extends its remit to disability discrimination cases.

these had succeeded in altering the balance of power between parents and local authorities. The tribunals in this field exist to hear appeals from parents of children with special educational needs/additional support needs in cases of disputes on specific grounds between parents and local authorities/schools. They also deal with complaints of disability discrimination towards children arising in schools. The outcomes of the tribunals are legally binding, unlike the outcomes from mediation; in Scotland, the remit of the tribunal was limited to children with CSPs, but has been extended to certain types of placing requests.

A questionnaire survey conducted with all local authorities in England and Scotland found that they tended to hold negative views of the tribunal. In England, almost half of them did not think that the tribunal made a positive contribution to dispute resolution. They did not object to the right of appeal per se, but they believed that it encouraged parental challenges to decisions or intensified disputes. They regarded the process as irksome and likely to go against them. Some thought that the tribunal was overly generous towards parents in the degree of procedural flexibility it allowed them, for example regarding time limits, and in helping some secure a high level of resources for their child, skewing resource allocation. In Scotland, there were concerns about the tribunal's rather adversarial hearing and variable approach. Parents, on the other hand, whose views were explored through case studies, were generally positive about the tribunal, seeing the process as somewhat stressful but feeling that, in general, fair outcomes were achieved.

Figures 2.6 and 2.7 illustrate the use of the SEN/ASN tribunals in England and Scotland.

Since its inception, use of the English tribunal has proved popular, although there have been fewer appeals from parents living in areas of social deprivation and those from minority ethnic backgrounds. In Scotland, use of the ASNTS has been much lower (only

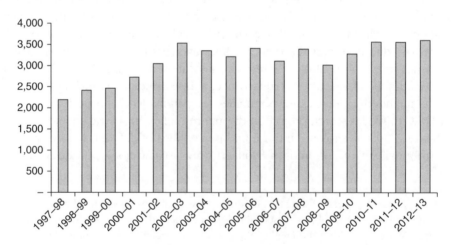

Figure 2.6 Total number of registered appeals to the Special Educational Needs and Disability Tribunal, 1997–2013. *Source*: www.gov.uk/government/statistics/tribunal-statistics-quarterly-july-to-september-2013

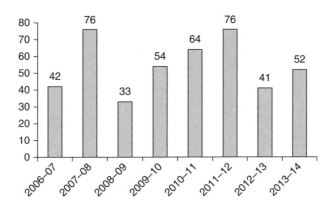

Figure 2.7 References to the Additional Support Needs Tribunal, 2006–2014. *Source*: ASNT, *Annual Reports*, see www.asntscotland.gov.uk

76 references were made in 2007/08, with fewer references in the subsequent years except in 2011/12. This is partly because references must relate to a CSP, but only a tiny proportion of children with ASN are deemed to meet the qualification criteria for a statutory plan (see Riddell and Weedon, 2009, for further discussion of this point).

Mediation has been strongly supported by government in preference to courts or tribunals on the grounds that it is a cheaper and less stressful means of resolving disputes between the citizen and the state. In addition to the duty placed on English local authorities to provide access to independent mediation, noted above, the ASL Act 2004 obliged Scottish local authorities to provide access to independent mediation and adjudication. In both England and Scotland, mediation has proved much less popular than hoped for by government (Riddell et al., 2010). Although there are no national figures on SEN or ASN mediation, our local authority survey suggested that in England there was an average of little more than one mediation per authority, compared to an average (based on national statistics) of approximately eight appeal hearings per authority. More than half of authorities (60%) reported no mediations that year. In Scotland, three-quarters of all authorities reported fewer than five mediations each. Reasons for the low uptake included a failure by local authorities to promote or publicise mediation, a reluctance to participate on the part of schools or local authorities, and suspicion by parents that mediation was a way of 'fobbing them off' rather than delivering justice, a view which was sometimes reinforced by parents' advisers and representatives. During the year 2006/07, there were only 12 cases of adjudication in Scotland, signalling parents' lack of knowledge of and confidence in this route.

Overall, the low uptake of alternative dispute resolution mechanisms (mediation and adjudication), and the apparent preference, at least in England, to take cases to the tribunal suggests that parents have little faith in less formal dispute resolution routes, which rely on trust between parties. However, it should be noted that the Parent Partnership Service (PPS) played a significant role in informal mediation. It was when this informal mediation failed that parents tended to opt for the tribunal rather than trying formal mediation. As noted above, Harris (2005) has argued that there has been little progress with regard to increasing parental participation in education decision-making, with local authorities and schools retaining control in many critical areas, including the field of SEN/ASN. This was reflected in the Lamb Inquiry which reported that parents lacked confidence in the system of decision-making and felt disempowered (DCFS, 2009), problems which the Coalition Government's reforms as enshrined in the 2014 Act, with their provision for increased information, personal budgets and other changes aimed at providing 'greater choice and control for young people and parents over support' (DfE and DoH, 2015: 1.2) are claimed to be aimed in part at addressing. Findings from the research reported here also suggest that the bureaucratic decision-making has continued to hold sway. Whilst this is contrary to the rhetoric of parental empowerment, it must be acknowledged that there is a genuine dilemma in managing the balance of power between parents and professionals, since local authorities can legitimately claim that if the pendulum swings too far in the direction of allowing parents to act as the ultimate arbiters in resource allocation decisions, then their role as independent arbiters in the fair allocation of resources becomes compromised.

Case studies

So far, we have discussed two particular dilemmas in the field of special and additional support needs. In the following section, we present two case studies drawn from the research project described above to illustrate the way in which these dilemmas are manifested in everyday life.

Mrs McIntosh – Placing request leading to independent residential special school placement

The McIntosh family lived in Sea City, an affluent Scottish city with a low use of CSPs and a high proportion of formal disputes. At the time of the research, Fraser McIntosh was 15 years of age and had a diagnosis of autistic spectrum disorder. His parents, both professionals, worked freelance in order to combine work and childcare. Fraser was placed in a special school, but during his teenage years his difficulties became more apparent, with attendant stresses for his family and teachers. His mother became convinced that school staff did not have the specialist training to manage his behaviour effectively. She researched the options independently, and eventually decided that placement in a residential Steiner school would best meet her son's needs, although she knew that the council was unlikely to agree because of the cost. Mrs McIntosh made a formal placing request, with a view to taking the case to tribunal as a last resort. Following advice from an advocacy organisation, Mrs McIntosh took on the role of lead professional and, prior to a review meeting, had private meetings with all 13 professionals involved with Fraser. Each confirmed in writing that Fraser's current school could not meet his needs, and that a residential special school placement was required. The placing request was granted, although the senior officer continued to maintain that the local authority was able to meet the child's needs and that the cost of the residential placement was unjustified and detrimental to other children's education because of its resource implications. This view was reinforced by the educational psychologist, who spoke of the danger of middle-class parents claiming more than their fair share of resources for their children.

Mrs Redgrave – Successful mediation led to a statement of needs and additional support for mainstream placement

Mrs Carole Redgrave, a single parent working as a care assistant, lived in Midshire, an English local authority spanning both urban and rural areas with a low use of statements. Her daughter Lucy was aged 10 at the time of the research and, from early on in her primary school career, had struggled with basic numeracy and literacy, leading to a diagnosis of 'non-specific special educational needs'. Lucy was placed on a School Action Plus programme, which delivered very little extra support, and she still failed to make progress. On the advice of an educational psychologist, Mrs Redgrave asked if she could be assessed for a statement of needs, since this would deliver dedicated support, but a request for a formal assessment was turned down twice, despite support from a range of professionals. Mrs Redgrave felt fobbed off by both the school and the local authority, but persisted in arguing Lucy's case because she was convinced that her daughter would thrive in mainstream education with extra help. The local Parent Partnership Service was recommended by a friend, and they supported her through mediation, after which a special needs statement was issued guaranteeing 10 hours of support from a teaching assistant. According to the PPS, the head teacher had wanted Lucy to be placed in a special school, since she thought this was the only place where additional support would be available, but according to the PPS worker, Lucy was 'nowhere near the criteria for special'. The additional support in mainstream education was successful, with marked improvements in Lucy's behaviour, confidence and attainment.

Summary

To summarise, a number of dilemmas characterise the field of special and additional support needs, in particular the dilemma of whether to emphasise difference or sameness and the dilemma of how much power to accord to parents or professionals in determining the type of appropriate education for a child with special or additional support needs. These dilemmas are interconnected, since they both have implications for resource distribution and identity. We noted that the educational reforms of the 1990s in England tilted the balance of power in the direction of parents, making professionals far more accountable and opening up accessible appeal and other redress routes. This process is arguably advanced further by the Children and Families Act 2014. In Scotland, the ASL Act was implemented more than a decade after SEN reforms in England, with the aim of widening the pool of children eligible for additional support and boosting parents' power to hold professionals to account. In both England and Scotland, there has continued to be a commitment to an inclusive educational system, underpinned by the presumption that a child will be placed in the mainstream unless there are compelling reasons for a special school placement. It is also worth noting that despite the willingness of many parents to 'fight' for their perceived entitlement to a particular form of education and sets of arrangements for their child, which our research confirmed, the judicial system, both internationally (the European Court of Human Rights) and domestically (the tribunals and courts in England and Scotland), has largely failed to uphold as a matter of human rights parental convictions as regards the type of placement their child should have (Harris, 2007; Harris and Riddell, 2011). This has led to disputes focusing on resource issues rather than broader issues of principle.

The analysis of official statistics on the identification of children with special and additional support needs in England and Scotland underlined some of the ongoing tensions in the system. Low-incidence normative difficulties, such as physical and sensory impairments, are identified across the social spectrum, and the issuing of, in England, a statement of needs or (now) an EHC plan – or in Scotland a CSP – releases additional resources, potentially helping the child to achieve his or her educational potential. By way of contrast, high-incidence non-normative difficulties, such as social, emotional and behavioural difficulties, which carry with them the risk of stigmatisation, are much more likely to be identified amongst children living in socially deprived areas. Children with special and additional support needs living in such areas are less likely to be allocated additional resources, which might outweigh the negative impact of a stigmatising label.

The brief case studies presented above also highlight the central dilemmas and the way in which they are manifested differently in particular circumstances. Mrs McIntosh wanted her son to be identified as unequivocally different from other children, so that the significant cost of the residential special school could be justified.Mrs Redgrave, on the other hand, was not seeking a specific label for her child's difficulties, but an assessment which would release additional support to be delivered in the mainstream rather than a special setting. Both parents were similar in wanting their voices to be heard and in being willing to use formal routes of redress if necessary, although Mrs McIntosh had greater social and cultural resources at her disposal. The response of the schools and local authorities was similar in both cases, as they expressed deep anxiety about the danger of preferential resource allocation to those who were most willing to fight their corner. These dilemmas are unlikely to be easily resolved, particularly since pressures on public sector funding are set to continue into the foreseeable future.

Discussion points

- What are the upsides and downsides of the broad definition of ASN employed in Scotland compared with the much narrower definition of SEN used in England?
- Through the recent Children and Families Act 2014, mediation has been promoted in England and Scotland as a better way of resolving SEN disputes compared with tribunals. What are the advantages of judicial and non-judicial forms of dispute resolution and how can mediation be promoted?
- What can be done to help parents of children with SEN/ASN in their efforts to ensure that their children get the support they need?

Further reading

Harris, N. (2013) Children and Education. In A. Bainham and S. Gilmore (eds), *Children: The Modern Law*, 4th edn. Bristol: Family Law, pp. 881–984.
This examines the evolving legal framework governing special educational needs, including the reforms now enacted in the Children and Families Act 2014, in the wider context of children and young people's rights to and in education.

Harris, N. and Riddell, S. (2011) *Resolving Disputes about Educational Provision: A Comparative Perspective on Special Educational Needs*. London: Sage.
This book discusses the nature of grievances and disputes in the field of SEN and the pros and cons of various dispute resolution mechanisms. It also focuses on SEN systems and approaches to dispute resolution in England, Scotland, the Netherlands and the USA.

Weedon, E. and Riddell, S. (2009) Additional support needs and approaches to dispute resolution: the perspectives of Scottish parents, *Scottish Educational Review*, 41: 62–81.
This paper provides an overview of provision for children with additional support needs in Scotland. It draws on survey findings which reveal parents' responses to the new additional support.

Wright, K., Stead, J., Riddell, S. and Weedon, E. (2012) Parental experiences of dealing with disputes in additional support needs in Scotland: why are parents not engaging with mediation? *International Journal of Inclusive Education*, 16(11): 1099–114, DOI: 10.1080/13603116.2010.548103.

(Continued)

(Continued)

Useful websites

England

www.gov.uk/government/policies/special-educational-needs-and-disability-send for an overview of policy documents.

www.legislation.gov.uk for access to statutes and regulations.

Scotland

www.educationscotland.gov.uk/inclusionandequalities/additionalsupportforlearning for an overview of support for schools and parents.

www.gov.scot/Topics/Education/Schools/welfare/ASL for an overview of provision for additional support needs.

enquire.org.uk/what-is-additional-support-for-learning/legislation for an overview of relevant legislation.

References

Armstrong, D. (2003) *Experiences of Special Education*. London: RoutledgeFalmer.

Ball, S.J. (2007) *Education plc: Understanding Private Sector Participation in Public Sector Education*. London: Routledge.

DCSF (2009) *Special Educational Needs and Parental Confidence* (The Lamb Inquiry). London: The Stationery Office.

DES (Department for Education and Science) (1978) *Special Educational Needs* (The Warnock Report). London: HMSO.

DfE (Department for Education) (1994) *Code of Practice on the Identification and Assessment of Special Educational Needs*. London: DfE.

DfE (Department for Education) (2013) *Special Educational Needs in England: January 2013, National Tables SFR 30/2013*. Available on: www.gov.uk/government/statistics/special-educational-needs-in-england-january-2013, accessed 18/08/2015.

DfE and DH (Department for Education and Department of Health) (2015) *Special Educational Needs and Disability Code of Practice: 0 to 25 Years*. London: DfE and DH.

Harris, N. (2005) Empowerment and state education: rights of choice and participation. *Modern Law Review*, 68(6): 925–7.

Harris, N. (2007) *Education, Law and Diversity*. Oxford: Hart.

Harris, N. (2009) Playing catch-up in the schoolyard? Children and young people's 'voice' and education rights in the UK. *International Journal of Law, Policy and the Family*, 23: 331–66.

Harris, N. and Riddell, S. (2011) *Resolving Disputes about Educational Provision*. Aldershot: Ashgate.

Lewis, A. and Norwich, B. (eds) (2005) *Special Teaching for Special Children? Pedagogies for Inclusion.* Maidenhead: Open University Press.

Minow, M. (1985) Learning to live with the dilemma of difference: bilingual and special education. In K.T. Bartlett and J.W. Wegner (eds), *Children with Special Needs.* Boulder, CO: Transaction Books pp. 375–429.

Norwich, B. (2008) *Dilemmas of Difference, Inclusion and Disability: International Perspectives and Future Directions.* London: Routledge.

Pearson, C. (ed.) (2006) *Direct Payments and Personalisation of Care.* Edinburgh: Dunedin Academic Press.

Phillips, A. (1999) *Which Equalities Matter?* Cambridge: Polity Press.

Riddell, S. and Weedon, E. (2009) Approaches to dispute resolution in additional support needs in Scotland. *European Journal of Special Needs Education,* 24(4): 355–69.

Riddell, S. and Weedon, E. (2015) Additional support needs policy in Scotland: challenging or reinforcing social inequality? *Discourse: Studies in the Cultural Politics of Education,* DOI: 10.1080/01596306.2015.1073012.

Riddell, S., Weedon, E. and Harris, N. (2012) Special and additional support needs in England and Scotland. In L. Peer and G. Reid (eds), *Current Dilemmas and Solutions in Special Educational Needs: A Guide for Inclusive Practice.* London: Sage, pp. 99–115.

Riddell, S., Harris, N., Smith, E. and Weedon, E. (2010) Dispute resolution in additional and special educational needs: local authority perspectives. *Journal of Education Policy,* 25(1): 55–71.

Scottish Executive (2005) *Supporting Children's Learning: Code of Practice.* Edinburgh: The Stationery Office.

Scottish Government (2008) *Pupils in Scotland, 2007.* Edinburgh: Scottish Government.

Scottish Government (2013) Pupil Census 2013 Supplementary Data. Available on: www.gov.scot/Topics/Statistics/Browse/School-Education/dspupcensus/pupcensus2013, accessed 18/08/2015.

Tomlinson, S. (1985) The expansion of special education. *Oxford Review of Education,* 11(2): 157–65.

Special Educational Needs: The State of Research

3

From Methodological Purism to Pluralistic Research Progress

Elias Avramidis and Brahm Norwich

Learning objectives

This chapter will help readers to:

- Understand the research implications of recent philosophical trends and developments in special education
- Appreciate the main paradigms (knowledge cultures) operating in educational research along with their methodological implications
- Recognise the impact of the Evidence-based Policy and Practice movement and its educational significance
- Explore the challenge of reaching consensus in the field and examine whether adopting multi-methodological research designs is a useful way forward

---

In an earlier version of this chapter (Avramidis and Norwich, 2011), we reviewed the range of diverse methodological approaches that then co-existed in the field of special needs and inclusive education and concluded that the state of research could be characterised as in some disarray. Although, some notable multi-method research studies have since been conducted in the field, we contend that there has only been moderate progress in reaching a consensus about the value of research approaches emanating from diverse disciplinary and philosophical backgrounds. In this respect, our previous call for tolerance, openness and mutual exchange between different research traditions leading to the formulation of coherent multi-method research designs remains as timely as ever.

This chapter begins by discussing some key developments in the field of special and inclusive education that have undoubtedly influenced the focus of research and, by extension, the methodologies employed by the research community. In so doing, the various methodological approaches utilised are critically reviewed and the current state of research in the field is appraised. The chapter concludes by presenting some illuminating examples of multi-method research projects that have certainly succeeded in transcending traditional dichotomies associated with exclusive philosophical positions and so-called research paradigms. Although the emphasis is largely placed on research developments in the UK, the issues discussed here have relevance to other national contexts and to researchers working in other strands of educational research.

Researching special needs and inclusive education

Although the title of this chapter refers to special educational needs, it is important to understand that this term itself reflects a particular construction of how education for children with learning difficulties and disabilities is organised. Historically, special education was associated with separate special schooling and class teaching. Placements in these specialist settings were based on the identification of specific kinds of deficits or difficulties and research tended to focus on analyses of the difficulties and their implications for specialist teaching (Thomas and Loxley, 2007). Much of the special education research focused mainly on a deficit perspective that located 'learning difficulty' or 'disability' within the individual, while ignoring the immediate teaching and wider institutional contexts. This research was within a particular kind of scientific style of psychological research based on abilities and dispositions, which ignored other theoretical approaches, such as functional and contextual ones. The introduction of the term Special Educational Needs (SEN) in the early 1980s (DES, 1981) reflected a functional and contextual psychological model, which viewed children experiencing difficulties in learning as 'special' within a particular educational context. In other words, it was acknowledged that it is the circumstances in which individuals find themselves that determine whether or not their individual characteristics are a cause of difficulty; and, more importantly, that other contextual factors (i.e. classroom organisation, teaching processes and teacher attitudes) also contribute to a child's underachievement.

One of the developments in research in the field of special needs and inclusive education over this period has been the turn towards more sociological analyses. Sociological analyses deriving from a sociology of education have tended to reflect a critique of psychological ones, especially the abilities/dispositional analyses, and to reflect critical perspectives on schooling for children with special educational needs and other vulnerable children. It is also important to be clear that just as there are different traditions of psychological research in this aspect of education, so there are different traditions within sociological approaches (Thomas, 2004). But, within the sociological tradition, there was also a development of theories about disability – disability studies – which drew on the critical or emancipatory tradition to represent disability as produced by an oppressive and exclusive society, and not as reflecting impairment or defects located in the person (Barnes et al., 1999). The field of disability studies was associated with the disability movement which has fought for the rights of disabled people, and in so doing set itself in opposition to the sociology of health and medicine (Bury, 1991).

The medical model was represented as not only locating 'impairment' or 'defect' in the individual, but as requiring a cure or alleviation that involved the intervention of medical and other professionals. By contrast, in the social model, people with impairments are seen as disabled by society's failure to accommodate their needs. Although the social model does not deny the presence of impairment in disabled people's lives, it denies that impairments have implications for disability, and sees disability as resulting from the barriers and discrimination society places on disabled people. In this respect, the social model views disability as socially created, and the explanation of its changing character is located in the social and economic structure of the society in which it is found (Mertens and McLaughlin, 2004). The significance of the origins of the social model is that it underpinned the development of ideas about inclusive education and critiques of what were portrayed as deficit models of special educational needs. Research relevant to the education of children with learning difficulties and disabilities came therefore to be undertaken within a social model based on inclusive education assumptions. Associated with these assumptions were emancipatory and participatory research approaches (Clough, 2000) that influenced research methodologies and specific research methods.

The important development of inclusive education as an international movement can also be traced back to the international organisations committed to global human rights. Here, the UNESCO World Conference on Special Education in Salamanca in 1994 was significant. The Salamanca Statement (UNESCO, 1994), which was signed by 92 governments and 25 international organisations, asserted the fundamental right of every child to education and advocated the development of inclusive mainstream schools which '*are the most effective means of combating discriminatory attitudes, creating welcoming communities, building an inclusive society and achieving education for all*' (Clause 5, 2nd paragraph, our emphasis). The achievement of an inclusive education system soon became a major priority in many countries around the world, including the UK.

The substantial reform of mainstream schooling that followed in many countries opened up new lines of research that co-existed with more traditional forms of research. In reviewing these research developments, Clough (2000) presented a framework of different approaches relevant to inclusive education, which included: (i) psycho-medical approach; (ii) sociological response; (iii) curricular approaches; (iv) school improvement approach; and (v) disability studies critique. This diversity of research assumptions has been characterised as fragmented, conflicting and not leading to productive dialogues (Dyson and Howes, 2009). For example, researchers influenced by the school effectiveness tradition embarked on a series of case studies in primary and secondary settings with a view to identifying organisational structures and practices which may be associated with facilitating or impeding the development of inclusion. These researchers saw special needs as arising from deficiencies in the way in which schools are currently organised; concomitantly, the solution advocated was to restructure schools to eliminate or reduce to a minimum the problem of students who fail to fulfil their learning potential in the schooling system. Accordingly, rich descriptions of exemplary inclusive schools were provided (Lipsky and Gartner, 1998; Clark et al., 1999; Kugelmass, 2001; Skidmore, 2004), alongside recommendations for developing inclusive school cultures. However, a caveat needs pointing out here: as Norwich and Kelly (2005) observe, the identified school factors conducive to inclusion were expressed in very broad terms which did not capture the ambiguity, tensions and complexity of schooling. Further, being descriptions of inclusive schools, it remained unclear whether these factors are causal of inclusive development or simply defining characteristics of inclusive schools.

Interestingly, writers operating within the disability studies perspective have taken a critical stance towards inclusion researchers. Oliver (1999), for example, characterises other approaches, called 'research as investigation' as 'parasitic' (p. 183). For Oliver, the solution to parasitic research is not just one of commitment: giving up 'the pursuit of objectivity in researching oppression and decid[ing] on which side we are on' (p. 184). His critique emanates from a critical or emancipatory research perspective that gives priority to social improvement over investigation, an improvement that can be achieved through uncovering social oppression and emancipating the research participants (e.g. disabled people) to take action to transform their lives.

Oliver's critique also reflects a dilemma which is, according to Hammersley (2003), inherent in educational research; that is, the commitment to the pursuit of knowledge versus the commitment to social improvement. This is especially relevant to inclusive education which, 'has not only become internationally pervasive but it has also come to be seen as self-evidently a "good thing" in a similar way that democracy or human rights have come to be self-evidently good' (Norwich, 2013: 3). To put it simply, if inclusion represents a value commitment, then it is not subject to empirical validation. From this perspective, if children with a disability in an ordinary class are performing less well academically or socially than similar children in a separate setting, then this implies the need to examine how the ordinary class can be adapted. It does not constitute evidence about the consequences of inclusion.

At this point it is worth noting that, despite the proliferation of descriptive studies of inclusive schools, the need for rigorous evaluation studies which shed light on the academic and social outcomes of the process remains. For example, while one of the main arguments for inclusion relates to the social benefits that pupils with SEN gain from their increased interaction with typically achieving peers, the results emerging from relevant empirical studies are very mixed. Indicatively, Lindsay's (2007) review on the social effects of inclusion on children with SEN found few differences between children educated in special schools and those in mainstream provision. Of the 16 different studies identified, 2 were positive, 2 were positive with some caveats, 8 showed no differences and 4 were negative. Similarly, Ruijs and Peetsma (2009) found 1 study with positive results, 2 with positive results with some caveats, 6 that showed no differences and 4 with negative results. We contend here that such discrepancies arise primarily because of the methodological limitations inherent in the research designs utilised in these studies and, to a lesser extent, because of socio-historical or contextual differences between these studies.

Equally mixed is the empirical evidence about the academic outcomes of inclusion for children with SEN and their peers. As Ruijs and Peetsma (2009) note in their comprehensive review, most studies examining academic effects are descriptive and concern children with mild to moderate learning disabilities, mild mental retardation, mild to moderate behavioural difficulties and mild psychosocial problems (these are the terms which they use). While the majority of these studies found positive or neutral results, some studies reported adverse effects on the achievement of children with mild SEN. A key limitation in most of these studies, however, was the absence of a 'control' group, which made a comparison between the effects of an inclusive versus a special placement impossible. Further, there was wide variation in the way in which inclusion was practised in these studies (i.e. some investigated the effect of full inclusion projects; others investigated the effect of inclusion programmes in which children are only included for some lessons during the day).

Notwithstanding the value of existing research in the field, it could be suggested that there is no clear endorsement of positive effects of inclusion, an observation that has led authors such as Farrell (2000) and Lindsay (2007) to conclude that inclusion has been advanced on the basis of socio-political arguments rather than empirical evidence. We contend here that the mixed results reported in the literature have arisen for several reasons. There are definitional issues about the nature of inclusion, methodological limitations inherent in the research designs utilised in the various studies and, to a lesser extent, historical or contextual differences between these studies. It is towards discussing more critically the kinds of research designs utilised in the field that we turn next.

Research paradigms and their application in special education

Although different methodological approaches in educational research are discussed in terms of paradigms, we prefer to talk about 'cultures of knowledge' (Kagan, 2009). Kagan departs from the typical two or three paradigm views to identify three cultures of knowledge: the physical sciences, the social sciences and the humanities. Educational research spans the social sciences and the humanities, and in doing so is distanced from the physical sciences. However, the point of his reference to cultures is to recognise the importance of members of these cultures adopting 'postures of humility' (p. 275). Special needs research has traditionally utilised scientific style quantitative research designs. One reason for this emphasis on quantification and generalised knowledge has been the concern for hard facts in the form of numerical information as a basis on which to measure the impact of an intervention in special education or to monitor the effectiveness of services (Mertens and McLaughlin, 2004). Moreover, special needs research in the UK has tended to be dominated by researchers trained in the disciplines of psychology and quantitative social sciences. These disciplines have characteristically used explanatory quantitative research strategies, such as surveys, which attempt to produce generalisations based on the statistical analysis of large samples, and experiments which establish cause-and-effect relations based on the control of selected variables.

Some educational researchers see scientific style quantitative research as rooted in a positivist/post-positivist paradigm, which holds that the purpose of research is to empirically test knowledge claims about educational or psychological phenomena (Cohen et al., 2007). Positivists are often characterised in educational research as adopting a realist-external ontology, whereby the social world exists 'out there' independently from the enquirer; and are committed to practising an objectivist epistemology, whereby 'reality' or 'truth' can be captured within a certain level of probability. However, scientific style methodologies do not have to adopt any ontological assumptions about reality; they need only assume that their theories can be constructed to predict effects that operate in education. Such a pragmatic philosophy judges scientific research in terms of its predictive usefulness, not its realistic ontological assumptions. Whether scientific style research in special education is positivist or pragmatic, there is still the common assumption that the claims or hypotheses posed about a particular phenomenon can be confirmed or refuted if rigorous scientific procedures are followed and an objective stance is maintained. However, there are, arguably, certain underlying assumptions of a scientific style approach that can restrict its application in special education (Avramidis and Smith, 1999). For example, in special education, low-incidence conditions such as deaf-blindness or cerebral palsy make it hard to find appropriate sample sizes. Further, the categories of disabilities often used in such research cover a diversity of differences, and individual children often have a pattern of difficulties that goes across different categories, making sample selection even more difficult (e.g. a child may have dyslexia and specific motor coordination disorder). The classification of difficulties and disorders themselves show variations within the category (e.g. dyslexia, Down syndrome, autism, etc.). Individuals with a syndrome or disorder share few, some or all of the stated characteristics with other similarly identified individuals. However, there are other traditions using scientific style research approaches that do not sample by diagnostic categories, but in terms of lower-level functional categories (e.g. below age-expected reading levels; Solity et al., 2000). This functional approach corresponds in special education practice to each student's programme being designed uniquely to satisfy that student's needs. In the UK context, this is reflected in the Code of Practice (DfES, 2001) which requires an Individual Education Plan (IEP) for each pupil identified with difficulties in learning tailored to their needs, thus resulting in a diversity of programmes and associated practices. These different styles of scientific study need to be taken into account in understanding scientific style research into special needs and inclusive education.

These considerations about scientific style research have led some researchers away from this approach to research towards qualitative research designs rooted within what is often called the interpretive/constructivist assumptions. However, the turn away from scientific quantitative research designs was not only because of the limitations with these designs and the limited application of the research findings to education practice, but it also reflected a widespread move towards more relativist and sceptical assumptions about the social sciences. Some researchers argued that the ontological and epistemological assumptions of interpretivism rendered this paradigm more appropriate for the study of special education. In its more radical relativist version, the interpretive paradigm purported that there was no one 'reality' waiting to be 'discovered', as the positivist paradigm was said to assume. Instead, realities were said to be multiple and socially constructed, so recognising that many interpretations can be made – a subjectivist epistemology (Cohen et al., 2007). Following these assumptions, the concept of 'SEN' or 'disability' was viewed largely as a socially constructed phenomenon, which was relative and context specific. Accordingly, the interpretivist researcher did not accept psychological categories and classifications (e.g. disorders and syndromes) as given and valid across individuals and contexts. Instead, the perceptions of teachers, learning support assistants, parents and, more importantly, children and young adults themselves were sought, with a view to enhancing understanding about the individual and their needs. There have been several problems with a relativist interpretivist style of research. Philosophically radical interpretivist assumptions undermine any claims that can be made for the research conclusions, if the findings of such research are open to many interpretations. However, as with scientific style research, there are different versions of interpretivist research, some versions recognise that some interpretations have priority over others because they fit the evidence better. Nevertheless, illuminating the findings produced by these interpretivist qualitative studies, the application of these research designs in special needs research has also been criticised on two further counts. First, most such studies were small-scale and highly context specific (i.e. case studies), and were thus said to produce findings not easily generalisable in other settings. Second, these studies have been said to be inappropriate for testing the effectiveness of therapeutic or teaching interventions and, therefore, of limited value in terms of influencing policy.

Moreover, as already mentioned, the emergence of the inclusive education movement resulted in the focus of research shifting from descriptive studies of children's conditions and disabilities to studies of the ways in which various educational needs might best be met. This, in turn, directed attention towards ways of improving the learning experiences of children, and evaluating and disseminating developments in teaching or provision in mainstream schools. Such a research agenda inevitably required a shift to a broader range of approaches, which included a range of quantitative and qualitative methods (Mertens and McLaughlin, 2004). The mix and balance between different kinds of research in the field were then influenced by what came to be called the Evidence-based Policy and Practice movement to be discussed next.

The Evidence-based Policy and Practice movement

In the mid-1990s, educational research in the UK came under fire for being idiosyncratic, sometimes ideologically driven and irrelevant to practitioners and policy makers alike. David Hargreaves (1999), for example, strongly argued that educational research needed to be redirected towards the systematic development of an accumulating body of knowledge that is capable of informing the practical judgement of teachers. In this way, the purpose of research ought to facilitate the development of evidence-based practice in education settings through providing research evidence that is decisive and conclusive for practice. Such a research agenda requires scientifically based research designs such as experimental studies and randomised controlled trials (RCTs) in search of cumulative knowledge of 'what works' in practice to produce the necessary improvements in educational outcomes (Slavin, 2002).

The evidence-based practice movement, which has a longer history and has had much influence in health services, can be seen to result from critiques about the quality of educational research and was quickly espoused by the UK government. The DfES Centre for Evidence-informed Policy and Practice in Education (EPPI-centre) was established to facilitate the carrying out of systematic reviews in education and the dissemination of such findings. The purpose of such reviews was to identify effective practice in educational settings and to pass this knowledge to professionals so their practice could be based on sound evidence of effectiveness. For example, Evans and Benefield's (2001) review of interventions to support primary aged pupils with emotional and behavioural difficulties (EBD) in mainstream primary classrooms aimed to describe and explain current knowledge about effective classroom practice related to EBD in order to guide professional practice. Similarly, Dyson et al. (2002) conducted a systematic review of the literature on school-level actions conducive to promoting the participation of all pupils. These 'systematic' reviews involved an exhaustive search of the literature and the establishment of strict criteria for including or excluding studies, in contrast to the more common 'narrative' or 'academic' reviews.

Indeed, as Evans and Benefield (2001) point out, the key difference between systematic and the more common narrative or academic reviews is that the former are explicit about the research question being addressed; the exhaustive and transparent search procedure followed; the setting of clear criteria for including or excluding studies; and the adoption of clear criteria for assessing the quality of the findings of the review. By contrast, the 'narrative' or 'academic' reviews tend to be more wide-ranging in their scope, less clear in reporting their search strategies or their criteria for including or excluding studies, have less explicit criteria for assessing the quality of the identified studies and do not generally make explicit their methodology for reviewing the studies included.

Notwithstanding the merits of adopting a systematic approach to research synthesis, systematic reviews have been criticised for adopting the over-simplified assumptions of scientific style research (Hammersley, 2001). Indeed, such reviews value randomised experimental research designs above all other research designs as the gold standard of research. Such a preference, coupled with the application of strict criteria for selecting and subsequently evaluating the research designs of the reviewed studies, results in a very limited account of the literature. For example, in Evans and Benefield's (2001) review, from the 265 articles, books, chapters and conference papers initially identified, only 33 fell within the scope of the review. Closer examination of these 33 studies resulted in the exclusion of another 22 studies, which failed to meet the criteria that had been set, thus bringing the final number of reviewed studies to 11. The systematic reviews can be interpreted differently depending on one's philosophical position. For those with interests in a cumulating body of knowledge about effective practices, the reviews can be seen to require more use of controlled trials (e.g. Gorard and Cook, 2007). For those who recognise the practical limits of such designs or who have an interpretivist orientation, the reviews show that there is more to educational research than seeking knowledge about evidence-based practice. It is also worth noting that there are certain epistemological problems in establishing a simple evidence base for classroom practice (Bridges, 2008; Issitt and Kyriacou, 2009). Without going into these in detail here, these critiques imply that there are contextual, relational and judgemental factors involved in classroom teaching which are not open to systematic and randomised controlled designs.

Leaving such philosophical debates aside, the particularities of the special education field outlined earlier (small sample sizes, diversity across categories of disabilities as well as within them, and the difficulty of matching and contrasting samples from different – mainstream and special – sectors) led most researchers in the field to resist adopting the experimental designs advocated by the evidence-based movement. It is notable that, in the few systematic reviews of classroom practices relevant to including pupils with special educational needs (Davis and Florian, 2004; Nind and Wearmouth, 2006), very few involved sophisticated randomised control designs. Instead, a range of diverse methodological approaches currently co-exist and the state of research in the field in the UK could be characterised as in some disarray.

Reaching consensus through multi-method research orientations

In considering the state of research in the field of special and inclusive education, two important observations should be noted. First, there has only been moderate progress in reaching a consensus about the value of research approaches emanating from diverse disciplinary and philosophical backgrounds. Indeed, more often than not, researchers in the field are firmly attached to particular paradigms or knowledge culture stances, thus reproducing sterile debates about the supremacy of particular methodologies (e.g. the scientific/quantitative vs interpretive/qualitative divide). Consequently, many researchers refuse to engage with research findings produced by researchers entrenched in different camps, thus resisting the development of an accumulating body of knowledge that is capable of informing policy making and stimulating further research. We believe that much of the confusion and debate in the field can be attributed to the oversimplified concept of 'paradigm' as currently understood and utilised in educational research. The term originates from Kuhn's (1962) analysis of scientific revolutions in physics published over 50 years ago, which has come to be used to refer to distinct social research approaches based on different ontological, epistemological and methodological assumptions. Moreover, paradigms are viewed as 'incommensurable'; that is, the quality of research can only be evaluated in terms of the assumptions of its own paradigm. The incommensurability assumption not only prevents communication and collaboration between researchers in the field, but it also makes it hard to assess quality and merit in educational research across different methodologies. This is where Kagan's call for greater humility across the cultures of knowledge is most relevant (Kagan, 2009).

A second important observation about the current state of research in the field concerns the prevalence of single methodological research designs, which provide a partial understanding of the phenomenon under study. Again, this methodological purism can also be attributed to the incommensurability between paradigms which precludes the mixing of methodologies and methods. Some researchers do not see value in asking different kinds of research questions about the same phenomena and do not draw on a range of methodologies and methods, being limited to a narrow repertoire of methods emanating from their basic knowledge affiliations. For example, scientific quantitative researchers can limit themselves to the collection of de-contextualised data using experimental and large-scale explanatory survey designs without undertaking any fieldwork in the organisations they study; and interpretivist qualitative researchers can utilise ecological methods (participant observations) without making any effort to access what is available about the performance or characteristics of the setting or organisation in which they research. We do recognise that there are different research orientations and interests; and that it is contradictory for research to be designed to produce scientific-style explanations or interpretivist illuminations in the same study. However, researchers can be flexible in their design and research orientations in different studies or different parts of their studies. We now present briefly two such recent studies along these lines, a large research project and a small-scale doctoral study to demonstrate that the judicious blending of diverse methodologies can be achieved irrespectively of the scale of the study.

The Deployment and Impact of Support Staff (DISS) project (Blatchford et al., 2009) examined the impact of support staff on SEN pupils' learning and academic progress. Specifically, the project sought to determine the impact of different amounts of support provided by teaching assistants (TAs) on SEN pupils' attitudes to learning and their attainment outcomes. Instead of adopting a traditional experimental design contrasting groups with and without support, the researchers opted for an alternative 'naturalistic' design that sought to measure support received by pupils under normal circumstances, and then examine relationships with academic and behaviour outcomes. In this study, attitudes to learning were operationalised as a set of eight different dimensions, measured on the basis of teacher ratings near the end of the school year: distractibility, task confidence, motivation, disruptiveness, independence, relationships with other pupils, completion of assigned work and the following of instructions from adults. Academic progress, on the other hand, was assessed by analysing effects on end of year attainment, controlling for start-of-year scores and SEN status. Accordingly, the design involved correlations between the main predictor variable (in this case, TA support) and the academic and behavioural outcomes. Although correlational analyses cannot establish causation, the longitudinal assessment of the academic progress and the controlling of prior attainment and SEN status meant that the effects of adult support on pupils' attainment could still be established. Additionally, the research involved the collection of a wide range of qualitative data, including observations of lessons and interviews, thus enabling the research team to gain rich insights into the deployment of support staff in schools and the nature of their interaction with pupils. In this way, the DISS project represents a large-scale multi-method design that is innovative and has wider significance for policy makers and practitioners.

In another multi-method study, Mammas (2009) sought in his doctoral research to determine the social status of children with special educational needs in Cypriot mainstream primary schools; and at a subsequent stage implement transformative steps to alter pupils' status at both the micro (school) and the macro (policy) level. As such, the study was informed by transformative assumptions, whereby the purpose of the research is not only to understand and explain social phenomena but to transform them. To achieve this, Mammas adopted a mixed-method sequential research design with two distinct phases. The first one involved the application of a classic sociometric approach using the peer nomination technique; while the second phase involved conducting semi-structured interviews with pupils and teachers as well as qualitative observations in the participating schools. In this respect, the outcomes of the quantitative phase were contextualised and interpreted through extensive qualitative fieldwork resulting in the formulation of a fuller understanding of the schools involved. The final stage of the study was dedicated to producing transformation through empowering the research participants at the school level and disseminating more widely the research outcome to influence policy making and stimulate further research.

It is our contention that the field of special needs and inclusive education research would benefit from the increased utilisation of coherent multi-methodological and multi-methods research designs of the type described here. The concluding section summarises the arguments put forward in this chapter and offers two different routes to overcoming the philosophical dilemmas confronting researchers in the field.

Summary

We have described some of the research in the field of special needs and inclusive education as being in some disarray. This is partly a matter of the clash of different research orientations reflecting uncompromising positions about what counts as knowledge and understanding in educational research. But, it is also partly about the general lack of research in this field, especially in the UK. Despite research funded through government agencies, charities and the Government Research Council, the systematic reviews in the field, as discussed above, show the paucity of UK research relevant to the big questions about inclusive practice and the future of special schools, for example (SEN Policy Research Forum, 2014). Indeed, one of the main conclusions of Lewis and Norwich (2004) in their work on SEN pedagogy was about the lack of rigorous pedagogic research.

Over a decade ago, Farrell (2000) concluded that more research was needed in the following areas:

1. Effective in-class support
2. The management, role and training of teaching assistants
3. The views of teachers in mainstream schools about inclusion, their training, etc.
4. The future of special schools
5. Factors affecting parental attitudes to inclusion
6. The views of pupils with special educational needs

Although there have been some notable research studies about questions relevant to these areas, it is clear from our review that there has only been moderate progress in constructing a consensus about what we know and understand in these areas. We suggest that research in the field over the next decade still needs to address questions and problems in these areas. Specifically, there is a need for larger-scale studies which employ coherent and, wherever possible, longitudinal research designs. Moreover, it is vital that a convergence and consensus about research methodologies and philosophical positioning is reached. We argue here that the mixing of methods within the same research study is a promising way forward and that there are at least two different views about how this can be achieved.

Some authors believe that the distinction between paradigms is a false one (Gorard, 2010), and maintain that research methodologies and methods can be detached from the epistemology from which they emerge. For Gorard, the key forgotten aspect of research is its design, which involves a choice based on the claims and conclusions to be drawn. Gorard also reminds us that the logic of analysis cannot be based on simple distinctions between quantitative and qualitative research. Commonalities are evident, for example inductive and deductive analysis are used in both traditions: qualitative methods imply concepts of the typical and degrees of frequency; and qualitative researchers often adopt quality checks on research that resemble those used in quantitative research.

From a different perspective, some authors see mixed methods as a third paradigm, which they have called 'pragmatic' (Johnson and Onwuegbuzie, 2004). Indeed, a growing number of authors, mainly from America, have written about the ascendancy of pragmatism as the philosophical foundation for mixed-methods research (Maxcy, 2003; Morgan, 2007;

Tashakkori and Teddlie, 2010). According to these authors, the selection of research strategy depends on its practical significance. In this respect, pragmatism has been presented as offering an account of research that is pluralistic and goes beyond simple dichotomies, such as theory and practice. It focuses on research (inquiry) as resolving problems that present themselves in experience and considers that practice is the driving force for inquiry rather than theory.

To sum up, there are problems with an a-paradigmatic view that adopts pragmatism as the philosophical basis for mixed-methods inquiry, which are beyond the scope of this chapter (see Norwich, 2013, for a more detailed discussion). Nevertheless, we would conclude that the field would benefit if researchers moved away from methodological purism towards embracing diverse approaches. This involves reaching consensus about the value and validity of different kinds of research questions, not just ones associated with exclusive philosophical positions and so-called research paradigms. The clash between scientific and interpretivist approaches can only be avoided if researchers respect and value theory and research approaches from diverse disciplinary and philosophical backgrounds and if they are flexible enough to use or collaborate with those who use different designs for different kinds of problems and questions. This requires tolerance, openness and mutual exchange between different research traditions. Within such a climate, coherent multi-method research designs should feature strongly in the field in its foreseeable future, provided that researchers' aims are consistent with the methodological principles they utilise. We contend that this is a route from disarray to tentative research progress.

Discussion points

- Research in the field of special needs and inclusive education was described in this chapter as being in some disarray. Discuss the reasons accounting for this state and possible ways forward.
- Discuss the contribution of research approaches emanating from diverse disciplinary and philosophical backgrounds in the field of special and inclusive education.
- Discuss the implications of adopting a particular paradigmatic stance with regard to designing, conducting and judging the quality of research in the field of special and inclusive education.
- Research paradigms are viewed by some authors as 'incommensurable', while others believe that the distinction between paradigms is a false one. Discuss the challenge of moving away from methodological purism towards embracing multi-methodological research approaches.

Further Reading

Slee, R. and Allan, J. (2008) *Doing Inclusive Education Research*. Rotterdam: Sense
 Publishers.
An interesting account of the ideological positioning of leading researchers in the field
and their reflections on their methodological decisions.

Tashakkori, A. and Teddlie, C. (eds) (2010) *Handbook of Mixed Methods in Social and
 Behavioural Research*. London: Sage.
A comprehensive overview of recent developments and contemporary issues in mixed-
methods research.

Useful websites

Research methods resources

BERA – methodological paradigms: www.bera.ac.uk/researchers-resources/
publications/methodological-paradigms-in-educational-research.

British Psychological Society website on qualitative research methods: www.bps.org.
uk/taxonomy/term/406.

National Centre for Research Methods: www.ncrm.ac.uk.

Research Methods Knowledge Base: www.socialresearchmethods.net/kb.

Sage Research Methods: srmo.sagepub.com/publicstart?authRejection=true.

Social Sciences Research Methods Centre: www.ssrmc.group.cam.ac.uk.

Research methods journals

International Journal of Quantitative and Qualitative Research Methods: www.eajournals.
org/journals/international-journal-of-quantitative-and-qualitative-research-methods-
ijqqrm.

International Journal of Research and Method in Education: www.tandfonline.com/toc/
cwse20/current.

International Journal of Social Research Methodology: www.tandfonline.com/toc/
tsrm20/current.

(Continued)

(Continued)

Journal of Mixed Methods Research: mmr.sagepub.com.

Methodology: European Journal of Research Methods for the Behavioral and Social Sciences: www.hogrefe.com/periodicals/methodology/about-the-journal-the-editors.

References

Avramidis, E. and Norwich, B. (2011) SEN: the state of research – compromise, consensus or disarray? In L. Peer and G. Reid (eds), *Special Educational Needs*. London: Sage, pp. 24–34.

Avramidis, E. and Smith, B. (1999) An introduction to the major research paradigms and their methodological implications for special needs research. *Emotional and Behavioural Difficulties*, 4(3): 27–36.

Barnes, C., Mercer, G. and Shakespeare, T. (1999) *Exploring Disability: A Sociological Introduction*. London: Polity Press.

Blatchford, P., Bassett, P., Brown, P., Martin, C., Russell, A. and Webster, R. (2009) *The Impact of Support Staff in Schools: Results from the Deployment and Impact of Support Staff (DISS) Project (Strand 2 Wave 2)*. DCSF Research Report 148. London: DCSF.

Bridges, D. (2008) Evidence-based reform in education: a response to Robert Slavin. *European Educational Research Journal*, 7(1): 129–33.

Bury, M. (1991) The sociology of chronic illness: a review of research and prospects. *Sociology of Health and Illness*, 13(4): 451–68.

Clark, C., Dyson, A., Millward, A. and Robson, S. (1999) Theories of inclusion, theories of schools: deconstructing and reconstructing the 'inclusive school'. *British Educational Research Journal*, 25(2): 157–77.

Clough, P. (2000) Routes to inclusion. In P. Clough and J. Corbett (eds), *Theories of Inclusive Education: A Students' Guide*. London: Sage, pp. 1–34.

Cohen, L., Manion, L. and Morrison, K. (2007) *Research Methods in Education*. Abingdon: Routledge.

Davis, P. and Florian, L. (2004) *Teaching Strategies and Approaches for Pupils with Special Educational Needs: A Scoping Study*. Research Report No. 516. London: DfES.

DES (1981) *Education Act*. London: HMSO.

DfES (2001) *Code of Practice: On the Identification and Assessment of Pupils with Special Educational Needs*. London: DfES.

Dyson, A. and Howes, A. (2009) Towards an interdisciplinary research agenda for inclusive education. In P. Hicks, R. Kershner and P. Farrell (eds), *Psychology for Inclusive Education*. London: Routledge, pp. 153–64.

Dyson, A., Howes, A. and Roberts, B. (2002) *A Systematic Review of the Effectiveness of School-Level Actions for Promoting Participation by All Students*. London: EPPI-centre, Social Science Research Unit, Institute of Education.

Evans, J. and Benefield, P. (2001) Systematic reviews of educational research: does the medical model fit? *British Educational Research Journal*, 27(5): 527–41.

Farrell, P. (2000) The impact of research on developments in inclusive education. *International Journal of Inclusive Education*, 4(2): 153–62.

Gorard, S. (2010) Research design as independent of methods. In A. Tashakkori and C. Teddlie (eds), *Handbook of Mixed Methods in Social and Behavioural Research*. London: Sage, pp. 237–42.

Gorard, S. and Cook, T. (2007) Where does good evidence come from? *International Journal of Research and Method in Education*, 30(3): 307–23.

Hammersley, M. (2001) On 'systematic' reviews of research literatures: a 'narrative' response to Evans and Benefield. *British Educational Research Journal*, 27(5): 543–54.

Hammersley, M. (2003) Social research today: some dilemmas and distinctions. *Qualitative Social Work*, 2: 25–44.

Hargreaves, D. (1999) Revitalising educational research: lessons from the past and proposals for the future. *Cambridge Journal of Education*, 29(2): 239–49.

Issitt, J. and Kyriacou, C. (2009) Epistemological problems in establishing an evidence base for classroom practice. *Psychology of Education Review*, 33(1): 47–52.

Johnson, R.B. and Onwuegbuzie, A.J. (2004) Mixed methods research: a research paradigm whose time has come. *Educational Researcher*, 33(7): 14–26.

Kagan, J. (2009) *The Three Cultures: Natural Sciences, Social Sciences and the Humanities in the 21st Century*. Cambridge: Cambridge University Press.

Kugelmass, J. (2001) Collaboration and compromise in creating and sustaining an inclusive school. *International Journal of Inclusive Education*, 5(1): 47–65.

Kuhn, T.S. (1962) *The Structure of Scientific Revolutions*. Chicago, IL: Chicago University Press.

Lewis, A. and Norwich, B. (eds) (2004) *Special Teaching for Special Children? Pedagogies for Inclusion*. Maidenhead: Open University Press.

Lindsay, G. (2007) Annual review: educational psychology and the effectiveness of inclusive education/mainstreaming. *British Journal of Educational Psychology*, 77(1): 1–24.

Lipsky, D.K. and Gartner, A. (1998) Factors for successful inclusion: learning from the past, looking forward to the future. In S.V. Vitello and D.E. Mithaug (eds), *Inclusive Schooling: National and International Perspectives*. Mahwah, NJ: Lawrence Erlbaum, pp. 98–112.

Mammas, C. (2009) 'Getting along with peers in mainstream primary schools: an exploration of the social status of pupils identified as having special educational needs in Cyprus'. Unpublished PhD thesis, University of Cambridge.

Maxcy, S.J. (2003) Pragmatic threads in mixed methods research in the social sciences: the search for multiple modes of inquiry and the end of the philosophy of formalism. In A. Tashakkori and C. Teddlie (eds), *Handbook of Mixed Methods in Social and Behavioural Research*. London; Thousand Oaks, CA: Sage, pp. 51–89.

Mertens, D. and McLaughlin, J.A. (2004) *Research and Evaluation Methods in Special Education*. London: Sage.

Morgan, D.L. (2007) Paradigms lost and pragmatism regained: methodological implications of combining qualitative and quantitative methods. *Journal of Mixed Methods Research*, 1(1): 48–76.

Nind, M. and Wearmouth, J. (2006) Including children with special educational needs in mainstream classrooms: implications for pedagogy from a systematic review. *Journal of Research in Special Educational Needs*, 6(3): 116–24.

Norwich, B. (2013) *Addressing Dilemmas and Tensions in Inclusive Education: Living with Uncertainty*. London: Routledge.

Norwich, B. and Kelly, N. (2005) *Moderate Learning Difficulties and the Future of Inclusion*. Abingdon: RoutledgeFalmer.

Oliver, M. (1999) Final accounts and the parasite people. In M. Corker and S. French (eds), *Disability Discourse*. Maidenhead: Open University Press, pp. 183–91.

Ruijs, N.M. and Peetsma, T.D. (2009) Effects of inclusion on students with and without special educational needs reviewed. *Educational Research Review*, 4(2): 67–9.

SEN Policy Research Forum (2014) Research in special needs and inclusive education: the interface with policy and practice. *Journal of Research in Special Educational Needs*, 14(3): 192–218. DOI: 10.1111/1471–3802.12070.

Skidmore, D. (2004) *Inclusion: The Dynamic of School Development*. Buckingham: Open University Press.

Slavin, R. (2002) Evidence-based education policies: transforming educational practice and research. *Educational Researcher*, 31(7): 15–22.

Solity, J., Deavers, R., Kerfoot, S., Crane, G. and Cannon, K. (2000) The early reading research: the impact of instructional psychology. *Educational Psychology in Practice*, 16(2): 109–28.

Tashakkori, A. and Teddlie, C. (eds) (2010) *Handbook of Mixed Methods in Social and Behavioural Research*. London; Thousand Oaks, CA: Sage.

Thomas, C. (2004) How is disability understood? An examination of sociological approaches. *Disability and Society,* 19(6): 569–83.

Thomas, G. and Loxley, A. (2007) *Deconstructing Special Education and Constructing Inclusion*. Milton Keynes: Open University Press.

UNESCO (1994) *The Salamanca Statement and Framework for Action on Special Needs Education*. Paris: UNESCO.

Inclusion and Special Educational Needs

A Dialogic Inquiry into Controversial Issues

Artemi Sakellariadis

4

Learning objectives

This chapter will help readers to:

- Bring to light the people behind the label of SEN
- Articulate a rationale for including disabled children and young people in ordinary schools
- Demonstrate benefits of inclusion for all
- Explore controversial issues from a range of perspectives
- Challenge conventional forms of academic writing

'I still don't get why you insist' Sophia chides. *'If you ask me, it's quite simple. Inclusion is all right for some, but there will always be those for whom it can never work. I wish you would just accept that and spare us all the hassle.'* I bite my lip and walk in silence, trying to conjure up a constructive response. She does not mean to be curt, I am sure. She probably thinks she understands obvious and insurmountable

difficulties, assumes that there is no merit in my position and sees no reason to discuss it. Sophia nudges me out of my thoughts.

'*Well ...?*' she raises an eyebrow expectantly.

'*Well ...*' I formulate my answer as I speak it, '*this brings back memories. Years ago, when I was a teacher in a special school, an adviser had said that my pupils would have benefitted more from a mainstream education. Thinking he was being deliberately unreasonable in order to provoke, I had refused to engage in conversation. And here I am now, making a similar claim and hoping you will discuss it with me.*'

'*Are you seriously telling me ...,*' she pauses and casts me an inquisitive look. '*No, you're teasing again. Come on, let's not waste our time, there are so many other interesting things to talk about.*'

'*Sophia, I promise you, I have never been more serious about this. I honestly think that the human rights agenda behind the call to include disabled children in ordinary schools is not yet widely understood. Please let us have this conversation now. You know that others are listening in, which makes this all the more important.*'

Discussion point

The question of whether education should be transformed so that disabled children, or those identified as having special educational needs, can be consistently included in their local schools continues to spark debate. Where do you stand? Take a few minutes to articulate what you see as the main advantages of mainstream schooling and of special schooling.

'*OK, let's go for it, it won't take long. Just tell me, what makes you think staff in mainstream schools are well equipped to teach children with profound and multiple learning difficulties?*'

She is evidently thinking about young people with high-level support needs, the preferred term put forward by disabled people (Alliance for Inclusive Education, 2001), but I decide not to challenge her choice of words. She is clearly embarking on this conversation determined to swiftly prove me wrong, so I must pick my words carefully to help her acknowledge her assumptions and explore alternative perspectives.

'*Who do you think is well equipped to teach those with the most complex needs and what is it that equips them?*'

'*Well, specialist SEN staff, of course. They've had all the necessary training.*'

'*Are you saying that it is only their training that equips them to do a good job?*' I ask, knowing that this lets her assume that 'training' is a matter of Initial Teacher Education.

'And their experience, naturally. Knowledge and experience make a good teacher. What are you getting at?'

I say nothing, allowing time for the circularity of her argument to dawn on her. Neither of us speaks and I let my mind follow my thoughts on what she has just said. Surely, it takes more than knowledge and experience to be a good teacher, but this is beside the point. I remember something I wrote many years ago, attempting to expose how the availability of experts can disempower those who have yet to engage with a new experience: At the dawn of the twenty-second century, a mother and her pregnant daughter are debating who will look after the baby. The daughter is adamant that, in line with current practice, her baby will be placed in a Baby Monitoring Institution (BMI) for at least one year. She argues that BMIs provide expert staff trained to attend to all health, nutritional, social and educational needs of babies and toddlers, whereas she is inexperienced and ill-equipped even to pacify a crying baby (Sakellariadis, 2003). Is there a parallel here? Does the availability and marketisation of 'specialist' special educators adversely impact on other teachers' confidence to support the learning and development of young people with high-level support needs? I make a mental note to suggest this as a discussion point for students considering how inclusion policies are put into practice.

'Are you going to tell me what you are getting at?' Sophia repeats her question, reminding me that she is not sufficiently engaged in this conversation to notice any discrepancies.

'I am just thinking that any teacher can access Continuing Professional Development and no teacher can become experienced in anything, unless they are afforded the experience in the first place.'

'Surely you are not suggesting that we all need to become specialists so that any of us can teach any child with any disability!' she presses on, apparently still oblivious to the circularity of her earlier statement. I bite my lip. If she had known what Richard Rieser says about the social model of disability (Rieser, 2000), she would have probably chosen a different form of words. Some people may have one or more impairments (long-term loss of physical or mental function), but that does not make them disabled. According to the social model, disability is an experience; people only become disabled when society fails to make adjustments or remove barriers. In this sense, a wheelchair user is not disabled by their physical impairment (they are able to move around, albeit by different means to most people) but may become dis-abled by an absence of ramps or by other physical barriers. I choose to say none of this to Sophia, who I sense is getting a little impatient. We need to wrap up on this issue of perceived competence of staff.

'No, Sophia, I am not suggesting that at all. All we need to do as teachers is realise that the basic pedagogic principles are the same, no matter what we are helping young people to learn; from how to make friends to how to solve complex mathematical equations. We are well equipped to help young people learn and should not freeze in the headlights of relative inexperience. Plus, of course, we should remember that "we are all ignorant; just about different things" [attributed to Mark Twain]. When the time is right, we can seek knowledge about how some children learn or seek advice on how to support the learning

and development of a particular child. So yes, maybe not everyone in the profession feels well equipped at the moment, but staff do not lack the skills; if anything, some people lack confidence that they already have sufficient skills to support any child's learning, alone or with the help of others.'

I choose to leave it at that, aware that this may be a lot for her to process right now. Even though she may find this to make sense at face value, it probably represents a considerable shift in how she perceives the capacity of ordinary local schools to respond to the full diversity of learners. I hope that she will engage with this sufficiently to realise the shift. If we had more time, I would have explained why seeking support is not an indication of weakness or inadequacy. I would also have reminded her of Gandhi's words that our ability to reach unity in diversity will be the beauty and test of our civilisation. I wonder if I should speak to her about the *Salt Review.* The final report (DCSF, 2010) confirmed that many teachers feel ill-prepared to teach learners with labels of severe or profound and multiple learning difficulties and suggested that this highlights a gap in initial teacher education. It also revealed a widespread perception that this group of learners requires 'carers' rather than educators. Sophia seems ready to pick up the conversation from where we left it and move us in a new direction.

'And why should teachers have to make time to gain more skills which only duplicate the expertise already available in special schools?'

I could raise the issue of children's rights and explain how they may be breached by segregated schooling. Or I could mention national and international legislation or policies calling for the development of inclusive education for all. But our time is limited, so I try something different.

'Did you enjoy your holiday in Portugal last year?'

'I beg your pardon?' she gives me a baffled look, understandably surprised at the question's apparent irrelevance.

'Please answer me. Did you enjoy your holiday in Portugal last year?'

'Yes thank you, as a matter of fact I did. Now what has that got to do with anything?'

'Well, I was just wondering why you chose a new hotel in Portugal, when there are other well established resorts all over the Mediterranean.'

'Ah, now you are being ridiculous. You know I was visiting my sister who lives there. It wasn't just a holiday – I was catching up with family and friends.'

'And would you say that going to school is just education? Shouldn't every child be spending their school days with their brothers, sisters, friends and potential friends from their local community?'

I think of my good friend Eva, a school friend whom I am still in touch with. Long-standing friendships are so precious! We have been there for one another in so many different ways over the years. I wonder if Sophia is still in touch with any of her school friends.

*'**But they need the specialist provision, you know they do.**'* Sophia interrupts my thoughts. I had intended to ask her how she might feel if she were to lose her sight, or her hearing or the use of her legs, and her employer transferred her to another site, making her travel a long distance every day, so that she could be with others that have lost their sight, hearing or use of their legs. But now the conversation is moving in a different direction.

'And just because they might need additional help with some things, you think it is all right to take something away from them? How come a perceived need for adult specialists is allowed to trump children's need to be with their peers and to belong in their local community?' I stop short of saying that this is like putting a child in hospital without allowing family or friends to visit, on the grounds that the child needs the medical intervention.

*'**Well, you've got to be realistic. You either deprive them of their peers or of the tailor-made provision. Which would you rather do?**'*

'Neither, Sophia. Neither.' I am unable to conceal a hint of impatience. I take a deep breath, then add in a calmer tone: *'With today's emphasis on personalised learning, there is no reason why tailor-made provision has to be offered in a separate place'* (CSIE staff and associates, 2009). I am painfully aware that many children and young people have been included in their local school without appropriate support and, consequently, have found the experience neither pleasant nor beneficial. Did anyone suggest that including everyone in ordinary schools is easy, or that schools can transform overnight? We know that there is a tendency in organisations and systems to resist change, but does that mean that we stop trying? I remember recently hearing Peter Farrell responding to parents who were praising special schools following their children's unpleasant experiences in mainstream education:

> We have good evidence that there are many children with a range of disabilities who are marginalised in mainstream schools, who are bullied in mainstream schools, who feel uncomfortable in mainstream schools. That is not to say that inclusion is not a good thing, it's just to say that we haven't actually got it right yet. (Farrell, 2010)

*'**Well that's a lovely rhetoric but we both know that the provision is not there. Children with severe learning difficulties simply cannot access the curriculum. What would they do all day in a mainstream school?**'*

I stop dead in my tracks. I lean against a tree, take off my right shoe and shake out a stone. I put my shoe back on, take it off again and shake it some more. Sophia seems ready to move on but I stay put. I take off my glasses and slowly clean both lenses. Without uttering a word, I hold them up to the light then clean them some more. With the corner of my eye I notice Sophia adjusting her hair band. Her eyes are focused at some point in the distance and she seems to be thinking. Good. She needs to make a mental leap that my words alone cannot engineer for her. She needs to realise that the proposal is not simply to place children in local schools as we know them; they have been set up with a narrower population in mind. What is called for is a critical examination of how we see disability, a radical reconsideration of how we organise teaching and learning in schools and an innovative mindset allowing us to perceive pupil progress in light of 'measuring what we value', if we must measure anything, instead of 'valuing what we can measure' (Ainscow, 2005). I look at my friend tenderly. She sounded impatient a few minutes ago. She probably thinks that parents who want their children with high-level support needs to go to their local school are unrealistic and that their choices are more sentimental than rational. One day she might understand that lived experience has led some parents to expand their sense of what is normal; not in the sense of what is average or what is shared by most people, but more in the sense of 'what can be considered a natural expression of our shared humanity' (Sakellariadis, 2012). For the time being, she, like so many others, is focusing on differences between disabled and non-disabled people and overlooks all of what we have in common. Sophia still seems absorbed in her thoughts. I wait patiently. A cat is sitting on a wall nearby, leisurely licking its paws. A welcome breeze brings the fresh scent of spring. We stay like this, almost frozen in time. Eventually, Sophia glances at me, her earlier look of concern gradually changing to a smile, as she sets us off walking again.

'I think I see what you are getting at. You are saying that whatever learning opportunities are available to children in special schools, could be made available to them in their local school. The option is not there … not because it cannot be done but because the capacity has not been developed.'

'Yet.' I interrupt. *'The capacity has not been developed yet.'* If only I could take her to Canada, show her some of the schools in the Hamilton-Wentworth Catholic District School Board, where they closed all of their special schools in 1969 and have been educating all children and young people in mainstream schools ever since (Hansen et al., 2006). Or if I could show her some of the excellent inclusive practice already unfolding in some schools over here. I wonder if Sophia knows how patchy the picture is in this country. The Centre for Studies on Inclusive Education (CSIE) has shown, through its Trends reports which date back to the 1980s, that in some areas much larger proportions of children are consistently sent to special schools than in other areas (Black and Norwich, 2014). I have written about this separately (Sakellariadis, 2014). It is not clear why this happens, but it seems to be linked to people's understandings of disability, and of disability equality. Whatever the reasons, it is intriguing that such a pattern of contrasting responses to diversity exists. Sophia is oblivious to my thoughts.

'OK, so the capacity has not been developed yet in mainstream schools. However …' She takes a deep breath and I can sense there is something else troubling her. *'… even if we agree that this is what we'd like in principle, surely in practice concentrating resources in one place makes more sense financially.'*

I knew this would come up sooner or later. Should I explain this or shall I let her work it out for herself? How difficult can it be to figure out that paying for staff to travel to mainstream schools is cheaper than paying for pupils to travel to special schools, often very long distances twice a day by taxi with a paid escort? Millions are spent each year for the sole purpose of getting children from home to a special school and back again. A recent report maintains that children's services rarely keep records in a way that enables them to evaluate the total cost of supporting an individual child. Transport costs and the costs of monitoring provision are identified as expenditure not being combined with the charges made by providers, since they come from separate budgets. The report suggests that without this financial information, it is not possible to make informed judgements about the most cost-effective placement for a particular child (Audit Commission, 2007). Transport costs aside, how hard can it be to realise that for every special school that closes, funds needed to run the school and maintain the buildings could enable the same staff to help develop more inclusive practice in ordinary schools? Sophia would probably say that the resources she had in mind are more than the human resources of my argument. That might not stand up to scrutiny either. For a start, as Micheline Mason has said (2007, personal communication), what better resource to support disabled children's learning and development than their non-disabled peers? An invaluable resource always available, absolutely free, in ordinary schools. Doesn't Sophia know that what children learn in school is not limited to the curriculum subjects but includes, for example, how to be a five-year-old, or a teenager, or any age for that matter? Yes, there is something to be said about physical resources, but my hunch is that Sophia's understanding would be different to mine. Am I ready to subject myself to the discourse of care and to assumptions about *Snoezelen* rooms or hydrotherapy pools as essential educational resources of unique benefit to disabled children alone? No, not now. I let her assumption about financial benefit lie and decide to explore another thought.

'*Are you saying that financial considerations alone should dictate decisions that affect the quality of people's lives?*' I am aware that articulating a vague concern can serve to clarify it and, occasionally, to expose it as unsound.

'Well, no, not exactly. I am not saying that finances should dictate where children go to school, only that cost should be taken into account.'

'*So, how should that impact upon a decision, if appropriate provision was available in either type of setting? Even if it was cheaper to send children to separate special schools, and therefore this question arose, would you see cost-cutting as sufficient justification for uprooting young people and keeping them apart from their local community, sometimes throughout their school lives?*' I stop short of asking her how she might feel if cost-cutting measures were affecting her own children. How would it seem if, responding to funding cuts, her local school removed art or maths from the curriculum? Maybe I should talk to her about Judith Snow, the Canadian activist, who compares the cost and effort of ensuring that a disabled child has a good education in their local school, to the cost and effort of ensuring an Olympic diver prepares and performs well (Snow, 2001).

Discussion point

Making available to disabled people facilities and services that most people take for granted, often necessitates additional expenditure (for example, the cost of providing hearing loops, accessible toilets, Braille signs or including disabled children in ordinary schools). What weight do you think such financial implications should carry? Who do you think should decide, and on what grounds, what facilities and services are made available to whom?

'But some may not benefit from being in their local community. Some of them are not in a position to make friends, are they?' Sophia naïvely questions the merits of togetherness and overlooks young people's emotional well-being.

'What?!? Of course they are! With all due respect, do you think you might be finding such friendships hard to imagine because you don't have any disabled friends yourself?'

'Well no, but ...'

'Or is there a particular mould in your mind that a friend has to fit in, in order to be called a friend?'

I had promised myself to remain calm throughout this conversation and I am not doing too well right now. But what is a friend, if not someone who loves you for who you are? And how are non-disabled youngsters to get to know and appreciate their disabled peers, if they are deliberately and consistently separated? Sophia has remained silent and I feel I owe her an apology.

'Look, I am sorry, I didn't mean to sound terse. Let's go back to my earlier question: would you see cost-cutting as a sufficient reason to uproot young people and keep them away from their local community?'

'I'm not sure. Why is it suddenly so bad to be away from your local community? Lots of children go to boarding school and that's not frowned upon, is it?'

'Well, in many ways it is, but I cannot see a sustainable comparison. Removing a young person from their local community to place them within a homogeneous smaller community of perceived privilege is hardly comparable to landing young people together in a disparate assemblage of ostracised youngsters, don't you think? Are you seriously comparing elitism with dismissal?'

'Whoa, you've said too much there! Why do you say disparate? They have their disability in common, don't they?'

She is confusing experience with impairment again. I let that go.

'Sophia, would you choose to work in a school deliberately staffed entirely by brunettes?'

'Now you are being flippant; we are talking about responding to children's needs. Children who share a disability also share similar special educational needs. What is wrong with organising schools around those needs?'

'*It would be like making all people with curly hair go to the same hairdresser.*' She is making sweeping assumptions again. If she has not yet grasped the full range of diversity, I cannot explain it here and now. But suggesting that everyone who has, for example, Down syndrome should be treated in the same way is as naïve as suggesting that everyone who lives on the same street learns in the same way. To think that people with a particular impairment have more in common with others who have the same impairment than with their peers who do not, is also an assumption that does not stand up to scrutiny.

'*No, no. Let's explore this.*' It is her that is pursuing the logic in the argument now, I am pleased to notice. '***Don't you think that children themselves would prefer to be in a school with others like them, rather than being thrown in a place where they are forever standing out as being different?***'

'*They might do. But what would this mean for them in the long term? Most children would rather eat sweets than vegetables, but would you raise them on a strict diet of nothing but sweets?*' If we had more time, I would have tried to deconstruct the notion of what is best for the child. Sophia may not have been seduced by the perception of a cosy bubble if she realised the extent of discrimination disabled people face. Does she know that the Equalities and Human Rights Commission (EHRC) has found that hundreds of thousands of disabled people regularly experience harassment or abuse but have come to accept this because of our society's culture of disbelief or 'collective denial' (EHRC, 2011)? Does she know that, as a means of putting this right, the EHRC has called for new research in order to better understand how segregated education, or inadequately supported inclusive education, impacts on attitudes towards disabled people and on disabled children and young people's life chances (EHRC, 2012)? The reciprocal link between ignorance and prejudice simply has to be broken. And if all this was not enough, we also know that separate special schools have lower expectations of children; diversity tends to get pathologised and young people are often destined for a life in day centres. If Sophia chose to engage with the bigger picture, would she still opt to commit people to a life of social isolation?

'***Come on, let us be serious. Let us take children who suffer from autism, for example.***'

I flinch, but say nothing. To suggest that anyone 'suffers' from autism, or Down syndrome for that matter, is little more than a projection of our own assumptions upon their lived experience. I smile at the fleeting memory of Temple Grandin saying that if she could snap her fingers and be non-autistic, she would not. 'Autism is part of what I am. … I would not want to lose my ability to think visually' (Grandin, 2008). To mention this now could spark off a long debate on individual perceptions of disability, which we do not have time for. Sophia is already halfway through her next sentence: '***What is wrong with putting them all in the same school with staff who really understand their needs and have developed appropriate provision? They would be in a happy, friendly and absolutely appropriate environment that fosters their development without the pressure of being different.***'

I could tell her about a number of adults with autism who fully support inclusive education in ordinary schools. I remember a keynote speech at a conference many years ago where the speaker, an adult with autism, described her parents' fight to get her into a mainstream school because they were adamant that autism doesn't need to see autism. I pick my words very carefully. '*At first glance the thought of a pressure-free environment may appear seductive. But if you think about it, a pressure-free environment is not a priority for everyone else, is it? Most children are subjected to the pressure of learning tough subjects and/or taking stressful exams; we justify this on the grounds that they are gaining knowledge and skills that will serve them well in adult life. Why should it be any different for disabled children? What exactly would we be protecting them from, by removing the pressure of being different, and how long do we think we can protect them for?*' She could have chosen to challenge me with the issue of schooling for deaf children and the need to respect deaf culture but, at the end of the day, I believe the same argument still holds. Surely, in the twenty-first century, everyone's right to belong in an inclusive society is no longer contested. If we want to live together as adults, we have to go to school together as children. When the London Borough of Newham was redesigning its educational provision in the wake of the 1981 Education Act, it sought an innovative solution to this challenge. Following extensive consultations and deliberations, the Council decided to 'build, develop and preserve deaf culture within the mainstream' (Jordan and Goodey, 2002): a primary and a secondary school were set up to offer resourced provision for deaf children, while every child had the choice of attending their local or one of the resourced schools.

Discussion points

- Do you believe that every child or young person should have the opportunity to spend time with other young people similar to them? If yes, who should be the best judge of which similarities between young people are significant?
- Do you believe that every child or young person has a right to be part of the local community in which they live?
- If you have answered 'yes' to both the above, how would you suggest that both considerations can be honoured?

Sophia has been walking in silence for a brief while, potentially thinking about what I have just asked her. She now takes a deep breath and seems ready to resume our conversation.

'*I'll tell you what we need to protect them from. Bullying. Children can be so cruel, why subject children with special needs to it?*'

I make a mental note to return to her choice of words but, for now, respond to her question directly.

'*Yes, children can be cruel and so can adults, if they think they can get away with it. Are you saying that bullying only happens in mainstream schools and, therefore, those who attend separate special schools are in a bully-free environment?*'

'How do you mean?'

I wonder if she has ever set foot in a special school, but don't want to embarrass her by asking. We seem to be dealing with a large number of assumptions here, so I decide to deal with them quickly, one at a time.

'Well, first of all let me tell you this: researchers have found that young adolescents said to have moderate learning difficulties were bullied just as much in either type of school.' In fact, this research put forward a far more disturbing picture:

> A notable emergent theme from the study was the high incidence of 'bullying' that was experienced. Though experienced in both settings, those in special schools experienced far more 'bullying' from children in other mainstream schools and from peers and outsiders in their neighbourhood. (Norwich and Kelly, 2004)

'But, even if we thought that bullying only happens in ordinary schools, are you seriously suggesting that we should send disabled children away rather than tackle the bullying? Is this what you would do about other forms of bullying?'

'What are you smiling at?'

'Nothing, sorry. The thought of removing children to protect them from bullying could be rather amusing in the context of other forms of prejudice-based bullying.' I manage to stifle a little giggle. *'What do you suggest we do about transphobic bullying, for example? Take transgender children and adults out of ordinary schools and send them somewhere else to keep them safe and protected?'*

'OK, I guess you are right. You'd have to tackle the bullying, wouldn't you?'

'M-hm.' If we had more time I would tell her about the recent Ofsted report which says that disabled children are among those who bear the brunt of bullying, even in schools where other forms of prejudice-based bullying are more effectively dealt with. Ofsted says that this happens because staff often dismiss offensive language as banter (Ofsted, 2012).

'Yes, OK, I'll give you that. Protection from bullying is not really a reason to turn children with special needs away from schools.'

Now is as good a time as any.

'Actually, Sophia, can we just stop and think for a moment who you might mean when you refer to children with special needs?' She throws me a baffled look, then takes a few moments to think.

'Well I can't give you a definition, but we both know who we are talking about, don't we?'

'We may or may not do. The point is, the words that we use serve to shape our thinking, and vice versa. I'm just wondering what we are doing to young people's sense of identity and what power structures we are supporting, by referring to a potentially undefined group of people as "children with special needs". Can you try to put into words for me who it is you think we are talking about?'

Sophia walks on in silence, squinting her eyes and tightening her lips. I am not surprised that she cannot come up with an easy answer. In the words of Baroness Warnock:

The definition, as you probably know, which comes in the 1981 Education Act, is the purest vicious circle you will ever know. A special need is defined as *'any need that the school needs to take special measures to meet'*. Well, that is not much of a definition but it is the only definition there is. (Warnock, 2005)

I am also reminded of the words of Alan Dyson: 'Special educational needs are needs that arise within the educational system rather than the individual, and indicate a need for the system to change further in order to accommodate individual differences' (Dyson, 1990). As I have written elsewhere, the difference between whether a child 'has' or 'experiences' difficulties is similar to whether a child 'brings' or 'finds' difficulties at school. To many this might seem like a futile word game; to others such differences are of paramount importance, not least because they can have a strong impact on young people's sense of identity (CSIE staff and associates, 2009).

'Look, sorry, I can't and I am beginning to worry that we are running out of time. Just tell me this: I can see some logic in including disabled children in ordinary schools, but we've got a system that works well. It has worked well for years. If it isn't broken, why fix it?'

'Because it doesn't serve us well. Not all of us. Disabled adults have been saying for years that being sent to separate special schools leads to adult lives at the margins of society.' The absence of disabled people's voices in debates about education for disabled children has been heavily criticised. Derrick Armstrong says these voices need to be taken seriously because 'they challenge both the homogeneity of experience and the social relations that have constructed difference as "abnormal"' (Armstrong, 2003: 116).

'So the people who designed this system were wrong?' She says this in a quiet voice, which might suggest that her steadfast support for the current system is beginning to waver.

'Well, yes and no. For a start, please don't imagine designers of education systems sat around a drawing board conjuring up the idea of mainstream schools for some and separate special schools for others. Far from it, this dual system is more the product of evolution than of conscious and deliberate planning.' On another day I might have said happenstance.

'What do you mean yes and no?' She seems troubled by the suggestion that we have arrived here more by chance than judgement.

'Only that it is a system that reflects the moral values of its time. I wrote about this recently. Current ideas about schooling were established over 100 years ago, when disabled people were thought to have no place in mainstream society. Although cultural norms have significantly shifted and disabled people are being increasingly valued as rightful members of our society, current educational practice has yet to embrace these changing attitudes [CSIE staff and associates, 2010]. *Today's schools have a moral and legal obligation to promote disability equality and to foster good relations between disabled and non-disabled people* [Equality Act, 2010]. *Inclusion for all is a fundamental human rights question, to which education is called upon to find an answer* [Sakellariadis, 2007].'

'But what can we do? We are talking about the need for massive change here. How can we begin to bring that about?'

'We don't need to begin anything; change is already underway. We simply need to embrace the transformation and use every opportunity to explore our assumptions and reflect on our practice.' I stop short of referring to a need to address our 'collective indifference' (Slee, 2010). *'We also need to share examples of good practice as widely as possible and remember that where there's a will there's a way.'* I remember an Ofsted report on the quality of provision for pupils said to have learning difficulties and disabilities, which concluded: 'Effective provision was distributed equally in the mainstream and special schools visited, but there was more good and outstanding provision in resourced mainstream schools than elsewhere' (Ofsted, 2006).

Case study: Emersons Green Primary School

Emersons Green Primary School in South Gloucestershire is a mainstream school with a resource base for pupils with physical and/or visual impairments. Purpose-built and first opened in 2000, the school has been set up so that provision in the resource base (which opened in 2001) forms an integral part of the school, intentionally moving away from earlier models of locating a 'unit' in a particular space of the school building, separate from the mainstream classes.

The school ensures that everyone is welcome and feels valued. Learning is organised in ways that are meaningful and relevant to every learner, while the school ensures that academic, social, physical and other forms of learning are all celebrated.

There is a high adult:child ratio at break times. Over and above supervising the children, adults facilitate cooperative play and other interactions in constructive ways. They often model ways for disabled and non-disabled children to play together, then gradually stand back and let the young people develop their own play and friendships.

Developing inclusive provision is seen as an ongoing process. Anywhere you look, you can find evidence of diversity being embraced. Situations which another school may have found challenging, if not impossible, here appear commonplace and ordinary. I was particularly struck by the 10-year-old peer mentor who fulfilled his duties with the help of an assistive communication device.

'That makes perfect sense, thanks. Are there any resources that you would recommend?'

We have now reached the station and are walking towards the platform. Are there more resources I would recommend? I certainly know of some excellent resources (Alderson, 1999; Booth and Ainscow, 2011; CSIE staff and associates, 2015; DfES and Disability Rights

Commission, 2006; Hayes, 2004; Pearpoint et al., 1992; Tashie et al., 2006), but I hesitate to go through them now.

'At the danger of sounding too simplistic, you don't need great big manuals lining your shelves. Developing inclusive education is not so much about what you do, as about how you do it. We are talking about a process, not a method.'

'What a wonderful note to finish our conversation on.' Sophia stops by the station entrance and turns to bid me farewell. We both understand the need to bring our conversation to an abrupt close. I wish her a constructive journey, the editors check her ticket and she is on her way. My trusted writing partner, albeit a figment of my imagination, has served her purpose. No doubt she will be conjured up again when I next choose to write something as a dialogue, attempting to be both scholarly and engaging. Walking away, I try to remember something I recently wrote. The words come to me and I recount them with significant trepidation, lest they get misconstrued as unappreciative of the effort, dedication and well-meaning of special school staff. They should not be:

> [We look] forward to the day when our society collectively and unanimously looks back in disbelief at the time when a small minority of young people were routinely ostracised from their local communities, in the name of their own good. (CSIE, 2010)

Summary

Disabled adults and their allies know that children who are sent to separate special schools often end up living adult lives at the margins of society. They are clear that, if we are to live our lives together in an inclusive society, disabled children should be included in ordinary schools. All children should be encouraged to learn and develop alongside their brothers, sisters, friends and potential friends from the local community.

Others maintain that special schools are needed, on the grounds that they offer specialised provision not available in ordinary schools and provide a better environment for the pupils who attend them. Instances where inclusion has been insufficiently resourced and/or poorly managed are sometimes cited as examples to support this claim.

These positions are not mutually exclusive. The former represents a human rights position, the latter a partial reflection on existing practice. The fact remains that including disabled children in ordinary schools is possible and can benefit everyone. If real choice is to be extended to all parents, as current and previous UK governments have pledged, the choice of mainstream education has to exist, therefore the capacity to include disabled children must be developed in ordinary schools. The effectiveness of this will depend, among other things, on the extent to which educators embrace the moral imperative to transform education.

Further reading

Personal narratives

Chib, M. (2011) *One Little Finger*. London: Sage.
This is the autobiography of Malini Chib, a personal friend and an amazing woman, who is a disability rights activist. Malini has cerebral palsy and a Master's degree in Gender Studies. She wrote this book over the course of two years, typing with one finger.

Higashida, N. (2013) *The Reason I Jump*. London: Sceptre Books.
The remarkable testament of a 13-year-old putting forward his personal experience of having autism.

Professional experiences

Hansen, J., Leyden, G., Bunch, G. and Pearpoint, J. (2006) *Each Belongs: The Remarkable Story of the First School System to Move to Inclusion*. Toronto: Inclusion Press.
The story of one local authority in Canada, which chose to close all of its special schools in 1969, and has been educating all children and young people in ordinary schools ever since.

Hart, S., Dixon, A., Drummond, M.J. and McIntyre, D. (2004) *Learning Without Limits*. Maidenhead: Open University Press.
Accessible and engaging, this book describes how a group of teachers uncomfortable with ideas of fixed ability developed teaching practices which avoid labelling by perceived ability.

Thomas, G., Walker, D. and Webb, J. (1998) *The Making of the Inclusive School*. London: Routledge.
Like other books telling similar stories (e.g. Jupp, 1992), this book explores philosophical arguments and presents the story of how a special school in South-West England transformed itself into an inclusive service, transferring all its pupils to ordinary local schools.

West, D. (2012) *Signs of Hope: Deafhearing Family Life*. Newcastle-upon-Tyne: Cambridge Scholars Publishing.
A creative and engaging representation of stories about resisting conventional discourses of deafness.

(Continued)

(Continued)

Theoretical perspectives

Goodley, D., Hughes, B. and Davis, L. (2012) *Disability and Social Theory: New Developments and Directions*. Basingstoke: Palgrave Macmillan.
A detailed exploration of disability from a range of theoretical perspectives.

Rieser, R. (2000) 'Disability discrimination, the final frontier: Disablement, history and liberation', in M. Cole (ed.), *Education, Equality and Human Rights: Issues of Gender, 'Race', Sexuality, Special Needs and Social Class*. London: RoutledgeFalmer.
In this chapter, Richard Rieser clearly explains the medical and social models of disability and explores ethical, political, social and educational challenges of inclusive education for all.

Rix, J. (2015) *Must Inclusion be Special? Rethinking Educational Support within a Community of Provision*. Abingdon: Routledge.
This book examines the discord between special and inclusive education.

Rustemier, S. (2002) *Social and Educational Justice: The Human Rights Framework for Inclusion*. Bristol: Centre for Studies on Inclusive Education.
This report articulates the human rights case for including disabled learners in ordinary schools and challenges traditional assumptions sustaining segregation.

Shakespeare, T. (2014) *Disability Rights and Wrongs Revisited*. Abingdon: Routledge.
This book offers an overview of the field of disability studies and proposes new research agendas.

Useful websites

www.anti-bullyingalliance.org.uk/send-programme The Anti-Bullying Alliance works to stop bullying and create safe environments for all children and young people. Part of its website is dedicated to reducing bullying of disabled children and young people and those identified as having special educational needs; it includes links to free resources and online training for professionals.

www.csie.org.uk The Centre for Studies on Inclusive Education (CSIE) is a national charity, founded in 1982, working to advance equality and eliminate discrimination in education. The Centre offers information and awareness-raising seminars; provides training and consultancy nationally and internationally; and produces a wide range of resources for schools, local authorities, parents and students, including student teachers.

www.worldofinclusion.com World of Inclusion is a consultancy that provides advice, resources and training in the UK and around the world to develop equality for disabled people especially in education.

References

Ainscow, M. (2005) Developing inclusive education systems: what are the levers for change? *Journal of Educational Change*, 6: 109–24.

Alderson, P. (1999) *Learning and Inclusion: The Cleves School Experience*. London: David Fulton Publishers.

Alliance for Inclusive Education (2001) *The Inclusion Assistant: Helping Young People with High Level Support Needs in Mainstream Education*. London: Alliance for Inclusive Education.

Armstrong, D. (2003) *Experiences of Special Education: Re-evaluating Policy and Practice through Life Stories*. London: RoutledgeFalmer.

Audit Commission (2007) *Out of Authority Placements for Special Educational Needs*. London: Audit Commission.

Black, A. and Norwich, B. (2014) *Contrasting Responses to Diversity: School Placement Trends 2007–2013 for All Local Authorities in England*. Bristol: Centre for Studies on Inclusive Education.

Booth, T. and Ainscow, M. (2011) *Index for Inclusion: Developing Learning and Participation in Schools*, 3rd edn. Bristol: Centre for Studies on Inclusive Education.

CSIE (2010) Some more equal than others? Posted 20 May 2010. Retrieved April 2015 from www.csie. org.uk/news/2010.shtml.

CSIE staff and associates (2009) *The Welcome Workbook: A Self-Review Framework for Expanding Inclusive Provision in Your Local Authority*. Bristol: Centre for Studies on Inclusive Education.

CSIE staff and associates (2010) *Developing a Single Equality Policy for Your School: A CSIE Guide*. Bristol: Centre for Studies on Inclusive Education.

CSIE staff and associates (2015) *Equality: Making It Happen – A Guide for Schools to Help Schools Ensure Everyone is Safe, Included and Learning*. Bristol: Centre for Studies on Inclusive Education.

DCSF (2010) *Salt Review: Independent Review of Teacher Supply for Pupils with Severe, Profound and Multiple Learning Difficulties (SLD and PMLD)*. Nottingham: DCSF Publications.

DfES and Disability Rights Commission (2006) *Implementing the Disability Discrimination Act in Schools and Early Years Settings: A Training Resource for Schools and Local Authorities*. Nottingham: DfES Publications.

Dyson, A. (1990) Special educational needs and the concept of change. *Oxford Review of Education*, 16(1): 55–66.

EHRC (2011) *Hidden in Plain Sight: Inquiry into Disability-Related Harassment*. Retrieved April 2015 from www.equalityhumanrights.com/sites/default/files/documents/disabilityfi/ehrc_hidden_in_plain_sight_3.pdf.

EHRC (2012) *Out in the Open: Tackling Disability-Related Harassment: A Manifesto for Change*. Retrieved May 2014 from www.equalityhumanrights.com/uploaded_files/disabilityfi/out_in_the_open_dhi_manifesto.pdf.

Equality Act (2010) Retrieved April 2015 from www.legislation.gov.uk/ukpga/2010/15/contents.

Farrell, P. (2010) *The Big Questions*, BBC programme, 9 May 2010. Retrieved May 2010 from www.bbc. co.uk/programmes/b007zpll.

Grandin, T. (2008) *Thinking in Pictures and Other Reports from My Life with Autism*. New York: Vintage.

Hansen, J., Leyden, G., Bunch, G. and Pearpoint, J. (2006) *Each Belongs: The Remarkable Story of the First School System to Move to Inclusion*. Toronto: Inclusion Press.

Hayes, J. (2004) Visual annual reviews: how to include pupils with learning difficulties in their educational reviews. *Support for Learning*, 19(4): 175–80.

Jordan, L. and Goodey, C. (2002) *Human Rights and School Change: The Newham Story*. Bristol: Centre for Studies on Inclusive Education.

Jupp, K. (1992) *Everyone Belongs: Mainstream Education for Children with Severe Learning Difficulties.* London: Souvenir Press.

Norwich, B. and Kelly, N. (2004) Pupils' views on inclusion: moderate learning difficulties and bullying in mainstream and special schools. *British Educational Research Journal*, 30(1): 43–65.

Ofsted (2006) *Inclusion: Does it Matter where Pupils are Taught?* London: Office for Standards in Education (Ofsted).

Ofsted (2012) *No Place for Bullying.* Retrieved April 2015 from www.gov.uk/government/uploads/system/uploads/attachment_data/file/413234/No_place_for_bullying.pdf.

Pearpoint, J., Forest, M. and Snow, J. (1992) *The Inclusion Papers: Strategies to Make Inclusion Work.* Toronto: Inclusion Press.

Rieser, R. (2000) Disability discrimination, the final frontier: disablement, history and liberation. In M. Cole (ed.), *Education, Equality and Human Rights: Issues of Gender, 'Race', Sexuality, Special Needs and Social Class,* 3rd edn. London: RoutledgeFalmer, pp. 159–89.

Sakellariadis, A.I. (2003) 'Confusion or inclusion? A comparative case study of individual perceptions of inclusion'. Unpublished MEd thesis, University of Bristol.

Sakellariadis, A.I. (2007) 'Voices of inclusion: perspectives of mainstream primary staff on working with disabled children'. Unpublished PhD thesis, University of Bristol.

Sakellariadis, A.I. (2012) A wider sense of normal? Seeking to understand Pierre Rivière through the lens of autism. *Emotion, Space and Society*, 5(4), Special Issue on Pierre Rivière: 269–78.

Sakellariadis, A.I. (2014) Issuing a ticket but keeping the door locked: the need for real change on disability equality. *Race Equality Teaching*, 32(2), Special Issue on Public Sector Equality Duty.

Slee, R. (2010) *The Irregular School: Exclusion, Schooling and Inclusive Education.* London: Routledge.

Snow, J. (2001) Diving for a Better World. Retrieved August 2015 from www.inclusion.com/artcreating whatiknow.html.

Tashie, C., Shapiro-Barnard, S. and Rossetti, Z. (2006) *Seeing the Charade: What We Need to Do and Undo to Make Friendships Happen.* Nottingham: Inclusive Solutions.

Warnock, M. (2005) Select Committee on Education and Skills: Minutes of Oral Evidence Taken on 31 October 2005. Retrieved April 2015 from www.publications.parliament.uk/pa/cm200506/cmselect/cmeduski/478/5103103.htm.

The Potential Impact and Influence of the Social Model of Disability

5

Charles Weedon

Learning objectives

This chapter will help readers to:

- Recognise the ways in which disabilities may be socially constructed and how this might impact within education
- Be aware of how socio-economic status interacts with the ways in which we respond to disabilities
- Understand how these factors may impact on assessment and examination arrangements, and of how issues of institutional and administrative convenience lead us sometimes to impose disabled identities on individuals who have no functional impairments – other than those imposed by the examination hall

Background: The context

In schools such as the one where I work, support-for-learning staff brace themselves for a perceptible surge of referrals at the start of the exam season each year. Almost continuous assessment is the hallmark of the exam years in schools: learners are subjected to a relent-less diet of learning outcomes, practice exams, 'prelims', national assessment bank tasks and, finally, the 'real' exam. It tends to commence when a learner is 14 or 15 years of age – and it continues until formal education is complete.

This sharp increase in the tempo of assessment has one inevitable and recurring conse-quence: experienced subject teachers report barriers to achievement that had apparently escaped detection until this point:

> Jamie may be a scatty and disorganised lad, but he's up there with the best of them in his grasp of plant reproduction/historical bias/subtle use of extended metaphor (or whatever). But he never performs at anything like the right level in formal exams …

The referral process leads, usually, to some formal assessment. The already over-assessed learner is subjected to a barrage of further assessment, standardised tests and data gathering – and to be sure, quite often some subtle but well-defined barrier to achievement is identified, and compensatory examination arrangements are put in place so that true levels of attainment may now be demonstrated in all these tests and examinations.

How did this happen? Had we been remiss in not identifying the difficulty earlier, much earlier? Or is it some kind of late-onset developmental difficulty that manifests itself in the mid-teens, then fades in the mid-twenties?

Or can it be argued perhaps more plausibly that educational institutions, driven by a bio-medical model of disability in combination with the demands and dynamics of the assessment industry, are creating these disabilities and barriers: have institutional imperatives habituated us into creating and accepting barriers that, for some learners, simply need not be there at all? For example, should the mildly dyslexic student who needs to use a word-processor and is allowed extra time in formal examinations be regarded as, or categorised as, 'disabled'? They certainly are categorised as such but only because of our assumption that we should measure mastery of a 'corpus of knowledge' by means of handwritten examinations that have to be completed in a limited period of time. To access the necessary accommodations, we are compelled to label the exam candidate as 'dyslexic'. Where the difficulty is a modest one, often the individual will need this label under no circumstances other than the examination hall. In doing this, we are causing these individuals to adopt a disabled persona, and for reasons it might be argued of doubtful validity. Crucially, if we were to dispense with that one assumption about the mode of assessing student competencies then – for some indi-viduals with dyslexia – we will have dispensed with the label of 'disability'.

What is a 'social model of disability'?

The social model of disability (e.g. Oliver, 1990; Barnes, 1991) suggests that many of the barriers faced by disabled people are environmental and societal – that certain individual characteristics and impairments that need not necessarily be disabling actually become disabling only because of the ways in which society responds to them. The barriers are therefore within the environment, not within the individual.

In contrast, a bio-medical model of disability will view those same characteristics, traits or impairments as disabling features intrinsically rooted within the individual, and which cause clear disadvantage to that individual. Our responses therefore focus upon the individual, rather than the context within which that individual is immersed.

It can be argued that many of the key professionals involved with barriers to learning at school level are still quite strongly influenced by a bio-medical model: while we may recognise and applaud the concept of lessening the environmental barriers, we find it hard to see just how it applies to our field – and for some of us, perhaps for most of us, the bio-medical concept of disabling individual differences influences much of our thinking and responses.

MacDonald (2009: 348), referring specifically to dyslexic students in higher education, captures the tension between the two models and challenges our thinking by stepping back from education. He quotes C. Wright Mills' reflections on unemployment: that when just one man in a city of 100,000 is unemployed, then 'that is his personal trouble … But when in a nation of 50 million employees, 15 million are unemployed, the very structure of opportunity has collapsed.'

Removed in this way from the context of education, the conflict between two contesting explanatory paradigms is immediately evident. Do the roots of an individual's difficulty lie primarily within that individual? Very few of us, if any, would be comfortable with such an assertion about unemployment – it clearly belongs to a long-gone era. Or do they lie, at least in part, in the structures within which that individual exists? For unemployment, this is clearly the case. MacDonald (2009: 347) argues that our perceptions of dyslexia are rooted firmly within the 'his personal trouble' paradigm; and that 'social class positioning and institutional discrimination shape the experiences of people living with this condition'.

In our teaching and learning in schools, we have come some way towards accepting a social model. We accept completely the need to differentiate and individualise learning so that the classroom is as truly inclusive as is possible, so that each learner, whatever their characteristics and individual traits, can learn and develop according to their own needs and attributes.

But in our formal assessment practice, that premise changes: we revert to thinking of learning difficulties as if they are intrinsic to the individual; and accordingly, in our attempts to help, we focus on those individuals rather than the context within which they function. We do this by assigning people to categories of disability (about which we often disagree, sometimes passionately); and then we make compensatory arrangements for those in our assigned categories with the intention that their 'disability' should not constitute a barrier to their achievement.

Barriers to learning

My work involves identifying and responding to different kinds of barriers to learning within the rather privileged context of an all-through, co-ed independent day school. It is privileged in terms of the socio-economic status of the service users. But it is privileged too in the opportunity it offers to engage with specific learning difficulties in a context that is support-ive and, importantly, longitudinal. For example, a difficulty identified in Year 3, and our responses to that difficulty, may be monitored and considered within a stable educational environment over a period of, perhaps, 10 years.

In such an environment, the more evident barriers to learning are likely to be understood relatively early in a learner's school life, and classroom practice is adapted to allow for them. It is the more subtle (and often later-emerging) barriers that are being considered here, bar-riers that have been allowed for effectively enough in the earlier years for them not to be 'disabling', in classrooms where differences between children are accepted and seen as the norm. Through their own efforts as well as an inclusive environment, a number of learners who will later be categorised as disabled compensate for their differences with some success in the earlier years (although often with considerable and unacknowledged effort).

Over time, though, two factors combine to change this. One factor is the lessening of the extent to which all learners are seen as unique, as being different each in their own way. Instead, as learning and teaching shifts from being child centred to subject centred, there emerges a sense that there is a 'normally learning' majority; and that in comparison with this majority there is a minority who are seen as not 'normally learning' – they come to be seen as being categorically different. The second factor may be the way that the effectiveness of a learner's compensating and masking strategies steadily diminishes as they encounter increasing thresholds of demand, and learning characteristics that have not been barriers until now become barriers. Often this may be at the onset of the 'exam years'; sometimes it may not be until the undergraduate years.

During those first 10 years of a child's education, then, there is arguably a perceptible and continuous shift in professional thinking. In the early years there is an almost instinc-tive inclusivity, and acceptance of a social model of disability. Each child is seen as a unique individual, and it is part of the teacher's craft to find ways for all of the individu-als in the class to share the learning. In the later years, where subject specialisation and formal assessment gain increasing influence, there is an increasing dynamic towards a bio-medical categorisation, an allocation of learners to categories in order that they might better fit the demands of the examination system.

Categorisation, complexity and subtlety

Categorising is what the human brain does, arguably what it is for. Learning is about pack-aging up all our accumulating experiences into usable schemata that allow us to respond to the seething and potentially overwhelming complexity that comprises any one moment of our lives. We categorise or we crash – and this drive to categorise can account for some of the challenges that we experience in responding to learners with a specific learning dif-ficulty (SpLD) (dyslexia).

The categories utilised in learning may be too crude to be fully fit for the purpose, and this seems especially true of our attempts to respond to SpLDs. It is an enormous, dynamic and complex area of study; and we simultaneously comfort and delude ourselves by organ-ising our limited understandings into deceptively tidy categories. There are at least five potential sources of confusion when we set out to categorise a specific learning difficulty (Weedon and Reid, 2008):

- *Overlap of characteristic features:* Pupils who present in the same ways in the classroom may have underlying needs that are very different.
- *Co-morbidity:* There is likely to be more than one SpLD present in the same pupil.
- *Meanings attached to labels:* Even when we decide upon a label, it may mean quite dif-ferent things to different people. There is a continuing lack of consensus about definitions.
- *Different professional perspectives:* The difficulties are compounded still further by the range of different professionals who may be involved with an SpLD child, each approach-ing the child from the standpoint of their own professional perspective.
- *A description, not a diagnosis:* Lastly, there is a spurious precision in our use of these labels. Affixing a label implies some kind of certainty about just what causes the difficulty, what it stems from. Yet the most rigorously derived label for a specific learning difficulty may still be no more than 'a description dignified as a diagnosis'. (Whitmore and Bax, 1999)

Despite quite long-standing recognition of all this, practice is changing only slowly. Research from Reading University (by Riddell and Cruddace, reported in *The Times Educational Supplement, Scotland*, 5 March 2010) estimates that 1 in 10 children have a dyslexic or reading disorder, of whom 50% have an overlapping speech and language disorder, 25% have an attention deficit disorder, and 25% a movement disorder. The more that pressure groups and charities for different difficulties and disabilities gain traction, the greater the danger that simplistic use of labelling may increase the extent to which co-morbid difficulties may be overlooked, co-morbid difficulties that may in some cases be a primary source of difficulty.

We categorise, then, and seem set to continue to categorise – but we are doing so in a way that we know to be sometimes disorganised, imprecise and too narrowly focused.

Barriers to learning: For whom are they likely to be identified, and when?

Schools are instrumental in creating barriers. We are complicit in the social construction of disability – but we have to be. Inevitably, the early school environment places much empha-sis on the acquisition of core literacy and numeracy skills – and for the children we are thinking about, this may be something that they cannot do quite as easily as would be expected. The happy pre-schooler becomes perhaps less happy in early primary. Edwards (1993) asks: 'if a person's ability to draw is extremely poor, why do we not call this "dyspic-toria"?'; then answers his own question: because 'reading and writing are culturally esteemed skills'. Early schooling is profoundly instrumental in the social construction of disability – but arguably it has to be, if it is to help individuals develop skills that are socially valued.

The evidently bright and extroverted child whose literacy is lagging behind the expected levels is likely to attract attention fairly early in his or her school career, and appropriate action taken. The underlying difficulties will be identified, and addressed; and any residual barriers will be known and allowed for as the child moves up the school. Focused extra tuition will be provided. If residual barriers persist, readers and scribes may be provided. Probably word-processing with spellcheck will be encouraged – and the learner understands their own strengths and weaknesses, and develops as a confident and reflective learner who is achieving at an appropriate level.

The child is encountering a socially constructed disability, and a category-driven response is proving effective. The two paradigms are working together harmoniously and symbiotically. But for others, whose individual learning characteristics and traits form less of a barrier during the earlier years, no such intervention is needed, and the child-centred and inclusive nature of early schooling allows learning to proceed appropriately and successfully. For these children, it will be some years before this changes, and the remorselessly increasing demands of the examination hall start to make themselves felt.

The role of social class positioning

Whether or not the barrier is later identified and acknowledged will depend on a number of factors – but one is likely to be social class positioning. Where teacher and parent expectations are high, and other masking factors are absent (deprivation, poor diet, lack of exposure to complex language, lack of books in the home, etc.), then the barrier may well come to light. The biology teacher may recognise that Sam has an excellent grasp of plant reproduction, but always underperforms in written tests; the English teacher may be impressed by the way Ahmed can talk about the ideas being explored in a poem, but not write about them nearly as well. Parents will share ideas with other parents about the kaleidoscope of sometimes competing therapies and programmes that aim to improve performance and lessen their children's difficulties. These dynamics are there in all schools and families, but they are arguably closer to the surface among more affluent communities and families than among the less socially advantaged.

It is suggested, then, that there may be a 'Matthew effect' in our responses to SpLDs ('For to all those who have, more will be given,' Matthew 25:29). If so, the implications for increasing educational inequity are evident: those with economic or social capital will leverage those resources to enhance their children's academic success.

Figure 5.1 draws on Scottish Government administrative data (Scottish Government, 2013) for 2013, and shows pupils per 1000 pupil population in local authority primary and secondary schools identified as *visually impaired (VI)*, being *dyslexic* or having *social/emotional/behavioural difficulties (SEBD)*. The differences between the authorities

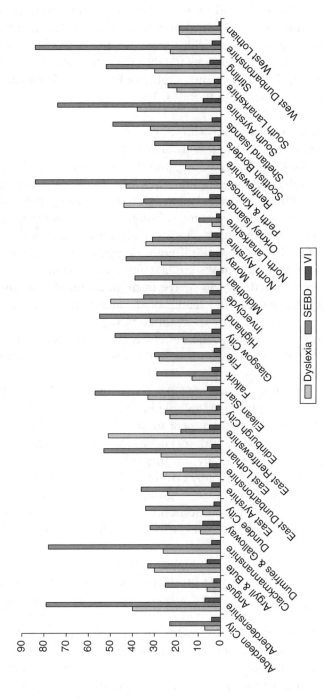

Figure 5.1 Pupils per 1,000 pupil population in local authority primary and secondary schools identified as visually impaired (VI), being dyslexic or having social/emotional/behavioural difficulties (SEBD). *Source:* Scottish Government (2013).

is striking, both in the numbers of children identified as having one of these needs, and in the hugely disparate prominence given to one or another of the needs.

The incidence of visual impairment provides some kind of a yardstick. Here, VI is certainly more measureable and objectively quantifiable than, for example, SEBD – it is not obviously context-specific, and it refers to measurable physical/physiological characteristics. It is relatively even across the different authorities. This is not true of SEBD, and only partly true of dyslexia.

The numbers are hard to interpret with any real confidence: for example, West Dunbartonshire has a great many pupils with SEBD and far fewer with dyslexic issues, while the reverse is true for East Renfrewshire, and that seems to support the notion that children from different socio-economic communities are dealt cards from different packs. But this is perhaps glib – other authorities' allocations do not seem to conform neatly to socio-economic status. What is intriguing and wholly evident, however, is the extent to which different educational communities allocate children to categories of difficulty in such very different ways, and to such very different degrees.

Educational communities and institutions are like any other community or institution, in that their beliefs, attitudes and actions will derive from an accumulation and organic synthesis over time of the beliefs, attitudes and actions of key individuals within the organisation. So to some extent it is not simplistic to expect different organisations to develop attitudes and behaviours that guide their actions in the same way that we expect different individuals to do so. Their actions are socially constructed, and these social constructions vary to an extent that is startling.

Scotland views itself as a country characterised by collectivism and commitment to social justice, with its education system playing a key role in promoting the tradition of democratic intellectualism (Devine, 2006) – but there appear to be indubitable links between the identification of additional support needs and social deprivation, and children identified as having learning difficulties in more socially advantaged schools have higher achievement levels than those so identified in less socially advantaged schools (Riddell et al., 2010).

Dyslexic students now form the largest single group of disabled students in higher education (Weedon and Riddell, 2007) – the proportion of dyslexic students in relation to those with other disabilities has risen from 15% in 1994/95 to 54% in 2004/05 (first-degree full-time students).

Weedon and Riddell found, too, that the highest proportion of dyslexic students was to be found in the more affluent, ancient and prestigious universities, and the lowest number in post-1992 institutions that served a lower socio-economic catchment. Interestingly (and perhaps part of the same dynamic of expectation and outcome), the first group of students were the most critical of the support they had been given. Disproportionately from independent rather than state schools, supported by families with high educational expectations, financially more likely to be able to pursue an independent identification of a dyslexic difficulty, well supported throughout their school years, students from the higher socio-economic groups appear more likely to be recognised as dyslexic; and then to make rigorous and demanding use of the support available.

In looking at dispute resolution procedures in Scotland, Riddell et al. (2010) found that parents from middle-class backgrounds appeared to use their social and cultural capital more effectively to challenge local authority decisions, and that these same parents were generally more successful than others in persuading professionals to provide additional resources. These students, from more advantaged backgrounds, are likely to have had enhanced experiences of support during the school years, and this in turn enhances their expectations of support through higher education.

Riddell and Weedon argue, too, that the situation is complex, in that certain categories of difficulty tend to be more stigmatised than others, and these tend to be assigned disproportionately to children living in the most socially disadvantaged neighbourhoods (2009). The converse seems likely also to be true – that other categories of disability, perceived as less stigmatising, will be disproportionately monopolised by those more socially advantaged. Dyslexia and attention deficit hyperactivity disorder (ADHD) are easier concepts to cope with and respond to than the broader categories of learning and/or behavioural difficulties.

The data and research for higher education are fairly clear, and in the public domain. The same insights for school-age children, and the public examinations through which they must go, appear not to be easily available at the time of writing. But there seems no reason to assume that a similar pattern does not exist, and it seems plausible that any inequities may be more pronounced during the years of compulsory schooling than they are among the smaller, self-selected and socially more uniform population that continues into higher education.

Encouraging a social model of disability: How might it help?

Riddell et al. (2005), writing about higher education, recognise the extent to which our understandings of disability are moving towards a socially constructed model – but recognise too the extent to which it remains the case that 'currently disabled students are forced to operate within a system which understands disability in terms of mental or physical deficit' (p. 17), perpetuated by 'a range of bureaucratic and administrative arrangements which promote a medicalised concept of disability'.

Simpson (2005) noted the extent to which, in schools, assessment is a process which is largely separated from teaching and learning. In the daily process of teaching and learning, practitioners are not faced by an 'either/or' choice, between a bio-medical or socially constructed response to learning difficulties. Most practitioners will, justifiably, draw on a blend of constructs in responding to a learner's needs. For most of us, most of the time, a wise response seems to lie (sometimes rather fluidly) somewhere in between the two. But that flexibility of choice terminates most abruptly when learning is formally assessed.

The Disability Discrimination Act (2005) (DDA) defines a 'disabled person as someone who has a physical or mental impairment that has a substantial and long term adverse effect on his or her ability to carry out normal day-to-day activities'. Clearly this cannot be wholly categorical, and a learner's characteristics might be considered in terms of a continuum, with placement depending upon the extent to which everyday function is impaired:

Everyday function impaired significantly ↔ Everyday function impaired to some extent ↔ Everyday function not impaired

Equally clearly, the critical factor in locating an impairment along this continuum must be the extent to which an individual's impairing difference is modest, or may be realistically compensated for.

With this in mind, it is easy to see how we may be comfortable with a social construction under some circumstances, where positioning on the continuum determines in a most obvious way whether or not an individual's characteristics might be regarded as a disability:

(Bio-medical model dominates, and categorising is helpful)

Blind ↔ Partially sighted ↔ Dependent on prescription glasses

(Socially constructed model dominates,

and categorising not needed)

A social construction of disability will be no help towards the left of the continuum – even the most evangelical supporter of inclusive practice will recognise the practical difficulties of teaching everyone Braille, and a bio-medical categorisation is clearly helpful. Equally no one would regard the use of prescription glasses as disabling for most wearers. Somewhere along the continuum we have shifted paradigm, enabled to do so by our acceptance of wearing glasses.

But consider for a moment an absurd scenario where the wearing of spectacles was seen to confer an unfair advantage in exams, and all candidates were expected to be spectacle-free unless certified by an optician to have needs that could be met only by allowing the candidate to wear glasses in exams. Suddenly, we create a whole new population of disabled learners, exactly as we do where a learner has, perhaps, weak spelling, slow reading and poor handwriting. For these learners, we have allowed individual differences to be institutionally transformed into disabling factors:

Severe dyslexia and consequent functional illiteracy

↔ Clearly defined dyslexic difficulty ↔

Accurate but relatively slow reader

with poor handwriting and spelling

Some impairments are arguably self-evidently disabling and sit fairly uncontroversially towards the left of any bio-medical/social construction continuum. But towards the right of the continuum, why accept spectacles and not word-processors?

The answer must be sought primarily among issues of institutional convenience ... and in an era where examination boards are commercial concerns, subject to market-place pressures, among issues of user-convenience and marketability. A mass education system has led to a mass assessment system. Examination boards compete for customers, and product marketability is likely to depend upon factors such as ease of administration. The logistical imperatives are undeniable: where several hundreds of candidates have to be processed through crowded examination halls to a remorselessly tight schedule, a single desk with pen, question paper and answer booklet comprises a formidably efficient process. It makes no difference if 20% of the candidates are wearing prescription glasses. It would make a lot of difference if large numbers chose to word-process their answers, or if an invigilator could not call out, at the scheduled time, 'Stop writing now. Please pass your completed answer papers.'

This chapter does not argue that one or another model of disability is better. It argues instead that both have relevance and value; but that it can only be helpful to generate a dynamic that seeks continuously and imperceptibly, to shift our perceptions a little further away from a bio-medical model whenever it is possible to do so, towards a socially constructed model; and continuously and imperceptibly away from a view that attributes a deficit to an individual, and to look instead at the barriers we construct within the environment.

Fuller and Healey (2009: 76) note the way in which 'the higher education establishment has defended the need for clear qualification criteria based on disability status in order to determine which students should be entitled to alternative forms of assessment', and go on to note the way in which this 'binary divide between disabled and non-disabled students' means that universities force students at some level to 'adopt a disabled identity to obtain the support for learning to which they are entitled'.

Educational practice is moving in the right direction. But there is some way to go, and the argument here is that a shift away from institutionally convenient assessment practices towards practices that are more genuinely inclusive would aid that 'paradigm-creep', to the advantage and gain of all concerned:

> If it is valid to assess one student in a certain way, why should it not be equally valid for all? If the quality of the thinking about biology may be validly assessed where candidates A, B and C have someone to read the questions, or have extra time, why should it not be equally valid for candidates D through to Z, should they opt to do so?

> It makes every sense. Fine judgments no longer have to be made, by people like me, about which candidates should receive such arrangements (and only the most passionate psychometrician would argue that the instruments used to quantify these difficulties are other than very approximate). It would also be inclusive in the best sense – it changes underlying structures in a way that militates against exclusion. (Weedon, 2006)

For policy makers, the issue is clear: for a number of our pupils and students, we are creating disabilities for no other reason than our own administrative convenience. In itself, this does not seem defensible; and by default seems likely to compound educational inequity, with all the social and economic correlates that such inequity must bring.

At the practitioner level, there is little direct action we can take, other than to be aware of what we are doing, and to broadcast that awareness to all concerned – to colleagues, students, parents, university and college admission staff, potential employers:

Yes, I am describing this individual as 'disabled' – but really only for the administrative convenience of the assessment industry, and because it is the only way to access fair examination arrangements. In no other way at all is there any 'disability'.

We can, too, seek to encourage the uptake of the compensatory arrangements more widely across the social spectrum. Exam boards do their best (and in the context of the Scottish Qualifications Authority it is a very effective best) to make available whatever compensatory arrangements are needed for every individual to demonstrate their true level of attainment. But exam boards can do no more than receive and respond to requests from schools and presenting centres. It is for staff within those schools and presenting centres to make full and assertive use of the available arrangements, so that no longer are they dominated by sectors of society already disproportionately empowered. Easier said than done – but worth trying to do.

Summary

- The continuing debates about the usefulness or existence of specific barriers to learning (such as dyslexia) are a function of our tendency to *categorise* the barriers experienced by learners; and then to seek to *compensate* for those barriers.
- This may be most true of those learners whose specific barriers are not of a severity that has led to early identification/categorisation.
- Learners from more advantaged sectors of society are more likely to have such modest difficulties identified/recognised by secondary schools and higher education institutions, and to have appropriate accommodation made for them.
- Failure to recognise such barriers among less advantaged learners impacts negatively on those learners as individuals, as well as on the economic well-being of the wider community.
- Emphasising a social model of disability should allow the development of more inclusive educational and assessment practices, thereby reducing the current social inequities of response.

Discussion points

- Do you think that your school or institution successfully identifies all those students who might validly request special examination arrangements?
- If so, is it conferring further advantage on an already privileged section of society?
- If not, what steps might you take to make more rigorous use of the special examination arrangements that are available?

Further reading

Burr, V. (2003) *Social Constructionism*. London: Routledge.
An in-depth but accessible introduction to the ways in which a broad range of personal experiences will in part be socially constructed. Burr also considers some of the limitations of this approach.

Lock, A. and Strong, T. (2010) *Social Constructionism: Sources and Stirrings in Theory and Practice*. Cambridge: Cambridge University Press.
Considers how contemporary social constructivism has developed and become a practical tool in understanding the everyday world.

Rapley, M. (2004) *The Social Construction of Intellectual Disability*. Cambridge: Cambridge University Press.
Explores in some depth the ways in which apparently individual problems of all kinds are in effect interactional and social products, at least in part.

Trevino, A.J. (2011) *The Social Thought of C. Wright Mills*. Newbury Park, CA: Pine Forge Press.
An examination of the beginnings of social constructivist thought. It focuses on Mills' interest in the interactions between personality and social structure, and on how bureaucratisation affects power relationships.

Useful websites

Bradnet

Bradnet aims to keep disability as a 'rights' issue, and promotes the Social Model approach to disability in all of its work.

www.bradnet.org.uk.

Health and Care professionals Council

The HCPC regulate a number of professions, including occupational therapists, practitioner psychologists, social workers and language therapists.

www.hpc-uk.org.

References

Barnes, C. (1991) *Disabled People in Britain: The Case for Anti-discrimination Legislation*. London: Hurst and Co.
Devine, T.M. (2006) *The Scottish Nation, 1700–2007*. London: Allen Lane.

Disability Discrimination Act (2005) www.opsi.gov.uk/acts/acts2005/ukpga.

Edwards, B. (1993) *Drawing on the Right Side of the Brain*. London: HarperCollins.

Fuller, M. and Healey, M. (2009) Assessing disabled students: student and staff experiences of reasonable adjustments. In M. Fuller et al. (eds), *Improving Disabled Students' Learning*. London and New York: Routledge, pp. 60–77.

MacDonald, S.J. (2009) Windows of reflection: conceptualising dyslexia using the social model of disability. *Dyslexia*, 15: 347–62.

Oliver, M. (1990) *The Politics of Disablement*. Basingstoke: Macmillan.

Riddell, S. and Weedon, E. (2009) Managerialism and equalities: tensions within widening access policy and practice for disabled students in UK universities. In M. Fuller et al. (eds), *Improving Disabled Students' Learning*. London and New York: Routledge, pp. 21–37.

Riddell, S., Tinklin, T. and Wilson, A. (2005) *Disabled Students in Higher Education*. London and New York: Routledge.

Riddell, S., Stead, J., Weedon, E. and Wright, K. (2010) Additional support needs reforms and social justice in Scotland. *International Studies in the Sociology of Education*, 20: 179–99.

Scottish Government (2013) *Pupils in Scotland, 2013*. Supplementary data. Retrieved from www.scotland.gov.uk/Topics/Statistics/Browse/School-Education/dspupcensus/pupcensus2013.

Simpson, M. (2005) *Assessment: Policy and Practice in Education*. Edinburgh: Dunedin.

Weedon, C. (2006) Exams, disabilities and natural justice. *The Times Educational Supplement, Scotland*, 13 January.

Weedon, C. and Reid, G. (2008) *Special Needs Assessment Profile: Specific Learning Difficulties v. 3 (SNAP–SpLD)*. London: Hodder and Stoughton.

Weedon, E. and Riddell, R. (2007) To those that have, shall be given? Differing expectations of support among dyslexic students. In M. Osborne et al. (eds), *The Pedagogy of Lifelong Learning*. London and New York: Routledge, pp. 26–40.

Whitmore, K. and Bax, M. (1999) What do we mean by SLD? A historical perspective. In K. Whitmore et al. (eds), *A Neurodevelopmental Approach to Specific Learning Disorders*. London: MacKeith Press, pp. 1–23.

PART II

Perspectives from Practice

6

Speech and Language

Janet O'Keefe and Janet Farrugia

Learning objectives

This chapter will help readers to:

- Understand what Speech, Language and Communication Needs (SLCNs) are and how to refer school-aged students and young people for an assessment
- Appreciate, through case histories, the positive impact that Speech and Language Therapy (SLT) can have on a student's ability to make progress, access the curriculum and reach their potential
- Explore a range of strategies that can support students with SLCNs at school and at home

One in ten children has SLCN. This is equivalent to three children in every primary school classroom (Law et al., 2000). SLCN is the most common type of special educational need (SEN) in children below seven years of age, and half of all children with SEN have SLCN (the Lamb Inquiry, DCSF, 2009a). Everyone living and working with children and young people enhances communication skills. As a result of this, several government-commissioned reports have commented on the support for pupils with SLCN in schools and emphasised the need for parents and professionals to work together to improve the educational and life attainments of this group.

The Bercow Report (2008) identified five key themes:

- Communication is crucial
- Early identification and intervention are essential
- A continuum of services designed around the family is needed
- Joint working is critical
- The current system is characterised by high variability and lack of equity

Bercow (2008) concluded that the support for pupils with SLCN is highly variable and therefore inequitable. The year 2011 was the National Year of Speech, Language and Communication. It was lead by Jean Gross, Communication Champion in England, to raise awareness and understanding of SLCN, share effective strategies for stimulating and strengthening language and leave, as its legacy, meaningful long-term benefits. Royal College of Speech and Language Therapists (RCSLT) Chief Executive Officer Kamini Gadhok said in September 2007 at a Speech, Language and Communication Provision Review:

> SLCN needs are the most common disability presenting in early childhood. We know many children are not currently receiving the services they need. Some areas have very long waiting lists and children and families struggle without crucial support. If left untreated, SLCN have a huge impact on the education achievement and the health of a child. The human costs can be devastating with up to a third of children with diagnosed communication problems developing mental illness if untreated.

Conti-Ramsden et al. (2002b, 2009) summarised the findings of the Manchester Language Study regarding the educational outcomes of young people with SLCN. This study has been following the progression of children who have attended language units since the age of seven.

The positive findings of the report relating to educational outcomes for language-disordered children are as follows:

- Some 44% obtained at least one GCSE equivalent at the end of secondary education
- On average, language disordered pupils were taking one more GCSE than they did in the 1990s
- Around 60% were provided with some type of support during their core examinations
- Some 90% remained in education after the age of 16 with support
- Some 40% had part-time employment in addition to their studies

The results indicate that significant progress has been made in the educational outcomes for language-disordered pupils in the last 10 years because Speech and Language Therapists (SLTs) are working with teachers and parents to help them differentiate their language and carry out SLT programmes at regular intervals throughout the school week – but more progress is needed. The critical period for progress for children with SLCN is 7–14 years (Botting et al., 2001). The data speak strongly for increased support for these young people and their families into adulthood and specific education and for SLT support being available at both primary- and secondary-school levels. In summary, social, emotional and behavioural risks seem to be associated with a history of communication impairment but a causal link should not be assumed (Botting and Conti-Ramsden, 2000). The increased risk seems to be related to the quality and quantity of education and therapy support received rather than the fact that the individual has a diagnosis of SLCN. The needs of young people with SLCN should be recognised and provided for in a wider range of ways as they reach adulthood too (Conti-Ramsden and Botting, 2008).

Pupils with SLCN may present in the classroom as:

- off-task
- intolerant of loud sounds
- not able to follow instructions
- not able to conform
- having poor discrimination of sounds (may show in spelling)
- 'in a world of their own' and often needing messages repeated
- copying peers and the last to carry out instructions
- continuously asking for help (if they are aware of their problems) or never asking for help (if they are unaware of their difficulties or are too embarrassed)
- having difficulty understanding the meanings of concepts such as 'more/less', 'same/different' or 'before/after', which can affect lessons such as maths, science, history and geography
- using the wrong word
- having poor grammar – often more obvious in written form
- having sequencing difficulties
- having difficulty categorising and grouping information
- having poor social skills
- very literal – getting hold of the wrong end of the stick
- having unclear speech and poor spelling
- dysfluent (stammering)
- having a continuous hoarse voice

In order to obtain a diagnosis of a student's SLCN, the student must be assessed by an SLT who is registered with the Health and Care Professions Council (HCPC). All SLTs must be registered with the HCPC to work in the UK as it is a protected professional title.

SLTs work with students with feeding, eating, drinking and swallowing needs; speech needs (pronunciation); verbal comprehension needs (understanding what is said); expressive language needs (using words to express themselves in meaningful and well-structured sentences verbally); and/or social communication/social thinking needs (understanding and using the rules of communication, such as how to start, maintain and finish conversations appropriately). They may also work with written language needs (dyslexia).

SLTs may be employed by NHS Trusts, Local Education Authorities (LEAs), schools, colleges, charities, independent services or be sole traders. There is open referral to all speech and language therapy (SLT) services in the UK, which means that any parent, carer, health, education or social services practitioner can, with the parents'/carers' consent, refer a student under the age of 16 for an SLT assessment if they have concerns about any aspect of a student's ability to understand spoken language, express themselves or use language socially. A young person over the age of 16 with capacity can refer themselves. This can be done via the local NHS SLT service or an assessment can be commissioned privately by a parent/carer, school or LEA from an independent SLT. The earlier in a student's life that SLCNs are identified, the earlier appropriate intervention and therapy can start, and the more effective it can be (Bercow, 2008). This is more likely to prevent educational and social needs in the future (Conti-Ramsden et al., 2001).

Assessment by an SLT typically involves a combination of the following:

- *Case history:* To ascertain any contributing medical, educational or social issues (such as hearing loss, family history, non-verbal cognitive skills)
- *Observation:* For example, symbolic development, attention, eye contact, functional use and understanding of language
- *Formal standardised assessments*
- *Information from all relevant professionals and carers*

Students with Education, Health and Care Plans (EHCP) may have their SLT provision funded by the LEA as part of their plan and this may be provided by an NHS or independent therapist or by the school as part of their fees for attendance. It is the integration of SLT with education that is the most effective in the progress of students with communication impairments, where therapy can inform teaching and teaching can inform therapy (Conti-Ramsden et al., 2009; Durkin et al., 2009). Parents and professionals report that students benefit when SLT is integrated into the curriculum (Reid et al., 1996).

SLCNs which affect a student's access to the curriculum

Attention and listening skills

If students are not paying attention, they cannot listen fully, and if they are not listening, then their understanding will be compromised. However, poor attention and listening can sometimes be the result and not the cause of problems with comprehension. This can be appreciated if we put ourselves in the position of having to listen to someone speaking a foreign language or somebody discussing a complicated topic. When we don't understand, we lose concentration and switch off.

Receptive language/comprehension/understanding skills

This includes understanding what others say (receptive language or comprehension). If a student is slow with understanding but is following normal developmental patterns, then this is called 'delayed receptive language'. If a student's language development is unusual and not following normal patterns, then it is described as 'disordered'. This could be due to the following.

Auditory processing

Auditory processing affects the ability to recognise and interpret sounds and impacts on the efficiency and speed of processing the meaning of spoken language.

This can result in misinterpretation and/or slow the speed of understanding. Consequently, students are unable to retain and understand everything that is said. Auditory processing disorders impact significantly on an individual's ability to process language and to focus on what is being said against background noise. There is evidence to suggest that background noise levels in the average classroom are higher than optimal conditions for understanding speech (Picard and Bradley, 2001).

Poor short-term auditory memory

This impacts on an individual's ability to process and retain lengthy verbal instructions/information. This difficulty can sometimes lead to the child or young person seeming disobedient or stubborn, when in fact they have not understood because too much information has been given to them at one time. As a consequence, messages need to be repeated and chunked into smaller units.

Often, this difficulty can be overlooked, as many learn to watch and follow what their peers are doing and therefore are the last to carry out an instruction. As they grow older their needs become more apparent as they cannot continue to 'get by' through copying their peers. Others may be continuously asking for help or conversely may never ask for help. They are likely to have difficulties transferring information from short-term auditory memory into working memory. This may result in inconsistencies in understanding and learning, so an individual may appear to have grasped something and understood it one day, but have completely forgotten it the next day.

Limited receptive vocabulary

This occurs when an individual finds it hard to learn new words. Learning vocabulary is more complex than it may at first appear. The child or young person has to be certain to what a new word is referring. When it is an object which is present and being pointed at, this difficulty is minimised. However, when more abstract words are used within a sentence, it can be much more difficult to work out what the word refers to and consequently its meaning (for example, 'The polar bear is an endangered species'). Many, might think that this means that the polar bear is dangerous because 'endangered' and 'dangerous' sound similar. An individual who has no language needs is likely to revise this opinion if they then hear, 'They therefore need protection'. This is because they will realise that their first interpretation of the meaning of the word 'endangered' is not consistent with this second sentence. They may ask the teacher to explain the meaning of the word 'endangered' or deduce it from the context. However, an individual with a receptive language disorder may not have understood the second sentence ('They therefore need protection') either because they would still have been trying to process the first sentence and/or because they also do not know the meaning of the word 'protection'.

Vocabulary deficits become cumulative: the less a child understands, the less they are going to understand; conversely, if the child or young person learns new words easily and has a good vocabulary, they are in a very good position to be able to extend this.

It is also important to appreciate that understanding a new word is of limited benefit if the child does not recognise it when they hear it again. Individuals with language needs find it hard to hold the phonological composition of words within their memory store. The normally developing individual can usually repeat a new word quite accurately and recognise it after hearing it several times. However, a child or young person with a language disorder may need to hear the word repeated many more times before they can recognise it. If they also have a speech difficulty, they will be unable to repeat the word in order to consolidate the sound patterns within it. This then makes it harder for them to remember it.

Speech

It is useful to be aware of the different stages that children commonly pass through on their route to full intelligibility, in order to judge the relative maturity of a student's speech compared with others of their age and whether a particular student's development is typical or not.

Delayed speech

Many children have immaturities with speech which can be considered part of normal development (such as 'th' pronounced as 'f' or 'r' as 'w'). Students with difficulties pronouncing sounds may be following normal developmental patterns but later than normal – this is 'delayed speech'. Most children with delayed speech will have grown out of this by the time they start school.

Students with disordered speech

Such individuals do not follow the typical pattern of normal speech development. Even though they may 'hear' a word correctly, they are unable to retain the correct phonological composition of the sounds within the word in order to lay down an appropriate motor pattern so they can repeat the word accurately. In its most severe form, a student can be virtually unintelligible. This is called a 'phonological disorder'.

The student with verbal dyspraxia

This student has normal muscle development in the oral area, but the neural connection from their brain to their oral muscles (tongue, lips and palate) is impaired, so they have difficulty pronouncing sounds and/or saying them at speed, particularly in complex words. Some students may also have difficulty moving their lips and tongue for non-speech activities such as licking, chewing and sucking. In its most severe form, a student may be unable to say an isolated sound at will and therefore effectively be unable to speak; in its milder form a student may struggle to pronounce complex combinations of sounds like 'str' or multisyllabic words such as 'hippopotamus'.

Unfortunately, there are some students who have such a severe form of dyspraxia (often referred to as apraxia) that they require alternative or augmentative communication systems. This can be in the form of signs/gestures (such as Makaton) and sign languages such as Signalong, Sign Supported English or Paget Gorman Signed Speech. Some students need the use of a voice output communication aid (VOCA), which is a computer-type device whose primary function is to use electronically stored speech as a means of communication.

Case study

Fred was diagnosed with verbal dyspraxia when he was at his infant school. He received blocks of SLT in his local clinic as well as within school but only made limited progress. When he was nine years old, his parents became increasingly concerned as he was struggling at school, both academically and socially, as he still could not communicate intelligibly. This was brought home to them on a school trip when his mother witnessed Fred raising his hand to ask a question to a museum guide and his teacher indicated that she should choose another pupil as she would not understand Fred. He was assessed by an educational psychologist as having average cognitive ability and an SLT carried out a detailed assessment making recommendations for a minimum of three sessions of SLT a week, delivered within a specialist school environment for children with specific speech and language disorders. His mother reports: 'Fred is now a happy and confident child who is starting to talk clearly and achieve the potential that he clearly has. At the end of Year 6 Fred achieved a Level 4 in SATs in science.'

Expressive language needs

The development of syntax or grammar is the structure of language of which speakers are often unaware. The learning of grammar does not come to an end until late childhood. Individuals learning language use simplified grammar, which becomes increasingly complex as the young person matures. Expressive language needs will impact on written language, too. There may or may not be an identifiable cause. Needs with expressive language include those that follow.

Delayed language

A student with delayed language speaks in an immature way like a younger person, and can nearly always be understood. Errors may include confusion with pronouns, immature forms and simplification of grammar and generally short sentences with little evidence of complex clauses, beyond those joined with 'and' (e.g. 'Mummy driving car. He gone to shops and buyed some Christmas things like a Christmas Tree').

Disordered language

A student with disordered language does not follow the normal patterns of language development and can produce some very unusual sentences, which often do not follow regular grammatical rules and as such cannot easily be understood. These are some examples of sentences from students with disordered language produced when trying to retell a simple story:

> Come here but he didn't pull his drivers and then he got in there and then he pushed him off. (Child aged six)

> When she … when monkey couldn't remember he have to find this treasure at once. That's a good idea thought the … she said. She thought … she find a pineapple. When she found there's a baraver she found a red long skirt and … and acourse there in things … the cage. (Child aged 10)

A child with a very severe language disorder may fulfil the diagnosis of specific language impairment.

Word-finding

This is when a student recognises a word if it is said to them, but is unable to recall it effectively. Word-finding may be due to a semantic error in that a student may call a 'banana' an 'orange' or a phonological error when they would say a nonsense word which often sounds like the target word. Phonological errors refer to when a student is unable to remember the exact sounds and/or sequences of sounds within a word. This is more likely to happen with lengthy words and/or phonologically complex words (such as 'anemone', 'statistics' or 'binoculars'). However, students with really severe word-finding may struggle to retrieve relatively simple words. Students with word-finding will be very hesitant when talking as they struggle to find the right words to use, which can cause them immense frustration.

Case study

Sophie was always a happy child but, when she was about two, her mother noticed that she wasn't putting words together as she should, and that she often couldn't understand Sophie. Sophie couldn't really talk in sentences and also found it hard to follow other people's conversation. She always struggled in school as she found it hard to follow the teacher. She also found making friends very hard because she couldn't follow their conversations and so became very isolated, and by the time she was 15 she came very close to a breakdown. Sophie's parents obtained reports from an SLT, an educational psychologist and a child psychiatrist as part of a statutory assessment. Her mother stated:

> I still remember the emotion of finally having my worries confirmed and explained – Sophie was *not* just shy, she *didn't* have learning difficulties, she had a severe expressive speech and language disorder and moderate difficulties with her receptive language including auditory recall and speed of processing – no wonder she couldn't follow the teacher or keep up in class.

Sophie now has a statement of special educational needs providing her with intensive SLT as part of her educational curriculum.

Speech and language disorder/specific language impairment may be associated with dyslexia/ written language disorder and may not be noticed until a child is at school. They may appear to have developed language and speech quite adequately but then teachers notice that they may find it difficult to understand certain things such as complex grammar, certain concepts or non-literal language. They may also find it hard to express themselves when trying to convey more complicated ideas and thoughts. These students may also have problems with word-finding.

Developmental written language disorder/dyslexia refers to problems with reading, writing and spelling. A student may be considered to have dyslexia if, in spite of adequate teaching, the student has specific persistent problems with reading and writing in comparison with their abilities in other spheres, to a degree sufficient to prevent school work from reflecting their true ability and knowledge. Early identification of dyslexia is essential in order to ensure that the student receives appropriate help. The earlier the difficulties are identified, the greater the likelihood of successful remediation. The case history of a dyslexic child may reveal early previously undiagnosed language needs that only become of recognised significance in the light of emerging reading and writing needs.

Snowling and Hayiou-Thomas (2006) state that: 'Children with Dyslexia and Specific Language Impairment typically share a continuity of risk for decoding deficits in reading that can be traced to phonological problems, whereas students who have wider language problems are at risk of reading comprehension deficits.' From available evidence they propose:

> that the probability of a child with oral language difficulties developing reading problems (and the nature of these problems) depends on a complex interaction of risk and protective factors. From the clinical perspective, an important protective factor is the availability of appropriate intervention, delivered at the right time, to foster oral and written language skills. (Ibid.)

Social communication and pragmatic language needs

Case study

James was diagnosed with autism (at the more severe end of the scale) at the age of 22 months. Following numerous appointments with various different professionals, James' parents were getting no further forward with making sense of anything. James was 'spiralling' out of control and it seemed as though there was absolutely nothing that his parents could do. James had weekly SLT over quite a substantial period of time and his parents carried out activities daily in between therapy sessions, following a speech and language programme which they could share with his nursery and primary school teachers. The SLT devised a 'list' of 10 or so items/activities each week that his parents were to work on. Using these 'positives', they worked forwards with a programme and after a few weeks, James could successfully complete most of the items on an A4 sheet.

With all this success, James' parents became much more motivated than they had been in the previous months. When James went to school, he had a statutory assessment and his LEA issued a statement of special educational needs and James' therapy transferred to his mainstream primary school with his teaching assistant attending SLT sessions with him and carrying out the daily programme activities.

Students with social communication/pragmatic language needs have problems using language to communicate effectively with others. They struggle to appropriately use language (such as requesting, informing and persuading) and to adapt their language appropriately in different situations and to different audiences. They find it difficult to provide relevant background information to unfamiliar listeners and may make inappropriate or off-topic comments. They generally understand things very literally and so struggle with sarcasm and idioms. They may appear to be rude or manipulative. For example, when told, 'We know that we don't push when waiting in line, don't we?' they may reply 'yes' or 'no' without changing their behaviour. They struggle to follow conversational rules such as turn taking (they often monopolise conversations on a favoured topic), to use appropriate facial expressions and eye contact and to maintain appropriate physical distance when communicating. This all has a significant impact on their social communication skills and their ability to make and maintain friends. They are at increased risk of bullying.

Students with pragmatic comprehension needs can have a good understanding of semantics (the meaning of words and language). However, they will have difficulty inferring from context which meaning is intended. For example, most children of 10 years of age, upon hearing expressions such as 'You'd better pull your socks up' or 'It's raining cats and dogs', are able to deduce that a literal interpretation is not plausible in the context in which it has been said. However, children with pragmatic comprehension difficulties may not.

Semantic–pragmatic language disorder refers to the individual who has difficulties with both understanding the meaning of words (semantics) and the development of the appropriate social use of language in different contexts (pragmatics). Many children with a diagnosis of semantic–pragmatic disorder have a diagnosis of an autistic spectrum condition.

Educational provision for students with SLCNs

Students who have SLCNs which are preventing them from accessing the curriculum need to be assessed and their needs described in a statement of special educational needs or Education Health and Care Plan so that SLT can be quantified and specified as an educational provision.

Direct SLT, no matter how intensive, is of limited benefit unless it is carried over into the student's school/college and home. This is because communication is something that goes on throughout the student's day and cannot be restricted to a few hours a week, when in the company of a SLT. Therefore, a great deal of any SLT's time will involve training teachers and parents to ensure the student is helped to practise their therapy techniques and strategies at various times throughout the day in a variety of different contexts as an educational provision. Law et al. (2000) have stated that:

> The emphasis is the embedding in the curriculum. It is important to ensure that therapists frame their intervention such that it is relevant to the student's educational experience and not something 'other' as has often been the case with clinic based models of delivery. This is not implying that the therapy should be indirect.

Students who have good speech and language skills are at an advantage when they learn to read and spell, as the development of spoken and written language skills is closely linked. Conversely, students who are having difficulties with speech and language development are at risk of having associated literacy needs. Frustration and evasion are understandable sequelae to the educational problems and daily ordeal of school work for these students.

Discussion points

The following discussion points arise from the case studies:

Fred

- Fred's verbal dyspraxia was so severe that his blocks of SLT were insufficient for him to make significant progress. A child like Fred often needs to practise speech sounds or words up to 1000 times before they are firmly established as motor engrams.
- Fred needed such intensive SLT that it became impossible for him to remain in a mainstream school for many reasons, including his consequential loss of self-esteem, limited friendships and the amount of time he needed out of the classroom in order to be able to work on his speech.

Sophie

- Despite her severe expressive speech and language and moderate receptive language disorders, Sophie 'managed' in mainstream education and obtained five low-grade GSCEs. However, does this academic achievement constitute success when she was unable to go into a shop, use public transport, make a phone call, establish friendships or go out socially with her peers? Consideration needs to be given to a child's functional communication and life skills. Consequently, Sophie required a specialist post-16 placement that offered her this as well as intensive SLT as an integral part of her curriculum. What could have been done differently for Sophie in the above case study when she was two? How would you intervene if Sophie was a young child within your setting? Do you think that there is more chance now for early identification of SCLNs?

James

- James' SLT, teachers and family worked closely together as part of a multidisciplinary team and, as a result, he had a successful mainstream placement for his primary school education.

Students with severe and significant receptive language disorder may need direct SLT as an educational provision focusing on specific areas, such as the development of the understanding of grammar, vocabulary and semantic knowledge and helping the student to learn strategies, such as visualisation, to support poor auditory memory. A great deal of the SLT's time should focus on training teachers in ways to simplify their language and provide visual support to enable students to understand the lesson delivery more effectively.

Students with severe dyspraxia and disordered speech generally require direct SLT as an educational provision. In order for this to be effective, the SLT needs to carry out a very detailed analysis of the student's speech in order to reach a hypothesis as to where the breakdown in speech development has occurred. Following this, the SLT should put together a very structured programme and work with the student on an individual basis, the frequency of which will depend on the severity of the student's needs. In order for this therapy to be effective and generalised into the student's everyday speech, it will be necessary for a teaching assistant, learning support assistant, learning mentor, SLT assistant or the parents to sit in on at least one session each week. A student with a severe speech disorder or dyspraxia will be affected in many ways in relation to their access to the curriculum.

Research has shown definite benefits from direct therapy for children with expressive language disorders as an educational provision (Law et al., 2003). The frequency of therapy depends on many factors, including the severity of the child's language disorder, the knowledge of their teachers and the educational environment in which the child is educated. However, as with all SLT, it has to be accompanied by educating the child's teachers and parents and ensuring the generalisation of the skills and strategies taught.

In therapy for written language disorders, the therapist must be aware of the relationship between spoken and written language disorder. The SLT's knowledge and skills (such as linguistics and phonetics) mean that they are ideally placed to contribute to the management of students with dyslexia. When providing therapy to students with a spoken language disorder, the SLT will consider written language skills as part of the overall intervention programme. The discharge of a student who is speaking, but not reading or writing or showing age-appropriate prerequisite skills, cannot be seen as a successful discharge. Intervention should be offered utilising the skills of teaching staff at all times.

To conclude, we agree with John Bercow that children with SLCN need to be identified early and SLT provision integrated across home and school settings by parents, therapists and teachers working together as part of the multidisciplinary team supporting the student to achieve their potential, because communication is crucial to every student's development for both educational attainment and successful life outcomes.

Table 6.1 lists some suggested strategies to help children with SLCN.

Table 6.1 Suggested strategies to help all students with SLCN and which impairments they specifically target

Activities	Attention and listening	Receptive language	Speech	Expressive language	Dyslexia	Pragmatic language
1. Familiar routines with a beginning, middle and end, so students always know where they are meant to be, what they are doing, for how long and what they will do next. Give plenty of notice of any planned changes (visual timetables)	X	X			X	X
2. Sit the student away from distracting areas (not facing windows/door/other students with attention problems) and keep the environment as quiet as possible. Position student near the teacher, away from outside noise	X	X			X	X
3. Say the student's name to ensure attention. Use a physical prompt if necessary and wait until the student is looking at you before speaking	X	X			X	X
4. Keep language simple and clear. Give instructions in the order in which they should be carried out avoiding 'before' and 'after'. Keep language relevant and concise. Make everything explicit for the child. Use key words	X	X			X	X
5. Break up longer paragraphs into shorter ones and then ask students to 'paraphrase' them in their own words before proceeding to the next part	X	X			X	X
6. Do not rely on verbal communication alone for expression or reception. Use and encourage visual aids or physical prompts wherever possible. Put instructions in writing or use pictures/symbols. Use and encourage body language and gesture	X	X	X	X	X	X
7. Speak slowly, clearly and loud enough	X	X			X	X
8. When teaching, explain the main content of the lesson before the teaching begins and refer back to previous associated lessons	X	X			X	X
9. Allow time for the student to process what has been said and give them time to respond (30 seconds as an average)	X	X	X	X	X	X

(Continued)

Table 6.1 *(Continued)*

Activities	Attention and listening	Receptive language	Speech	Expressive language	Dyslexia	Pragmatic language
10. Encourage the student to ask for help/repetitions (e.g. 'Please can you repeat that') or a visual means of communicating this request (symbol or picture)	X	X			X	X
11. Teach concept words in pairs (e.g. 'big' in contrast to 'small')	X	X			X	X
12. Introduce new vocabulary beforehand and practise use	X	X	X	X	X	X
13. Question with real interest, comment on what the student is doing and encourage emphatically			X	X		
14. Actively stimulate conversation beyond the here and now			X			X
15. Try not to finish the sentence for them/interrupt while they are speaking … and try to stop others in the class from doing so			X	X		
16. Rephrase correctly what the student has said by saying it back to them (modelling)			X	X		
17. Use 'scaffolding' (verbal and written) (e.g. who/what/where/when/how; beginning/middle/end)			X			X
18. Have discreet signals for when to stop talking (e.g. 'stop' gesture with hand)						X
19. Run social communication/social thinking skills groups (explicit teaching programme)			X			X
20. Introduce a buddy system (with a socially able student)	X		X			X

Summary

- The SLCNs that occur in school-aged children and that affect access to the curriculum are attention and listening; receptive language/verbal comprehension/understanding; speech (pronunciation); expressive language; and social communication.
- SLT should be an integrated educational provision to enable the student with SLCN to achieve their potential.
- There are key strategies for the home and school that can help support a student with SLCN.

Further reading

Attwood, T. (2008) *The Complete Guide to Asperger Syndrome*, revd edn. London: Jessica Kingsley.
This is a fully comprehensive, must-have and easy-read text for anyone living or working with individuals with Asperger syndrome.

Birnbaum, R. (2010) *Choosing a School for a Child with Special Needs*. London: Jessica Kingsley.
This gives advice to parents of children with all sorts of SEN on how to choose a school for their child.

Bowen, C. (2014) *Children's Speech Sound Disorders*, 2nd edn. Oxford: Wiley-Blackwell.
An exceptionally practical book. It has a superb companion website which is open access, and packed with all manner of useful resources and routes to further information.

Gross, J. (2013) *Time to Talk: Implementing Outstanding Practice in Speech, Language and Communication*. Abingdon: David Fulton/NASEN.
A practical and accessible book from the UK government's former Communication Champion for children.

Hatcher, C. (ed.) (2011) *Making Collaborative Practice Work: A Model for Teachers and SLTs*. Guildford: J. & R. Press.
Hilari, K. and Botting, N. (eds) (2011) *The Impact of Communication Disability across the Lifespan*. Guildford: J. & R. Press.
Trott, K., Stackhouse, J. and Clegg, J. (2011) *Children's Language and Literacy Groups: A Practical Resource for Students and Staff in Nurseries and Schools*. Guildford: J. & R. Press.
Roulstone, S. and McLeod, S. (eds) (2011) *Listening to Children and Young People with SLCN*. Guildford: J. & R. Press.
These are the most up-to-date and pertinent books for SLCN.

Howell, P. and Van Borsel, J. (2011) *Multilingual Aspects of Fluency Disorders*. Bristol: Multilingual Matters.
Provides a comprehensive coverage of the multilingual aspects of fluency disorders. The book reviews how formal language properties affect stammering in English, and then compares these findings to work on stammering in a variety of languages.

Kersner, M. and Wright, J.A. (2012) *Speech and Language Therapy: The Decision-making Process when Working with Children*, 2nd edn. London: Routledge.
This book helps the reader to understand the decision-making process in the assessment and management of children with speech and language problems. It also

(Continued)

(Continued)

illustrates how decision-making can change within different environments and with different client groups. In addition, it describes ways in which speech and language therapists work with other professionals. This book is relevant to speech and language therapy students and NQTs, specialist teachers in training and SENCOs in particular.

Logue, M. and Conradi, P. (2010) *The King's Speech: How One Man Saved the British Monarchy.* London: Quercus.
This book, of course, epitomises why speech and language therapy is so important as a profession. It truly makes a difference to the educational and life outcomes of individuals for ever.

Row, S. (2009) *Surviving the Special Educational Needs System: How to Be a Velvet Bulldozer.* London: Jessica Kingsley.
This book gives a parent's perspective on having a child with SEN and accessing the help and support they need in school.

Wells, B. and Stackhouse, J. (1997) *Children's Speech and Literacy Difficulties: A Psycholinguistic Framework.* Oxford: Wiley-Blackwell.
This book is useful to show how a psycholinguistic approach can be used in assessing speech processing in children. It uses case studies to interpret a child's performance within a psycholinguistic model and, at the end of each section, it has questions to test the reader's understanding of what they have read. It will be of interest to all professionals working with children with speech and language difficulties to help them understand the importance of detailed assessment to ensure appropriate therapeutic intervention.

Useful websites

www.afasic.org.uk.

www.comunicationsforum.org.uk.

www.helpwithtalking.com.

www.ican.org.uk.

www.janetokeefe.co.uk.

www.rcslt.org.

www.senconference.co.uk.

www.talkingpoint.org.uk.

www.theclaritypartnership.org.uk.

www.thecommunicationtrust.org.uk.

References

Bercow, J. (2008) *A Review of Services for Children and Young People (0–19) with Speech, Language and Communication Needs.* London: DCSF.

Botting, N. and Conti-Ramsden, G. (2000) Social and behavioural difficulties in children with language impairment. *Child Language Teaching and Therapy*, 16: 105–20.

Botting, N., Faragher, B., Simkin, Z., Knox, E. and Conti-Ramsden, G. (2001) Predicting pathways of specific language impairment: what differentiates good and poor outcome? *Journal of Child Psychology and Psychiatry and Allied Disciplines*, 42: 1013–20.

Conti-Ramsden, G. and Botting, N. (2008) Emotional health in adolescents with and without a history of specific language impairment (SLI). *Journal of Child Psychology and Psychiatry*, 49: 516–25.

Conti-Ramsden, G., Botting, N., Simkin, Z. and Knox, E. (2001) Follow-up of children attending infant language units: outcomes at 11 years of age. *International Journal of Language and Communication Disorders*, 36: 207–19.

Conti-Ramsden, G., Durkin, K., Simkin, Z. and Knox, E. (2009) Specific language impairment and school outcomes: I. Identifying and explaining variability at the end of compulsory education. *International Journal of Language and Communication Disorders*, 44: 15–35.

Conti-Ramsden, G., Knox, E., Botting, N. and Simkin, Z. (2002) Educational placements and National Curriculum Key Stage 2 test outcomes of children with a history of specific language impairment. *British Journal of Special Education*, 29: 76–82.

DCSF (2009a) *Special Educational Needs and Parental Confidence* (The Lamb Inquiry). London: HMSO.

DCSF (2009b) *Independent Review of the Primary Curriculum* (The Rose Report). Nottingham: DCSF Publications.

Durkin, K., Simkin, Z., Knox, E. and Conti-Ramsden, G. (2009) Specific language impairment and school outcomes: II. Educational context, student satisfaction, and post-compulsory progress. *International Journal of Language and Communication Disorders*, 44: 36–55.

Law, J., Garrett, Z. and Nye, C. (2003) SLT interventions for children with primary speech and language delay or disorder. *Cochrane Database of Systematic Reviews*, Issue 3 (Art. No. CD004110; DOI 10.1002/14651858.CD004110).

Law, J., Lindsay, G., Peacey, N., Gascoigne, M., Soloff, N., Radford, J., Band, S. and Fitzgerald, L. (2000) *Provision for Children with Speech and Language Needs in England and Wales: Facilitating Communication between Education and Health Services.* DfES Publications (www.dfes.gov.uk/research).

O'Keefe, J. (ed.) (2011) *Towards a Positive Future: Stories, Ideas and Inspiration from Children with Special Educational Needs, their Families and Professionals.* Guildford: J&R Press.

Picard, M. and Bradley, J.S. (2001) Revisiting speech interference in classrooms. *Audiology*, 40: 221–44.

Reid, J., Millar, S., Tait, L., Donaldson, M., Dean, E.C., Thomson, G.O.B. and Grieve, R. (1996) *Pupils with Special Educational Needs: The Role of SLTs, Interchange* 43. Edinburgh: SOEID.

Snowling, M.J. and Hayiou-Thomas, M.E. (2006) The dyslexia spectrum: continuities between reading, speech, and language impairments. *Topics in Language Disorders*, 26: 110–26.

Auditory Processing Disorder

7

Tony Sirimanna

Learning objectives

This chapter will help readers to:

- Understand the current definition of Auditory Processing Disorder (APD)
- Grasp the various forms of assessment of a child with suspected APD
- Recognise diagnostic criteria and differential diagnosis
- Have an outline of management

Introduction

APD has been known since the initial publication by Myklebust (1954), although over the years there has been confusion between APD and language processing. The American Speech-Language-Hearing Association (ASHA), as early as 1992 and subsequently in 1996, defined auditory processes that are likely to be deranged in those with APD. Following a consensus conference in Dallas in April 2000, Jerger and Musiek (2000) published its proceedings describing the nature of APD, co-morbidities, screening and diagnosis, and management. This led to the production of a Technical Report on (Central) Auditory Processing Disorder in 2005 by ASHA, followed by a number of further documents (www.asha.org). In 2015, the National Acoustic Laboratory (NAL) in Australia published their Position Statement (http://capd.nal.gov.au/capd-position-statement. shtml). They defined APD as: 'a deficit in the way the neural representation of sounds are processed by the brain, resulting in a distorted neural representation of the auditory signal within the auditory nervous system' creating 'difficulty in listening'.

In the UK, APD has been known over many decades under different names, e.g. 'obscure auditory dysfunction, 'auditory disability with normal hearing', in addition to 'auditory processing disorder', 'central auditory processing disorder' and '(central) auditory processing disorder'. Following discussions in the British Society of Audiology (BSA) Council in 2002, the author was instrumental in establishing the 'BSA APD Interest Group' and at an inaugural meeting in 2003, was elected as the founder Chair of the group. Professional and public awareness of APD has significantly grown since, with the APD Interest Group publishing its Position Statement and also Practice Guidelines. This not only led to an increased demand on a handful of services providing APD diagnosis but also a significant burden on the already overstretched educational services for children with additional needs. Over the years, disagreement amongst professionals has continued, but the understanding of the underlying processes, the effect of disordered auditory processing on academic achievement of children and young adults, the longer-term effect of continuing APD on people in employment, and how APD affects individuals' ability to function in day-to-day life has significantly improved. Especially over the last decade there has been a surge of good quality research on understanding the nature of APD, and screening, diagnosis and management of this condition. APD is categorised under the International Classification of Diseases (ICD) within the diseases of the nervous system as ICD-9–CM Diagnosis Code 388.40 and ICD-10–CM H93.29. Over the last five years or so, some education authorities have begun to recognise APD as an entity and started to respond to the demand by supporting those children who suffer from APD and require help in order to achieve their best. However, in spite of this, there has been a continuing limitation of comprehensive APD diagnostic services in the UK that has led to frustration amongst the public, especially parents.

Although the British Society of Audiology has made continuing attempts to resolve these issues and progress through its APD Interest Group (www.thebsa.org.uk), there is still a lot more work required to be done, and this chapter will provide an overview of the current understanding of APD in children from the UK perspective.

Definition of APD

Over the last 15 years, there has been considerable scrutiny of the definition of APD, with attempts to increase clarity and remove ambiguity. Since the ASHA's description of central auditory processes in 1992 and subsequently in 1995, the Dallas Consensus Conference in April 2000 (Jerger and Musiek, 2000) convened for agreeing on 'Diagnosis of APD in school-aged children' was probably the first such attempt and the group defined APD as 'a deficit in the processing of information that is specific to the auditory modality'. They agreed that there are other conditions with similar presentation such as ADHD (Attention Deficit Hyperactivity Disorder) or ADD (Attention Deficit Disorder), ASD (Autistic Spectrum Disorder), SLI (Specific Language Impairment) and cognitive impairment, and therefore the tests that were available at that time might not diagnose APD unless a minimum battery was used.

In early 2002, the author raised APD as an important developing area in the field of pae-diatric audiology in the UK, at a BSA Paediatric Audiology Interest Group (PAIG) meeting that led to establishing an APD Interest Group in October 2003 under the auspices of the BSA. One of the first actions of this group was to discuss, debate and agree on a definition for APD. This led to the working definition: 'Hearing disability resulting from impaired brain function and characterised by atypical recognition, discrimination, segregation or ordering of non-linguistic auditory stimuli,' thus dissociating auditory from language processing.

In 2005, ASHA released a position statement that defined APD as:

> difficulties in the processing of auditory information in the central nervous system (CNS) as demon-strated by poor performance in] one or more of the following skills: sound localisation and lateralisation; sense of movement of sound, auditory discrimination; auditory pattern recognition; temporal aspects of audition, including temporal integration, temporal discrimination (e.g. temporal gap detection), temporal ordering and temporal masking, auditory performance in competing acous-tic signals (including dichotic listening), and auditory performance with degraded acoustic signals

thus describing the complex auditory functions beyond what is determined by Pure Tone Audiometry (PTA) reiterating the fact that PTA does not really examine a person's ability to hear in normal listening conditions. They went on to state that: 'diagnosis of APD requires demonstration of a deficit in neural processing of auditory stimuli that is not due to higher order language, cognitive, or related factors'.

More recently, the BSA APD steering group have reviewed their definition of APD and have agreed that APD is due to impaired neural function involving the auditory pathways leading to 'poor perception of speech and non-speech sounds'. Their Position Statement is being reviewed at present and the reader is encouraged to visit the BSA website for an update and also to follow the latest publications by the UK APD Interest group.

The current classification of APD consists of three categories:

1. *Developmental APD*: This is the commonest presentation with APD present from early life and most likely to continue
2. *Secondary APD*: Secondary to periods of auditory deprivation, e.g. following long-standing periods of 'glue ear'
3. *Acquired APD*: Due to known neurological events, e.g. hypoxia, brain injury, tumours and their treatment, etc

Prevalence of APD

In 1997, Chermak and Musiek estimated prevalence in children to be 2–3%. This rises to 10–20% in adults (Cooper and Gates, 1991) probably due to neurological and neuro-degenerative disorders, suggesting that prevalence may increase with age. Prevalence of APD in children in the UK is unknown but it is likely to be many times more frequent than permanent congenital hearing impairment (PCHI).

Processing of auditory information

Hearing difficulties are often associated with a measurable deficit (impairment) on pure tone audiometry. The incidence of permanent hearing impairment in children increases from 1 per 1000 at birth to 1.6 per 1000 in 9–16 years of age (Fortnum et al., 2001), with a larger number having temporary hearing loss due to middle ear effusions ('glue ear') or acute middle ear infections during the first 5–7 years of life. As pure tone audiometry, the main measure of hearing impairment, is carried out in a sound-treated or soundproof room, it does not reflect the child's functioning in a normal day-to-day listening environment. There are a comparatively large number of children, as indicated by prevalence studies, who have significant difficulties with hearing in such adverse acoustic conditions, and these children may have disabilities similar to those experienced by children with permanent or temporary hearing loss.

The processing ability of the human brain is unimaginable and the complexity of the sensory systems in place to sense the world we live in is enormous. At any given time, the human brain receives multiple information through various sensory systems including hearing and vision. Each sensation is physically different and therefore requires to be transformed into a language that the brain can understand before being processed.

Every word we hear has a three-dimensional pattern consisting of loudness (intensity) and pitch (frequency) that changes in time. Each word therefore has a unique pattern, and we store these patterns in our long-term memory through repeated exposure for future use along with associations such as pictures, experiences, etc. The auditory system should have the capability of transporting these patterns from the ear to the place in the brain where these are held within the short-term memory for finding the matching pattern from the long-term memory. Correct recognition and accurate interpretation of the original sound signal relies on the auditory pathways not distorting the signal and losing its characteristics. Any distortion or gaps in the pattern will lead to the 'processor' taking a longer time to find a match, thus leading to a processing delay. Such delay in processing auditory patterns will lead to significant difficulties in hearing and understanding, especially of longer strings of information.

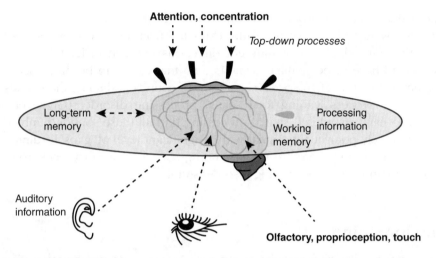

Figure 7.1 Sensory processing: Simplified model and top-down influences

Poor temporal resolution ability (i.e. not being able to sense acoustic changes in a word) leads to 'gaps' in what is heard, again requiring extra time to identify a correct pattern match. Sensing loudness and pitch changes in time is vital for recognising prosodic characteristics such as rhyme, rhythm, stress and intonation that can give a different meaning to the same word (e.g. desert vs dessert).

Extracting speech from background noise occurs at different levels within the auditory pathways. The inner ear has a sophisticated arrangement where the outer hair cells act as an 'amplifier' for quieter sounds and a 'damper' for louder sounds, while the inner hair cells transform the mechanical energy (pattern) reaching the inner ear into an electrical pattern. The brain scans information that comes through the auditory channel continuously, identifying relatively static sounds as 'noise', as opposed to sounds that change as 'speech', and uses the outer hair cells to dampen down noise through a neural feedback pathway called the 'olivo-cochlear bundle'. This mechanism acts as the first level of filtering background noise.

Further filtering of background noise occurs with the processor (brain) using binaural information (dichotic listening). The binaural functions are therefore extremely important in helping individuals to extract speech from background noise. Those children with a unilateral hearing loss have significant difficulties with hearing in background noise as they have lost the binaural function. Noise within a speech signal leads to gaps in what the individual hears and therefore those who have difficulties in 'filling the gaps' will struggle with hearing in spite of normal pure tone audiometric thresholds.

Often static noise in the background is easy to ignore or discard compared to fluctuating noise, e.g. classroom noise or multi-talker babble noise (Ferguson et al., 2010) that has significant variation in the acoustic characteristics (i.e. 'speech-like noise').

In a normal listening environment sounds come from different directions. The signal (sound that we want to listen to) has to be extracted from noise (other sounds that come from either the same direction or different directions), and in order to do this different streams of sound have to be spatially separated so that each can be processed differently. Binaural functions help in such spatial separation of sounds and some individuals have difficulties with this process leading to a spatial processing disorder (Glyde et al., 2011). Individuals who have disordered spatial processing find all these sounds 'jumbled up', thus creating an extremely poor-quality signal with a significant level of 'gaps' leading to extreme difficulties in hearing and therefore understanding speech in a noisy background (http://capd.nal.gov.au/capd-spatial-processing-disorder.shtml).

Discussion point

It is important to separate 'peripheral auditory functions' from 'central auditory processes', although there is some central control of the peripheral auditory system. What are these peripheral auditory processes and how do the central auditory processes depend on having good peripheral auditory function? Can children with peripheral auditory dysfunction, either temporary or permanent, have central auditory difficulties as well?

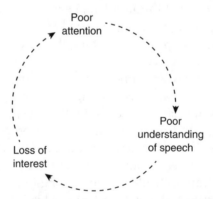

Figure 7.2 Relationship between attention and the ability to understand speech

There are other mechanisms that play a part in a child's ability to hear and of these, top-down processes such as attention and concentration are extremely important. These lead to creating gaps in what is heard, thus producing a similar delay in processing auditory information. This often results in a vicious circle, making it even more difficult to focus, listen and therefore understand (secondary attention difficulties).

Attention and ability to sustain concentration on complex sounds such as speech is an essential part of listening. Often children are able to have sustained concentration on tasks they are fond of or like doing (e.g. playing a computer game), yet will not have the same focus in the class. Such auditory attention is vital for understanding spoken instructions and verbal information and therefore some believe that these children have attentional APD (Moore et al., 2010).

Attention thus forms an important part of a child's ability to hear auditory information, and therefore poor attention leads to difficulties in hearing. Other factors described above can augment these difficulties, highlighting the importance of understanding the complexity that plays a part in a particular child's inability to hear and understand in adverse listening conditions.

A past history of Otitis Media with Effusion (OME) or 'glue ear' is commonly found in children referred for APD assessment. Moore et al. (2003) studied a cohort of children and found that those who have had OME have poor binaural release from masking (a test of binaural function) and therefore the likelihood of experiencing difficulty with hearing in background noise. These difficulties continue into the latter half of the first decade and the first half of the second decade before beginning to improve in most children. It is now considered that in this group APD is a secondary phenomenon due to periods of auditory deprivation.

Maturation of the auditory pathways starts from the periphery. Although the inner ear is fully developed at birth, the auditory nerve may take on average four to six weeks to fully mature (myelinate) but the synaptic function of the auditory brainstem fibres improves until about three years of age (Cox, 1985). The central auditory pathways take considerably more time to mature with myelination of inter-hemispheric auditory pathways in the corpus callosum spanning into the teenage years. This means that the central (or more complex) auditory functions are not fully developed in the first decade and are still developing in the second, a period when children start pre-school nursery and go through their primary and secondary education. Maturation of the auditory pathways (Jiang, 1998; Ribeiro Fuess et al., 2002; Pronton et al., 2002) can be physiologically delayed in some children and in a small number the delay could well be due to some pathological reason (Starr et al., 2003). It is therefore quite possible for some children to have rather immature or delayed auditory functions in spite of normal sensitivity to sounds in acoustically optimum conditions.

The brain has the ability to change through stimulation (i.e. neuroplasticity), and this is greatest when individuals are younger. Various environmental factors lead to establishing new neural networks and shutting down those unwanted during this period. This can be used for remediation, especially using various forms of auditory training.

The ability to hear an unknown language, or nonsense syllables or words and repeat them correctly requires just the initial processing of auditory information; while making a correct pattern match and attaching meanings to what is heard requires language processing. Once the auditory patterns are recognised, matched and labelled, and meanings are attached, these are passed onto the next stage for processing in the language domain, along with other sensory information. This level of processing is dependent on language and cognitive abilities. Once the auditory information is processed in the language domain and integrated with processed information coming through other sensory modalities (i.e. sensory integration), a learned (as opposed to reflex) response can be produced by the individual.

Discussion point

Auditory processing occurs within auditory pathways. However, these processes are dependent on a number of other factors and processors – from attention, concentration and distractibility to language and cognition. How do these 'other' factors influence or affect the child's ability to process information coming through the auditory system? How and why do these factors lead to a compounding effect on each other?

Clinical presentation

A child with APD may present with a range of symptoms, of which at least some are common to a number of other neurodevelopmental disorders such as ADD/ADHD, dyslexia, specific language disorder and autism. Furthermore, it is also possible for these conditions to co-exist with APD (Dawes and Bishop, 2010) and therefore it may not be possible to differentiate them on the basis of presenting features. A percentage of children will give a past history of a fluctuating hearing loss due to 'glue ear' and most will present with hearing difficulties when there is background noise. They also may show other symptoms of hearing difficulties such as asking for repetition, 'day dreaming' and some may even show phonological difficulties. A small percentage of children present with acquired APD from various neurological conditions such as certain forms of epilepsy (e.g. Landau-Kleffner syndrome), vascular events involving the brain (e.g. hypoxia or haemorrhage), brain trauma following accidents and intracranial tumours.

In a cohort of 1200 children seen by the author for APD assessment, 76% had difficulty in hearing when there is background noise as the main presenting complaint. Of the same cohort, 30% had difficulty in understanding verbal instructions especially sequential information, 21% also had a diagnosis of dyslexia and 19% had SLI. In the same cohort, 21% had increased sensitivity to loud sounds and 43% gave a past history of OME. In addition, 48% presented with poor short-term memory. This cohort clearly illustrates the commonest presenting feature – difficulty with hearing in a noisy environment. It also shows the co-morbidities that exist between APD and conditions such as dyslexia, and the relationship between significant periods of auditory deprivation during the early years of life and auditory processing.

Children with APD may behave like those with a peripheral hearing loss, in spite of normal pure tone audiometry. The difficulties experienced by children with APD include not being able to hear when there is background noise, asking for repetition, taking a longer time to respond to verbal instructions, inability to attend or focus on instructions that may result in disruptive behaviour in the class, distractibility and sensitivity to loud sounds.

It is important to separate true APD from conditions that present with similar symptoms due to poor auditory memory, attention, concentration, and language and cognitive difficulties. Those with poor short-term auditory memory may have limited ability in remembering sequential auditory information, while those with language and cognitive difficulties may show poor understanding of verbal as well as non-verbal information. In addition to language impairment, there are other co-morbid conditions such as reading disability (Sharma et al., 2006, 2009).

Case study 1

Kirsten, aged seven years, presented with poor academic performance, difficulty with hearing in background noise, poor short-term memory, hypersensitivity to louder sounds compared to peers, distractibility and difficulty in concentration when there is background noise, dyslexia and language difficulties. She came with speech and language and cognitive assessments that showed a significant receptive and expressive language deficit with cognitive abilities within the normal range.

She had already benefitted by being in a class of 11 pupils at a specialist school for dyslexic children. She was finding it difficult to understand long strings of information, struggled to take notes and listen simultaneously during lessons and felt that the teacher's voice blended in with the noise from a nearby road and also from children in the playground. Being an inner-London school, the playground was not large enough for all children to have a break at the same time and therefore playtime was staggered, leading to a steady level of noise during most of the school day.

Measure	Average Score for Age	Cut-off Score (dB)	Client's Score(dB)	Normal Limits	Variants from Average in StdDev
Low-Cue SRT	−0.5	1.4	0.6	Within	−1.1
High-Cue SRT	−11.9	−7.0	−4.1	Outside	−3.8
Talker Advantage	5.7	1.4	2.8	Within	−1.3
Spatial Advantage	9.6	6.3	4.1	Outside	−3.3
Total Advantage	11.4	8.3	4.7	Outside	−3.4

(Continued)

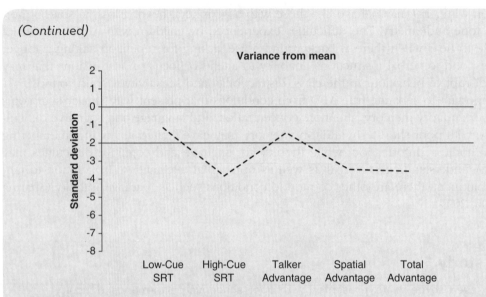

(Continued)

Figure 7.3 Spatial processing ability assessed by listening in spatialised noise

Her short-term memory was at the 9th percentile, and APD tests confirmed that she was able to hear clearly spoken words in a soundproof room without any difficulty but her ability to hear clear words in multi-talker babble background noise and degraded (low redundancy) speech (filtered words) in a quiet environment were at 1st percentile (disordered) and 5th percentile (borderline abnormal), respectively. Her temporal processing and auditory pattern sequencing were perfectly normal but binaural integration functions were disordered. Her spatial processing ability assessed by Listening in Spatialised Noise – Sentence test was disordered (see Figure 7.3).

She was diagnosed with an auditory processing disorder with disordered auditory decoding and closure, and spatial processing, co-existing with and compounded by poor short-term memory and language difficulties, although the latter would have been, at least to some extent, secondary to APD.

She had memory training and specific training to improve her spatial processing ability using the LiSN & Learn auditory training package. The diagnosis was useful, and the school changed the educational environment by minimising background noise that helped Kirsten to progress well.

Research has shown that poor auditory attention is one of the main reasons for deficits in auditory processing (Moore et al., 2010). Lack of attention leads to poor listening ability and therefore not being able to hear and understand spoken instructions. The work by Facoetti et al. (2002) has also shown the importance of auditory attention in phonemic perception in a group of dyslexic children. There is increasing evidence of cognition and attention (Dawes and Bishop, 2009) playing a major role in processing information presented through the auditory domain (Moore et al., 2010). Understanding these co-morbid factors and how these interact and compound the difficulties is therefore extremely important.

Screening for APD

A number of questionnaires and a few audiological tests are used for screening children for APD. These include Fisher's auditory problems checklist, Children's Auditory Performance Scale (CHAPS; Smoski, 1990), SCAN-3 test (C & A; Keith, 2000), Test of Auditory Perceptual Skills-Revised (TAPS-R). Some of these tools have been validated, e.g. SCAN-3, CHAPS (Amos and Humes, 1998; Wilson et al., 2011), albeit using a small number of normal subjects, but none of these can be used with reasonable specificity to identify those who might have APD, although the sensitivity is reasonably high.

Assessment of a child with APD

Multidisciplinary assessment

Often a careful history of the difficulties faced by the child will point the clinician in the right direction. Clarity of speech, pronunciation, receptive and expressive verbal and non-verbal language abilities, cognitive abilities, attention and concentration, and short-term and sequential auditory memory will help the clinician to understand the area of difficulty the child has. Finding out whether the child has other neurodevelopmental conditions, a family history of similar difficulties and pre- and perinatal problems (including a detailed description of past health issues) are all useful components of the initial assessment, thus requiring medical including neurological, cognitive and language assessments.

Audiological assessment and diagnosis of APD

Hearing difficulties in spite of normal pure tone audiometry and middle ear function are due to dysfunction of complex auditory processes such as binaural resolution (separation, fusion and integration), spatial processing, temporal resolution, frequency and intensity coding difficulties leading to poor auditory closure (ability to fill the gaps in speech), difficulties with localisation, lateralisation and sensing direction of movement of sounds and extracting speech from background noise. None of these functions are checked by pure tone audiometry and therefore assessment of APD requires a range of specialised tests that help us to examine these processes.

There is a vast range of audiological tests available that are used to assess auditory processing. Although reviewing and comparing these is not the aim of this chapter, understanding the principles would be beneficial. Therefore some of these are described as examples of the tests used to examine a particular function and to give the reader a basic understanding of the components evaluated.

Before various auditory processing tests are used, it is extremely important to confirm that the peripheral auditory mechanisms are functioning well. This includes examination of the ears and other relevant anatomy, and assessing the middle ear function and the functioning of the outer hair cells within the inner ear.

Although it is possible for APD to occur in individuals with a permanent peripheral hearing loss (Singh et al., 2004), it may not be easy to further examine this unless specific tests are used.

Ideally, non-linguistic tests should be employed to test for APD in order to minimise the effect of any language deficit on the outcome. If linguistic tests are used, it is important to understand the individual's language abilities before interpreting the results. Furthermore, as all behavioural functions are dependent on top-down processes, it is extremely important to ensure the child's maximum attention during testing.

Most audiological tests used for assessment of APD have a lower age limit of seven years but a few can be used in six- to seven-year-olds. However, as all younger children have very variable abilities, the normative dataset for tests in this age group usually has large confidence intervals, making it difficult to diagnose APD unless the scores (for the tests) are well below the mean.

The auditory tests currently available to test for APD can be grouped as in Table 7.1.

Table 7.1 Auditory tests for APD

Test group	Test	Function assessed
Monoaural low redundancy speech tests	Filtered words	Auditory closure
	Speech in noise/auditory figure ground	Auditory decoding
	LiSN (Listening in Spatialised Noise)	Auditory decoding
Dichotic tests	Dichotic digits	Binaural integration
	Competing sentences	Binaural separation
	Staggered spondaic words	Binaural integration
	Binaural fusion test	Binaural interaction
	Rapid alternating sentence test	Binaural interaction
	Masking level difference	Binaural interaction
	Listening in Spatialised Noise – Sentence test	Spatial processing
Temporal processing tasks	Random, gap detection test	Temporal resolution
	Gaps in noise test	Temporal resolution
	Pitch pattern sequence test	Frequency discrimination, temporal ordering +/- linguistic labelling
	Duration pattern sequence	Duration discrimination, temporal ordering +/- linguistic labelling

There are also a number of objective tests that are used in a selected number of patients. These include:

1. Auditory brainstem responses
2. Transient Evoked Otoacoustic Emissions (TEOAE) (outer hair cell function)
3. TEOAE contralateral suppression test (test of cochlear feedback mechanism, i.e. olivo-cochlear pathways)
4. Mismatch negativity (event related potential, objective evidence of processing sound at sub-cortical level)

The aim of the assessment of a patient with suspected auditory processing disorder is to exclude dysfunction of the peripheral auditory system and identify deficits in complex auditory functions so that appropriate measures can be put in place to help the individual. This should only be carried out by those with sufficient knowledge of auditory processes and access to a team of professionals able to provide medical, cognitive and language assessments when required.

Discussion point

What are the differences between screening and diagnostic tests for auditory processing and their importance? Are there specific presenting features that are unique to an auditory processing disorder and are there others that are common to a number of co-morbid conditions? What are the limitations of audiological tests available for diagnosis of APD, and which non-audiological assessments might help this process in a child with a complex presentation? Management is dependent on precise diagnosis confirming exact mechanisms that are disordered. What are the key steps in arriving at the diagnosis of APD and what investigations help in understanding the exact processes that are disordered?

Management of APD

There are no universally agreed criteria for diagnosis of APD at present, although some services use their own. Often the diagnosis of APD is made when there is more than one abnormal test result. When the results are clearly abnormal in only one functional area (e.g. auditory closure) the term 'auditory processing issues' or 'auditory processing difficulties' is used.

The purpose of identifying conditions or areas of difficulty is to help the individual child to achieve his or her best potential and maximise their life chances, so that the individual can make an optimum contribution to society. Class sizes are ever-increasing in the UK, with reduced pupil to teacher ratios and diminishing discipline within classes leading to disruption and poor attention, to the detriment of the child achieving their best unless APD is identified early and interventions made. Auditory attention is extremely important and distractions, either auditory, visual or other sensory, would affect the child's ability to concentrate and grasp essential information during lessons. Often acoustic conditions in the class are sub-optimal for most children, with high levels of background noise generated within or from external sources and also sometimes with an unacceptable level of reverberation (echoing), especially in classrooms with high ceilings. Although most children may be able to cope with these adverse conditions those with APD will struggle. Most professionals look for diagnostic labels before help is provided, to the detriment of children who have difficulties with hearing and/or understanding when in a specific educational environment.

Case study 2

Sam was a 12-year-old who had just started being home educated, and was referred to the APD clinic by the community paediatrician (audiology) with a history of unexplained behavioural difficulties. The teachers suspected a hearing loss when he was in the primary school but a screening hearing test by the school nurse showed normal hearing.

The suspicions continued when deteriorating school performance and a referral to local ENT was made by the GP at the request of the parents. Audiological tests including pure tone audiometry, middle ear function tests, transient otoacoustic emissions and speech audiometry in quiet surroundings were all normal and therefore he was discharged from the clinic with a diagnosis of 'normal hearing'.

However, he continued to have difficulties with his educational progress and was showing disruptive behaviour in the class. He was often seen disturbing those seated next to him leading to him being seated at the front with other children who had been misbehaving in the class. His educational progress and behaviour further deteriorated and after several meetings with the parents, and an assessment by the local second-tier audiology and community paediatric services he was excluded from the class.

APD tests clearly highlighted his difficulty, with extremely poor ability to hear when there was background noise and marginal temporal processing difficulties (speech in noise test score at 0.1 percentile, filtered words at 1st percentile and a gap threshold of 20 ms). His cognitive abilities were excellent with superb non-verbal skills and an above average IQ. He also had poor auditory memory with good memory for visual events. His language scores were below average and thought to be secondary to his auditory difficulties. When asked, Sam said that he often could not understand instructions and therefore had to ask his friends for clarification.

Various recommendations were made including those for improving memory and attention, placing him in a better educational environment with good acoustics (minimum background noise and reverberation), preferential seating, a smaller class and eventually a personal FM system. Sam continued to make significant progress with close supervision and additional help initially, and passed his GCSE and 'A' Level examinations with excellent grades, enabling him to complete university education.

The most common deficits seen in those with confirmed APD are with auditory closure and auditory decoding functions and spatial processing. These children struggle to hear when there is background noise and also with low redundancy (poor-quality) speech (e.g. someone talking in a different accent). Very few children with APD have temporal processing difficulties and it is important that these are identified, as specific auditory training may have to be considered. A significant proportion of children have co-existing conditions such as disordered language, dyslexia, ADD, ADHD and autism. Language processing difficulties may also co-exist but can be secondary to APD. Top-down processes such as attention and concentration (specifically auditory attention) are of paramount importance in understanding spoken language. Poor attention could be due to a primary attention disorder or secondary to auditory difficulties. It is therefore important to understand every aspect of the child's difficulties and take a holistic approach to management (Bamiou et al., 2006). It must be remembered that, although individually each of these deficits may not reach a level of significance, collectively they can have a disabling effect on the child's performance. The following section discusses the auditory aspects of management, but as described earlier, this should be implemented with recommendations for managing other conditions, deficits, difficulties and impairments in areas such as memory, attention, language and cognition.

Managing a child with poor auditory closure and decoding deficit

Not being able to fill in the gaps created by poor listening, poor-quality speech or poor auditory attention and inability to extract speech from background noise makes it difficult for children to understand speech. Such difficulties will lead to the individual taking a longer time to process spoken instructions (i.e. processing delay):

1. *Improving acoustic environment*: The aim here is to improve the speech (signal) to noise ratio (SNR) so that the teacher's voice is heard fully by the affected pupil. As it is impractical and unsustainable for the teacher to raise their voice throughout the lesson, it is extremely important to make every effort to minimise the background noise. This should be achieved by a combination of classroom discipline, identifying the source(s) of noise and dealing with it and improving acoustics within the classroom by using

sound absorbing material (softer material and avoiding hard surfaces that reflect sound, e.g. carpets, curtains, rubber shoes for the furniture that will help to reduce the background noise). These measures will also minimise reverberation within the classroom.

2. *Improving speech to noise ratio*: This can be achieved by using sound-field systems or personal FM systems in combination with the above. Children are more likely to listen and therefore stay quiet during lessons if they are able to hear and follow the teacher. With sound-field systems (e.g. Phonak dynamic SF system), the child benefits as long as he or she remains within the class, but a personal FM system can be carried with the child to be used in most places (e.g. in the playground or on field trips). These systems require the teacher to wear a microphone and a transmitter system and in group discussions it is possible to use an additional roving microphone that can be passed around for individual speakers to use, so that the APD child is never left out of a discussion. If a personal wearable FM device (e.g. Phonak Roger Focus – www.phonak.com, ReSound minimicrophone – GN Resound) is used, a trial period before purchasing a system is recommended.

   Getting the child to sit nearer the teacher will also improve the loudness of the teacher's voice over the background noise but this helps only if the teacher stands in front and does not move around in the class.

3. *Clarity of voice and accents*: An individual's auditory system is programmed to identify the voices of familiar people such as their parents with the greatest ease. Although most individuals will manage to understand different accents by drawing in functions such as increased attention and lip reading, those with APD are unlikely to cope. These factors have a synergistic effect (e.g. if the teacher has a different accent the child with APD is unlikely to manage with levels of background noise that other children are able to cope with).

Managing a child with a spatial processing disorder

These children find it extremely difficult to process multiple streams of sound coming from different directions. Spatial processing disorder can be improved by specific auditory training (Cameron et al., 2012) (LiSN & Learn – Cameron and Dillon, 2006), although completing this programme takes about three months in total. Immediate measures include preferential seating of the child, minimising background noise and using personal FM systems (http://capd.nal.gov.au/capd-spatial-processing-disorder.shtml).

Managing a child with a temporal processing disorder

Ability to sense changes in loudness and pitch is extremely important for identifying complex sounds such as speech. Not being able to do so will lead to an unacceptable number of 'gaps' in the speech sound, making it difficult for the child to understand speech or take a longer time to process it. These children may present with dyslexic features and be diagnosed as having dyslexia (Cameron and Dillon, 2006). However, the number of children who have a temporal processing disorder among those presenting with a diagnosis of dyslexia is small (personal experience from over 600 children with suspected APD).

Although temporal processing disorders are not very common, it is important to identify these as auditory training (both formal and informal) can make a significant improvement in a relatively short period of time (Depeller et al., 2004). However, the sustainability of such improvements has been questioned. More research is needed to further investigate the effectiveness of these programmes.

Case study 3

James was in the first year in secondary school when he was referred for assessment of auditory processing function. He had significant difficulties in junior school for years and had been on School Action Plus, but in spite of this he was a few years behind his peers in a number of areas by the time he transferred to secondary school. He had cognitive and language assessments as a part of a community paediatric evaluation which showed concerns in both areas with a strong suspicion of auditory factors playing a major role, while excluding dyslexia, ADD, ADHD and autism. Audiological assessment showed a picture compatible with a temporal processing disorder (phonological difficulties, poor auditory decoding and closure, and gap thresholds of 80 ms). Formal auditory training was recommended with a choice of auditory training packages in addition to measures for managing some of the other difficulties in the short term. A commercially available auditory training package was used by the school with direct support from a specialist overseeing the programme. Significant improvement was noted by three months and James continued to improve over the next year to 18 months, to a point where he was performing at an age-appropriate level. His temporal processing ability was assessed using the Gaps in Noise test at the age of 15 and was found to have significantly improved, although still outside the normal range with a gap threshold of 10 ms.

Informal auditory training also has a place in managing a child with APD but administering it requires a good knowledge of the methods and also experience.

Managing poor auditory attention

As mentioned earlier, attentional deficits can be primary or secondary to auditory deficits (or a combination). It is crucial to identify these and manage them appropriately. At the extreme, primary attentional deficits may require medication for control of poor attention.

Other methods and tactics to sustain the child's attention for longer periods of time include didactic or interactive teaching, using visual material to help understanding, use of simple language, breaking down information into smaller chunks, pre-teaching. Listening programmes with enhanced music (e.g. The Listening Programme that claims to improve auditory processing abilities, Esteves et al., n.d.), has been recommended by some professionals and has a varying degree of success, but can help to improve the child's ability to listen and sustain concentration.

Managing auditory short-term memory difficulties

In order to understand spoken instructions (or for that matter any sensory information that changes in time), it is essential that the individual has the ability to retain these auditory events in the working memory sequentially so that meaningful interpretation can take place. Those with limited working memory can take longer to process information. Improving sequential short-term auditory memory can be attempted using various memory games (e.g. Simon game, mind maps, memory booster and attaching visual imagery).

Discussion points

Management of APD consists of understanding the exact auditory processes that are disordered and having a clear perception of co-morbid factors, if there are any, so that a 'multi-pronged' approach to intervention can be considered. This leads to 'tailor-made' intervention strategies covering all areas of dysfunction so that the child is helped in a most cost and time effective manner. What are the key aspects of such interventions? Why is it important for everyone involved with the child's education to understand, not only the diagnoses, but also how these affect the child's performance in day-to-day situations?

Summary

Understanding of APD is improving and research is leading us to a clearer definition, better understanding of the effects of APD, co-morbid conditions and the interactions and methodical approach to managing affected individuals in order to give them the best opportunity for achieving the optimum from education and life. Figures 7.4 and 7.5 show the parent-reported outcomes for a cohort of over 700 children seen at a major tertiary hospital.

As professionals, we have a responsibility to understand the complexity of this condition, its diagnosis and recommendations for its management, and find the optimal solution for a particular child. It is important to realise that a proactive approach pays off much more than waiting

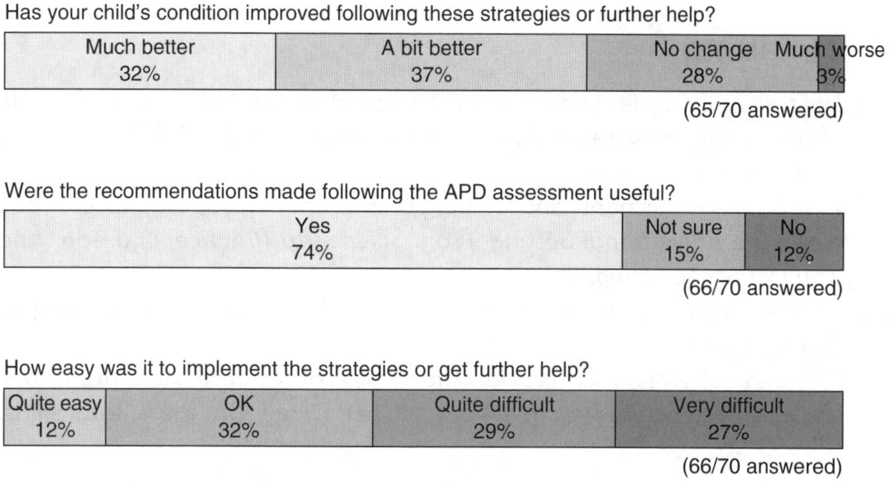

Has your child's condition improved following these strategies or further help?

Much better 32%	A bit better 37%	No change 28%	Much worse 3%

(65/70 answered)

Were the recommendations made following the APD assessment useful?

Yes 74%	Not sure 15%	No 12%

(66/70 answered)

How easy was it to implement the strategies or get further help?

Quite easy 12%	OK 32%	Quite difficult 29%	Very difficult 27%

(66/70 answered)

Figure 7.4   Parents reported outcomes following APD diagnosis (a)

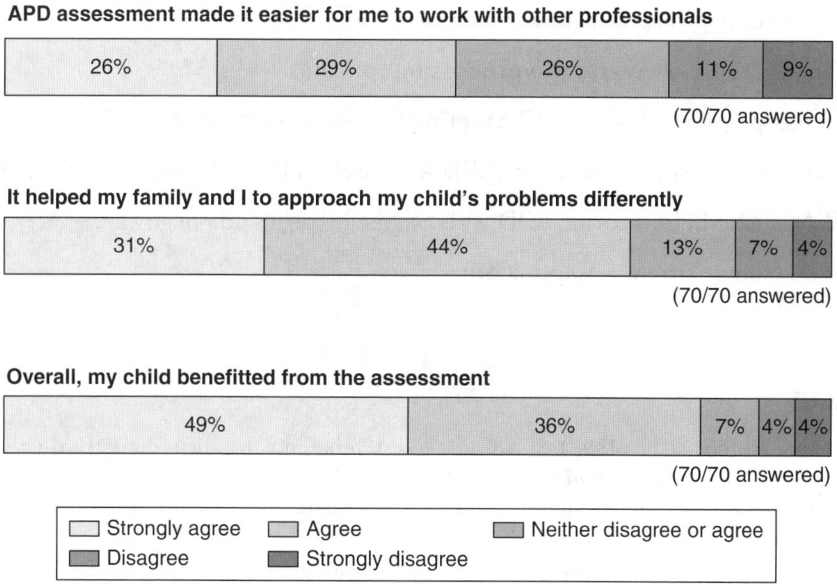

APD assessment made it easier for me to work with other professionals

26%	29%	26%	11%	9%

(70/70 answered)

It helped my family and I to approach my child's problems differently

31%	44%	13%	7%	4%

(70/70 answered)

Overall, my child benefitted from the assessment

49%	36%	7%	4%	4%

(70/70 answered)

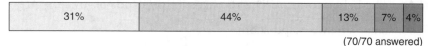

☐ Strongly agree   ☐ Agree   ☐ Neither disagree or agree
☐ Disagree   ☐ Strongly disagree

Figure 7.5   Parents reported outcomes following APD diagnosis (b)

for a child to fail before help is provided. Initial signs of APD (or any other neuro-developmental condition) should be recognised, and early diagnosis and appropriate management advice should be sought in order to achieve the best for the child, the family and society as a whole.

Further reading

Auditory Processing Disorder (April 2004) Published by the MRC Institute of Hearing Research (available in portable document format on the BSA/APD special interest group web pages, see below).

Bellis, T.J. (2002) *Assessment and Management of Central Auditory Processing Disorders in the Educational Setting: From Science to Practice*, 2nd edn. Andover: Thompson Delmar Learning.

British Society of Audiology APD Interest Group publications, www.thebsa.org.uk/bsa-groups/group-apdi.

Musiek, F.E. and Chermak, G. (2006) *Handbook of Central Auditory Processing Disorders: From Science to Practice*, Vols. 1–2. San Diego, CA: Plural Publishing Inc.

Useful websites

American Speech-Language-Hearing Association: www.asha.org.

Auditory Processing Disorder, New Zealand Review: www.health.govt.nz/publication/auditory-processing-disorder-new-zealand-review.

Australian APD site: www.auditoryprocessing.com.au.

British Society of Audiology – APD Steering Group: www.thebsa.org.uk.

MRC Institute of Hearing Research (APD Research in the UK): www.ihr.mrc.ac.uk.

National Acoustic Laboratories APD web pages: http://capd.nal.gov.au.

UK APD consumer site: www.apduk.org.

References

Amos, N.E. and Humes, L.E. (1998) SCAN test-retest reliability for first- and third-grade children. *Journal of Speech, Language, and Hearing Research*, 41(4): 834–45.

Bamiou, D., Campbell, N. and Sirimanna, T. (2006) Management of auditory processing disorders. *Audiological Medicine*, 4(1): 46–56.

Cameron, S. and Dillon, H. (2006) Remediation of spatial processing issues in central auditory processing disorder. In G.D. Chermak and F.E. Musiek (eds), *Handbook of Central Auditory Processing Disorders: Comprehensive Intervention. Vol. 2*. San Diego, CA: Plural Publishing.

Cameron, S., Glyde, H. and Dillon, H. (2012) Efficacy of the LiSN & Learn auditory training software: randomized blinded controlled study. *Audiology Research*, 2(1): e15.

Chermak, G.D. and Musiek, F.E. (1997) *Central Auditory Processing Disorders: New Perspectives*. San Diego, CA: Singular Publishing Group.

Cooper, J.C. Jr and Gates, G.A. (1991) Hearing in the elderly – the Framingham cohort, 1983–1985: Part II. Prevalence of central auditory processing disorders. *Ear and Hearing*, 12(5): 304–11.

Cox, L.C. (1985) Infant assessment: developmental and age related considerations. In J. Jacobsen (ed.), *The Auditory Brainstem Response*. San Diego, CA: College Hill Press, pp. 296–316.

Dawes, P. and Bishop, D.V.M. (2009) Auditory processing disorder in relation to developmental disorders of language, communication and attention: a review and critique. *International Journal of Language & Communication Disorders*, 44: 440–65.

Dawes, P. and Bishop, D.V.M. (2010) Psychometric profile of children with auditory processing disorder and children with dyslexia. *Archives of Disease in Childhood*, 95: 432–6.

Depeller, J.M., Taranto, A.M. and Bench, J. (2004) Language and auditory processing changes following Fast ForWord. *Australian and New Zealand Journal of Audiology*, 26(2): 94–109.

Esteves, J., Stein-Blum, S., Cohen, J. and Tischler, A. (n.d.) *Identifying the Effectiveness of a Music-Based Auditory Stimulation Method on Children with Sensory Integration and Auditory Processing Concerns: A Pilot Study* (downloaded from www.advancedbrain.com).

Facoetti, A., Lorusso, M.L., Paganoni, P. et al. (2002) Auditory and visual automatic attention deficits in developmental dyslexia. *Cognitive Brain Research*, 16: 185–91.

Fortnum, H.M., Summerfield, A.Q., Marshall, D.H., Davis, A.C. and Bamford, J.M. (2001) Prevalence of permanent childhood hearing impairment in the United Kingdom and implications for universal neonatal hearing screening: questionnaire based ascertainment study. *BMJ*, 323(7312): 536–40.

Glyde, H., Hickson, L., Cameron, S. and Dillon, H. (2011) Problems hearing in noise in older adults: a review of spatial processing disorder. *Trends in Amplification*, 15(3): 116–26

Jerger, J. and Musiek, F. (2000) Report of the consensus conference on the diagnosis of auditory processing disorders in school-aged children. *Journal of the American Academy of Audiology*, 11: 467–74.

Jiang, Z.D. (1998) Maturation of peripheral and brainstem auditory function in the first year following perinatal asphyxia: a longitudinal study. *Journal of Speech, Language, and Hearing Research*, 41: 83–93.

Keith, R.W. (2000) Development and standardization of SCAN-C Test for auditory processing disorders in children. *Journal of the American Academy of Audiology*, 11(8): 438–45.

Moore, D.R., Hartley, D.E. and Hogan, S.C. (2003) Effects of otitis media with effusion (OME) on central auditory function. *International Journal of Pediatric Otorhinolaryngology*, 67(Suppl. 1): S63–7.

Moore, D.R., Ferguson, M.A., Edmondson-Jones, A.M., Ratib, S. and Riley, A. (2010) The nature of auditory processing disorder in children. *Pediatrics*, 126: e382–90.

Myklebust, H. (1954) *Auditory Disorders in Children*. New York: Grune & Stratton.

Pronton, C., Eggermont, J.J., Khosla, D. et al. (2002) Maturation of human central auditory system activity: separating auditory evoked potentials by dipole source modeling. *Clinical Neurophysiology*, 113(3): 407–20.

Ribeiro Fuess, V.L., Ferreira Bento, R. and Medicis Da Silveira, J.A. (2002) Delay in maturation of the auditory pathway and its relationship to language acquisition disorders. *Ear, Nose and Throat Journal*, 81(10): 706–12.

Sharma, M., Purdy, S.C. and Kelley, A.S. (2009) Comorbidity of auditory processing, language, and reading disorders. *Journal of Speech, Language, and Hearing Research*, 52: 706–22.

Sharma, M. et al. (2006) Electrophysiological and behavioral evidence of auditory processing deficits in children with reading disorder. *Clinical Neurophysiology*, 117(5): 1130–44.

Singh, S., Liasis, A. and Rajput, K. et al. (2004) Event-related potentials in pediatric cochlear implant patients. *Ear and Hearing*, 25(6): 598–610.

Smoski, W. (1990) Use of CHAPPS in a children's audiology clinic. *Ear and Hearing*, 11: 53S–56S.

Starr, A., Michalewski, H.J., Zen, F.G. et al. (2003) Pathology and physiology of auditory neuropathy with a novel mutation in the *MPZ* gene (Tyr145Ser). *Brain*, 126(7): 1604–19.

Wilson, W.J., Jackson, A., Pender, A. et al. (2011) The CHAPS, SIFTER and TAPS-R as predictors of (C)AP skills and (C)APD. *Journal of Speech, Language, and Hearing Research*, 54(1): 278–91.

Occupational Therapy and Developmental Coordination Disorder/ Dyspraxia

8

Jane Abdullah

Learning objectives

This chapter will help readers to:

- Understand the role of the Occupational Therapist (OT)
- Understand the difference between Developmental Coordination Disorder (DCD) and dyspraxia from an OT perspective
- Gain a general overall view of DCD characteristics
- Describe how some of these difficulties can impact on daily function
- Provide some supportive strategies

The role of occupational therapists

Occupational Therapy (OT) is defined as a client-centred health profession, with the primary goal of enabling people to participate in everyday life (World Federation of Occupational Therapists, 2013). OT's are health and social care professionals and can be based within the

NHS, Social Services, Education Authorities, charities or as independent practitioners. In order to practise within the United Kingdom, they are required to be registered with the Health and Care Professions Council (HCPC). As a profession, OT's aim to develop, restore and maintain the skills, strategies, behaviours and relationships needed for safe, functional and dignified independent living, as appropriate to the age and priorities of clients referred to them.

They use standardised and non-standardised assessments, clinical observations and task analysis to identify difficulties that impact on everyday performance. They then, in partnership with the client, set goals, and offer treatment, strategies, environmental modifications, adaptations, advice and information as deemed necessary. They work as members of an interdisciplinary team that can encompass health, social and educational parameters. They play a key role in educating parents/carers and professional colleagues concerning the functional challenges that individuals can face.

Using professional expertise, across a variety of settings, and in collaboration with the client, family, carers and educators, the OT can decide how best to deliver therapy interventions (Case-Smith and O'Brien, 2010), as discrepancies in behaviour can occur in different settings (Buitendag and Aronstam, 2012).

Therapy can be provided through direct and indirect intervention. Direct intervention provides focused, intensive and face-to-face input via individual or group sessions, whilst indirect or consultative treatment involves other people following specified advice, programmes or adaptations to the environment, as directed by the OT (Case-Smith and O'Brien, 2010).

Nowadays, when implementing treatment goals, many OT's favour a 'top-down' approach. This assumes that the necessary or required skills are developed due to interaction between the individual, the task and the environment (Mandich et al., 2001). Top-down approaches emphasise client centred input and focus on the analysis of functional performance and its context in real-life situations such as learning to ride a bike, make a snack, tie shoelaces or style hair.

More traditional process-orientated or 'bottom-up' approaches concentrate on remediating underlying problems, so that improvements in occupational performance can occur (Coster, 1998). Bottom-up treatments therefore focus on developing components such as strength, balance, visual perception or sensory processing with a view to developing the core skills needed for functional activities.

Depending on the presenting difficulties, needs and desires of each client, therapists can decide whether to adopt a top-down, a bottom-up or a combined approach to treatment (Brown and Chien, 2010). They then use their professional skills to ascertain whether the individual requires direct or indirect intervention.

Because OT's are skilled in the observation of fine and gross motor task performance, along with other multiple factors that contribute to movement difficulties, they can assist with identifying and providing information on the severity of presenting problems, and establish the impact they can have on daily functioning. Using standardised and non-standardised interviews, questionnaires and observation, OT's can assess and determine the effect that motor skill delays and poor coordination have on:

- personal independence (dressing, eating, toileting, personal hygiene)
- leisure (sports, arts, crafts, outings, socialising)
- educational activities (academic progress, peer relationships, access and participation in class, work production)

Following skilled activity analysis, OT's then provide intervention that can: modify tasks; teach strategies or skills; educate, thereby altering unrealistic demands and expectations; and coach others so that consistent approaches to tasks occur during relevant situations (Missiuna et al., 2011).

What is developmental coordination disorder?

Developmental Coordination Disorder (DCD) is classified as being a specific developmental disorder of motor function (DSM-5, 2013) where there is a delay in motor (movement) skill development, or when problems in coordinating movement affect the ability of individuals to perform everyday tasks with the efficiency or effectiveness expected for their age, within their homes, educational environments and community settings.

Historically, the terms DCD and dyspraxia have been used interchangeably (Gibbs et al., 2007). Confusingly, in the UK, such difficulties are still often referred to as dyspraxia; however, in 2011, the European Academy for Childhood Disability (EACD) recommended that the term DCD should be used (Blank et al., 2012). DCD is therefore now the recognised term used.

DCD can be formally diagnosed using the DSM-5 (2013) and ICD-10 (2004) criteria, as summarised below:

- *Criterion A*: a marked impairment in the development of motor control
- *Criterion B*: the impaired motor development significantly affects educational progress and/or activities of everyday life
- *Criterion C*: the difficulties demonstrated cannot be explained by a general medical condition (e.g. cerebral palsy, muscular dystrophy) and do not meet the criteria for a pervasive developmental disorder
- *Criterion D*: if learning difficulties are present, the problems with movement and coordination are in excess of those usually associated with the level of learning difficulty identified

DCD is, therefore, not really a single disorder as there is no single known cause, typical developmental pathway or known outcome, and people with DCD do not have identifiable medical or neurological conditions that explain their coordination difficulties. The manifestations of DCD consequently vary from individual to individual and with age and development. In addition, DCD can exist co-morbidly with a spectrum of other diagnoses such as: Attention Deficit Hyperactivity Disorder (ADHD); Asperger's syndrome; Autistic

Spectrum Disorder (ASD); Deficit of Attention and Motor Perception (DAMP); sensory processing disorder; speech and language difficulties; and specific learning difficulties such as dyslexia (Hellgren et al., 1993).

Generally, individuals with DCD perform functional activities at a slower developmental pace and in less effective ways than their peers. Common characteristics include:

- 'clumsy' or awkward gross and fine motor coordination
- inconsistent performance and discrepancy in motor skill ability
- delayed motor skill development
- problems learning new motor skills
- poor balance
- difficulty coordinating both sides of the body
- handwriting problems
- difficulty with activities that require constant change or adaptation

DCD can therefore have a major impact on daily life function as illustrated below.

Discussion points

Imagine what it would be like if you could not dress yourself or wear clothes of your choice because your fingers were too fumbly to manage the fastenings. How would it feel to find holding and using a pencil uncomfortable and difficult, and that despite trying your hardest to write neatly, the work you produce always looks messy and is usually illegible? How would it feel to be consistently chosen last for team games, or ostracised from playground or sporting activities because you can never get to the ball in time? How would you manage to concentrate in class or at work, when the sound of a lawn mower outside the window keeps distracting you, the feeling of the collar on your shirt is continually irritating you, you are unable to balance or sit still on your chair, or you cannot keep up with what the teacher is saying? How do you make and sustain friendships when you are slower to learn games and are unable to keep up with your peers? How would you manage to participate in out-of-school clubs or social activities when you are completely exhausted and drained by the end of the day?

Daily life can consequently be a constant struggle, with school/college/work performance; self-esteem; and age-appropriate activities of daily living being severely limited. Associated poor self-regulation, anxiety, attention and poor working memory can also impact on skill acquisition. When not recognised and properly managed during a child's development, DCD can lead to academic failure, mental health problems, poor physical fitness (Gaines et al., 2008), and reduced self-esteem (McWilliams, 2005; Watson and Knott, 2006).

DCD is one of the most common disorders amongst school-aged children, and boys are more affected than girls (Zwicker et al., 2012). Between 5 and 10% of school-aged children are thought to have DCD, with 2% being severely affected. International studies suggest that DCD is present in 6% of children between the ages of 5 and 12, which equates approximately to one child in every class at primary school level (Kaplan et al., 2000).

DCD is now known to persist from childhood into adulthood (Kirby et al., 2010, 2011), and difficulties with posture, movement and coordination have been found to impact significantly on daily function, occupational performance and emotional well-being (Kramer and Hinojosa, 2010). Frustrations caused by DCD are described as having a negative influence on adolescent relationships within school, with peers and with family members (Missiuna et al., 2007) and consequently emotional health is affected. DCD impacts on social and leisure choices, and studies (Kirby et al., 2011; Cousins and Smyth, 2003) have shown that affected adults demonstrate continued difficulty with writing, driving coordination and participating in sport.

The manifestations of DCD, resulting from a delay in the development of motor skills and coordination, can therefore create functional difficulties when everyday tasks are undertaken. Because the level of difficulties experienced by individuals varies, each person with DCD will present with their own set of strengths and weaknesses.

What is dyspraxia?

Dyspraxia is a term that has a number of meanings according to the context in which it is used. Confusingly, it is still used to describe DCD. Unlike DCD, dyspraxia has no formal diagnostic criteria; however, it is a very real, albeit often hidden disability which impacts on many areas of daily life.

To an OT, DCD and dyspraxia depict different things. OTs view DCD as an umbrella term, with dyspraxia as a sub-category within this. This is particularly true when viewing dyspraxia from the sensory integrative viewpoint, which is a particular model based on the theory and treatment originated by A. Jean Ayres (1979).

Dyspraxia derives from the words 'dys' (indicating impaired ability) and 'praxis' which is 'the ability to interact successfully with the physical environment, to plan, organise and carry out a sequence of unfamiliar actions and to do what one needs and wants to do (Kranowitz, 1998).'

In order to understand the OT's perspective on dyspraxia, it is important to understand 'praxis'. Praxis consists of three components:

- ideation – forming ideas and knowing what to do
- motor planning – organising and planning the sequence of movements
- execution – carrying out the movements (plan) in smooth sequence

Praxis affects every aspect of life, including behaviour, language, daily living skills, learning and movement: from playing with toys, using a pencil, building a structure, straightening up a room to engaging in many other activities and occupations (Ayres et al., 1987).

The term dyspraxia therefore refers to 'a breakdown of praxis (action)' and 'the inability to utilise voluntary motor abilities effectively in all aspects of life from play to structured skilled tasks' (S. Chu and N.R. Milloy, cited in Bowens and Smith, 1999). In order to be regarded as having dyspraxia by an OT the individual must present with deficits in one or more of the three practice processes: ideation, motor planning or execution, when undertaking new or unfamiliar activities (Kramer and Hinojosa, 2010; Bundy et al., 2002; Schaaf and Roley, 2006).

Thus, although the components of a movement might be present, individuals with dyspraxia are not able to generalise movement sequences or skills outside a familiar context, due to difficulties with the organisation, planning and execution of physical movement (Miller et al., 2007). Dyspraxia is therefore seen as a sub-category within the much wider group of children with DCD. Consequently, many people who fulfil the criteria for DCD do not have 'dyspraxia' in its true sense.

Characteristic features of DCD

DCD can impact on

- physical ability
- sensory processing
- behaviour
- emotion
- social participation
- education
- personal independence

Whilst there are many commonly occurring characteristic features found in individuals with DCD, its manifestations will vary with age and development. It is also important that DCD features should not be taken in isolation, as many elements can be observed in people who have no marked or apparent difficulties. However, when a number of characteristics combine together, they can cause significant and very real difficulty with everyday function (Table 8.1).

Not all individuals demonstrate all these difficulties, but it can be seen that problems associated with both DCD and dyspraxia have a direct impact on both daily living and learning in many areas of life within the home, in educational settings, socially and in the community. DCD can cause the individual to be viewed with frustration and scorn, which in turn has an indirect impact on siblings, parents, the wider family, friends and teachers.

Table 8.1

Physical characteristics

To be able to learn and move we need to be aware of our body and its position in space (proprioception); balance; coordinate and integrate the two sides of the body (bilateral integration); plan and undertake unfamiliar activities (praxis); and grade the amount of strength and force needed to perform skilled movements. Common physical difficulties include:

Hypermobile joints and 'low muscle tone' (hypotonia)	• causes instability and reduced strength • affects postural control, agility, balance and stamina
Reduced co-ordination	• gross and fine motor skills below the expected age level • huge effort produces little result • 'soft' neurological features i.e. posturing of the hands, arms or face when moving or concentrating
Gross motor skills (large movements)	• poor timing, rhythm, fluency and sequencing • movement looks awkward and uncoordinated • retention of primitive reflexes, affecting movement performance • poor balance, slow saving reactions • difficulty controlling movement changes
Fine motor skills (small movements)	• immature grasp • problems constructing or manipulating items • clumsiness during art and craft • difficulty using utensils or tools • difficulty applying cosmetics, styling hair, or shaving
Dyspraxia	• difficulties planning, organising and carrying out movement sequences in the correct order • problems with sequencing, timing, organisation and orientation • extended practice and step-by-step instruction necessary
Poor body awareness (proprioception) and spatial awareness	• poor orientation towards items; knocking things over; bumping into people accidentally; poor sense of direction; difficulty imitating actions • difficulty perceiving speed, distance and direction accurately • trouble grading strength and force • poor tactile discrimination
Laterality and bilateral integration	• problems determining left from right • non-automatic crossing the body midline – twisting body in chair or swopping hands during tasks to compensate • poorly developed hand dominance; cross-laterality; ambidexterity • difficulty coordinating both sides of the body when undertaking different but complementary movements
Eye movements	• poor tracking and scanning • poor localisation, looking quickly and effectively from object to object • poor eye/hand coordination
Visual perceptual functions / visual motor difficulties	• poor registration and interpretation of visual information • trouble with visual memory, spatial organisation/orientation • difficulty discriminating differences between similar shapes/letters/numerals • problems creating or copying visual information
Speech and language	• impaired or delayed language • poor auditory memory and discrimination • difficulty collating and organising language to form written or spoken thoughts

(Continued)

Table 8.1 *(Continued)*

Sensory processing characteristics

Individuals with DCD can have difficulties processing the information they receive from their senses. Sensory processing, or sensory integration, is the ability to register, organise and interpret sensory information from the sensory systems of sight, sound, smell, taste, touch and movement. There are also three other senses which provide vital information to enable efficient and effective interpretation of sensory input. These are the:

- *Tactile* (somatosensory) system: which interprets and processes information regarding discriminatory touch and unexpected/ light touch received through the skin
- *Vestibular* system: which interprets and processes information related to movement, balance and gravity, which is received through the inner ear
- *Proprioceptive* system: which interprets and processes information about body position, parts of the body and grading of force. It receives information through the muscles, ligaments and joints

The development of sensory integration is an on-going process. It enables interpretation of sensory information from the surrounding environment and integration of this information with the other sensory systems to produce a response. If sensory information is perceived inaccurately, faulty sensory integration occurs resulting in some individuals being over-aware (hypersensitive), or under-aware (hyposensitive), to environmental sensory stimuli, such as noise, light, textures and movement. Efficient and effective sensory processing has an essential role to play in the ability to regulate attention levels, and in controlling emotional and behavioural control.

Common difficulties include:

Hypersensitivity	<ul><li>distress at loud noises, discomfort with textures, tactile defensiveness</li><li>over-reaction to seemingly normal stimuli</li><li>easily overwhelmed, leading to either withdrawal or aggressive reactions</li><li>preference to follow own agenda and operate within their comfort zone</li></ul>
Hyposensitivity	<ul><li>decreased discrimination of vestibular, proprioceptive and tactile information</li><li>under-responsive to pain or temperature</li><li>not tuning into name being called</li><li>presents as a 'bystander', misses contextual sensory input</li><li>appears tired, lethargic and uninterested</li><li>some individuals seek sensation to counteract their under-responsiveness, so crave touch or movement</li></ul>
Somatodyspraxia	<ul><li>caused by poor tactile and proprioceptive processing</li><li>causes poor organisation, 'clumsiness', tripping, bumping into objects</li><li>difficulty with fine motor and manipulation skills</li></ul>
Gravitational insecurity	<ul><li>fear of movement that is out of proportion to the movement being undertaken</li><li>limited participation in movement activities, avoidance/fear of escalators, resistance to feet leaving the ground</li></ul>

Behavioural and emotional characteristics

Frustrations caused by DCD are known to impact on self-esteem and emotional well-being resulting in a variety of behaviours. Common difficulties include:

Variability	<ul><li>'good days and bad days', performs well one day but not the next</li><li>inconsistency in performance: confusing, highly frustrating and demoralising to the individual</li><li>inexplicable to family or educators</li></ul>

(Continued)

Table 8.1   *(Continued)*

Behavioural and emotional characteristics

Organising and sequencing tasks	<ul><li>praxis difficulties</li><li>disorganisation</li><li>tendency to lose things</li><li>difficulty with time concepts</li><li>difficulty remembering instructions in sequence</li></ul>
Poor attention and concentration	<ul><li>poor on-task attention</li><li>concentration fluctuates throughout the day</li><li>poor listening skills</li><li>difficulty tuning out non-relevant stimuli (birds singing) and tuning into relevant stimuli (teacher's voice)</li><li>problems in multi-tasking: listening to the teacher whilst writing down homeworkpoor sensory processing affecting regulation of alertness levels</li></ul>
Emotional problems	<ul><li>accused of poor effort despite trying very hard</li><li>poor self-esteem and lack of confidence</li><li>high levels of frustration</li><li>reduced motivation</li><li>unhappiness, loneliness and social isolation</li><li>anxiety</li></ul>
Behaviour	<ul><li>non-compliance, whining, tantrums or aggressive behaviour</li><li>restless and lacking in control</li><li>adept at avoiding or 'opting out' of tasks</li><li>prefers to follow own agenda or engage in familiar learnt activities</li><li>controlling of activities to ensure they remain within their comfort zone</li><li>seeks out adults or younger children as unable to manage at an age-appropriate level</li></ul>

Social characteristics

In order to communicate and interact with each other, both verbally and non-verbally, we need to be able to present ourselves in a socially acceptable manner, interpret speech and language accurately and understand and use body language appropriately. Common difficulties include:

Independence	<ul><li>immature independence skills: problems dressing, eating, grooming, toileting and in personal hygiene</li><li>use of adapted items, which whilst necessary for independence, can increase isolation from peers</li><li>increased adult support or assistance, which increases social isolation and emphasises difficulties</li></ul>
Social difficulties	<ul><li>poor social interactions, difficulty making friends and interacting with age peers</li><li>social activities with peers avoided, due to low self-esteem, introversion and anxiety</li><li>ostracised by peers as they do not 'fit in'</li><li>reduced physical fitness affecting leisure choices</li><li>preference to talk rather than do</li><li>vulnerable to teasing and bullying</li></ul>

(Continued)

Table 8.1   *(Continued)*

Educational characteristics

The need to think and respond quickly, write legibly and keep up with the language and social demands of school/ college can be problematic for DCD individuals. These difficulties can combine to hinder independent function within the class/work situation and bring the individual to the attention of his/her peers. Common difficulties include:

Classroom difficulties	<ul><li>slower and less independent than peers</li><li>problems reading, writing or spelling</li><li>problems with numbers, rote learning, and sequencing</li><li>poor sequencing and organisation of movements</li><li>visual perception and auditory processing difficulties</li><li>poor language skills impact on organising thoughts into written work</li></ul>
Handwriting	<ul><li>unusual pencil grasp, hand discomfort, variable size and quality of letters or words, illegible writing, inability to space or place the writing between the lines</li><li>necessitates technology use: laptops, tablets and specialised software</li></ul>

The impact of DCD and dyspraxia on daily life

Because many of the difficulties mentioned above can combine together to hinder function, numerous aspects of daily life and independence can be severely affected. The following case studies highlight some of these difficulties.

1 Functional difficulty with self-care

In the following self-care situations, the OT can offer advice, strategies and specific activities following a thorough task analysis, to help develop the skills necessary for efficient and effective functioning.

Case study
Dressing

Alex has poor balance and struggles to stand on one leg to put on trousers; his fine motor difficulties impact on him fastening buttons, zips and buckles; his poor motor planning affects his ability to put clothes on in the correct order and the right way round; his poor body awareness affects his ability to know when clothes are pulled down or tucked in correctly; his difficulties with bilateral integration, where one hand does one movement and the other a different but complementary movement affects tying shoelaces; and poor attention and concentration impact on him staying focused.

He knows that he needs far more help and assistance than other children his age which he finds demoralising and frustrating. He can become very stubborn and resistant to trying to dress himself on school mornings, as he knows he cannot manage in the time available, so he relies on his mother to lead him through the task, which he resents.

Possible solutions

- Allow extra time for practising
- Break the activity into small parts
- Arrange clothes in the correct order
- Use pictures to depict the dressing sequences
- Use clothing without fastenings, e.g. elasticated waistbands, T-shirts
- Use elastic sewn onto buttons to avoid unfastening them
- Choose clothing that is easy to manage, e.g. terry sports socks, large openings, raglan sleeves, velcro on shoes
- Buy items a size larger to give extra room
- Provide visual cues for front/back/right/left, e.g. motifs on the front of garments, coloured dots in shoes, coloured tape sewn around the inside of armholes

Case study

Toileting

Joe has a poor awareness of internal body rhythms and difficulty in registering and responding to the signals that indicate the need to use the toilet. This is causing constipation and overflow problems, can result in 'accidents' which make him smelly, and is affecting his socialisation at school. Due to poor body awareness, he cannot locate the correct part of his bottom to wipe and he struggles to manage the fastenings on clothes due to poor fine motor ability.

Possible solutions

- High fibre diet
- Regular toilet breaks throughout the day
- Use clothing that is easy to put on and off
- Use wet wipes to help with wiping
- Place a mirror next to the toilet, angled so he can check wiping

2 Functional difficulty with sports

Individuals with DCD find movement hard and have low strength and stamina. Consequently they are less likely to be physically active, which results in lower levels of physical fitness.

Case study

Serena has poor motor planning and difficulties with gross motor skills so has difficulty participating in PE and sport, particularly ball sports. Her low muscle tone and reduced postural control affect balance, strength and stability. She needs supportive insoles and struggles with barefoot tasks such as dance. Her poor motor planning impacts significantly on sport, as extra time is needed to plan, organise and execute her movements, and during team sports she cannot do this quickly enough which leads to her hindering, rather than helping her team. Her reduced upper limb strength and weak hand and finger muscles cause problems when throwing and catching a ball, or holding a bat or racket. Due to poor eye movements, she struggles to track a ball and her reduced hand/eye coordination impacts on catching or hitting it.

Possible solutions

- Break the activity into small parts. Practise one part of the activity at a time
- Use hand-over-hand instruction
- Practise a skill before starting a particular sport, e.g. ball throwing prior to playing cricket
- Emphasise fun, activity and participation rather than proficiency
- Encourage socially based lifestyle activities, e.g. swimming, sailing, golf, instead of team-based sports

3 Functional difficulty with handwriting

Handwriting is a complex skill with perceptual, cognitive and motor components that all combine together to produce efficient and effective writing ability. Different writing tasks require differing emphasis on these components, e.g. simple copying tasks are less cognitively demanding than following dictation. DCD individuals frequently struggle with handwriting as it involves motor control, praxis and visual-motor integration.

The OT is able to trial different shapes and weights of pen, provide activities to develop muscle strength and stability, develop strategies to help with motor planning and advise teachers on how best to present and refine written work.

Case study

Sam has poor postural control and difficulty holding his body upright when writing or sitting at a table. His weak shoulder stability affects holding his arm, hand and fingers in a steady position. Fine motor problems holding and controlling the pencil and motor planning difficulties impacting on the ideation and execution of the writing, mean that due to the physical effort needed to write, his train of thought is interrupted. Sam has additional difficulties remembering which movements are needed to form letters (motor memory).

Possible solutions

- Reduce the amount of written work required through use of handouts
- Photocopy notes from class and teach him how to pick out key meanings while peers are copying from the board
- Explore the use of different or adapted writing implements, e.g. rollerball instead of pencil, 'Twist 'n Write' pencil
- Use an angled writing board to promote better hand position
- Use laptops, tablets or voice-to-text software and allow dedicated time for practice
- Movement breaks
- Use wiggle cushions to assist with positioning
- Allow extra time to complete in-class assignments

4 Functional difficulty with academic skills

Due to underlying problems with sensory processing, praxis, visual perceptual function and motor coordination, problems in acquiring the expected academic skills at the same speed as peers can occur.

Case study

Ali's motor planning difficulties make it difficult for him to follow multiple-part directions and to remember regular routines at college. He is frequently disorganised and late. Due to handwriting and processing difficulties he is slower to take down written material and due to the concentration required for writing, he often misses instructions. Because many tasks require increased effort, he frequently has difficulty completing set tasks within the allocated time frame.

(Continued)

(Continued)

Possible solutions

- Use of smartphone and tablet apps for organisation
- Colour-coded timetable
- Use handouts
- Use laptops, tablets or voice-to-text software and allow dedicated time for practice
- Provision of lecture notes
- Allow more time to complete the task

Summary

Individuals with DCD generally have difficulty learning motor tasks that other people learn automatically. In collaboration with the goals of the individual, family and educators, the OT can determine the intervention approaches and set of strategies that will best help each individual reach his/her full potential.

Discussion points

- Discuss the differences between diagnosing DCD and dyspraxia from an occupational therapist's perspective.
- What are the key observational differences between DCD and dyspraxia?
- Discuss some of the key everyday difficulties those with DCD and dyspraxia experience. As a practitioner, how could you help them to overcome these?

Further reading

Ball, M. (2002) *Developmental Coordination Disorder: Hints and Tips for the Activities of Daily Living.* London: Jessica Kingsley Publishers.

Boon, M. (2014) *Can I Tell You about Dyspraxia?* London: Jessica Kingsley Publishers.

Cairney, J. (2015) *Developmental Coordination Disorder and Its Consequences.* Toronto: University of Toronto Press.

Drew, S. and Creek, J. (2005) *Developmental Co-ordination Disorder in Adults.* London: Whurr.

Kamps, P. (2005) *The Source for Developmental Coordination Disorder.* East Moline, IL: Linguisystems.

Kirby, A. (1999) *Dyspraxia: The Hidden Handicap.* London: Souvenir Press.

Kirby, A. and Peters, L. (2007) *100 Ideas for Supporting Pupils with Dyspraxia and DCD.* New York: Continuum.

Missiuna, C. (2001) *Children with Developmental Coordination Disorder: Strategies for Success.* New York: Haworth Press Inc.

Morgan, J., Brookes, G. and Ashbaker, B.Y. (2015) *The Paraprofessionals Guide to Dyspraxia: Clumsy Child Syndrome or Developmental Coordination Disorder.* Kindle.

Nichol, T. (2003) *Stephen Harris in Trouble: A Dyspraxic Drama in Several Clumsy Acts.* London: Jessica Kingsley Publishers.

Patrick, A. (2015) *The Dyspraxic Learner: Strategies for Success.* London: Jessica Kingsley Publishers.

Polatajko, H.J. and Mandich, A. (2004) *Enabling Occupation in Children: The Cognitive Orientation to Daily Occupational Performance (CO-OP) Approach.* Ottawa: CAOT-ACE Publications.

Portwood, M. (1999) *Developmental Dyspraxia: Identification and Intervention. A Manual for Parents and Professionals:* London: David Fulton Publishers.

Useful websites

The Alert Programme – How Does Your Engine Run?: www.alertprogram.com.

CanChild Centre for Childhood Disability Research: http://dcd.canchild.ca/en.

Cognitive Orientation to Daily Occupational Performance, The CO-OP approach: www.ot.utoronto.ca/coop.

The Dyscovery Centre: http://dyscovery.newport.ac.uk.

The Dyspraxia Foundation: www.dyspraxiafoundation.org.uk.

The Listening Programme (TLP): www.learning-solutions.co.uk.

Movement Matters: www.movementmattersuk.org.

Occupational Therapy on Hand: www.albertahealthservices.ca/4819.asp.

References

Ayres, A.J. (1979) *Sensory Integration and the Child.* Los Angeles: Western Psychological Services.

Ayres, J., Mailloux, Z. and Wendler, C. (1987) Developmental dyspraxia: is it a unitary function? *Occupational Therapy Journal of Research*, 7: 93–110.

Blank, R., Smits-Engelsman, B., Polatajko, H. and Wilson, P. (2012) European Academy for Childhood Disability (EACD) recommendations on the definition, diagnosis and intervention of developmental coordination disorder. *Developmental Medicine and Child Neurology* 54: 54–93, 63.

Bowens, A. and Smith, I. (1999) *Childhood Dyspraxia: Some Issues for the NHS.* Nuffield Portfolio Programme Report No. 2. Leeds: Nuffield Institute for Health.

Brown, T. and Chien, C. (2010) Top-down or bottom-up occupational therapy assessment: which way do we go? *British Journal of Occupational Therapy*, 73: 95.

Buitendag, K. and Aronstam, M. (2012) The relationship between developmental dyspraxia and sensory responsivity in children aged four years through eight years (Part 2). *South African Journal of Occupational Therapy*, 42(2): 2–7, 6.

Bundy, A., Lane, S. and Murray, E. (2002) *Sensory Integration: Theory and Practice*, 2nd edn. Philadelphia: F.A. Davis Company, pp. 477–8.

Case-Smith, J. and O'Brien, J. (2010) *Occupational Therapy for Children*, 6th edn. Maryland Heights: Mosby, pp. 355–64, 352.

Coster, W. (1998) Occupation-centred assessment of children. *American Journal of Occupational Therapy*, 52: 337–45.

Cousins, M. and Smyth, M. (2003) Developmental coordination impairments in adulthood. *Human Movement Science*, 22: 433–59, 454.

DSM-5 (2013) *Diagnostic and Statistical Manual of Mental Disorders*, 5th edn. Arlington, VA: American Psychiatric Publishing, pp. 74–7.

Gaines, R., Missiuna, C., Egan, M. and McLean, J. (2008) Educational outreach and collaborative care enhances physician's perceived knowledge about Developmental Coordination Disorder. *BMC Health Services Research*, 8: 21. DOI: 10.1186/1472-6963-8-21.

Gibbs, J., Appleton, J. and Appleton, R. (2007) Dyspraxia or developmental coordination disorder? Unravelling the enigma. *Archives of Disease in Childhood*, 92(6): 534–9.

Hellgren, L., Gillberg, C., Gillberg, I.C. and Enerskog, I. (1993) Children with deficits in attention, motor control and perception (DAMP) almost grown up. General health at 16 years. *Developmental Medicine and Child Neurology*, 35: 881–92.

ICD-10 (2004) *International Statistical Classification of Diseases and Related Health Problems*, 10th revision (ICD-10), 2nd edn. Geneva: World Health Organization.

Kaplan, B.J., Wilson, B.N., Dewey, D.M. and Crawford, S.G. (2000) Does "pure ADHD" exist? *Journal of the International Neuropsychological Society*, 6: 153.

Kirby, A., Edwards, L. and Sugden, D. (2011) Emerging adulthood in developmental coordination disorder: parent and young adult perspectives. *Research in Developmental Disabilities*, 32: 1351–60.

Kirby, A., Edwards, L., Sugden, D. and Rosenblum, S. (2010) The development and standardisation of the Adult Developmental Coordination Disorders/Dyspraxia Checklist (ADC). *Research in Developmental Disability*, 31: 131–9.

Kramer, P. and Hinojosa, J. (2010) *Frames of Reference for Pediatric Occupational Therapy*, 3rd edn. Baltimore: Lippincott, Williams and Wilkins, pp. 115–16.

Kranowitz, C.S. (1998) *The Out of Sync Child.* Cheltenham: Skylight Press, 290.

Mandich, A., Polatajko, H., Macnab, J. and Miller, L. (2001) Treatment of children with developmental coordination disorder: what is the evidence? *Physical and Occupational Therapy in Pediatrics*, 20(2/3): 51–68.

McWilliams, S. (2005) Developmental coordination disorder and self-esteem: do occupational therapy groups have a positive effect? *British Journal of Occupational Therapy*, 68(9): 394.

Miller, L., Anzalone, M., Lane, S., Cermak, S. and Osten, E. (2007) Concept evolution in sensory integration: a proposed nosology for diagnosis. *American Journal of Occupational Therapy*, 61(2): 135–40.

Missiuna, C., Pollock, N. and Rivard, L. (2011) *Children with Developmental Coordination Disorder: Adolescents with Motor Difficulties: A Resource for Educators*. Hamilton, ON: CanChild. (Retrieved 26 October 2014 from http://dcd.canchild.ca/en/EducationalMaterials/resources/MATCH20JK-SK20Dec209.pdf).

Missiuna, C., Moll, S., King, S., King, G. and Law, M. (2007) A trajectory of troubles: parents' impressions of the impact of developmental coordination disorder. *Physical and Occupational Therapy in Pediatrics*, 27(1): 81–101, 99.

Schaaf, R. and Roley, S (2006) *Sensory Integration: Applying Clinical Reasoning to Practice with Diverse Populations*. Austin, TX: PRO-ED, 21.

Watson, L. and Knott, F. (2006) Self-esteem and coping in children with developmental coordination disorder. *British Journal of Occupational Therapy*, 69(10): 451.

World Federation of Occupational Therapists (WFOT) (2013) *Definitions of Occupational Therapy from Member Organisations*, revised October 2013.

Zwicker, J.G., Missiuna, C., Harris, S.R. and Boyd, L.A. (2012) Developmental coordination disorder: a review and update. *European Journal Paediatric Neurology*, 16: 573–81.

9

Vision and Learning

Keith Holland and Clare Holland

Learning objectives

This chapter will help readers to:

- Understand the role played by visual processing in learning
- Appreciate the view that issues with vision can impact enormously upon learning
- Explore issues relating to research, identification and intervention for visual difficulties
- Recognise support strategies and resources that can be used to minimise the impact of visual difficulties

---

Introduction

Mention vision in the context of learning difficulties and these days most people will immediately think 'colour' – coloured lenses or coloured overlays. But visual problems have a much larger role in special educational needs than most people realise, with 'colour' being but a very small – but currently rather popular – part of this. Almost 100 years ago, the first description of dyslexia was of a 'congenital word blindness', described by a Scottish eye surgeon, James Hinshelwood in 1917, and the literature on dyslexia has had a close – and at times controversial – association with vision ever since. Many children suffer from subtle visual difficulties which can affect learning, sometimes coexisting with other learning difficulties.

There is perhaps no other area in special needs where more confusion exists than that of vision. This arises partly because there are several professional groups involved in assessing visual difficulty, approaching the area from very different perspectives. The child, who passes a standard eye test, being able to read clearly at distance with healthy eyes, may be regarded as having no visual difficulty. The same child may, however, experience difficulties with convergence and tracking that make reading difficult and tiring. Identifying and taking appropriate corrective action can have a significant impact on this child's educational progress, and make a big difference to their quality of life. To complicate the situation further, this same child may cope with a visual difficulty through some periods of their education, but be symptomatic and experience difficulties at other times. This visual difficulty may be caused by: 1) a structural or physical issue (refractive error of sight); 2) a visual efficiency problem relating to eye movement, focus and binocular vision issues; or 3) a visual perceptual problem (what we do with the information provided by the eyes) – or indeed any combination of the three. How, then, should these difficulties be identified? How should they be assessed? How should they be treated?

The visual system

Light enters the eye through the cornea, a clear fixed membrane which provides much of the refractive or focusing element of the eye, before passing through a variable aperture (known as the pupil) and thence through a flexible lens that can alter focus to produce a focused image on the rods and cones of the retina.

The rods and cones convert incoming light into electrical signals which are transmitted via the optic nerve to an area of the brain known as the occipital cortex. This is located at the rear of the brain, but has links to every other area of the brain – indeed, visual information is represented in over two-thirds of the brain area. Thus, vision is intimately linked with other sensory systems, such as balance and hearing.

The two eyes are each controlled by six muscles, which can move the eyeballs up, down and to either side, and can also rotate the eyeballs relative to head tilt. These muscles themselves are controlled by 3 of the 12 cranial nerves that leave the brain – highlighting the importance of eye movement control. A complex mechanism exists to ensure that both eyes are looking at the same point in space (this is known as convergence), and that the lens inside the eye is focused to that same point or distance (this process is known as accommodation). This focus/convergence relationship is crucial for efficient visual function, but is impacted on by stress – an important point to realise in children with learning difficulties, who are often under undue stress in learning situations, and whose visual efficiency may consequently be reduced.

Of late, much attention has been paid to visual information processing, and what has become known as the 'dual-channel' or 'parallel pathway' theory. To understand this best, it is important to realise that the retina is not only a light receptor but also an extension of the central nervous system with a great deal of processing of visual information occurring at the retinal level. There are several pathways conducting information from the retina to the visual cortex, the two main pathways known as the parvocellular (p) and magnocellular (m) pathways.

Table 9.1 illustrates the main differences between these two pathways. The magnocellular system is the rapid visual-awareness system, picking up change in the visual environment at a subconscious level and directing the attention of the slower parvocellular system for detailed analysis. There is so much visual information in the world that we would not be able to process everything we can see, all the time, all at once, without massive overload! On entering a room, a brief magnocellular survey of the room builds a virtual model of the space, while the parvocellular system acts to fill in detail. Any change in the environment is detected by the m system, attracting attention, that then directs the p system for detailed analysis. In this way, we can subconsciously be aware of our visual world all the time, but only directing attention to the interesting bits, or where change occurs.

Table 9.1   Key features of the magnocellular and parvocellular pathways

Magnocellular pathway (m system)	Parvocellular pathway (p system)
Responsible for peripheral and background awareness	Detail/speech-grabbing system
Response to change – responds when something alters in the visual field	Analytical – what is it? System responsible for interpretation of what we are attending to
Subconscious	Conscious awareness
Fast, instinctive response to stimulus (takes less than 150 ms)	Slow response (takes 600 ms–2 s to respond)
Stimulus processing – takes in our entire space world at once	Awareness of specific items in our world at any moment

Visual system anomalies

Researchers have identified anomalies in the relationship between these two systems, and have related these to dyslexia. A team at Oxford University have identified significant anomalies in the magnocellular system in particular, and has identified a genetic basis for this centred around chromosome 6 (Stein, 2001). Stein's hypothesis (known as the dual-channel hypothesis) has met with widespread acceptance, and goes some way to explain the visual issues experienced by many dyslexics. Sensory information transmitted by the m and p channels needs to remain in synchrony with each other, and Stein has identified a mis-timing in the relationship between the two channels in many dyslexics, due to a fault in the magnocellular pathway.

Stein has demonstrated that changing the relationship between the two channels is possible through the use of colour (light of differing wavelengths at opposite ends of the spectrum can increase or decrease the response speed of the magnocellular channel), and this provides one explanation for the effect of coloured lenses in enhancing reading skills. Stein's team has shown that blue or yellow tints can significantly improve visual stability (Ray et al., 2005) – in one study one third of dyslexic students improved their reading age by two months for every month in which coloured filters were worn.

For a number of years, many optometrists have recognised inefficient visual skills as a major cause of reading difficulty, and have found that improving visual dysfunction through a combination of lenses and eye exercises (known as vision therapy) can have a significant impact on reading and learning. From an optometric perspective, assuming a child has appropriate spectacles in place for any significant long- or short-sightedness, there are three main areas of visual difficulty that can affect learning.

Convergence

First, a child needs to maintain stable convergence over time and in an effortless way in order to attend to near-vision activity. The convergence mechanism really only kicks in within a 1m range, and children can have excellent visual skills beyond this distance (for instance, excelling in sport) yet have major difficulties at near, affecting their learning. Children with convergence problems complain of eyestrain and discomfort associated with close work, impacting on concentration and leading to distractibility. One study has shown that 25% of children diagnosed with attention deficit disorder (ADD) have poor convergence control (Granet, 2005). In the light of this, it is good clinical practice for all children with attention difficulties to undergo careful testing for convergence difficulties before a formal diagnosis of ADD is made.

Poor convergence may not be obvious in young children where reading demands are of short duration and text size is large with good spacing. It may only start showing up as reading demands increase, with text becoming smaller and reading taking place over longer periods of time. Children with good verbal skills avoid reading by talking or asking questions, thus masking their difficulty. It is possible for convergence difficulties not to have a great impact on reading until a child is at secondary school, if they are able to use other strategies in compensation.

Some children may adopt unusual head postures and tilts, or even resort to allowing their hair to cover one eye as a form of patching to prevent double vision! As many children can be confused over the meaning of 'double vision', it is helpful to be able to demonstrate this. A simply made tool for the classroom teacher or assessor can consist of a passage of text photocopied on to two acetate sheets, which are precisely laid over each

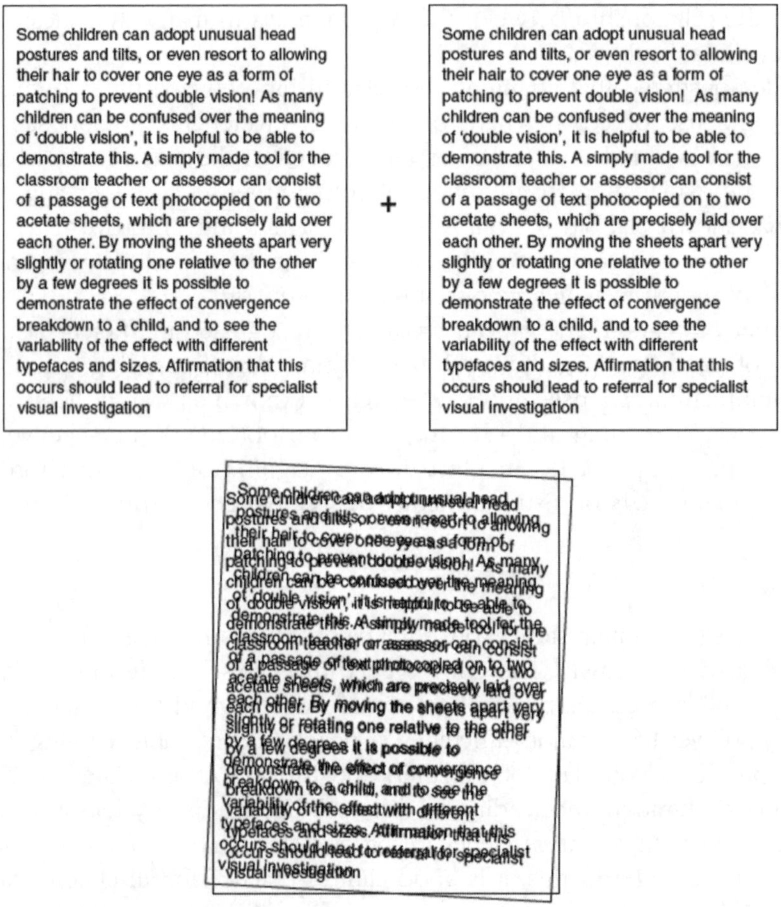

Figure 9.1 Overlaying two identical photocopy acetates allows a demonstration of how text can double when convergence breaks down

other. By moving the sheets apart very slightly or rotating one relative to the other by a few degrees it is possible to demonstrate the effect of convergence breakdown to a child, and to see the variability of the effect with different typefaces and sizes. Affirmation that this occurs should lead to referral for specialist visual investigation (see Figure 9.1).

Convergence difficulties respond well to appropriate spectacles that stabilise visual control, and this would normally be an initial treatment to provide immediate relief. Vision therapy exercises usually provide excellent longer-term correction and stabilisation but do require concentration and skilled direction over some months to take effect. A recent series of studies has shown vision training to be the best long-term solution to convergence difficulties and to impact significantly on reading abilities (Scheiman et al., 2005).

Focusing

Poor focus control will similarly impact on reading and can take two forms. Children can show a significantly reduced range or amplitude of focus, making it difficult to sustain accurate focus at a normal working distance – and it should be remembered that young children will tend to be working much closer to their paper than teenagers or adults! Children may also experience difficulties in switching focus rapidly and effortlessly from far to near, and back again, and this can impact on copying skills in the classroom. If a child also has reduced short-term memory skills, this issue can become a major problem in a very didactic learning environment. The typical symptoms of focus difficulty include eyestrain and visual discomfort with close work, transient blurred vision at near and fatigue. The solution is often similar to that for convergence problems – and indeed it is very common to see reduced focusing associated with poor convergence. Spectacles to ease focusing at near and vision training exercises to increase focus flexibility both work well and can easily be carried out at home.

Children experiencing difficulties with focus and convergence will often find close work effortful and uncomfortable and not unnaturally will 'switch off', losing concentration and becoming disinterested in the learning process. They may compensate by relying on listening and verbal skills, and on television and other visual means of learning. Thus, they can often present a puzzle in the classroom, working well within the class yet underachieving when it comes to paper-based activity and learning. This should be a warning sign that further investigation is needed.

Eye movement

The eyes also need to be able to move around, tracking and scanning their visual world. In the context of reading, a very specific pattern of eye movements is required to enable sequential movements in a left-to-right direction and on a line-by-line basis for efficient cognition. This type of movement, known as saccadic eye movement, is distinct from the pursuit eye movements required when following moving targets.

Pursuit eye movements involve locking on to a target that is moving and maintaining fixation on the target, even when the rest of the visual world appears to be moving relative to the target (try looking at your thumb and moving it about and you will see that the world behind the thumb seems to move in the opposite direction and is ignored while you are concentrating on the thumb). Pursuit eye movements are therefore all about ignoring the periphery while maintaining attention on the central target. This is important when we are moving about in the world and following targets such as a ball in sport. Problems with pursuit eye movement can affect spatial awareness and coordination, and can also have social implications, such individuals sometimes finding it difficult to interact with the moving world around them.

Saccadic eye movement requires an individual who is fixing one point to use their peripheral awareness to gauge where to move to for the next fixation. As we read, this

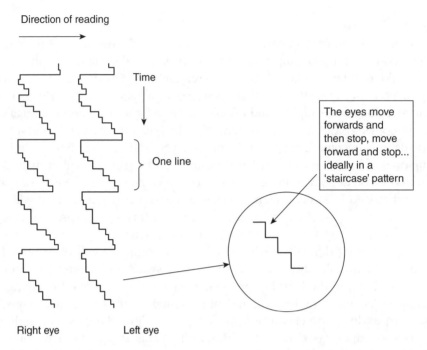

Direction of reading

Time

One line

The eyes move forwards and then stop, move forward and stop... ideally in a 'staircase' pattern

Right eye   Left eye

Figure 9.2 The horizontal, or saccadic, eye movements of a competent reader, recorded with an infrared eye-tracking device

involves moving from the point we are looking at to an appropriate point some way ahead in order for cognition of the next word or words to occur – an efficient adult reader will typically move between 12 and 15 letters forward at a time, while a nine-year-old child will typically move only 5 or 6 letters forward at a time. A characteristic pattern of saccadic eye movements is desirable in reading, with occasional regressions or backward movements taking place to double check what we have read (see Figure 9.2).

During the 1970s and 1980s, it was suggested by Pavlides (1981) that disorders with saccadic eye movement control were the likely cause of reading difficulties, and thus the possible cause of dyslexia. While there is no doubt that many children with reading problems have poor-quality saccadic eye movements, it is not likely that this is the cause of dyslexia. However, it is important to recognise poor eye movement skills and to investigate these further. Typically, children with poor-quality saccades are also likely to have issues with convergence and focusing skills, and these areas all need to be treated in an integrated fashion. Technological advances have meant that it is quite possible to analyse the eye movements required for reading in a clinical setting and to compare these with established norms. This also means that treatment can be monitored and progress measured objectively (see Figure 9.3).

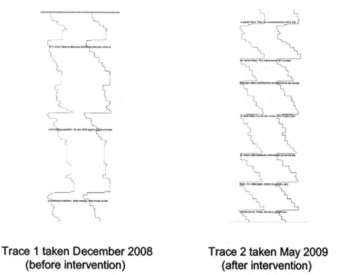

Trace 1 taken December 2008
(before intervention)

Trace 2 taken May 2009
(after intervention)

Figure 9.3 Two examples of eye movement recordings taken for the same child (aged 14 for trace 1), showing the dramatic changes possible after stabilising visual problems through spectacles and vision therapy

Visual problems and learning

The existence of visual issues affecting convergence, focusing and eye movement skills can have a significant impact on visual perception. Children with such difficulties may show reduced skills in the way they assess visual information. Most commonly, poor visual figure-ground skills and poor visual-closure skills are seen. Visual figure-ground skill is the ability to analyse detail (the figure) in a busy background, and this affects the ability rapidly and effortlessly to find detail on a 'busy' page. Visual closure refers to the ability to 'fill in' incomplete detail that is seen and is an essential component of reading and scanning information. The two skills are intimately linked, and difficulties here will affect both comprehension when reading and the acquisition of information quickly and accurately when scanning through pages. These problems are also likely to reduce visual processing speed. While there can be other causes for this, reduced visual perceptual skills of this nature can often contribute to lower-than-predicted results in the subtests of some intelligence testing (for example, in the coding and block design subtests of the Weschler intelligence scale).

Early and persistent visual difficulties can impact on how well we rely on visual recall or visualisation skills, and this in turn can affect the way we choose to learn spellings. Children with visual problems will often find it hard to recall spellings as visual images and rely heavily on phonetic spelling. They may be able to learn by rote and use this to achieve success in spelling tests, but this often fails to transfer well to long-term memory, and they may appear to make 'careless' and inconsistent errors soon after.

Problems with visual perceptual abilities can be quite fluid, and stabilising visual input, either through appropriate spectacle lenses or following a course of visual training, can sometimes have an immediate and dramatic impact on visual perception, making it easier for a child to acquire visual information and to maintain attention on near tasks. This can sometimes be seen in a child's handwriting, with almost immediate increased fluency and consistency when visual factors are eliminated (see Figure 9.4).

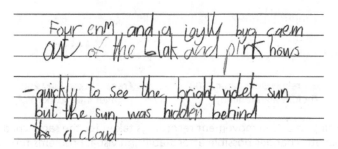

Figure 9.4   A handwriting sample before, and immediately after, insertion of lenses to stabilise poor convergence control

Incidence and identification of visual problems

The incidence of visual problems that affect learning is quite variable in the research literature, but a good estimate would be of between 10 and 15% of the child population having visual inefficiencies that are impacting on learning. This translates to between one and two children in every average classroom, with a significantly higher figure in groups of children with learning difficulties. It is essential, therefore, that class teachers and parents work together to recognise these children and that appropriate mechanisms exist for referral, analysis and treatment.

Once a visual issue has been initially identified, appropriate referral for specialist investigation needs to be arranged. There is no longer any national school eye-examination service in the UK and, where screening does take place, it does not normally involve visual skills for learning. One should therefore not assume that because a school 'eye test' has been carried out – and probably passed – that appropriate testing has taken place.

In the UK, all children under the age of 16, and under the age of 19 if in full-time education, are entitled to a basic sight test paid for by the National Health Service. Unfortunately, this service is essentially geared around the need for spectacles to correct refractive error, and there is no guarantee that an eye examination will investigate the visual factors that affect learning. Restricted funding of the service over many years has meant that there are considerable time pressures on optometrists when examining children, and subtle issues with binocular vision control and eye movement skills are unlikely to be looked at.

More detailed investigation of the visual factors that affect learning is available on a private basis. One group of optometrists who specialise in this work is the British Association of Behavioural Optometrists, and their website identifies practitioners who have completed considerable additional training in this specialism and offer expert evaluation and treatment (www.babo.co.uk). Binocular vision anomalies are also investigated by orthoptists working within the hospital eye service, and referral for such investigation can normally be arranged through a child's GP.

Before a specialist eye examination, it is useful to complete a checklist that allows identification of the symptoms relating to visual difficulties, and this may be carried out by either teachers or parents (ideally, by both), and it provides a useful overview of the child's difficulties. It should be remembered that parents do not necessarily see their children in a normal learning environment in order to identify many of these issues and, in a classroom setting, children may sometimes hide symptoms from their teacher for fear of the response, or being thought of as being 'stupid'. Nonetheless, questionnaires are probably the most useful initial screening approach. A suitable questionnaire which can be used in the classroom or by parents is given below. This is used by the authors to identify children with possible visual difficulties. Any positive responses should lead to referral for visual investigation:

- Often loses place when reading
- Misses out words or rereads the same word
- Needs to use a finger or marker to keep their place
- Quickly becomes tired when reading
- Experiences transient blurred or double vision during close work
- Complains of words 'moving about', 'shimmering' or 'dancing' when reading
- Has difficulty copying from the board down on to paper
- Complains of headache (usually around the temples) after close work
- Has poor concentration for close work
- Short and often decreasing working distance
- Continuous reading is inaccurate, yet can read single words quite easily
- Has difficulty 'taking in' what he or she is reading, and has to read something several times for meaning

In addition, the following more general symptoms may also suggest visual problems:

- Poor coordination at near, typically shown as bumping into, or knocking things over, yet may be good at sports (this may be identified as 'dyspraxia', but may simply be a vision problem)
- Reluctance to play with jigsaws and similar puzzles
- Difficulty with spatial concepts in maths

- Irregular and untidy handwriting
- Travel sickness
- A strongly phonetic pattern to spelling

Visual correction

Glasses and contact lenses

It is normal for adults with poor focusing skills (which typically occurs from the mid-forties onwards) to wear bifocal or varifocal spectacles, in order to provide optimum correction at both distance and near. It is perhaps surprising, therefore, that children, who will frequently have the same need for different prescriptions at near and far, are rarely prescribed bifocals.

Once optimum visual correction is in place with glasses or contact lenses, there is a need to develop underlying visual skills through vision-training exercise programmes, and these have been proven to be very effective in improving convergence, focusing and eye movement difficulties. Vision training can be somewhat time-consuming and does require dedication from both child and parent. Some optometrists overcome this by offering in-practice training programmes where much of the work is done by the optometrist or a vision therapist working in conjunction with the child. Some computer-based training programmes are also available which can be particularly useful for children in boarding school situations – especially as these computer programs often have Internet links which allow an optometrist to monitor progress remotely, but there are limitations to what can be trained via a computer. One study has shown that regular use of a computer-based tracking programme typically produces a six-month improvement in reading age with a six-week intervention programme CME of 15 minutes' computer-based training a day (Hoover and Harris, 1997).

Coloured lenses

There has been much talk and hype about the use of coloured lenses in treating dyslexia and, as noted at the beginning of this chapter, they are perhaps now the most well-known 'treatment' for visually based reading difficulties. There is certainly a place for the use of judiciously tinted lenses to stabilise the magnocellular/parvocellular anomalies described earlier, and the work of Stein has shown how blue or yellow tints can be beneficial (Ray et al., 2005). The first person to recommend the use of tints was Helen Irlen, an American psychologist, and her programme of tinted spectacles included many claims of dramatic cures when introduced in the late 1980s. Further work by Arnold Wilkins (Wilkins and Neary, 1991), at the time Professor of Applied Psychology at Cambridge University, led to a more systematic and structured approach to the use of tints, and a device (the intuitive colorimeter) was developed to formalise the testing and prescribing of tints. Wilkins, together with Bruce Evans who cooperated in his research, coined the term 'Meares–Irlen' syndrome to describe the visual difficulties they felt benefited from coloured lenses. Wilkins also developed several tools which allow screening with simple coloured overlays to see if colour may be beneficial (Wilkins, 1994).

The evidence for coloured lenses is, however, arguable as to the long-term impact they have on reading. Although many studies have been carried out showing the short-term benefits of coloured lenses on reading, very few have adequately allowed for the presence of other visual difficulties. Indeed, in one major review of the literature it was found that 95% of patients considered appropriate for coloured lenses had significant undetected and uncorrected vision disorders that were ignored within the studies (Blaskey et al., 1990). There is little information on the longer-term impact of coloured lenses, and their use is certainly not straightforward.

Modifications to books and computers

Children with visual difficulties often have increased sensitivity to glare and to repetitive patterns, such as may occur with many lines of text on a page. Reducing contrast may aid this, and the use of off-white paper may be particularly helpful to such individuals (a cream colour is used by Barrington Stokes for their range of dyslexia-friendly books). Similarly, modifying the background colour on computer monitors may reduce glare problems for screen users. A useful computer program can be downloaded without cost, allowing modification of screen background colour, and many students report this to be helpful (the program can be downloaded from www.thomson-software-solutions.com).

Modifications to the classroom

Within the classroom or work environment, there are several modifications that can be made to reduce visual stress. First the use of a slightly sloping desk surface (to approximately 20°) has been shown to lead to an increased working distance which, in turn, can reduce visual demands. We typically angle material to match the plane of our face and older-style sloping desks are ideal for this, encouraging both good posture and working distances. The more recent use of horizontal desk surfaces can lead to moving forward and dropping the head down towards the desk, in turn leading to a reduced working distance – as well as increasing stress on the neck muscles. Portable desk slopes that sit on the desk and angle text to an appropriate 20° are becoming widely available and can be carried from classroom to classroom by students who need them.

The surroundings of classrooms are often overlooked, but children with visual difficulties are often more sensitive to peripheral distractions. Excessive amounts of brightly coloured material displayed in front of and to the side of children, with objects hanging from the ceiling around the classroom, can be the cause of major distraction. Studies have shown that subdued, plain-coloured backgrounds are conducive to better study and do minimise distraction effects for children, as well as having a calming effect on the class as a whole.

Lighting in the classroom can also play an important role and should be even and flicker-free, ideally using high-frequency fluorescent lighting rather than conventional fluorescent lights, which will often produce flicker at the end of tubes for a considerable part of the lights' life. While this may not be a big issue for many children, those with visual difficulties – and particularly those with magnocellular dysfunction – will be unduly sensitive to this, and can find them a source of irritation and distraction.

High-frequency fluorescent tubes do not normally produce any flicker of this nature. Optimal lighting for a classroom would involve the use of halogen up-lighting, thus producing the closest lighting to natural daylight; however, the energy requirements of these lights preclude their use in these environment- and energy-conscious times (but they are ideal in the home).

Recent work has been carried out on typefaces and type layouts to reduce visual demands, and several typefaces have been designed specifically for individuals with dyslexia and other reading problems (such as the Sassoon font). As long ago as 1878, researchers postulated that poor typography could cause visual difficulty, and the use of serifs has been shown to diminish legibility of text. Some researchers have also suggested that ragged margins are easier for poor readers to cope with than fully justified text, providing greater reference as to where you are on the page. Text size would also appear important, and many children, particularly those with tracking difficulties, avoid 8- or 10-point text wherever possible, preferring instead 12- or even 14-point material which reduces visual demands.

It is important to ensure when photocopying material in a classroom that copies are clear and sharp, and not reduced in size to get more on the page. Copying coloured material into black and white can also cause problems of reduced legibility and contrast.

The increasing use of display screens, both from a teaching perspective and from home use in computer games and on the Internet, is a controversial area. Studies point to both the benefits and pitfalls of excessive screen use, and the research is really not clear on the overall impact. The quality of screens has improved enormously in the last three to four years, and some of the early negative research carried out with monochrome CRT computer displays is perhaps no longer valid. However, there is increasing evidence that excess screen use can both impact on perceptual development and restrict time that could otherwise usefully be spent on more motor-based activity and play. It is perhaps beyond the scope of this chapter to expand into motor training, but the role of motor activity in developing the skills needed for learning is well documented, and anything that detracts from this is regarded by the authors as being detrimental to well-rounded learning.

Most classrooms now make use of interactive whiteboards, allowing the use of computer-projected material and PowerPoint slides alongside free writing on the board itself. There would appear to be very little work carried out on the potential risks and difficulties associated with the interactive whiteboard, but children frequently complain to their optometrist of glare problems and visual discomfort due to the very high light levels of the screen compared with the surroundings. Contrast on the screen itself can often be poor and causes difficulties with copying. Teachers should regularly check the clarity of screens themselves from different areas of the classroom and ensure that all children are comfortable in using such screens. One very practical aspect to the use of technology is with the simple task of copying – in the days of roller blackboards, children who were slow at copying could keep going as the board rolled around. This is not possible with the interactive board where, at a touch of a button, material changes. This can be a cause of considerable stress to some children who struggle with copying, and should be borne in mind by the teacher! Children with focusing difficulties, who also have problems with short-term memory, are likely to find copying off boards particularly difficult, and it is important to ensure that printed copies of material are available for them.

Summary

Most of the information we take in and learn from is acquired through the visual system. Small, subtle difficulties in the area of eye movements, focusing or convergence can massively impact on the ease with which reading skills are acquired, and on the fluency and comfort of readers as they progress from learning to read to reading to learn. This can then impact on all areas of the curriculum.

Reversals, eye strain, poor place keeping and distractibility are all common, and may simulate specific learning difficulties, including a slower than average processing speed. Visually related learning difficulties should be excluded by careful examination.

Some children have poor central visual skills in that their system is more geared to awareness of the periphery of their visual field. These pupils may perform better in a plainer environment with fewer visual distractions such as work hanging from the ceiling around them.

Children are unlikely to complain directly about the blurred or double vision they may experience, since what they see is, to them, entirely normal and un-remarkable. Mature readers whose vision starts to blur at near in their mid-forties know to get their eyes checked and to seek reading glasses. Children, who have never seen differently, do not know that print should be clear and stable, and finding a practitioner with a special interest and training in how vision affects learning is very important for the underachieving youngster.

The text size and layout in first reading books is generally large and spaced out, so small degrees of blur or 'wobble' may not inhibit the early reading development of some children, who then start to struggle when moving onto more advanced books with smaller print size, fewer illustrations and more compact layout of text. To the surprise of their teachers and parents, some excellent early readers start to struggle and lose enthusiasm for reading around Year 3, in which case visual issues should be suspected.

Poor copying from the board, with frequent errors and never finishing in time with their peers may well indicate slow re-focusing skills. Ensure the child sits straight onto the board, so that only glances up and down are required, not turning the head as well. Interactive boards, whilst exciting and versatile, can be difficult to see from certain angles in a classroom, with bothersome reflections from windows or lights and poor contrast between background and pixilated writing. Do check the visibility of your board from different areas of the classroom.

Other signs for the observant teacher to look out for include a child who is seen to frequently rub their eyes, or whose eyes or lids appear red, and those who complain of headaches or unusual tiredness as the day progresses. Some can 'hold things together' for the mornings, but lack the visual stamina to maintain focus through the afternoon. Untidy handwriting, often small and poorly spaced which does not improve greatly with practice, and mistakes in maths because digits are misaligned, are also common.

Discussion points

- How do you think modern technology affects those with visual learning difficulties?
- From a practitioner's perspective, what are the key signs that a learner may have visual learning difficulties?
- How do you think teachers and parents can work together to help those with visual learning difficulties?

Further reading

Hellerstein, L. (2010) *See It, Say It. Do It! The Parent's and Teacher's Action Guide to Creating Successful Students and Confident Kids*. Denver, CO: Hi Clear Publishing.
This is a bang up-to-date guide for parents and teachers on how to develop visual skills in children – both at home and in the classroom.

Scheiman, M. and Rouse, M. (2006) *Optometric Management of Vision Related Learning Problems*. St Louis, MO: Mosby.
This is the leading textbook in the field and, although designed for eye-care professionals, contains a wealth of information that would benefit other professionals.

Useful websites

www.acbo.org.au/for-patients/about-vision.

The Australasian equivalent site has particularly well-explained sections for parents, for example developmental games to play with babies and young children to aid visual development.

(Continued)

(Continued)

http://babo.co.uk/signs-of-a-visual-problem/.

The official site of the British Association of Behavioural Optometrists, with a list of common signs and symptoms.

http://www.covd.org/?page=Vision_Learning.

This links to one of the two main USA (but also international) organisations which teach and accredit optometrists working in this area. There are links to research under 'Patients & Parents' on the home page.

www.keithholland.co.uk/vision_and_learning.html.

Our own site, with parent-friendly information and links.

www.oepf.org/reference_articles.

The other teaching organisation in the USA, with some access to research and book suggestions and information for parents.

https://visionhelp.wordpress.com.

This has some excellent writing; follow the 'Dr Fortenbacher PESI Visual Processing and Therapy Lecture Resource Links' at the top of the home page for more in-depth info.

References

Blaskey, P. et al. (1990) The effectiveness of Irlen filters for improving reading performance: a pilot study. *Journal of Learning Disability*, 23: 604–12.

Granet, D.G.C. (2005) The relationship between convergence insufficiency and ADHD. *Strabismus*, 13: 163–8.

Hoover, D. and Harris, P. (1997) The effects of using the Readfast computer program on eye movement abilities as measured by the OBER2 eye movement device. *Journal of Optometric Vision Development*, 28: 227–34.

Pavlides, G.T. (1981) Do eye movements hold the key to dyslexia? *Neuropsychologia*, 19: 57–64.

Ray, N. et al. (2005) Yellow filters can improve magnocellular function: motion sensitivity, convergence, accommodation and reading. *Annals of the New York Academy of Science*, 1039: 283–93.

Scheiman, M. et al. (2005) A randomised clinical trial of treatments for convergence insufficiency in children. *Archives of Ophthalmology*, 123: 14–24.

Stein, J. (2001) The magnocellular theory of developmental dyslexia. *Dyslexia*, 7: 12–36.

Wilkins, A.J. (1994) Overlays for classroom and optometric use. *Ophthalmic and Physiological Optics*, 14: 97–9.

Wilkins, A.J. and Neary, C. (1991) Some visual, optometric and perceptual effects of coloured glasses. *Ophthalmic and Physiological Optics*, 11: 163–71.

Good Practice in Training Specialist Teachers and Assessors of People with Dyslexia

10

Sheena Bell and Bernadette McLean

Learning objectives

This chapter will help readers to:

- Understand the current climate in the training of dyslexia specialists in England
- Appreciate the key skills needed by specialist teachers
- Gain an overview of the knowledge and skills needed to support people with dyslexia across all phases of education and employment
- Reflect on the value of evaluation as a crucial element in training courses
- Understand the support needed for teachers undertaking specialist training

Training for dyslexia specialists: Where are we now?

The field of training specialist teachers and assessors is evolving both in terms of our understanding of dyslexia and literacy difficulties, and in systems and protocols of teaching and learning for people with special educational needs within the school system and beyond. In England, although the network of specialist teachers and assessors is expanding, government policy states clearly that *every* teacher is a teacher of children with SEN (special educational needs) (Department for Education and Department of Health, 2014). The SEN Code of Practice covers students aged 0–25 and emphasises the responsibility of schools to assess and support all learners who are not making progress in line with national expectations. This means that schools, colleges, universities and other training providers now need to develop the skills of specialists within their teams. As part of this provision, Education and Health and Care Plans are intended for those children or young people with SEN who need education provision. Trained specialist teachers are likely to be key players in the process. A recent national report in England warned that: 'we cannot currently be confident that those who are charged with making a judgement about the quality of the education provided for pupils with SEN can do so on the basis of a good understanding of what good progress is or how best to secure it' (Lamb, 2009: 7). This report reinforces the need for the English school inspection body to report specifically on the quality of the education provided for children with SEN and disabilities. Dyslexia training in England is regulated by bodies which include expert representatives of national dyslexia organisations that are currently developing a national qualifications framework in order to ensure that all trained and qualified specialist teachers and assessors have the necessary competences to carry out their roles effectively.

Whilst demanding that the needs of students with dyslexia and other SEN are met in mainstream schools and classrooms alongside their peers, the inclusion agenda nevertheless requires institutions to respond to individual learning styles of learners with dyslexia who may need individualised teaching and support. Definitions of dyslexia are not internationally agreed although there are common characteristics. In England, the British Psychological Association (BPS) definition has been widely used as a baseline for intervention, focusing specifically on a failure to read and spell single words despite appropriate teaching (British Psychological Society, 1999). For over ten years, there have been constraints on identifying people with dyslexia because of the narrow focus of this definition. Rose's report into dyslexia teaching (Rose, 2009) effectively widened this by proposing a working definition that embraced a number of other dyslexia characteristics such as verbal memory and processing speed.

Although all teachers should be equipped to teach the wide range of learners they encounter in their classrooms (Department for Education and Department of Health, 2014), there is a need to train expert teachers who can respond on an individual level to learners with dyslexia. A structure of dyslexia support is proposed to schools and local authorities in England which is based on a pyramid of support (Rose, 2009). At the first level, classroom teachers should develop core skills for recognising children with risk factors for dyslexia and put in appropriate interventions immediately. At the second level, more experienced or qualified specialist teachers should assess the child's difficulties and use assessment to plan focused teaching programmes. At the third level, specialist teachers with appropriate qualifications or other professionals should carry out a full diagnostic assessment to decide if the child has dyslexia, and make recommendations for teaching and support. In England, teachers trained to this level may now hold professional practising certificates which require an appropriate qualification and evidence of continuing professional development and practice to ensure national standards are met.

Students with dyslexia may not need pedagogical approaches that are essentially different from other learners, but they will need individually focused programmes of learning involving 'greater planning and structure, more time for reinforcing learning and more continuous assessment' (Lewis and Norwich, 2001: 2). This attention to very specific individual needs necessitates training specialist teachers and providing opportunities for them to work with individual students. Specialist teachers require still more complex knowledge, understanding and skills to carry out diagnostic assessments for learners with dyslexia. In England, in recent years, a range of training courses have been developed to equip specialist teachers to fulfil both the role of specialist teacher and diagnostic assessor:

> The course has opened my eyes to the particular difficulties faced by dyslexic children and particularly to how many pass through their school days with no recognition and no support. (Experienced SENCo (Special Educational Needs Coordinator)

However, specific one-to-one provision for individual students with dyslexia may not be available in all schools, or may be delivered by practitioners with little or no specific training. Many schools who manage to support their teachers and teaching assistants in completing training courses report immediate feedback:

> After only one term, the course has helped teachers to build up a bank of useful resources in their schools. It has enabled trainees to develop evaluative thinking and self-evaluation, informing their current practice. Already this new learning is impacting – it's like a ripple effect! (Local Authority inclusion consultant)

Regrettably, financial constraints may prevent schools from investing in specialist training for their teachers. Once trained, there may also be issues over deploying specialists across the institution. Schools may not have sufficiently large SEN budgets to allow for individual or small group teaching programmes with specialist practitioners and if such teaching is carried out at all it may be with teaching assistants whose qualifications, experience and expertise are highly variable. It is imperative that teachers with specialist qualifications are prepared to disseminate their knowledge and competence to others. Communication and presentation skills should be embedded in the training now offered to specialists (Rose, 2009):

> I have led teacher and support assistant training to highlight how best to support dyslexic children in the classroom. We are now better able to identify children and to use appropriate strategies to give them the support they need. (Experienced SENCo)

Courses should equip and inspire trainees to pass on their newly acquired knowledge and skills:

I want to cascade as much information as I can to colleagues so that everyone realises how students can be affected by the difficulties they have and how something simple, like a worksheet on coloured paper, can make a big difference to their achievements and subsequently self-esteem. (Experienced SENCo)

Despite recognition of the need for early identification and intervention (Rose, 2009), there is inconsistency of provision across educational phases. For example, in the higher education phase in England, a Disabled Student Allowance (DSA) provides funding directed towards the individual with dyslexia after a rigorous process of assessment and identification of individual need (Jamieson and Morgan, 2008). This system is currently under review. Notwithstanding, no such funding stream exists in the school system and provision of specialist tuition is highly variable.

The contrast between protocols for dyslexia assessment and support in schools and higher education may contribute to the fact that most students with dyslexia in higher education are not formally diagnosed until after entry into higher education training (Singleton, 1999). Across the compulsory education sector there are many excellent teachers and schools, but without clear legislative requirements and targeted, ring-fenced funding, identification and provision for dyslexia is likely to remain inconsistent. In addition, the current global recession is probably not conducive to increasing funding for these vulnerable learners. It was recognised by the last UK government (2010–15) that there was a need for a specialist dyslexia teacher in every school and funding for a limited period was allocated to train such teachers, using existing, high-quality training courses (DCSF, 2009). If and when such targets for specialist teachers are achieved, each English school must decide on priorities for the use of their SEN funding in relation to dyslexia and this will depend on the school pupil population and their diverse needs. This has been reinforced by a requirement under the recent Code of Practice (Department for Education and Department of Health, 2014) for all Local Authorities in England, to collaborate with schools and other agencies, to publish a 'Local Offer' outlining SEN support. This sets out provision available for children and young people with SEN in the area.

Key skills needed for specialist teachers

Even in primary school settings, where literacy acquisition is a key overriding target, specialist teachers are different from classroom teachers: classroom teachers are trained to deliver a national curriculum, but specialist teachers need liberation from this to respond to the individual needs of children.

Teachers need to develop the confidence to use their imagination to 'pick and mix'. For children with dyslexia, there is no one programme which can fulfil the needs of every individual, therefore evaluation of what works for a particular learner is essential. Learners who access support will have struggled with the learning environment of a mainstream classroom.

Some learners with dyslexia have floundered after being placed in remedial settings and given more of the same style of teaching which led to their failure in their mainstream class.

Learners with dyslexia require far more repetition and overlearning than other students; therefore, specialists need to have a vast repertoire of attractive and engaging activities which can be adapted to focus on particular learning preferences and key targets, whilst tapping into the child's own interests and goals. Courses for specialist teachers must show participants how to make teaching more multisensory. 'Death by Worksheet' can be a dire fate; specialist teachers learn to teach in a much more creative and three-dimensional manner. Multisensory methods require teachers to use all the sensory channels to help their students acquire literacy. For example, letter shapes do not have to be learnt simply by writing them. Teachers can plan lessons where a range of senses are used to enable the participant to maximise their strengths and scaffold weaker channels. In Table 10.1 the list is by no means exhaustive, but shows how course participants may be encouraged to respond to the needs of learners.

Naturally, not all the activities will be suitable for all phases. However, even adults can respond well to multisensory activities when they are developed in a suitably non-childish way. For example, many adult learners respond well to using three-dimensional letters, small whiteboards with large felt tip pens, highlighters and image association.

In the mainstream classroom, it can be easy to miss signs of specific learning difficulties, particularly when students disguise these with bad behaviour, or by keeping a low profile

Table 10.1

Sensory channel	Teaching points	Activities to combine sensory channels
Auditory (oral)	Say the letters (sounds or names, depending on target)	Drawing picture with memory cues to associate letter
		Saying letter sounds/phonemes/words
Visual	Use colour, shape associations (such as S for snake), images	
		Painting
Kinaesthetic/ tactile	Use three-dimensional letters	Sticking string shapes
	Making the letters	Writing in sand
		Alphabet arc activities
Taste/smell (olfactory)	Although more unusual, associations can be made for students with difficulties in other channels, e.g. J with JAM	Finger writing in modelling clay
		Make biscuits
		Write on playground in water
		Fernald methodology (Doveston and Cullingford Agnew, 2006)
		Matching games
		Acting
		Making shapes with the body/dance

enabling them to remain undetected in a busy classroom. Many adults with dyslexia are well-practised at concealing weaknesses at work and therefore do not receive the appropriate support and possibly simple adjustments to their working practice which would help them carry out their roles more efficiently, and reduce stress and anxiety about exposure.

For many trainees, training courses challenge the way they assess their learners. In early stages of courses, some teachers make comments such as *careless mistake*, and *you should read more slowly and carefully* on students' scripts, showing that even motivated and interested teachers need to understand how dyslexia can affect reading and writing behaviours. Even specialist teachers can make assumptions that learners are careless, simply reading too fast and therefore stumbling on words. They may, however, be exhibiting errors symptomatic of the underlying difficulties of dyslexia.

Discussion point

On a training course for specialist teachers, one of the participants is teaching a secondary school level learner who is having difficulty sequencing ideas for an essay. He is unable to plan by using headings and subheadings. Multisensory methods, such as mind mapping, using Post-its to brainstorm ideas and sticking these on a large piece of paper, moving them around to form logical sequences, have been used. What other ideas might be suggested to help this teacher respond to the learner's needs?

Skills can be taught to teachers across educational and other professional contexts

Course providers should consider the context of their participants, but should also ensure that teachers understand the challenges that people with dyslexia face throughout their lives. Teachers need to be aware of the implications of changing legislation and policy at national and local levels for trajectories of students with dyslexia in the education system. People with dyslexia must deal with highly complex twenty-first century social structures combined with increasingly mobile populations on national and international levels. Choices in terms of education and employment are rapidly evolving. Students with dyslexia and their families should be informed and included in decisions about support structures and transition planning, so that they can fulfil their potential in the long term. Recent national policy changes reinforce the importance of the involvement of young people and their families in the choices that are available to them. For some students with intractable dyslexic difficulties, integrated settings may not provide the most suitable environment either for skills acquisition or the development of a positive self-concept. Nevertheless, the opportunity to choose a specialist setting may be available only to students whose parents have the financial means to pay for private education.

Teachers must look ahead to facilitate the students' future progression through the education system and employment. Thus, teachers in primary school need to be aware of the direct challenges presented to the dyslexic learner in a wide secondary curriculum.

Assistive technology is potentially enormously helpful to students with dyslexia as they move into secondary education and the information-technology-driven workplaces of the twenty-first century. Many would benefit from learning to touch type as early as possible, to provide easy access to computer technology:

> From this course I have also learnt of the benefits of making sure learners are competent in basic ICT skills. I can also now see the benefits of encouraging them to learn to touch type. (Specialist teacher)

Technical problems need technical solutions; such solutions can ease the lot of people with dyslexia and their families but this is not all. People with dyslexia tend to have adaptive problems requiring them or the people and environment around them to devise adaptive solutions. Where typing is not a solution, voice-to-text software and touch screen technology should be investigated. Technical solutions may not allow people with dyslexia to listen and process oral information more quickly, but teachers and other presenters of oral information can adjust the speed at which information is delivered. Such adjustments can be used alongside digital recorders, screen readers, digital notebooks and other technological solutions to increase accessibility for all learners, not just those with dyslexia.

The affective needs of children moving from a supportive primary school with one key teacher into the more challenging world of the secondary school can put additional strains on those who may have hitherto been able to cope with academic work. In all phases of education, and employment, the specialist teacher may need to play the role of advocate for learners with dyslexia, explaining their issues to non-specialists to ensure that their needs are met through 'reasonable adjustments' enshrined in English disability legislation (Equality Act, 2010).

Similarly, specialist teachers in secondary schools should be aware of possible funding for support and access as students move into higher education. Transition planning for students is a long-term project, to be addressed before the final year prior to moving into post-compulsory education or the workplace, and teachers have a key role to play in this process. Specialist teachers must be prepared to discuss issues of disability disclosure and enable students to assess the range of factors involved in choosing dyslexia-friendly institutions. In England, higher education students with dyslexia must accept the label of disability to access funding, which may not sit comfortably with their self-concept (Armstrong and Humphrey, 2009).

High-quality training in assistive software should be available before the student with dyslexia progresses into higher education with its high demands on organisation skills and novel learning formats such as lectures (involving note-taking, a huge challenge to dyslexic learners with information processing difficulties) and seminars (which may involve reading aloud or quick responses to written information, often highly stressful for the learner with dyslexia).

It is an advantage for courses to attract trainees from a range of backgrounds to bring a variety of perspectives to the course. This can be exploited within the training group in discussions and information sharing. Teachers in primary school must understand how to prepare dyslexic learners for the change of teaching style they will encounter in secondary school. Conversely, a support teacher from a university setting needs to understand how previous educational experience may have affected learners in terms of motivation and skills acquisition, as well as self-esteem.

Teachers can bring a wealth of experience of working with learners. They need opportunities during and after the course to practise their skills as part of their personal development as specialist teachers. Although they have a role in the dissemination and training of other non-specialist professionals, it is important that dyslexia specialists are given the opportunity to work with individuals or small groups where they are able to use their skills. Increasing pressures on resources in schools may be a barrier to this taking place.

Teaching – What trainees need to know

Crucial to any teaching programme for learners with dyslexia is that it should be individualised. Trainees learn how to direct learning programmes towards students' particular strengths and weaknesses. They should be based on a clear view of what students can do already, taking into account progression and relating clearly to their individual learning contexts, which can be as diverse as a primary school classroom, a university, a business enterprise or a prison. Course tutors must respond to the demands of these contexts and should also ensure that the skills and needs of trainees are carefully audited to ensure responsive individualised teaching.

Discussion point

Many existing courses for specialist teachers and assessors train teachers across age ranges. Dyslexia may be mitigated by good teaching and the environment in which learners develop their skills, but the underlying difficulties remain the same. An understanding of learner context and motivation is key to developing a teaching programme.

On courses for specialist teachers, trainees are the 'piggy in the middle': they are both receiving and giving teaching (Figure 10.1).

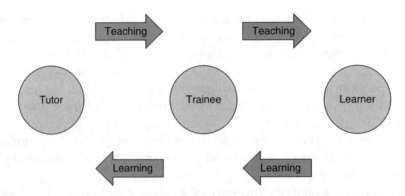

Figure 10.1   Teaching and learning on specialist teacher courses

Course tutors can model good teaching in the way they work with their trainees, for example giving them manageable targets. It is essential that any specialist courses integrate observations of the participants' teaching in their own settings. Ideally, more than one observation should be included so that teachers are given the chance to develop skills as they extend knowledge. Positive feedback and reflection on feedback is highly beneficial, as it helps develop a habit of self-evaluation, an important part of the one-to-one teaching process (Figure 10.2).

In the light of a recent observation, I now have many more ideas of how to incorporate multi-sensory teaching into lessons. (Support teacher)

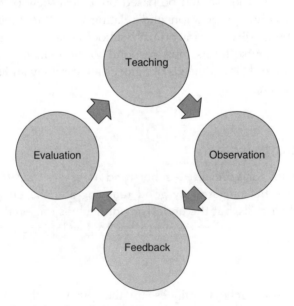

Figure 10.2   The cycle of training for observations

Detailed records of this process enable trainees to track back and review progress, just as they do with their own students. Continuing to use this process of critical evaluation and adapting teaching as they gain more experience develops professional competences:

> I also understand that my own learning in this specialist field will not stop. I will have to continue to update my reading and learning to stay in touch with changes and new techniques. I felt confident in most areas of assessment and I do recognise that this will improve, again with practice, as my tutor informed me 'you wouldn't expect to know everything by the end of this course – that comes with experience'. (Teaching assistant)

Building a knowledge and skills base for assessment

Trainees need a clear understanding of the underlying processing difficulties which are causal factors in dyslexia. If students are not learning, it is essential for teachers to have a hypothesis of where difficulties lie in order to offer appropriate support:

> I had not fully realised how important working memory and processing speed is in those learners with traits of dyslexia or how important phonological processing is. (Teaching assistant)

Although teachers do not need detailed knowledge of medical research, an awareness of current advances in neuroscience and genetics is important because of their practical applications to practice. For example, the fact that there are genetic links for dyslexic traits (Pennington and Olson, 2005) has implications for how teachers approach the families of students with disabilities; parents may not offer literacy support as they themselves have similar difficulties. Similarly, a specialist teacher's awareness of issues such as visual processing difficulties (Singleton, 2008) may affect not only the nature of support offered but also generate recommendations for referrals. Such intervention can have a huge effect on a learner's progress.

Courses must include the normal development of literacy skills, an area which is now not generally included in teacher training, even at primary level. Teachers should also be taught simple, qualitative assessments for working memory, sequencing and phonological awareness and how to observe and comment on functional expressive and receptive language skills of learners. Specialist teachers should be trained to administer detailed individual assessments including the mastery of non-standardised tests. They should be equipped to devise and use questionnaires and checklists to collect relevant background information. They need to understand and interpret the results of screening tests and reports. All teachers and supporters should be aware of the language of statistical standardised tests and implications for learners to prevent common misunderstandings of the significance of age equivalents and problems with misinterpretation of percentiles. Initial teacher training does not generally provide training in this area and yet the English education system appears to rely increasingly on the results of such tests both to classify students and justify educational support. Specialist teachers should share this knowledge with colleagues:

> I have always been in the habit of reading dyslexia reports and educational psychologist's reports prior to working with a learner if at all possible. However, in the past I had only looked at the recommendations as I had not understood many of the other areas. But now I can understand percentiles and scores which are considered 'normal' and those scores able to receive access arrangements. (Specialist teacher)

Whilst the development of literacy skills is not the remit of this chapter it is important to stress that effective literacy skills specialists experienced in teaching synthetic phonics may not be successful in teaching those skills to those dyslexics whose phonological difficulties make them unreachable by this approach:

> I want to learn to teach all children how to read not just those who respond to synthetic phonics. (Teacher applying for specialist teacher training)

Training diagnostic assessors

Formal diagnostic assessment differs from teaching. They have a similar knowledge base but two different skill sets. Both specialist teachers and qualified assessors of dyslexia need to understand the underlying cognitive differences that play a part in specific learning difficulty (Philips et al., 2013; Boyle and Fisher, 2007). There is a distinction between the subjective tests which should be in the battery of any specialist dyslexia teacher and the specialised psychometric tests required for a full dyslexia report.

In England, full diagnostic reports may be needed to pinpoint a learner's difficulties and to access and justify the provision of support. Skills for dyslexia assessors can be quite different: teachers are trained to help and enable learners, but assessors have to push students to the edge of their competence which can be uncomfortable for both tester and testee. A good teacher is concerned with helping a student achieve targets and become an independent learner in a safe, supportive environment where strengths are celebrated and weaknesses supported. However, administering dyslexia assessments not only requires thorough understanding of psychological testing, both theory and practice (British Psychological Society, 2007), but involves deliberately placing learners in situations both challenging and difficult.

Psychometric tests required for full diagnostic assessments are standardised by testing large samples of the population in an identical way so that results can be compared. This presents a number of challenges for trainee assessors. For example, testers must adhere meticulously to scripts and procedures to ensure that all testees receive identical instructions. Many tests demand that testees perform to the limit of their abilities, possibly to the point of failure. For example, one reading test in England (WRAT4) requires a learner to make 10 single-word spelling errors before it is stopped (Wilkinson and Robertson, 2006). This can be as unpleasant and uncomfortable for the teacher as for the testee, and seemingly in direct conflict with the teacher's training, experience and indeed instincts to support and help a learner.

Discussion point

Many highly competent teachers sign onto courses covering specialist assessment and find it difficult not to offer help to children when they are carrying out formal standardised tests which require complete objectivity. Learners are pushed to the limit of their ability or attainment, which can be very uncomfortable for tester and testee. In what way are the contrasting skills of teaching and diagnostic assessment in conflict, and how can trainers help participants to overcome the inherent contradictions in this change of roles?

Courses at this level develop trainees' clear understanding of statistical terms and their use, and also their ability to interpret standardised tests. Diagnostic testing for dyslexia requires a blend of tests, depending on the level and needs of the student. Dyslexia diagnosis remains an art, not a science, and the diagnosis is made by the tester and not by the tests (Jones and Kindersley, 2013). In England, there are national standards for assessment set up by a body of experts. Once trained, assessors can apply to hold a practising certificate which require a high standard of expertise and must be supported by continuing professional development (www.sasc.org.uk).

Trainees should understand and carefully consider the hopes and aspirations of the testee. Participants should anticipate that testees and sometimes their carers have an expectation of a result different from reality. Reporting and feeding back from tests requires sensitivity and tact. Even when results meet expectations, the reaction may be hugely emotionally charged. For example, older learners may be delighted to find a reason why they have suffered throughout their schooling but this may also lead to feelings of anger and disappointment about lost opportunities in their previous lives.

Evaluation: A key skill at all levels

Trainees should be prepared carefully to measure and evaluate learner progress against measurable targets and to give equal attention to learner progress in 'soft' outcomes, not just measurable skills. Teachers and testers should be able to evaluate their own performance; self-evaluation is a key skill both in terms of evaluation of teaching and assessment. It is only by this process that specialist teachers will be able to map their methodology to individual learners' needs continually as teaching progresses.

Another facet of evaluation crucial to the professional development of teachers and testers is choosing and using published materials. There are a huge range of commercially produced materials available, many of which are excellent but many of which may well need adapting for use with particular learners (Brooks, 2013). Trainees learn to evaluate critically materials in order to choose carefully from an expanding and expensive market (McPhillips et al., 2009). This is equally true for standardised tests.

It is also important that trainees learn to evaluate the wealth of research so that they can distinguish between reliable, evidence-based teaching programmes and tests and the 'snake oil' miracle treatments for dyslexia often marketed (Carter and Wheldall, 2008).

Supporting the trainees

Training courses are demanding. Aimed at teachers and supporters already in full-time employment, there are conflicts between providing rigorous training and allowing trainees time to complete. SENCos now have management roles in English schools with many conflicting demands on their time. But all SENCos need to be trained in how to recognise and support individual difficulties within the dyslexic spectrum.

Dyslexia is not the only specific difficulty on the syllabus; the growing awareness of co-occurring difficulties, such as dyspraxia, attention deficit, speech and communication problems, and dyscalculia necessitates study of these areas so that teachers can learn to make referrals to other agencies if any of these conditions are suspected:

> This course was a 'must' for all SENCos and extremely useful for all class teachers who want to improve the understanding and attainment of all children in their classroom. (Experienced SENCo)

Course providers can employ a variety of organisational training models to meet participants' needs, including twilight, whole days, and using e-learning to supplement face-to-face tuition. Teachers undertaking the training may already be in full- time work with family commitments. Course providers must take care to support participants, many of whom may be returning to academic study after a break:

> I wasn't sure about studying again initially – it had been 20+ years since I last wrote an essay! But I needn't have worried. I thoroughly enjoyed every moment of Year 1 – in fact, it was great to study again. I wasn't as rusty as I thought I would be! (Experienced SENCo)

Tutors can encourage peer support and ensure that these courses welcome and embrace the wide range of experience and achievement of trainees:

> During this course I have been made to feel not only welcome, but also part of a group of like-minded people. (Teaching assistant)

Discussion point

It is not unusual for teachers who themselves may have dyslexic tendencies to be attracted to specialist training. Many of these are excellent practical teachers but may have difficulty in producing written assignments. Whilst it is essential to make reasonable adjustments to enable teachers with dyslexia to complete specialist courses, it is also vital that they should be able to teach the necessary literacy skills at whatever level they are working.

Summary

This is an optimistic period for training dyslexia specialists. In the past ten years the profession has become more recognised. Through a series of national policies and protocols backed up by legislation, dyslexia is increasingly recognised in educational establishments, and, to some extent, within the wider population. The professional competences of teachers and assessors are currently a subject of debate at national level which will result in an agreed raft of learning outcomes to inform course providers. However, the nature of good practice has not changed radically: with the exception of an increasingly expanding range of assistive technology on offer, the basics of good teaching and assessments remain the same. Training for specialist teachers is effective for teaching *all* students with literacy difficulties, not just those who have been diagnosed as dyslexic. Dyslexia is present across all levels of ability, and language backgrounds, so it is vital that specialists are employed in all schools to help equip everyone with the skills needed to survive in a world increasingly driven by text. As we move into the future, it is vital that economic constraints do not prevent us from training the teachers and assessors who can make such a difference to the lives of people with dyslexia at all levels.

Further reading

Carter, R. (2010) *Mapping the Mind,* 2nd edn. London: Orion Publishing.
This book relates current medical neurological research to learning in an accessible way.

Jones, A. and Kindersley, K. (2013) *Dyslexia: Assessing and Reporting.* London: Hodder Education.
This book covers a range of knowledge and skills which would be a good basis for a course for specialist assessors of dyslexia.

(Continued)

(Continued)

Reid, G. (2016) *Dyslexia: A Practitioner's Handbook*, 5th edn. Oxford: Wiley/ Blackwell.
A very comprehensive guide to dyslexia teaching and assessment.

Rose, J. (2009) *Identifying and Teaching Children and Young People with Dyslexia and Literacy Difficulties*. London: Department for Children, Schools and Families.
This report provides a clear overview of the training needs for specialist teachers and assessors.

Useful websites

Dyslexia-SpLD Trust: www.thedyslexia-spldtrust.org.uk.

International Dyslexia Association: www.interdys.org.

PATOSS (Professional Association of Teachers of Students with Specific Learning Difficulties): www.patoss-dyslexia.org.

Acknowledgements

With thanks to participants on courses for specialist teachers and assessors of learners with specific learning difficulties (dyslexia) at the Helen Arkell Centre, Farnham, and the School of Education, University of Northampton, who generously shared their words for the quotations in this chapter.

References

Armstrong, D. and Humphrey, N. (2009) Reactions to a diagnosis of dyslexia among students entering further education: development of the 'resistance–accommodation'. *British Journal of Special Education*, 36: 95–102.
Boyle, J. and Fisher, S. (2007) *Educational Testing: A Competence Based Approach*. Oxford: Blackwell.
British Psychological Society (1999) *Dyslexia, Literacy and Psychological Assessment*. Leicester: BPS.
British Psychological Society (2007) *Code of Good Practice for Psychological Testing*. Leicester: Psychological Testing Centre.
Brooks, G. (2013) *What Works for Pupils with Literacy Difficulties?* 4th edn. London: Dyslexia–SpLD Trust.
Carter, M. and Wheldall, K. (2008) Why can't a teacher be more like a scientist? Science, pseudoscience and the art of teaching. *Australian Journal of Special Education*, 32: 5–21.
Department for Children, Schools and Families (DCSF) (2009) Sir Jim Rose presents findings of review into dyslexia, 22 June 2009. Press Notice 2009/0114. London: DCSF.

Department for Education and Department of Health (2014) *Special Educational Needs and Disability Code of Practice: 0 to 25 Years*. London: DfE.

Doveston, M. and Cullingford-Agnew, S. (2006) *Becoming a Higher Level Teaching Assistant: Primary Special Educational Needs*. Exeter: Learning Matters.

Equality Act (2010) London: The Stationery Office.

Jamieson, C. and Morgan, E. (2008) *Managing Dyslexia at University*. Abingdon: Routledge.

Jones, A. and Kindersley, K. (2013) *Dyslexia: Assessing and Reporting*. London: Hodder Education.

Lamb, B. (2009) *Report to the Secretary of State on the Lamb Inquiry: Review of SEN and Disability Information*. London: DCSF.

Lewis, A. and Norwich, B. (2001) Do pupils with learning difficulties need teaching strategies that are different from those used with other pupils? *Topic*, 26: 1–4.

McPhillips, T., Bell, S. and Doveston, M. (2009) Identification and intervention for primary pupils with dyslexia in Ireland and England: finding a path through the maze. *REACH: Journal of Special Needs Education in Ireland*, 22(2): 67–81

Pennington, B.F and Olson, R.K. (2005) Genetics of dyslexia. In M.J. Snowling and C. Hulme (eds), *The Science of Reading*. Oxford: Blackwell, pp. 453–72.

Phillips, S., Kelly, K. and Symes, L. (2013) *Assessment of Learners with Dyslexic-type Difficulties*. London: Sage Publications Ltd.

Rose, J. (2009) *Identifying and Teaching Children and Young People with Dyslexia and Literacy Difficulties*. London: Department for Children, Schools and Families.

Singleton, C. (1999) *Dyslexia in Higher Education: Policy, Provision and Practice (Report of the National Working Party on Dyslexia in Higher Education)*. Hull: University of Hull.

Singleton, C. (2008) Visual factors in reading. *Educational and Child Psychology*, 25: 8–20.

Wilkinson, G.S. and Robertson, G.J. (2006) *Wide Range Achievement Test 4 Professional Manual (WRAT4)*. Lutz, FL: Psychological Assessment Resources.

11

Literacy

Margaret Crombie

Learning objectives

This chapter will help readers to:

- Understand how literacy and literacy difficulties fit into the context of the twenty-first century
- Consider the political and educational implications of treating literacy as a topic of debate
- Appreciate how literacy has come to be viewed as it is, and the impact this has had on those learning to become literate
- Recognise how early intervention can minimise or prevent failure in literacy development
- Understand what can be done to assist learning and ensure accessibility to literacy for those who experience difficulties

Background

Literacy and literacy difficulties in the twenty-first century are the subjects of much discussion. Everyone seems to have a view on how literacy should be dealt with, and how illiteracy should be eliminated. While most people would agree that an end to illiteracy would be desirable, there is absolutely no agreement on how this might be done. Politically literacy is richly debated (Commons Select Committee, 2013; Goodwin and Fuller, 2011; Rose, 2006; Scottish Government, 2010; Scottish Parliament, 2012; Wyse and Styles, 2007), practitioners and researchers discuss methodologies, governments invest large amounts of money in it, schools spend considerable time dealing with it, newspapers give much column space to it, the media more generally consider it a topic of widespread interest, and across the world, countless millions are spent researching it, yet the problems associated with low literacy levels remain!

Before considering what literacy (and therefore illiteracy) is, and looking at the reasons for the widespread disagreement on how to deal with literacy difficulties, it is worth emphasising that there are many different literacies: in addition to text, we have financial literacy, emotional literacy, spiritual literacy, scientific literacy, health literacy, game literacy, media literacy, visual literacy, digital literacy to name but a few. Defining literacy can, it seems, be problematic with all these areas to cover. The National Literacy Trust view literacy as being more than reading and writing and include listening and speaking (Jama and Dugdale, 2012). In their State of the Nation document which gives a 'picture of literacy in the UK today', they stress that '42% of employers are not satisfied with the basic use of English by school and college leavers'. Jama and Dugdale emphasise the importance that literacy has for employment prospects, and promotion in the workplace (CBI, 2011).

The Scottish Curriculum for Excellence defines literacy as 'the set of skills which allows an individual to engage fully in society and in learning, through the different forms of language, and the range of texts which society values and finds useful' (Education Scotland, 2014: 1). The intention of this definition is to make it general enough to be 'future proofed' and take account of the developments we may not yet have considered in the current digital age. In England, though the literacy curriculum has been founded on developing oracy skills alongside reading and writing, political planning is very clearly focused on decoding and encoding text through developing phonics as the route to becoming literate (Department for Education, 2013, 2014). This seems likely to continue (Standards and Testing Agency, 2015).

Wells states that: 'to be fully literate is to have the disposition to engage appropriately with texts of different types in order to empower action, feelings, and thinking in the context of purposeful social activity' (Wells, 1990: 14). Engaging with texts suggests a form of literacy focusing on reading and writing or typing in a range of media. Soler (2010) considers that: 'from a socio-cultural perspective literacy learning can be viewed as embedded in culturally crafted, meaning making practices and discourses taking place within social groups' (p. 180).

Almost half of UK employers report weaknesses in employees in the core skills of literacy with two-fifths feeling the need to provide '"remedial" training to school and college leavers' (CBI, 2011). The literacy to which they are referring includes writing, reading and oral skills. While acknowledging all of the literacies that do exist and accepting that being literate in each case means being able to talk, listen, read and write in a reasonably competent fashion, in this chapter I will focus on discussion of the text-based literacies that allow us to access information, culture and knowledge through reading and writing – the literacies that everyone who went to school has been taught (for better or worse), and which help give us access to the wide range of other literacies.

The range of literacy

While speaking and listening seem to happen 'naturally' before children enter nursery or school, either because the skills are innate – as Chomsky (1965) suggests in proposing that every child is born with a language acquisition device (LAD) – or absorbed through the support and social experiences of growing up in a social community or family – as Bruner (1983) proposes in his LASS (Language Acquisition Support System) – it is consequently reading and writing that are politically and educationally more controversial. Although the development of oracy and listening skills are undoubtedly important, politically speaking reading and writing appear more important with regard to pedagogy (Ofsted, 2012; OECD, 2014a, 2014b; Scottish Government/ADES, 2014).

What then does it really mean to be literate in the twenty-first century? And for those who are not considered to be literate and cannot extract or embed meaning in and from text, what can be done? While acknowledging the inextricable links that there are between all four elements (speaking, listening, reading and writing), this chapter will consider text-based literacies and what happens when the processes which normally develop these literacies break down, and children fail to learn to read and write adequately. In addition, the chapter looks at various perceptions of why literacy and illiteracy (lack of abilities in reading and writing) may be problematic and also acknowledges the role now played by the various technologies in helping to circumvent and overcome literacy difficulties.

Over the years, literacy and academic writing on the subject tend to have fallen into distinct and different camps with those who consider the cognitive within-person factors, those who value the psycholinguistic traditions that have developed largely from the work of Chomsky, and those who see literacy as a socio-cultural activity, being in their own distinct camps! While there has been some individual movement between camps, in general these divisions have got us nowhere in terms of eradicating illiteracy and those at the centre, the 'illiterates' and 'semi-literates' for want of better words, gain very little. These are the people who are in danger, through their lack of literacy, of becoming demotivated, disengaged and if not wisely counselled, can sink into a life of depression, crime, isolation or worse (Cree et al., 2012).

Educators interested only in improving the lot of their charges, and politicians interested in their electorate, find it difficult to know which camp to join, so over the years we have seen policies swing widely between extremes with teachers drawn up in the mood of the moment. These swings from phonics to 'real' reading (without phonics) to an integration of the two, and again back to a domination of phonics are changes which come with scant consideration for the huge range of factors that influence each and every one of our students in the real world. Adams, in her book *Beginning to Read: Thinking and Learning about Print*, which reviews, evaluates and integrates a vast body of research and its implications for children learning to read, uses headings such as 'Reading Words and Meanings: From an Age-old Problem to a Contemporary Crisis', in describing the concerns and conflicts around the learning and teaching of reading (Adams, 1994: iii). Even the titles of the research, stretching far beyond the UK, tell us that all has not been unity and harmony in the field of reading research. Only when we agree to acknowledge the whole range of perspectives and take account of the views of those who adopt different views from ourselves, and look at the needs of developing learners will we gain greater harmony and the insights we need to improve literacy levels overall.

Literacy difficulties

Children can have difficulties in learning to read and write for a multitude of reasons, some of them within the child (e.g. cognitive functioning problems) and others external to the child (e.g. lack of exposure to books at home). When discussing literacy and literacy difficulties, one must consider the possibility of dyslexia, as it is claimed that somewhere between 2% and 15% of the population are dyslexic to some degree (Parliamentary Office of Science and Technology, 2004). The particular degree will of course depend on how you view dyslexia and how you define it. The 15% is likely to cover those who have mild difficulties and the 2% only those who have severe difficulties.

There are a multitude of views and debates on whether it is possible to distinguish dyslexia from other difficulties with literacy (Crombie, 2002, 2005; Elliott and Grigorenko, 2014; Stanovich, 1988, 1996). These arguments inevitably centre on definitions of both literacy and dyslexia and whether through a definition of dyslexia we seek to look for discrepancies and differences as well as difficulties (Reid, 1996, 2009). Though there are important distinctions to be made, for the purposes of this chapter, those debates will remain academic as the most important factor is not what we call the difficulties, it is the impact these difficulties have on individuals and what we do about them.

Identifying literacy difficulties

Screening and subsequently assessment are important means of determining a young person's strengths and weaknesses. Early identification of concerns is beneficial in ensuring that everything that can be done to prevent or overcome any difficulties is done before the learner begins to realise failure. However, appropriate intervention and support must follow from the identification of concerns. Knowing how to support children is therefore vital for their progress. Knowledge of the range of possible approaches and when to employ them can make the difference between success and failure in school learning. Goswami (2010) emphasises the importance of children's phonological understanding in the early years and its relation to the later development of literacy. 'The brain develops phonological "representations" in response to spoken language exposure and learning to speak, and the quality of these phonological representations determines literacy acquisition' (p. 103). This makes it quite clear that the better the exposure to language, and the more the child is encouraged to participate in activities such as rhyming, alliteration and generally listening to, and participating in all types of language 'games', the more likely success in later literacy will be (Muter et al., 2004). Specific problems in the phonology sphere are likely to lead to difficulties in the acquisition of literacy.

For those learners who do have literacy difficulties, how then is it possible to marry up the various approaches previously mentioned to facilitate the reading process? If we consider firstly the psycholinguistic tradition, we think of the guessing games that Goodman (1967, 1992) describes, as children, seeking to understand the words they are reading on the page before them, consider the context and insert a meaningful word if they are unsure. If they can do this (e.g. saying pony for horse), they are considered to be using their knowledge of semantics appropriately. If however they insert a word that is phonically similar in appearance (e.g. starts with the same letter, or has a similar letter pattern), but is not meaningful in context, then they are said to be over-relying on graphophonic cues and not fully understanding what it is they are reading about. Syntactic errors (such as omission of 'can' in a phrase like, 'I can read') would indicate an acceptable miscue as the meaning is largely maintained. Goodman termed the reading errors as miscues rather than mistakes perhaps to indicate that the child was at least partially correct in coming to terms with the complexities of reading. If we then combine the sociolinguistic models with the application of phonic approaches, we may get a clearer view of the reading process.

From an analysis of the miscues that an individual makes, we can determine where we need to focus attention. Do they have the phonic knowledge to self-correct errors that don't make sense? Can the learner recognise when something does not make sense, but can't use graphophonic knowledge to help increase accuracy and thence, understanding? Does the learner carry on regardless of omissions and substitutions if the sentence makes some kind of sense? If a word fits into the context of the story, will the learner read on regardless? Though some aspects of miscue analysis have been criticised and discredited as not identifying skill needs in the area of word recognition and being too dependent on context (McKenna and Picard, 2006), there are aspects which teachers can use to help them understand the process the young person is going through, and so gain 'a window into the mind' of the reader (Farrington, 2007). What kind of help will enable the learner to produce the desired reading accuracy to gain more precise meaning from the text? How can we help the learner to adopt a more accurate approach to reading without affecting their confidence for reading? How can the learners themselves be sure of what they are reading and have confidence in their own abilities to decode and understand as the author intended?

The notion of miscue analysis was developed to help understand the processes that learners go through in their efforts to make sense of the world of reading and language, and as such can be a tool for educators to use to gauge how a learner approaches reading, and to identify precise areas that may require attention and direct teaching support. Thus the psycholinguistic approach, with its emphasis on making meaning through being able to guess, and then self-correct when a wrong guess is made can be useful, but what if …? What if a learner simply does not know where to start, and doesn't get to the point of being able to insert meaningful words? What if the learner misreads a word or two, and then guesses – what will happen to the context clues then? Here the psycholinguistic 'guessing game' can make a learner the target of ridicule from classmates who simply don't understand why their peer isn't able to 'catch on', and can destroy confidence for a lengthy period of time.

Perhaps then for these learners a cognitive approach might have more to offer. If the learner can grasp letter–sound combinations and has some mastery of phonics, then the possibilities of being able to get started onto the reading process are realisable. However, if they have failed to learn to read through psycholinguistic guessing, then time will be required to form automatic responses to visual symbolic language cues – initially that is letter–sound combinations. These responses need to reach the point of automaticity before the learner will be able to cope competently with decoding and understanding reading matter at the same time. 'Automaticity frees cognitive resources for the more difficult task of integration and comprehension. If attention and effort are devoted to low-level processes, like decoding the pronunciation of a letter string, there may be insufficient resources to execute processes needed for comprehension' (Klein and McMullen, 1999: 3). Reaching automaticity with phonics is vital as these learners struggle to make connections between the symbols they see and the sounds they make.

Intervention

The conditions that cause reading difficulties are undoubtedly complex, with social factors clearly influencing the literacy learning of many poorer children. A child who grows up in a home where there are no books or magazines and where no value is given to being able to read and write, is unlikely to have the same desire to learn to read as those from literate homes with an endless ready supply of meaningful literature. Although children growing up in depressed areas are less likely to be motivated to adopt positive images of literacy and learning, it is important to remember that there is much that can be done. We must not fall into the trap of assuming that poor social circumstance means that children are doomed to failure from the start. 'Poor performance does not automatically follow from low socio-economic status' (Clark and Akerman, 2006: 1). We must take care and consider the old adage that 'correlation does not necessarily imply causation'. Statistics tell us that children from poorer backgrounds have lower levels of literacy than those in better-off circumstances. Social circumstances can undoubtedly impact on children's prospects and motivation to learn (Cree et al., 2012). Helping disadvantaged students to overcome negative feelings about their environment can contribute greatly to literacy learning.

Engagement is critical, but how to engage children and young people can be a problem when reading skills are weak and in danger of preventing the young person's access to the curriculum and to literature more generally. Parents can be a huge source of support to children when learning. 'Attracting parents to participate actively in educational and school endeavours can serve to form social networks where parents get to know and help each other' (OECD, 2010: 157). Involving parents can also be a source not just of support to the school, but also of support to individual children who may struggle to learn to read. Epstein and co-workers (1995, 2009) emphasise the importance of schools working with parents and not assuming that parents will automatically know how to help their own children.

School–parent partnerships

'School, family, and community partnerships cannot simply produce successful students. Rather, partnership activities may be designed to engage, guide, energise, and motivate students to produce their own successes' (Epstein, 1995: 703). Where children struggle in specific areas such as literacy, home-school reading partnerships, paired reading with appropriately trained volunteers and other supportive practices can ensure that no child is left struggling without understanding and empathetic help for their difficulties (Topping, 2004; Wolfendale and Einzig, 1999). Schools, however, do need to learn how to organise parental support sensitively so that no child becomes stigmatised through inappropriate comments or lack of consideration (Epstein et al., 2009). Teachers and managers may not be able to change children's environments as some would like, but they can work within social boundaries to encourage parents to value their children's efforts and to ensure parents feel welcome in schools to discuss any problems and get involved in supporting not just their own children, but the whole school, in whatever ways they are able (Department for Education, 2010).

Kellett and Dar (2007) trained and employed 11-year-olds from two UK schools – one from an area of deprivation and the other from a socio-economically advantaged area – as researchers. Findings common to both areas were that throughout the studies, 'themes of enjoyment, choice and ownership came through strongly as being effective ways for children to engage with literacy' (p. 40). Consideration was given to how the schools could bridge gaps and compensate for their areas of difference relating to their varying socio-economic statuses. It was felt that homework clubs, adult literacy classes and the teaching of lifelong learning skills, such as information and communications technology, could help.

Case study

Carolann has experienced difficulties with literacy development since starting school. Carolann is now 14, and her school, in a deprived area of London, has recently started a parental involvement scheme whereby parents are welcomed into school, and can work with teachers and other volunteers on a paired reading scheme. Though Carolann is still not a fluent reader, she has started to enjoy books, and is increasing her skills. Teaching staff mentioned recently that Carolann can now access some information from the Internet which would previously have been unlikely. Though Carolann still struggles with written work, teaching staff are hopeful that the increase in reading skills will lead to an overall improvement in literacy more generally.

Literacy access

In the twenty-first century, it is becoming more and more important that students can use their literacy skills and access text-based material not just through printed matter such as books and magazines, but also through the vast knowledge basket that is the World Wide Web. The skills of decoding and understanding are supplemented by skills of skimming and scanning to find information quickly. The need for students to be discriminating and critical in what they 'read' is vital if they are not to be lead astray by irrelevant and misleading information and extraneous matter! For those with low reading skills, the effort required can be enormous.

'Metacognition in reading refers to the awareness of and ability to use a variety of appropriate strategies when processing texts in a goal oriented manner' (OECD, 2010: 72). Metacognitive skills are necessary for all types of reading in this information age. Students need to learn to consciously question, identify the main ideas, monitor their own comprehension, check and clarify as they go. However, the good news on metacognition is that it 'can be taught' (OECD, 2010: 23). It seems, too, that the teaching of metacognition to students has a positive effect on their reading literacy.

Reading and writing are two sides of the same coin. The processes of decoding and encoding, though different, are therefore inextricably linked. For learners who find decoding difficult, it is likely that encoding will be equally or more difficult, relying not just on recognition processes as are necessary for reading, but also on memory for shape for letter formation, linking letters, spacing words and so on. Inputting letters and words into digital technology may not represent quite such a large challenge as handwriting, but there are still issues of putting together letter combinations to form words rather than just being able to recognise the words as they appear on the page or screen. Students today have to deal not just with handwriting and book reading but also with screen reading and word processing – vital skills for the digital era in which we live.

For young people with reading difficulties, the need to read lengthy texts can be minimised through digital books and journals, and screenreaders. In Scotland the *Books for All* project (CALL Scotland, 2015) is working with publishers and teachers to ensure that textbooks are made available to anyone who finds difficulty in accessing books through reading. Material available on screen can be read through screenreading technology, or material can be copied and read aloud by a computer. Similarly the necessity to write has become less pressured through computer programs such as *Dragon NaturallySpeaking* speech recognition software (Nuance Communications, 2015). Technology, while it presents us with challenges, is constantly evolving new approaches and possible solutions.

Digital recording of homework simply presents the same material differently and can be assessed and commented on by teachers. Teachers can record notes in digital format for pupils to listen to at any time, thus easing the burden on the pupils in class, and enabling parents' awareness of what their children are studying. For learners listening to MP3 players or their mobile phone, there is no stigma attached to lack of reading ability as teachers make reading accessible to those who are having difficulties. For those who cannot overcome their early difficulties, their lives need not be impaired by lack of reading and writing abilities. The need to read and write in exams, is now also being overcome through the use of digital technology:

> Candidates can read the question paper 'on screen', using text-to-speech technology, where appropriate. Also, where the format of the question paper is a question/answer booklet, such candidates can also write/speak their responses 'on screen' (Scottish Qualifications Authority, 2015)

thus lightening the load of reading and writing for pupils who have significant literacy difficulties.

Although reading and writing problems can often be circumvented or overcome by the use of technology, it is still desirable for learners to read and write to the best of their abilities. Linking literacy teaching to the needs of individual learners with difficulties is no easy matter. The famous quote by Huey (1908) that:

> to completely analyse what we do when we read would almost be the acme of a psychologist's achievements, for it would be to describe very many of the most intricate workings of the human mind, as well as to unravel the story of the most remarkable specific performance that civilization has learned in all its history

is no less important today than it was over a century ago. An understanding of reading in the context of literacy development across the curriculum is absolutely vital for all teachers in the twenty-first century to ensure that students are prepared for the breadth of literacy they will meet now and in the future. It would seem that we still have a considerable way to go before we can claim to be able 'to completely analyse what we do when we read'. Moreover, we still have a considerable way to go before we can claim to be able to completely analyse what happens when those who fail to learn to read appear in our classrooms and work places. Neuroscience and research still have a way to go before we reach the point of 'unravelling' the whole 'story' with regard to reading and literacy.

However, from the educators' perspective, the reason we have not 'unravelled' this story may be that we are searching for something that isn't there, like a mythical creature. We can imagine mythical creatures but they don't really exist – their invisibility means that we are in fact searching for something we will never find. In the case of reading, we are seeking to find the way in which children learn to read, and hence how we can help them. This is not to say that we can't help them, but to find just one way is not going to be the solution. If it had been we'd already have discovered our 'mythical creature'. One size most definitely doesn't fit all! As educators, we must consider the individuality of every reader, in particular, every failed reader or every reader we have failed, and ask ourselves:

- Is there anything we can do in our classrooms to help ensure access to the curriculum for all our students with literacy difficulties?

We can further break down this question:

- Is each and every student paying attention?
- Do we use language that every learner can understand?
- Can each and every learner follow what we are saying at the pace we are saying it?
- Do we direct each student appropriately, or do we assume that because most students learn from us, that is the way we should teach?
- Do we know how each of our students learns best?
- Is our manner in approaching each student conducive to the learning of that student?
- Are there learners who seem to have cognitive processing factors that are blocking out specific types of learning?
- Does this individual want to learn?
- Are there emotional factors that are influencing learning?
- What can we do in one period of 50 minutes that will help (if that is all the time we have in one session)?
- Can we organise our learners so that each student with specific learning needs can receive the help they need (either independently through the use of aids and minimal guidance), or with help (peers, teacher, teaching assistant) or simply by an increase in our understanding and empathy of what works well for these particular individuals?

There are also some quite basic factors that might be influencing learning, too:

- Has this learner had breakfast this morning? Did s/he go to bed last night?
- Do we know if this young person or adult is a carer who has to look after someone at home before coming to school or work?
- Is there a space at home where the individual can work?

Some of these questions may sound basic, and we may feel we are powerless to influence home and cognitive processing factors, but as a result of answering these questions, can we improve matters for all our students? Can we adapt to the changing needs of our learners? (What works today will not always work tomorrow.) Can we perhaps through influencing whole-school or college policy or the working environment, improve learning and literacy?

Managing literacy in the classroom

Though managing the individual learning needs of a whole group of learners is difficult, it is a task which must be mastered if teaching is to succeed in the classroom situation. However, just as teachers differ, the learning process is sufficiently different for each and every learner that if a student does not learn to read, pushing in one direction by one approach is not likely to be the answer. We have research that tells us that phonics works (Ehri, 1998; Rose, 2006, 2009; Johnston and Watson, 2005), that 'real reading' works (Goodman, 1992; Waterland, 1989), that specific programmes are the answer (Kelly and Phillips, 2011), but for whom, to what extent? It is for literacy teachers, and therefore every teacher, to evaluate the research that does exist, not just on the teaching of literacy, but on teaching and learning more generally. Each piece of research exists in a context, but each only gives us partial answers. The more possible answers the greater the likelihood of finding the right one for each individual.

Literacy, and therefore teaching literacy, are complex issues with many processes involved (Adams, 1994; Ehri, 2002; OECD, 2010; Rassool, 2009; Stuart et al., 2009). If learners do not respond to one particular approach, then another should be tried in order that all can somehow be included in literacy practices (Crombie, 2002; Reid, 2009). It is important then for teachers to have a full range of approaches at their fingertips, to acknowledge that there is no one way that will work for all and to explore all the factors that are involved – classroom, teaching, support, cognitive, social, emotional, interactional, and also to look at their own teaching needs and who can help with those.

Summary

- Literacy teaching is complex but should involve every teacher and educator if young people are to be adequately prepared for life in the twenty-first century.
- There is a considerable body of research on all aspects of literacy and teaching literacy.
- No one approach has all the answers and some approaches raise further questions.
- Developing children and young people's literacy abilities for life in today's world of digital as well as traditional literacies presents opportunities and challenges for all.
- Technology poses new challenges, but also offers new solutions.
- Educators must have a range of evaluative skills to enable them to approach literacy teaching and learning in a solution-focused way.

Discussion points

- Does the use of digital technologies by those who have difficulties with literacy encourage a dependency culture and discourage new learning?
- Debates over the teaching of reading, and the 'Reading Wars' as they have become known, have not resolved the issues around how reading should be taught. The relationship between writing and reading is a complex one. There are issues around 'code' and 'meaning' in learning to read and to write. Bearing in mind that every individual is different, can these issues ever really be resolved?
- Does giving those with literacy difficulties additional time for reading and writing in exams give them an advantage?
- Although literacy learning at the early stages is particularly important for school learning, difficulties with literacy can exist at any age. What are the critical factors that are different for older learners?

Further reading

Hall, K., Goswami, U., Harrison, C., Ellis, S. and Soler, J. (eds) (2010) *Inter-disciplinary Perspectives on Learning to Read*. Abingdon: Routledge.
Considers a range of perspectives relating to literacy and reading.

Larson, J. and Marsh, J. (2005) *Making Literacy Real: Theories and Practices for Learning and Teaching*. London: Sage Publications Ltd.
Relates literacy theory to practical aspects of teaching – grounded in social and cultural perspectives.

Palmer, S. and Corbett, P. (2001) *Literacy: What Works?* Cheltenham: Nelson Thornes.
Practical information to assist the primary practitioner.

Wolf, M. (2007) *Proust and the Squid: The Story and Science of the Reading Brain*. New York: HarperCollins.
Considers our understanding of how the human brain has developed the ability to read.

Useful websites

Adult Literacy Core Curriculum: rwp.excellencegateway.org.uk/Literacy/Adult %20literacy%20core%20curriculum.

(Continued)

(Continued)

BBC Literacy (for 4–11-year-olds): www.bbc.co.uk/schools/websites/4_11/site/literacy.shtml.

British Dyslexia Association: www.bdadyslexia.org.uk.

National Literacy Trust: www.literacytrust.org.uk.

For older learners: www.bbc.co.uk/skillswise.

Skills for Life – Literacy Learning Materials: rwp.excellencegateway.org.uk/Literacy/ Literacy%20teaching%20and%20learning%20materials/Entry%201.

UK Literacy Association: www.ukla.org.

References

Adams, M.J. (1994) *Beginning to Read: Thinking and Learning about Print.* Cambridge, MA: MIT Press.

Bruner, J.S. (1983) *Child's Talk: Learning to Use Language.* New York: W.W. Norton and Co.

CALL Scotland (2015) *Books for All,* University of Edinburgh. www.callscotland.org.uk/What-we-do/ Projects/Books-for-All.

CBI (Confederation of British Industry) (2011) *Education and Skills Survey 2011.* www.cbi.org.uk/ media/1051530/cbi__edi_education___skills_survey_2011.pdf.

Chomsky, N. (1965) *Aspects of the Theory of Syntax.* Boston, MA: MIT Press.

Clark, C. and Akerman, R. (2006) *Social Inclusion and Reading: An Exploration.* London: National Literacy Trust.

Commons Select Committee (2013) *Debate on Adult Literacy and Numeracy.* www.parliament.uk/ business/committees/committees-a-z/commons-select/backbench-business-committee/news/ debate-on-adult-literacy-and-numeracy.

Cree, A., Kay, A. and Steward, J. (2012) *The Economic and Social Cost of Illiteracy: A Snapshot of Illiteracy in a Global Context.* Melbourne: World Literacy Foundation.

Crombie, M. (2002) Dealing with diversity in the primary classroom – a challenge for the class teacher. In G. Reid and J. Wearmouth (eds), *Dyslexia and Literacy: Research and Practice.* London: Wiley, pp. 229–40.

Crombie, M. (2005) Dyslexia is all too real for sufferers. *Times Educational Supplement Scotland, 2030,* Scottish Opinion, p. 21.

Department for Education (2010) *Parental Opinion Survey 2010.* London: The Stationery Office.

Department for Education (2013) *Learning to Read through Phonics: Information for Parents.* www. gov.uk/government/uploads/system/uploads/attachment_data/file/194057/phonics_check_leaflet_ 2013_.pdf.

Department for Education (2014) *Teaching Phonics: Information for Schools.* London: The Stationery Office.

Education Scotland (2014) *Curriculum for Excellence: Literacy across Learning: Principles and Practice.* www.educationscotland.gov.uk/learningandteaching/learningacrossthecurriculum/responsi- bilityofall/literacy/principlesandpractice/index.asp.

Ehri, L.C. (1998) Grapheme–phoneme knowledge is essential for learning to read words in English. In J.L. Metsala and L.C. Ehri (eds), *Word Recognition in Beginning Literacy.* Mahwah, NJ: Erlbaum, pp. 3–40.

Ehri, L.C. (2002) Reading processes, acquisition, and instructional implications. In G. Reid and J. Wearmouth (eds), *Dyslexia and Literacy: Theory and Practice*. Chichester: John Wiley and Sons, pp. 167–86.

Elliott, J.G. and Grigorenko, E.L. (2014) *The Dyslexia Debate (Cambridge Studies in Cognitive and Perceptual Development)*. New York: Cambridge University Press.

Epstein, J.L. (1995) School/family/community partnerships: caring for the children we share. *Phi Delta Kappan*, 76(9): 703.

Epstein, J.L. et al. (2009) *School, Family, and Community Partnerships*, 3rd edn. Thousand Oaks, CA: Corwin Press.

Farrington, P. (2007) A window into the mind: using miscue analysis. *Literacy Today*, 52: 10–11.

Goodman, K.S. (1967) A psycholinguistic guessing game. *Journal of the Reading Specialist*, 6: 126–35.

Goodman, K.S. (1992) Why whole language is today's agenda in education. *Language Arts*, 69: 354–63.

Goodwin, A. and Fuller, C. (eds) (2011) *The Great Literacy Debate*. Abingdon: Routledge.

Goswami, U. (2010) Phonology, reading and reading difficulties. In K. Hall, U. Goswami, C. Harrison, S. Ellis and J. Soler (eds), *Interdisciplinary Perspectives on Learning to Read*. Abingdon: Routledge, pp. 103–16.

Huey, E.B. (1908) *The Psychology and Pedagogy of Reading*. Cambridge, MA: MIT Press.

Jama, D. and Dugdale, G. (2012) *Literacy: State of the Nation: A Picture of Literacy in the UK Today*. London: National Literacy Trust.

Johnston, R.S. and Watson, J. (2005) *A Seven Year Study of the Effects of Synthetic Phonics Teaching on Reading and Spelling Attainment*. Edinburgh: Scottish Executive Education Department.

Kellett, M. and Dar, A. (2007) *Children Researching Links between Poverty and Literacy*. York: Joseph Rowntree Foundation.

Kelly, K.S. and Phillips, S. (2011) *Teaching Literacy to Learners with Dyslexia: A Multi-sensory Approach*. London: Sage.

Klein, R.M. and McMullen, P. (eds) (1999) Introduction: The reading brain. In R.M. Klein and P. McMullen (eds), *Converging Methods for Understanding Reading and Dyslexia*. Cambridge, MA: MIT Press, pp. 1–22.

McKenna, M.C. and Picard, M.C. (2006) Revisiting the role of miscue analysis in effective teaching. *Reading Teacher*, 60(4): 378–80.

Muter, V., Hulme, C., Snowling, M.J. and Stevenson, J. (2004) Phonemes, rimes, vocabulary, and grammatical skills as foundations of early reading development: evidence from a longitudinal study. *Developmental Psychology*, 40(5): 665–81.

Nuance Communications (2015) *Dragon NaturallySpeaking*. Burlington, MA: Nuance. http://shop.nuance.co.uk/store/nuanceeu/en_GB/Content/pbPage.201408_PS_UK_DNS13?gclid=CMe_z8D10sECFY_ItAodMV0AGA.

OECD (Organisation for Economic Cooperation and Development) (2010) *PISA 2009 Assessment Framework: Key Competencies in Reading, Mathematics and Science*. Paris: OECD.

OECD (Organisation for Economic Cooperation and Development) (2014a) *A Profile of Student Performance in Reading, in PISA 2012 Results: What Students Know and Can Do* (Vol. 1, Revised edition, February 2014): Student performance in mathematics, reading and science, OECD Publishing. http://dx.doi.org/10.1787/9789264208780-8-en.

OECD (Organisation for Economic Cooperation and Development) (2014b) *PISA 2012 Results in Focus: What 15-year-olds Know and What They Can Do with What They Know*. www.oecd.org/pisa/keyfindings/pisa-2012-results-overview.pdf.

Ofsted (Office for Standards in Education, Children's Services and Skills) (2012) *Driving up Standards of Literacy*. www.gov.uk/government/news/ofsted-chief-inspector-calls-for-rapid-improvement-in-literacy.

Parliamentary Office of Science and Technology (2004, July) Dyslexia and dyscalculia. *Postnote*, No. 226, p. 1.

Rassool, N. (2009) Literacy: In search of a paradigm. In J. Soler, F. Fletcher-Campbell and G. Reid (eds), *Understanding Difficulties in Literacy Development: Issues and Concepts*. London: Sage, pp. 7–31.

Reid, G. (2009) *Dyslexia: A Practitioner's Handbook*, 4th edn. Chichester: John Wiley and Sons Ltd.

Reid, G. (ed.) (1996) *Dimensions of Dyslexia: Assessment, Teaching and Curriculum*. Edinburgh: Moray House Publications.

Rose, J. (2006) *Independent Review of the Teaching of Early Reading (Rose Review)*. Nottingham: Department for Education and Skills.

Rose, J. (2009) *Identifying and Teaching Children and Young People with Dyslexia and Literacy Difficulties: An Independent Report from Sir Jim Rose to the Secretary of State for Children, Schools and Families*. Nottingham: DCSF Publications.

Scottish Government (2010) *Literacy Action Plan* (scotland.gov.uk/Publications/2010/10/27084039/0).

Scottish Government/ADES (Association of Directors of Education in Scotland) (2014) *Review of Scottish Government Literacy Hub Approach*. www.scotland.gov.uk/Resource/0044/00449063.pdf.

Scottish Parliament (2012) *Members' Business: Dyslexia*. news.bbc.co.uk/democracylive/hi/scotland/newsid_9762000/9762239.stm.

Scottish Qualifications Authority (2015) *Assessment Arrangements: Digital Question Papers*. (www.sqa.org.uk/sqa/30030.html).

Soler, J. (2010) Dyslexia lessons: The politics of dyslexia and reading problems. In K. Hall, U. Goswami, C. Harrison, S. Ellis and J. Soler (eds), *Interdisciplinary Perspectives on Learning to Read*. Abingdon: Routledge, pp. 179–92.

Standards and Testing Agency (2015) *National Curriculum Assessments: Future Arrangements*. www.gov.uk/government/publications/national-curriculum-assessments-future-test-dates.

Stanovich, K.E. (1988) Explaining the difference between the dyslexic and the garden-variety poor reader: the phonological-core variable-difference model. *Journal of Learning Disabilities*, 21: 590–612.

Stanovich, K.E. (1996) Toward a more inclusive definition of dyslexia. *Dyslexia*, 2: 154–66.

Stuart, M., Stainthorp, R. and Snowling, M. (2009) Literacy as complex activity: Deconstructing the simple view of reading. In J. Soler, F. Fletcher-Campbell and G. Reid (eds), *Understanding Difficulties in Literacy Development: Issues and Concepts*. London: Sage, pp. 53–66.

Topping, K.J. (2004) *Thinking, Reading, Writing: A Practical Guide to Paired Learning with Peers, Parents and Volunteers*. London: Continuum Practical Education.

Waterland, L. (ed.) (1989) *Read with Me: An Apprenticeship Approach to Reading*. Stroud: Thimble Press.

Wells, G. (1990) Talk about text: where literacy is learned and taught. *Curriculum Inquiry*, 20(4): 369–405.

Wolfendale, S. and Einzig, H. (1999) *Parenting Education and Support*. London: Routledge.

Wyse, D. and Styles, M. (2007) Synthetic phonics and the teaching of reading: the debate surrounding England's 'Rose Report'. *Literacy*, 47(1): 35–42.

Mathematical Learning Difficulties and Dyscalculia

12

Steve Chinn

Learning objectives

This chapter will help readers to:

- Relate the research into effective learning to the learning difficulties of dyscalculia
- Understand which are the factors that can contribute to learning difficulties in mathematics
- Appreciate the role of mathematical strategies in supporting problems with mathematical memory
- Consider the principles of effective intervention

Introduction

Specific learning difficulties could be viewed in the light of Howard Gardner's theory of multiple intelligences and that it is possible for intelligences not to be uniformly distributed in an individual. For example, a deficit in logico-mathematical intelligence could be significant enough to be described as a mathematical learning difficulty or severe enough to be judged as dyscalculia. A complementary perspective is for a learning difficulty to be considered as a consequence of many interacting factors that may be detrimental to effective learning. For example, factors that are characteristic of an individual, such as working memory and anxiety or external factors such as an inappropriate curriculum or embedded beliefs that can be part of the culture of mathematics education. A third consideration could be a mismatch between the way a student learns and the way she is taught. The apparently weak specific intelligence might well be the consequence of a specific learning difficulty. A key hypothesis of this chapter is that mainstream mathematics education has much to learn from adjustments and interventions that have been effective for the outliers (Murray et al., 2015).

However, research (Hattie, 2009) shows that any intervention will improve learning, but only for a while. This makes students with learning difficulties at risk of exploitation or over-enthusiastic interpretations of the efficacy of an intervention. My own experience of 24 years of teaching students with specific learning difficulties, coupled with the essential optimism of a teacher who believes that appropriate teaching can make a positive difference seeks, and finds, more from Hattie's meta-analysis of educational research. The objective is not to just make a temporary improvement, but to maximise long-term learning.

Dyscalculia definitions and some implications

Although Bronner hypothesised the existence of a specific learning difficulty for mathematics in 1917, this was followed by years of minimal attention. However, recently dyscalculia is beginning to attract more research. This, in turn is slowly drawing more attention to mathematical learning difficulties (Gersten et al., 2007; Chinn, 2015), a broader concept, which may be timely in the light of the recent conclusion from the DSM-5 Neurodevelopmental Work Group that 'the many definitions of dyslexia and dyscalculia mean those terms would not be useful as disorder names or in the diagnostic criteria'.

Nevertheless, it is of value to reflect on some definitions. If we take a parallel with dyslexia, also a specific learning difficulty, the definition proposed by the Department for Education and Skills (DfES, 2001) has some resonance:

> Dyscalculia is a condition that affects the ability to acquire mathematical skills. Dyscalculic learners have a difficulty understanding simple number concepts, lack an intuitive grasp of numbers, and have problems learning number facts and procedures. Even if they produce a correct answer or use a correct method, they may do so mechanically and without confidence.

In the USA Developmental Dyscalculia (DD) was defined as:

> a specific learning disorder that is characterized by impairments in learning basic arithmetic facts, processing numerical magnitude, and performing accurate and fluent calculations. These difficulties must be quantifiably below what is expected for individuals' chronological age, and must not be caused by poor educational or daily activities or by intellectual impairments. (American Psychiatric Association, 2013)

Both definitions focus on early mathematical skills. They do not look at higher levels of mathematics such as algebra. This makes sense for several reasons. Mathematics is very developmental. Concepts build and develop as numeracy progresses. For example, addition is rooted in counting, multiplication is rooted in repeated addition and algebra is rooted in arithmetic. If learners do not understand numbers, they are not likely to learn number facts. Compounding this difficulty, they are not likely to develop linking strategies that would support deficits in long-term memory for these facts. This combination of poor retrieval of facts and poor number sense, which inhibits the development of compensatory strategies, has a hugely negative influence on learning mathematics and often depresses motivation.

At the start of my lectures for teachers I often ask them about lack of motivation from students in mathematics lessons and when this occurs in enough pupils for them to notice. The modal response I get, and this is the same for many countries worldwide, is at seven years old. The cognitive problems create affective problems such as worry, shame, anxiety, low self-esteem and poor motivation. This vicious circle, which often leads to learned helplessness, starts far too soon in children's mathematical learning history.

There are implications with the focus on early arithmetic in these definitions of dyscalculia. Mathematically, it means that pupils who fall behind in the early years will be handicapped by the impact of dyscalculia and mathematics learning difficulties on learning the fundamental facts and concepts, and thus on future attempts to learn mathematics (Geary, 2013). It also means that intervention for older (and adult) learners will almost certainly have to go back to basic concepts.

Dyscalculia, mathematics learning difficulties and research

A thorough review of the research into dyscalculia was provided by Ramaa and Gowramma in 2002. Their review remains apposite today in that it highlighted the key factors that contribute to dyscalculia (and thus also mathematics learning difficulties):

- A deficiency in retrieval of number facts and the ability to solve story problems (Russell and Ginsberg, 1984)
- Perseveration of counting strategies and counting errors (Geary, 1990)
- Persistence of fact retrieval deficits (Ostad, 1997)
- Fact retrieval deficits due to speed of processing (Ackerman and Dykman, 1995)
- Difficulties with story problems (Parmer et al., 1996)
- A delay or difficulty with conservation, seriation and classification (Ramaa, 1990)
- Extra stress, anxiety and depression (Magne, 1991)

And, from Kaufman et al. (2003), the specific problems exhibited by children having arithmetic difficulties are:

- Mastering the skills pre-requisite for arithmetic achievement
- Mastering the basic computational skills, time and money concepts
- Acquiring conceptual knowledge

A further review of research identifies the main factors involved in dyscalculia and mathematical learning difficulties as:

- Perseveration of counting strategies
- Recall of basic facts
- Speed of working (including speed of retrieval of facts and procedures)
- Working memory and short-term memory
- A lack of understanding of place value
- Word problems and problem solving

These are addressed in more detail below.

Perseveration of counting strategies and an understanding of place value

The first procedure that is taught in arithmetic is counting. Children learn how to count forwards, one at a time, probably using their fingers as tallies. This may well start as a task for memory rather than as an introduction to the base 10 system and place value. Children are more likely to practise counting up than counting down. Counting on fingers restricts the number of tallies to 10, whereas tallying on paper enables the child to use as many tallies as he or she needs. Our 10 fingers are, of course, the reason we have a base 10 system of numbers. If we counted like the Babylonians, we would use our thumb as the pointer to count the segments of the remaining four digits (fingers) on a hand, giving base 12.

Counting up is adding one each time and sets the foundations for addition. Counting down is subtracting one each time and sets the foundations for subtraction. As the child's skills develop, then he or she should be able to count up and back in chunks, for example, in twos or tens. This is a further stage in developing the concepts and skills of addition and subtraction and may well be linked to the ability to subitise.

Once counting goes beyond nine, the last single-digit number, then an understanding of place value is essential. If the child does not progress from counting in ones then he or she will not develop arithmetical skills, nor will he or she understand later topics in mathematics, such as algebra. Unfortunately, failure in mathematics is usually cumulative and this has consequences for intervention. As an example of the extension of place value knowledge, to measurement, my research in the UK (Chinn, 2013) showed that only 51% of 15-year-old students could correctly convert 5.67 km to metres. This figure, and others that are uncomfortably similar, add evidence for the extent of mathematical learning difficulties in the UK.

Speed of working (including speed of retrieval of facts and procedures)

From the perspective of knowing and understanding what children need to learn in order to become proficient in arithmetic and mathematics, it is clear that a deficit in any one of the factors listed on the previous page will create learning problems, but the extent of the impact may also depend on the interactions of several factors. For example, the culture of mental arithmetic is that the computation should not only be done accurately, but quickly. The same culture of answering quickly applies to the retrieval of basic facts. It is an expectation that they will be retrieved accurately and quickly. Many learners with special cognitive needs, whatever those needs may be, are slower than average to process information. If success and positive feedback is dependent on speed, then many children, and adults, with learning difficulties will fail. And anxiety can exacerbate the problem. Anxiety often has a debilitating effect on performance. The demand to do things quickly, especially things a pupil finds difficult, is likely to create anxiety, and anxiety can depress working memory (Ashcraft et al., 1998)

Recall of basic facts

One of the 'Key Findings' from the National Research Council's seminal book *How People Learn* (Bransford et al., 2000) is that learners 'must have a deep foundation of factual knowledge' (but also see later). What we may have never discussed for mathematics is just what constitutes the essential knowledge needed to create this deep foundation. In terms of basic facts, it seems that the understanding of what constitutes a deep foundation is based on convention and mathematics culture, rather than scientific investigation. For example, prior to decimalisation in the UK, knowing via rote learning the 12-times facts was considered as essential. Surprisingly, our current Ministry of Education (2015) considers this to remain an essential requirement in this age of decimalisation. So, first, we have to ask from the point of view of mathematical necessity, 'What facts are essential?' Then we have to ask, 'What facts do many people find difficult to retrieve from memory?' Well, the answer lies in what people can memorise. My experience, working in the UK and abroad, of asking teachers which multiplication facts they have found most children and adults remember is that these are the 10×, 5×, 2× and 1× facts. Just how much the inability to learn all the other basic facts contributes to a learning difficulty will depend on the specific demands of the mathematics curriculum and the way it is taught. This particular issue is a good test of the attitude, empathy and understanding of teachers and tutors (and curriculum designers) towards their learners. If they believe that practice and rote learning alone will eventually triumph, then reality will disappoint and the consequences may well be to create significant anxiety, low self-esteem and poor motivation in many learners, irrespective of their age.

Word problems and problem solving

Bryant et al. (2000) surveyed 391 teachers in the USA, asking them what they considered to be the most significant weaknesses for students with learning difficulties in mathematics.

The results remain illuminating and pertinent for the education of all children. The first three items, out of 33, were:

1. Has difficulty with word problems
2. Has difficulty with multi-step problems
3. Has difficulty with the language of mathematics

Although the research was carried out in the USA, the results are echoed in many other countries.

Word problems should test the learner's understanding of numbers and mathematics concepts. Unfortunately, as Boaler (2009) observes for mathematics problems:

> Students come to know that they are entering a realm in which commonsense and real world knowledge are not needed.

The objective of testing understanding by using word problems may not be achieved if the learner is not engaged in the task. It could be that a student's perception is that word problems are written to confuse, or to catch them out when they are tempted to use simplistic, formulaic strategies. For example, the problem:

> Mark has two more pens than James. Mark has eight pens. How many pens does James have?'

involves only two numbers and thus no distracting number or extra numbers that suggest the probability of a (much more challenging) two-step problem. The numbers, eight and two, are simple and the vocabulary is easily decoded. A pupil may seek out the 'operation word', in this case 'more' and then add the two numbers without any deeper analysis. The question actually requires a subtraction, 8 − 2 = 6. It's not the vocabulary. The reading level is quite low. It's the comprehension. It's spotting the trap. It's about being bothered about who has how many pens.

Multi-step problems are not open to such simple, expedient (even if imperfect) strategies.

The vocabulary of maths creates at least two problems. First there is the problem that everyday words, for example 'and' take on a new meaning in mathematics, so learners have to abandon their previous interpretation and adopt to how mathematics uses the vocabulary. They have to translate English into Mathematics. Imprecise words take on precise meanings in mathematics. It is the nature of the subject.

Secondly there are some inconsistencies in the vocabulary of mathematics. Unfortunately, for this aspect of mathematics, we all seek consistency (Cialdini, 2007) because consistency helps us to focus on important new issues. Insecure learners seem to have a particular need for consistency. For example, in mathematics the vocabulary for the first two-digit numbers after 10 is inconsistent. This starts with 'eleven' and 'twelve' which are exceptions and then moves on to the words we use for the 'teen' numbers. Their linguistic structure gives the unit digit before the 10 as in sixteen (six-ten), but we write the symbols as 16 (ten-six). The vocabulary does not support the logic of place value in the first two-digit numbers that children encounter.

Another choice and consistency issue is that in English we also have a range of words that can mean add and subtract, and choices for multiply and divide. Insecure learners would be more comfortable if there were only one word for each operation so that they could focus on the computation.

Both of the examples above feature in children's early experiences of mathematics. As they seek to make sense of information and find patterns, the language and vocabulary confounds them. Teachers have to be skilled at mediating this potentially influential insecurity in learning.

Working memory and short-term memory

There is little doubt that good working and short-term memories are essential pre-requisites for many areas of mathematics, most notably, mental arithmetic. Gathercole and Alloway (2008) note that 'mental arithmetic requires the storage of arbitrary numerical information, but the retrieval and application of number rules that may not have yet been securely learned'. The questions asked for mental arithmetic will demand short-term memory in order to recall the question accurately and working memory will be necessary at a level that matches the number of steps required to solve the problem. A poor retrieval of basic facts will exacerbate working memory problems.

The prevalence of dyscalculia

It is difficult to make a precise judgment of the prevalence of dyscalculia since there is not an 'absolute' definition as yet. Bugden and Ansari (2015) describe the current situation for developmental dyscalculia (DD):

> It is evident that current findings in the DD literature are contradictory, and there is no clear conclusion as to what causes DD. Furthermore, there is no universally agreed upon criteria for diagnosing children with DD, and as a result, it is difficult for researchers to make conclusions about what underlying cognitive mechanisms impair DD children's ability to learn basic arithmetic.

However, the research shows a range of values, varying, in part, because of the lack of an authoritative definition. The consensus of research papers is that prevalence is around 5%. One of the earliest studies by Lewis et al. (1994) in the UK suggested that prevalence was around 3.3%. Hein et al. (2000) in Germany found a prevalence of 6.6%. Ramaa and Gowramma (2002) carried out two studies in India using different criteria and found 5.5–6.0%

of their subjects were dyscalculic. In these studies the percentage of girls presenting with dyscalculia was approximately equal to the percentage of boys. This is not usually the case with other learning difficulties and special needs.

In the USA, the term, 'mathematics learning difficulties' is used to describe the bottom quartile of achievers. The existence of this cohort is, sadly, undeniable in the UK. Government-funded research in England (Rashid and Brooks, 2010) into the levels of attainment in literacy and numeracy, 1948–2009, showed that 22% of 16–19-year-olds were functionally innumerate and that this has remained at the same level for at least 20 years. It seems that England has not been able to address the problem of mathematics learning difficulties.

Being good at mathematics

To complement the initial focus on difficulties in mathematics, it is useful to consider what skills and knowledge are considered necessary for success. Krutetskii (1976) listed the 'Components of Mathematical Ability' as:

- An ability to formalise maths material (to abstract oneself from concrete numerical relationships)
- An ability to generalise and abstract oneself from the irrelevant
- An ability to operate with numbers and other symbols
- An ability for sequential, segmented, logical reasoning
- An ability to shorten the reasoning process
- An ability to reverse a mental process
- Flexibility of thought
- A mathematical memory
- An ability for spatial concepts

Unfortunately, these skills are often weak in children with specific learning difficulties, for example, dyspraxia (developmental coordination disorder) is often associated with poor spatial abilities. As with other comments of this nature that are written in this chapter, this is not meant to imply that nothing can be done to alleviate or circumvent problems. What students with learning difficulties need are teaching methods that do not assume that everyone is a perfect learning-machine. They need methods that are relevant and appropriate to their learning profile.

Diagnosis

Diagnosis is another circular concept. Diagnosis will depend on the definition used for dyscalculia. This is not an issue for mathematical learning difficulties. Butterworth (2005) considers 'numerosity' to be the underlying factor that causes dyscalculia. His 'Dyscalculia

Screener' (2003), a computer-based tool, has test items that assess subitising (dot enumeration) and number comparison (numerical stroop) as pre-requisite skills that underlie ability with numbers. Chinn (2012) suggests using a range of tests and informal diagnostic activities that probe many of the underlying problems that may result in mathematical learning difficulties. A critical part of the protocol is a dialogue with the child or adult.

If we want to know how a learner thinks and approaches mathematics, it makes sense to ask them rather than guess. An educational diagnosis should also guide intervention. Diagnosis is something you do *with* the student. Assessment is something you do *to* the student.

Intervention and programmes for learning

Intervention and indeed all teaching, since there will inevitably be students, often undiagnosed, with different levels of different learning difficulties in every class (and very few perfect learners) should take into account learning profiles. If the programme does not cater for poor working memory, a limited long-term mathematical memory and speed of working then, just because of these three factors alone, many students with learning difficulties will fail. The most efficacious way of addressing these factors is to teach for understanding, drawing on an empathetic understanding of these issues. This should include, for example, the inter-linking of facts and procedures to support memory deficits. As with all expectations and targets, these should be individual, flexible and realistic. At this time we do not have sufficient evidence as to what is efficacious and with which learner profiles.

One of the hardest challenges for teachers, especially when working with older students, is to persuade their learners that intervention is going to be most effective if it starts at the point where learning is secure, partly to address the situation identified by Buswell and Judd (1925). The programme will have to be based on a clear understanding of the structure of the numeracy which has to be delivered, but with the learning profiles of the students clearly in mind. A teacher at one of my training courses explained that she had tried division by 'chunking' but it didn't work because her students could not subtract. Subtraction is an integral component of the traditional division process, so the student was not ready for division. Progression has to follow a full pathway of relevant, pre-requisite topics.

There is another problem in England. School students have to take a national examination at age 16 years. If they enter secondary school at age 11 years with a mathematics age of, say, 8 years, the inference from this is that they have made approximately six months' progress per school year to date. If the intervention increases the progress rate to twelve months per school year, they will still be three years behind as they approach the examination. Catch-up is a challenging undertaking. This situation makes it clear that precision, small step-by-step teaching cannot be the main answer. It is just too slow for catch-up.

Any teaching programme will have to consider a number of key issues. The research found in two key sources is extensive and compulsive. 'How People Learn' (Bransford et al., 2000) provides the findings of a two–year study conducted by the Committee on

Developments in the Science of Learning of the National Research Council (NRC) of the USA. The three key findings are:

1. Students come to the classroom with preconceptions about how the world works. If their initial understanding is not engaged they may fail to grasp the new concepts and information that are taught, or they may learn them for the purposes of a test but revert to their preconceptions outside the classroom.

This finding reflects, again, the conclusions of Buswell and Judd (1925) that the first learning experience of a new topic provides strong input to the brain. If the first learning is wrong, it is hard to correct later. This should be a major caution about an overzealous application of the pedagogy of 'mastery' to all learners (Chinn, 2014).

2. To develop competence in an area of inquiry, students must: (a) have a deep foundation of factual knowledge, (b) understand facts and ideas in the context of a conceptual framework, and (c) organise knowledge in ways that facilitate retrieval and application.

It is parts (b) and (c) that make this key finding apposite for learners who are unable to achieve the commonly held perception of 'a deep foundation of factual knowledge'. The characteristic of mathematics that makes this the case is the potential to interlink facts and operations to work out those facts that are so difficult to remember.

3. A 'metacognitive' approach to instruction can help students learn to take control of their own learning by defining learning goals and monitoring their progress in achieving them. Learners need to be encouraged to think about their thinking.

John Hattie (Hattie, 2009) carried out a meta-analysis of thousands of research papers on what made for effective educational programmes. He found that the highest effects accrued when teachers provided feedback data or recommendations to the students and that the programmes with the greatest effects used strategy-based methods.

Although Hattie's findings are aimed at the whole learning spectrum, they have particular relevance for students with special needs in mathematics.

Returning to the first key finding of the NRC. It concerns pre-conceptions. Learners try to make sense of what they are trying to learn. Often this involves looking for patterns and relating the new information to something they already know. Unguided learning can result in misconceptions. I started teaching in the 1960s when learning by discovery was the big educational thing. These were dangerous times in education, especially when the law of unintended consequences is ignored. If the child discovers incorrectly, then once again, the Buswell and Judd findings become very pertinent.

As an example of lack of pattern in number, consider a child's first encounter with two-digit numbers. Two-digit numbers are the first experience of place value, a sophisticated concept which is vital to understanding numbers and how mathematics develops. The symbols, 11, 12, 13 and so on, have logic, as symbols, but as English words they do not make semantic sense.

With fractions the situation is reversed. It is the symbols that create the problem. The semantics of 'one fifth plus two fifths' suggest an answer of 'three fifths'. The symbols,

$$\frac{1}{5} + \frac{2}{5} \text{ suggest an answer of } \frac{3}{10}$$

There is a danger that, without developing their understanding of mathematics, children will simply rely on their memory of a previous concept and rely on consistency. In this fraction example the child is likely to apply the belief that, '+ means add' and apply that to both the numerator and the denominator.

Manipulative materials, for example Dienes base-10 blocks, are often advocated as a way of helping learners with learning difficulties. However, the connection between materials and learning is far from straightforward. Hattie's research survey found that the use of manipulatives had a medium impact on learning. Different manipulatives have different characteristics and may work well for illustrating some concepts but not others. Also, not every learner 'sees' what the manipulatives are meant to show. Hart (1978) noted that for some children, 'bricks are bricks and sums are sums'. A skilled teacher selects the appropriate manipulative, links it to the symbols and the mathematics vocabulary, and makes it a stage in the learning process. The Singapore Model Method (Kho et al., 2009) resulted in significant gains when first introduced, but children became dependent on the models and reluctant to move to the exclusive use of symbols. The creators adjusted the method. It is the skill of the teacher and his or her empathy with the learners that makes manipulatives work. Manipulatives should be used to help learners develop concepts and not keep them at the concrete stage of learning.

Hattie found that the maths programmes with the greatest effect were strategy-based methods. It is noteworthy that research by Gray and Tall (1994) quoted in Boaler (2009) found that the lowest-achieving mathematics students did not use strategies, whereas the high achieving students did.

Linking facts can help retrieval, but can also help understanding. For example, computing 12×8 as $10 \times 8 = 80$, plus $2 \times 8 = 16$, giving 96 as the answer has benefits. It uses key (and easily remembered) products to access another product, by a method that is applicable to many other products. It rehearses the key facts, topping up memory. It introduces the concept of partial products for multiplication. There seems to be no reason why the 12× facts should be retrieved from memory rather than computed using a strategy that reinforces a mathematical concept.

Another examples of concept building is knowing that 10×8 is a development from $8 + 8 + 8 + 8 + 8 + 8 + 8 + 8 + 8 + 8$. Using 10×8 replaces nine additions with one multiplication. A large part of the early mathematics curriculum is about computing numbers in an efficient way. It is an important benefit of much of mathematics.

It is possible to look at the logical and inter-dependent progressions in mathematics and thus find where a learner is failing as well as where gaps in learning occur, but it is often the gaps that are low in the hierarchy that are likely to have the greatest impact. Knowing the structure, that is knowing both where the topic is heading and where it is rooted, is a key element in making the teaching of mathematics an ongoing diagnostic procedure. This reflects Hattie's observation (paraphrased) that teachers need to listen to learners, either directly or through the use of diagnostic worksheets. Teachers need to be able to analyse errors and to design worksheets using this skill. For learners with specific learning difficulties, this is even more efficacious if the teacher understands the profile of each learner. It makes communication, teaching and learning more empathetic and effective.

Summary

- Dyscalculia is a specific learning difficulty.
- Dyscalculics are a heterogeneous group.
- Dyscalculia is at the extreme end of a spectrum of mathematical learning difficulties.
- Wherever learners lie on that continuum, they require teaching that actively acknowledges their cognitive and affective profiles.
- More of the same, whether it be the procedures or the reliance on rote, will not work.
- Motivation will depend heavily on success, so the pedagogy has to be structured for success and structured to address failures in a way that does not destroy resilience in the learner.

Discussion points

- Do maths beliefs such as 'You have to answer quickly' handicap learning for children with difficulties?
- Is mastery an efficacious pedagogy for such learners?
- Why is an over-emphasis on rote learning still dominant in maths education when maths is a subject which allows learners to use core factual knowledge and concepts to develop and support learning more facts and knowledge?
- Can the mainstream learn from the 'outliers'?
- What can be done to make early learning more effective?
- What is the future for manipulatives in the digital age?

Further reading

Ashlock, R.B. (2010) *Error Patterns in Computation*, 10th edn. Boston: Allyn and Bacon.

Berch, D.B. and Mazzocco, M.M. (eds) (2007) *Why is Math so Hard for Some Children?* Baltimore: Paul Brookes.

Boaler, J. (2015) *The Elephant in the Classroom*, 2nd edn. London: Souvenir Press.

Bransford, J.D., Brown, A.L. and Cocking, R.R. (eds) (2000) *How People Learn*. Washington, DC: NRC.

Chinn, S. (2012) *More Trouble with Maths: A Complete Guide to Identifying and Diagnosing Mathematical Difficulties*. Abingdon: Routledge.

Chinn, S. (ed.) (2015) *The Routledge International Handbook of Dyscalculia and Mathematical Learning Difficulties*. London: Routledge.

Cialdini, R. (2007) *Influence: The Psychology of Persuasion*. New York: Collins.

Dowker, A. (2005) *Individual Differences in Arithmetic*. Hove: Psychological Press.

Hattie, J. (2009) *Visible Learning*. Abingdon: Routledge.

Useful websites

www.bdadyslexia.org.uk.

www.dyscalculia.org.

www.dyslexicadvantage.org.

www.mathsexplained.co.uk.

www.stevechinn.co.uk.

References

Ackerman, P.T. and Dykman, R.A. (1995) Reading disabled students with and without cormorbid arithmetic disability. *Developmental Neuropsychology*, 11: 351–71

American Psychiatric Association (2013) *Diagnostic and Statistical Manual of Mental Disorders*, 5th edn. Arlington, VA: American Psychiatric Association.

Ashcraft, M.H, Kirk, E.P. and Hopko, D. (1998) On the consequences of mathematics anxiety. In C. Donlan (ed.), *The Development of Mathematical Skills*. Hove: Psychology Press, pp. 175–96.

Boaler, J. (2015) *The Elephant in the Classroom*, 2nd edn. London: Souvenir Press.

Bransford, J.D., Brown, A.L and Cocking, R.R. (eds) (2000) *How People Learn*. Washington, DC: National Academy Press.

Bronner, A.F. (1917) *The Psychology of Special Abilities and Disabilities*. Boston: Little, Brown and Co.

Bryant, D.P., Bryant, B.R. and Hammill, D.D. (2000) Characteristic behaviours of students with LD who have teacher identified math weaknesses. *Journal of Learning Disabilities*, 33: 168–73.

Bugden, S. and Ansari, D. (2015) How can cognitive developmental neuroscience constrain our understanding of developmental dyscalculia? In S. Chinn (ed.), *The Routledge International Handbook of Dyscalculia and Mathematical Learning Difficulties*. London: Routledge, pp. 18–43.

Buswell, G.T. and Judd, C.M. (1925) Summary of educational investigations relating to arithmetic. *Supplementary Educational Monographs*. Chicago, IL: University of Chicago Press.

Butterworth, B. (2003) *The Dyscalculia Screener*. London: NFER-Nelson.

Butterworth, B. (2005) The development of arithmetical abilities. *Journal of Child Psychology and Psychiatry*, 46(1): 3–18.

Chinn, S. (2012) *More Trouble with Maths: A Complete Guide to Identifying and Diagnosing Mathematical Difficulties*. Abingdon: Routledge.

Chinn, S. (2013) Is the population really woefully bad at maths? *Mathematics Teaching*, 232: 25–8.

Chinn, S. (2014) Explainer: what is the mastery model of teaching maths? The Conversation. http://theconversation.com/explainer-what-is-the-mastery-model-of-teaching-maths-25636.

Chinn, S. (ed.) (2015) *The Routledge International Handbook of Dyscalculia and Mathematical Learning Difficulties*. London: Routledge.

Cialdini, R. (2007) *Influence: The Psychology of Persuasion*. New York: Collins.

DfES (2001) *The National Numeracy Strategy: Guidance to Support Children with Dyslexia and Dyscalculia*. London: DfES.

DSM-5 Neurodevelopmental Work Group. www.dsm5.org/Documents/Specific%20Learning%20Disorder%20Fact%20Sheet.pdf.

Gathercole, S. and Alloway, T.P. (2008) *Working Memory and Learning: A Practical Guide for Teachers*. London: Sage.

Geary, D.C. (1990) A componential analysis of an early deficit in mathematics. *Journal of Experimental Child Psychology*, 49: 363–83.

Geary, D.C. (2013) Early foundations for mathematics learning and their relation to learning disabilities. *Current Directions in Psychological Science*, 22(1): 23–7.

Gersten, R., Clarke, B. and Mazzocco, M.M. (2007) Historical and contemporary perspectives on mathematical learning disabilities. In D.B. Berch and M.M. Mazzocco (eds), *Why is Math so Hard for Some Children?* Grand Rapids, MI: Paul H. Brookes Publishing Co, pp. 7–28.

Hart, K. (1978) *Children's Understanding of Mathematics*. London: John Murray, pp. 11–16.

Hattie, J. (2009) *Visible Learning: A Synthesis of Over 800 Meta-analyses Relating to Achievement*. Abingdon: Routledge.

Hein, J., Bzufka, M.W. and Neumarker, K.J. (2000) The specific disorder of arithmetic skills. Prevalence studies in a rural and an urban population sample and their clinic-neuropsychological validation. *European Child and Adolescent Psychiatry*, 9 (Suppl. 2: II).

Hong, K.T., Mei, Y.S. and Lim, J. (2009) *The Singapore Model Method for Learning Mathematics*. Singapore: Ministry of Education.

Kaufman, L., Handl, P. and Thony, B. (2003) Evaluation of a numeracy intervention programme focusing on basic numerical knowledge and conceptual knowledge. *Journal of Learning Disabilities*, 36(6): 564–73.

Krutetskii, V.A. (1976) In J. Kilpatrick and I. Wirszup (eds), *The Psychology of Mathematical Abilities in School Children*. Chicago, IL: University of Chicago Press.

Lewis, C., Hitch, J.G. and Walker, P. (1994) The prevalence of specific arithmetic difficulties and specific reading difficulties in 9- to 10-year-old boys and girls. *Journal of Child Psychology and Psychiatry*, 35: 283–92.

Magne, O. (1991) *Dysmathematics – Facts and Theories Concerning Mathematics Learning for Handicapped Pupils*. Lund: Department of Educational and Pyschologic Research, Lund University.

Murray, E., Hillaire, G., Johnson, M. and Rappolt-Schlichtmann, G. (2015) Representing, acting, and engaging: UDL and mathematics. In S. Chinn (ed.), *The Routledge International Handbook of Dyscalculia and Mathematical Learning Difficulties*. London: Routledge, pp. 393–404.

Ostad, S.A. (1997) Developmental differences in addition strategies: A comparison of mathematically disabled and mathematically normal children. *British Journal of Educational Psychology*, 67: 345–57.

Parmer, R.S., Crawley, J.R. and Frazita, R.R. (1996) Word problem solving by children with and without mild disabilities. *Exceptional Children*, 62: 415–29.

Ramaa, S. (1990) *Study of Neuropsychological Processes and Logico-mathematical Structure among Dyscalculics*. NCERT Project Report. Mysore: Regional College of Education, NCERT.

Ramaa, S. and Gowramma, I.P. (2002) A comprehensive literature survey into dyscalculia and two thorough research studies. *Dyslexia*, 8(2): 67–85.

Rashid, S. and Brookes, G. (2010) *The Levels of Attainment in Literacy and Numeracy of 13–19-year-olds in England*. London: National Research and Development Centre for Adult Literacy and Numeracy.

Russell, R.L. and Ginsberg, H.P. (1984) Cognitive analysis of children's mathematic difficulties. *Cognition and Instruction*, 1: 217–44.

PART III

Syndromes and Barriers

Students with Down Syndrome in Inclusive Classrooms

Using Evidence-Based Practices

Iva Strnadová and David Evans

13

Learning objectives

This chapter will help readers to

- Understand the diagnostic criteria for Down syndrome
- Identify and discuss the differing patterns of development for students with Down syndrome
- Appreciate strategies that assist the cognitive, social and emotional development of a child with Down syndrome
- Consider educational practices and supports that assist students with Down syndrome access quality curriculum and post-school options
- Critically examine the transition processes for students with Down syndrome across school and beyond

---

Down syndrome is a genetic condition, and its development is established in the early development of cells at conception. Our bodies are made up of cells, and each of these cells comprises 23 pairs or 46 chromosomes. These chromosomes contain the genetic material that determines the functioning of our bodies. A person with Down syndrome is born with an additional chromosome; that is, the twenty-first 'pair' contains additional chromosomal material (World Health Organization, 2014). Down syndrome is often referred to as Trisomy 21; about 95% of people diagnosed with Down syndrome are born with an additional chromosome on the twenty-first 'pair'. Other types of Down syndrome include Translocation Down syndrome (i.e. the additional chromosome 21 has attached to another chromosome), and Mosaic Down syndrome (i.e. some cells have an additional chromosome).

The presence of an additional chromosome is where similarities between persons with Down syndrome end. All persons with Down syndrome beyond this point have their own unique characteristics, motivations, interests and preferences – like us all. Getting to know a person with Down syndrome on the basis of a label is something that should be avoided at all costs.

Persons with Down syndrome, as a result of their chromosomal structure, are diagnosed with an intellectual disability (Cunningham, 2011) and demonstrate a developmental delay (van Gameren-Oosterom et al., 2011). The extent of this disability differs across all persons with Down syndrome. Down Syndrome Victoria (www.downsyndromevictoria.org.au), for example, report that 120 physical features are used to describe a person with Down syndrome – and none of them are constant between each person. A child with Down syndrome may have low muscle tone, a single crease across the palm of the hand, a larger tongue, slanted eyes and rounded face with a flat profile. All these features are different between persons, and many can be addressed (e.g. low tone through physiotherapy sessions) or children grow out of these (e.g. difficulty with mouth and tongue).

Young persons with Down syndrome experience a number of health issues from birth, and throughout life, that occur at greater frequency than for many others in our community. A number of babies are born with heart conditions that can be treated soon after birth and managed through regular monitoring of their health (Cohen and Spenciner, 2009); young persons with Down syndrome may also experience various gastrointestinal problems (e.g. reflux, imperforate anus) (van Gameren-Oosterom et al., 2011). Throughout life, persons with Down syndrome require regular monitoring of their thyroid as this gland can result in a hormone imbalance leading to a range of difficulties (e.g. lethargy, weight gain, mental health issues). Amongst other health issues associated with Down syndrome is atlantoaxial insatiability. This occurs in a minority of children with Down syndrome, and is characterised by a hyper-mobility of the two bones in the neck just below the skull (Norberto, 2013). As with health issues with any child, educators should collaborate with parents, and with professionals in the area (e.g. medical staff, specialist staff).

Like all young children, a child with Down syndrome needs to engage in regular physical activity. During their formative years, children with Down syndrome sometimes develop physically at a different rate than other children, so activities may need to be adjusted to meet their needs (Cunningham, 2011).

As children with Down syndrome develop, they may experience delays in developing social behaviour (e.g. social skills, emotions). While not all young persons with Down syndrome develop social and emotional difficulties, it is more prevalent than in other groups within the community (Silverman, 2007; van Gameren-Oosterom et al., 2011). Young persons with Down syndrome are reported to show a reduced prevalence rate in relation to anxiety and depression (van Gameren-Oosterom et al., 2011).

Down syndrome is not hereditary. The prevalence of Down syndrome has been constant over the years/decade at about one in every 700–800 babies born (Guralnick et al., 2011; Silverman, 2007; van Gameren-Oosterom et al., 2011). Throughout history, babies with Down syndrome have been part of civilisation. Down syndrome is not a disease, and cannot be caught. Its chromosomal basis means that it can be identified prior to birth, and soon after birth. As a result, families make decisions about how they will prepare to raise a child with Down syndrome. Recent history tells us that persons with Down syndrome can lead a life like that of us all – given the opportunity and right to access quality services, education and support.

Learning characteristics of students with Down syndrome

As mentioned earlier in the chapter, most students with Down syndrome have intellectual disability. Among learning characteristics of these students belong increasing difficulties with keeping up academically, which can be caused by struggling with recalling what they previously learned. These difficulties in memory development have been referred to by a number of researchers (Richards, et al., 2015). Silverman (2007) and Davies (2008) furthermore refer to problems with verbal memory experienced by students with Down syndrome, while visuospatial memory is similar to in the mainstream population.

Difficulty in applying previously learned material to new tasks and situations is amongst learning characteristics of students with Down syndrome (Beirne-Smith et al., 2006; Cohen and Spenciner, 2009; Woodcock et al., 2013). This area of difficulty is usually referred to as problems with 'transfer and generalisation of knowledge and skills' (Richards et al., 2015: 162). Students with Down syndrome also need support in understanding abstract constructs and applying these to real-life situations (Parmenter, 2011). They are capable learners, but may require instruction to be systematic and explicit, including purposefully planned repetition in order to acquire skills (Woodcock et al., 2013). Teachers also need to be aware of the short attention span of these students, and that they have fewer learning strategies, but that this can be easily resolved in a mainstream school setting (Beirne-Smith et al., 2006; Bowman and Plourde, 2012; Woodcock et al., 2013). Teachers can address this by using Task Analysis, within which they break a complex task into a step-by-step instruction (Draper Rodriguez et al., 2015), and which was successfully used with this population for teaching academic skills (Courtade et al., 2010; Jimenez et al., 2008). Other learning strategies successfully used with this population include mnemonic strategies, graphic organisers and problem-solving strategies (Richards et al., 2015). It is crucial that teachers introduce diverse learning strategies to students with Down syndrome, and allow them opportunities to become acquainted with these and see which ones work for them. This is important: as evidenced by research, students with intellectual disabilities, including those with Down syndrome, use fewer learning strategies than their peers without this disability (Richards et al., 2015).

In terms of literacy and numeracy, students with intellectual disability (including those with Down syndrome) typically acquire reading, writing and mathematical skills with a delay (Beirne-Smith et al., 2006). This can be addressed by systematically promoting literacy (e.g. phonemic awareness, decoding, vocabulary, comprehension) and numeracy (e.g. number sense, problem-solving) across school, home and the community (Beirne-Smith et al., 2006). In terms of reading, a particular strength of students with Down syndrome is word identification, while word attack and reading comprehension are areas that require carefully developed and delivered programs (Fidler and Nadel, 2007).

Language development in students with Down syndrome has been a subject of research for decades. These students have stronger receptive language skills when compared to their expressive language skills (Fidler and Nadel, 2007). Speech intelligibility is often an issue, as it may lead to people lacking understanding of what a student with Down syndrome said, resulting in several repetitions. This can impact on social relationships of students with Down syndrome. Having knowledge about language development in this population of students is important for educators, so that they don't pitch their instruction only at the expressive language level.

Students with Down syndrome from birth may experience motor development delays (Lloyd et al., 2010) primarily due to hypertonia and hyperflexia (Davies, 2008). Ongoing early health issues (e.g. congenital heart disease, respiratory illness) can adversely influence motor development in the early years through restricted opportunity for movement, and hospitalisation (Pitetti et al., 2013). The development of gross motor milestones is delayed, but this does not prevent achievement of key motor milestones. Once the health of a young child with Down syndrome settles it is important, as for all children and youths, to undertake regular physical activity (e.g. play, sporting activities). Some of this activity may be best planned in collaboration with a physiotherapist and/or occupational therapist. This collaboration can help build professional knowledge about how to address the impact of non-typical motor tone, and how physical activity can be adapted to allow students with Down syndrome to access regular physical activity. Achieving good physical health is strongly linked to children and youths with Down syndrome achieving emotional and social success across the life span.

Social development is referred to as one of the strength of students with Down syndrome, mainly due to their eagerness to be involved and engaged in social interactions (Guralnick et al., 2011). Sociability and empathy are among a number of features that are described in literature as a behavioural phenotype of students with Down syndrome (McGuire and Chicoine, 2006; Wishart et al., 2007). However, students with Down syndrome also display difficulties with understanding social situations. Wishart (2007) focused on socio-cognitive skills of students with Down syndrome to conclude that these students experience difficulties in some aspects of socio-cognitive skills. Many students with Down syndrome struggle with developing age-appropriate social behaviours (Cohen and Spenciner, 2009), and in developing friendships (D'Haem, 2008). As a result, some people with Down syndrome experience social isolation and loneliness in their lives. One of the approaches that many mainstream schools take is establishing the Circle of Friends. This approach enhances inclusion of a student experiencing difficulties in establishing social relationships by involving his/her peers. An established Circle of Friends provides a support to a student with Down syndrome, and a space to learn and practice social skills, as well as problem-solving strategies useful in everyday life situations (Inclusive solutions, n.d.). However, relationships developed within these Circles may not continue outside of the school environment (D'Haem, 2008).

Students with Down syndrome worldwide engage in education programmes within the mainstream school environment. This is academically beneficial but students may remain isolated in their classes unless specific action is taken to engage them socially (McGuire and Chicoine, 2006). A contributing factor to success might be the presence of a teacher assistant, whose role is to support students with Down syndrome in mainstream classrooms and to facilitate peer interaction (Dolva et al., 2011). However, a teacher assistant can become a barrier between a student with Down syndrome and his/her peers (Broer et al., 2005). Dolva et al. (2011) concluded in their study of interactions between students with Down syndrome and their peers that one of the barriers to peer interactions is the difference in interests of students with Down syndrome and their peers without disability. Group work and teacher's planning for academic learning within these groups was commonly used in this study to facilitate peer and social relationships in mainstream classrooms.

Educational provision for students with Down syndrome

An early feature of the newborn child with Down syndrome (as it is with any child) is the development of relationships with the parents and family members (Landy, 2009). This development can be difficult for families; the family – if not prepared for the birth of a child with Down syndrome – may be working their way through stages of grief and/ or rejection. This in turn can impact on the relationships they build with the newborn child. On the other hand, the newborn may be irritable, may have other health issues (e.g. cardiac conditions requiring surgery) and not be welcoming of attention. These multiple sources of stress can lead to a breakdown in the development of attachment between the newborn and mother and family (van Hooste and Maes, 2003). Developing this attachment is important for longer-term relationships and learning (Bernardo et al., 2014; Landy, 2009).

In the early years, learning is best enhanced through the newborn being part of the family and extended community. It breaks down attitudinal barriers and builds opportunities for support of the child and family. An early intervention programme will provide some of these opportunities – where mother and newborn may be part of a supportive playgroup and a therapy group. These groups can assist in the development of key milestones through modelling and therapy (e.g. language development, mobility, gross and fine motor skills, play skills, social skills). These family-centred sessions can assist a newborn overcome some of the physical difficulties associated with Down syndrome (e.g. low muscle tone, difficulties with learning to walk), as well as address possible health issues. Well-organised experiences within the family, and the community, can have a positive, long-term impact on intellectual, physical and social development of a young child with Down syndrome (Guralnick, 2005).

It is key to remind oneself that young children with Down syndrome are more like their peers without Down syndrome than unlike. They learn by doing, by being provided supports to develop the full range of skills, all of which are inter-related. The best group to undertake the integration of areas of development is the family unit – with the support of early intervention or education agencies (Guralnick, 2008). These groups will also assist families in the transition of their child to school.

Students with Down syndrome have the same rights as all other students to an education. The right of equal access is mandated by a number of international documents, such as The Convention on the Rights of the Child (CRC) (UN General Assembly, 1989) and the Convention on the Rights of Persons with a Disability (CRPD) (UN General Assembly, 2006). And yet it was not that long ago that a child born with Down syndrome did not access an education 'on the same basis as' their peers without Down syndrome (Attorney-General's Department, 2006). It was only three decades ago that persons with Down syndrome spent every part of their day within the confines of an institution without contact with their family, or social opportunities with other members of the wider community.

Many young children with Down syndrome attend their neighbourhood or local main-stream school. A key consideration in transitioning to a school setting is maintaining the focus of the early childhood setting (e.g. language development, physical and motor programmes). There is no reason why a student with Down syndrome entering school should not be working towards the same content as their peers, maybe with adjustments and/or modifications (Ryndak et al., 2014). Students may benefit from new skills and knowledge being broken into smaller steps, presented on a regular basis to allow the student to retain them for later use. Presenting new tasks in a number of representations (e.g. visual, auditory, concrete materials, pictorial) can assist learning and memory. The use of visual cues and prompts can be of specific assistance for students with Down syndrome – as well as for a number of other students in the classroom.

A benefit of the student with Down syndrome attending the local school is the multiple opportunities to have social skills and conventions modelled (Hollingsworth et al., 2009). The student with appropriate supports can learn how language is used and interpreted; they can have social skills and conventions demonstrated so that they have the opportunity to examine the context in which they are used. Taking advantage of these opportunities does not emerge by itself, as the teacher and school community are a key part of this context.

They need to be prepared to support the inclusion of the student with Down syndrome, and be firmly committed to the idea that this student has the right to participate and benefit from an education like all other students.

As the years go by, the gap in learning between the student with Down syndrome and other students may become more evident (Buckley and Bird, 2002). It is at this time that the school culture, and links with the student and family, become important. The attitude of the wider community plays an important role – it can be barrier or a support. School programmes may well become more individualised (e.g. focusing on transition beyond school, self-care). This is where teachers and school staff may need professional support in working to meet the diverse needs of a young person with Down syndrome (e.g. development of alternative ways to present learning, use of technology to assist communication).

Discussion point

What can teachers do to make sure they are supporting a child or young person with Down syndrome effectively in their education? What challenges might they face?

The education of a young person with Down syndrome in the mainstream school setting can have significant benefits, or disadvantages. Proactive approaches to promoting social behaviour and peer interactions by classroom teachers can assist in the development of social behaviour (Guralnick et al., 2011). As students move through school, and mature, they develop their own social groups, independence and motivations. In a secondary school setting, for example, a young person with an intellectual disability may be accepted in the school setting but ignored in a social setting (e.g. not invited to birthday parties and social events) (Sipperstein et al., 2007). Family is important, but so is the chance to develop relationships with persons with similar backgrounds and interests. The school can play a part, but the family in many instances is left to pursue these activities alone. It is key, however, that the opportunity to engage with and be part of a community is maintained so that the young person with Down syndrome can develop as an individual.

Opportunities for education and lifelong learning do not have to – and, in fact, should not – end at the secondary education level. Traditionally, post-schooling life of people with intellectual disabilities (including those with Down syndrome) was depicted by restricted employment or day centre options. Despite the inclusion and human rights movement, it is still this population which is the least likely to participate in postsecondary education (Thoma et al., 2011), especially tertiary education or training (O'Brien et al., 2009). According to Neubert and Moon (2006), there are number of postsecondary education models, such as segregated, mixed and inclusive-individualised ones. In a segregated model, students with intellectual disabilities only attend courses designed and run for this population of students. An example of a mixed model of postsecondary education would be a separate course run for people with intellectual disabilities within a college or university campus (Westling et al., 2013). Within an inclusive-individualised model, students with intellectual disabilities receive tailored support 'in college/university courses for audit or credit' (O'Brien et al., 2009: 286).

Evidence-based practices

There are a number of evidence-based practices that can be used in mainstream schools to support all students, including those with Down syndrome. As mentioned previously, students with Down syndrome might need support to develop their social skills and age-appropriate behaviours. Among evidence-based practices that can be easily utilised in a classroom setting is video modelling. Video modelling is a well-established evidence-based practice, used especially (but not exclusively) with people with intellectual disabilities and autism spectrum disorders across their lifespan (Cumming et al., 2013). This evidence-based practice is based on a student watching a video of behaviours or skills s/he needs to develop, with the aim of him/her performing these behaviours/skills later on (Burton et al., 2013). Within this approach, both video modelling and self-video modelling approaches can be used. Advances in technology make this evidence-based approach even more accessible in mainstream schools. Mobile technology, such as tablets or smart phones, can be easily used, especially given the existing range and growing number of mobile applications (Draper Rodriguez et al., 2015).

In order to develop positive peer relationships, as well as to support students' learning; cooperative learning and peer-tutoring are evidence-based practices that benefit any students in a mainstream classroom, including those with Down syndrome. Cooperative learning is a strategy based on a number of components, such as interdependence among the group members, individual accountability of each and every member of a group, cooperation and evaluation (Mitchell, 2014). Peer-tutoring is used to practise acquired knowledge and skills, rather than to learn these. Peer-tutoring is used in different forms, from cross-age to class-wide tutoring (Mitchell, 2014). When using peer-tutoring, teachers need to train the tutors in approaches they will be using, set up the tutoring sessions, and supervise these.

When discussing evidence-based practices, parent involvement and support cannot be omitted. The research shows that when schools have a high level of collaboration with parents, test scores were 40% higher compared with other schools. Furthermore, students with actively involved parents are more likely to have better test results, and are more likely to continue on to further education (Henderson and Mapp, 2002). Mitchell (2014) distinguishes five different levels of parent involvement: (a) being informed; (b) taking part in activities; (c) dialogue and exchange of views; (d) taking part in decision making; and (e) having responsibility to act. There are a number of programmes supporting home–school collaboration, such as the Incredible Years Programme, and the Triple P-Positive Parenting Programme (Mitchell, 2014). There are various ways in which schools can support and nurture parents' involvement, such as recognising that parents are involved in their child's learning, irrespective of families' socio-economic and religious backgrounds. Finding ways to develop collaborative communication between parents and schools is of upmost importance (Carter et al., 2014).

Transition to post-school life

Transition to post-school life can be very exciting but also a challenging time for students with Down syndrome and their families. There are a number of evidence-based practices that can be used to optimise the transition process and the post-schooling outcomes for students with intellectual disabilities. Well thought-through transition planning is essential for students' post-school life success, and should start as early as possible. Transition planning needs to be student-focused, with the student having knowledge about the transition process, and being actively involved in it (Mazzotti et al., 2014). Yet, it is often students with intellectual disabilities, including those with Down syndrome, who have minimal or even no participation in transition planning (Davies and Beamish, 2009; Strnadová and Cumming, 2014). There are a number of instruction strategies that can be used to support students' active involvement, such as *Whose Future is it Anyway?* (Wehmeyer et al., 2004). It is essential that schools, parents and the student collaborate in a transition planning process and in developing a transition plan.

Development of students' academic, social, self-determination and functional life skills is another important component of a transition process (Mazzotti et al., 2014). The development of these skills needs to start as early as possible, and across all environments. It is important that parents provide opportunities for their children with Down syndrome to take responsibility for some of the household chores. Volunteering in the community is another option for developing employment and social skills. Self-determination skills are of primary importance for students' positive post-school outcomes (Davies and Beamish, 2009), and should be a primary component of transition planning (Gil, 2007).

A focus of transition planning may be to examine potential employment opportunities for students with Down syndrome. There is strong evidence to suggest that adolescents with Down syndrome can benefit from supported employment opportunities (Wehman et al., 2014). With community and agency support, persons with intellectual disability are employed in open settings (e.g. local supermarkets, office-based positions). Employers are empowered to support persons with disability who in turn are supported to advocate for themselves about their work experience (Wehman et al., 2014).

Another feature of the transition process may be to address issues of independence and self-care (Kellems and Morningstar, 2010). Through engaging with the person with Down syndrome, their family and other interagency groups, plans can be put in place to build long-term security. While employment has been shown to be important in post-school life, the skills needed to live independently as well as to be social and engaged with one's community are also important. Achieving this outcome can be enhanced through including it as part of transition planning.

Case study

Nathan is a 16-year-old student with Down syndrome, attending a mainstream high school. He lives with his parents and younger sister in a town house in a metropolitan city. Nathan plans for the future are to have a family and to work in a café, as he loves meeting new people. Nathan's transition team is established, consisting of Nathan, his parents, his class teacher, and his speech and occupational therapists. Nathan's teacher explains to all parties involved the purpose of the team, as well as what is expected from all involved. Nathan delivers a PowerPoint presentation he has prepared about himself, his interests, strengths, preferences and dreams for future. This starts a discussion and development of Nathan's Individual Transition Plan (ITP), which is mainly focused on Nathan's self-determination, and social skills. An agreement is made with a café owner in his neighbourhood for Nathan's work placement. In order to practise his social skills, Nathan uses two mobile applications: *The Conversation Builder Teen*, which allows him to further develop his conversation skills in his own time; and *The Personal Social Skills – Workplace*, with which he can practice skills related to appropriate behaviour at the workplace.

Future considerations

As discussed in this chapter, students with Down syndrome are more alike to other students than different. Through being involved in their own life development, and provided with adequate and evidence-based support, they are most likely to succeed and live to lead a productive, quality and meaningful life in our society. Teachers need to keep reflecting on their professional knowledge and how best to provide a quality programme for students with Down syndrome. Parents can engage with other families and groups outside of the education environment through support groups found in most countries worldwide (see Useful websites below).

Summary

- Students with Down syndrome have learning strengths, as well as challenges, which can be addressed by using evidence-based practices.
- It is vital to ensure that the person with Down syndrome is at the centre of all planning to develop self-determination skills and independence.
- Evidence-based practices are desirable to use, not only for students with Down syndrome, but also for all students.
- Transition planning is essential for the successful transition of students with Down syndrome into a post-school life.

Further reading

Research articles

Abbeduto, L., Warren, S.F. and Conners, F.A. (2007) Language development in Down syndrome: from the prelinguistic period to the acquisition of literacy. *Mental Retardation and Developmental Disabilities Research Reviews*, 13: 247–61.

Bruce, S., Parnell, E.P. and Zayyad, M. (2008) Assessment and instruction of self-recognition. *Teaching Exceptional Children*, 41(1): 36–41.

Buckley, S., Bird, G., Sacks, B. and Archer, T. (2006) A comparison of mainstream and special education for teenagers with Down syndrome: implications for parents and teachers. *Down Syndrome Research and Practice*, 9(3): 54–67.

Bull, E. (2008) Handling the transfer to secondary school. *Down Syndrome Research and Practice*, 12(2): 112–77.

Davis, A.S. (2008) Children with Down syndrome: implications for assessment and intervention in the school. *School Psychology Quarterly*, 23(2): 271–81.

De Graaf, G., Van Hove, G. and Haveman, M. (2013) More academics in regular schools? The effect of regular versus special school placement on academic skills in Dutch primary school students with Down syndrome. *Journal of Intellectual Disability Research*, 57(1): 21–38.

De Graaf, G., Van Hove, G. and Haveman, M. (2014) A quantitative assessment of educational integration of students with Down syndrome in the Netherlands. *Journal of Intellectual Disability Research*, 58(7): 625–36.

Dolva, A.S., Hemmingsson, H., Gustavsson, A. and Borell, L. (2010) Children with Down syndrome in mainstream schools: peer interaction in activities. *European Journal of Special Needs Education*, 25(3): 283–94.

(Continued)

(Continued)

Gallagher, K.M., van Kraayenoord, C.E., Jobling, A. and Moni, K.B. (2002) Reading with Abby: a case study of individual tutoring with a young adult with Down syndrome. *Down Syndrome Research and Practice*, 8(2): 59–66.

Lightfoot, L., and Bond, C. (2013) An exploration of primary to secondary school transition planning for children with Down's syndrome. *Educational Psychology in Practice*, 29(2): 163–79.

Virji-Babul, N., Kerns, K., Zhou, E., Kapur, A. and Shiffrar, M. (2006) Perceptual-motor deficits in children with Down syndrome: implications for intervention. *Down Syndrome Research and Practice*, 10(2): 74–82.

Books

Bruni, M. (2006) *Fine Motor Skills for Children with Down Syndrome: A Guide for Parents And Professionals*, 2nd edn. Woodbine House.

Cunningham, C. (2011) *Down Syndrome: An Introduction for Parents and Carers*. London: Souvenir Press.

Horstmeier, D.A. (2004) *Teaching Math to People with Down Syndrome and Other Hands-On Learners: Basic Survival Skills*, 1st edition. Bethesda, MD: Woodbine House.

Kumin, L. (2012) *Early Communication Skills for Children with Down Syndrome: A Guide for Parents and Professionals*, 3rd edn. Bethesda, MD: Woodbine House.

Winders, C.P. (2013) *Gross Motor Skills for Children with Down Syndrome: A Guide for Parents and Professionals*, 2nd edn. Bethesda, MD: Woodbine House.

Useful websites

Down Syndrome Association: www.downs-syndrome.org.uk.

Down Syndrome Education International: www.dseinternational.org/en-us.

Down Syndrome Victoria: www.downsyndromevictoria.org.au.

Down Syndrome Western Australia: dsawa.asn.au/children/education/teaching-strategies.html.

National Secondary Transition Technical Assistance Center: nsttac.org.

Universal Design for Learning: www.cast.org/udl.

World Down Syndrome Day: www.worlddownsyndromeday.org/about-wdsd.

References

Attorney-General's Department, Australian Government (2006) *Disability Standards for Education 2005, plus guidance notes*. Canberra: Commonwealth of Australia.

Beirne-Smith, M., Patton, J.R. and Kim, S.H. (2006) *Mental Retardation. An Introduction to Intellectual Disabilities*. Upper Saddle River, NJ: Pearson, Merrill Prentice Hall.

Bernardo, S., Rennie, M., Little, C. and Evans, D. (2014, August) 'Investigating attachment and young children with complex needs'. Paper presented at the Early Childhood Intervention Australia Conference, Gold Coast.

Bowman, S.L., and Plourde, L.A. (2012) Andragogy for teen and young adult learners with intellectual disabilities: learning, independence, and best practices. *Education*, 132(4): 789–98.

Broer, S.M., Doyle, M.B. and Giangreco, M.F. (2005) Perspectives of students with intellectual disabilities about their experiences with paraprofessional support. *Exceptional Children*, 71(4): 415–30.

Buckley, S. and Bird, G. (2002) Cognitive development and education: perspectives on Down syndrome from a twenty-one year research programme. In M. Cuskelly, A. Jobling and S. Buckley (eds), *Down Syndrome across the Life Span*. London: Whurr, pp. 66–80.

Burton, C.E., Anderson, D.H., Parter, M.A. and Dyches, T.T. (2013) Video self-modeling on an iPad to teach functional math skills to adolescents with autism and intellectual disability. *Focus on Autism and Other Developmental Disabilities*, 28(2): 67–77.

Carter, E., Brock, M. and Trainor, A. (2014) Transition assessment and planning for youth with severe intellectual and developmental disabilities. *Journal of Special Education*, 47(4): 245–55.

Cohen, L.G. and Spenciner, L.J. (2009) *Teaching Students with Mild and Moderate Disabilities. Research-based Practices*, 2nd edn. Upper Saddle River, NJ: Pearson Education, Inc.

Courtade, G.R., Browder, D.M., Spooner, F. and DiBiase, W. (2010) Training teachers to use an inquiry-based task analysis to teach science to students with moderate and severe disabilities. *Education and Training in Autism and Developmental Disabilities*, 45: 378–99.

Cumming, T., Draper Rodriguez, C. and Strnadová, I. (2013) Aligning iPad applications with evidence-based practices in inclusive and special education. In S. Keengwe (ed.), *Pedagogical Applications and Social Effects of Mobile Technology Integration*. Hershey, PA: IGI Global, pp. 55–78.

Cunningham, C. (2011) *Down Syndrome: An Introduction for Parents and Carers*. London: Souvenir Press.

Davis, A.S. (2008) Children with Down syndrome: implications for assessment and intervention in the school. *School Psychology Quarterly*, 23(2): 271–81.

Davies, M.D. and Beamish, W. (2009) Transitions from school for young adults with intellectual disability: parental perspectives on 'life as an adjustment'. *Journal of Intellectual and Developmental Disability*, 34(3): 248–57.

D'Haem, J. (2008) Special at school but lonely at home: an alternative friendship group for adolescents with Down syndrome. *Down Syndrome Research and Practice*, 12(2): 107–11.

Dolva, A.S., Gustavsson, A., Borell, L. and Hemmingsson, H. (2011) Facilitating peer interaction – support to children with Down syndrome in mainstream schools. *European Journal of Special Needs Education*, 26(2): 201–13.

Draper Rodriguez, C., Strnadová, I. and Cumming, T. (2015) Implementing iPad and mobile technologies for students with intellectual disabilities. In N. Silton (ed.), *Recent Advances in Assistive Technologies to Support Children with Developmental Disorders*. Hershey, PA: IGI Global, pp. 27–44.

Fidler, D.J. and Nadel, L. (2007) Education and children with Down syndrome: neuroscience, development and intervention. *Mental Retardation and Developmental Disabilities Research Reviews*, 13: 262–71.

Gil, L.A. (2007) Bridging the transition gap from high school to college: preparing students with disabilities for a successful post-secondary experience. *Teaching Exceptional Children*, 40(2): 12–15.

Guralnick, M. (2005) Early intervention for children with intellectual disabilities: current knowledge and future prospects. *Journal of Applied Research in Intellectual Disabilities*, 18: 313–24.

Guralnick, M. (2008) International perspectives on early intervention: a search for common ground. *Journal of Early Intervention*, 30: 90–101.

Guralnick, M.J., Connor, R.T. and Clark Johnson, L. (2011) Peer-related social competence of young children with Down syndrome. *American Journal of Intellectual and Developmental Disabilities*, 116(1): 48–64.

Henderson, A.T. and Mapp, K.L. (2002) *A New Wave of Evidence: The Impact of School, Family, and Community Connections on Student Achievement*. Austin, TX: Southwest Educational Development Laboratory.

Hollingsworth, H., Boone, H. and Crais, E. (2009) Individualised inclusion plans at work in early childhood classrooms. *Young Exceptional Children*, 13(1): 19–35.

Inclusive Solutions (n.d.) What is a circle of friends? Downloaded from: http://inclusive-solutions.com/circle-of-friends.

Jimenez, B.A., Browder, D.M. and Courtade, G.R. (2008) Teaching an algebraic equation to high school students with moderate developmental disabilities. *Education and Training in Developmental Disabilities*, 43: 266–74.

Kellems, R. and Morningstar, M. (2010) Tips for transition. *Teaching Exceptional Children*, 43(2): 60–8.

Landy, S. (2009) *Pathways to Competence: Encouraging Healthy Social and Emotional Development in Young Children*. Baltimore, MD: Paul H. Brookes Publishing Co.

Lloyd, M., Burghardt, A., Ulrich, D. and Angulo-Barroso, R. (2010) Physical activity and walking onset in infants with Down syndrome. *Adapted Physical Activity Quarterly*, 27: 1–16.

Mazzotti, V.L., Test, D.W. and Mustian, A.L. (2014) Secondary transition evidence-based practices and predictors: implications for policymakers. *Journal of Disability Policy Studies*, 25(1): 5–18.

McGuire, D. and Chicoine, B. (2006) *Mental Wellness in Adults with Down Syndrome. A Guide to Emotional and Behavioural Strengths and Challenges*. Bethesda, MD: Woodbine House.

Mitchell, D. (2014) *What Really Works in Special and Inclusive Education: Using Evidence-based Teaching Strategies*. London: Routledge.

Neubert, D.A. and Moon, M.S. (2006) Postsecondary settings and transition services for students with intellectual disability: models and research. *Focus on Exceptional Children*, 39(4): 1–8.

Norberto, A. (2013) Atlantoaxial instability in Down syndrome. Downloaded from: http://emedicine.medscape.com/article/1180354–overview.

O'Brien, P., Shelvin, M., O'Keefe, M., Fitzgerald, S., Curtis, S. and Kenny, M. (2009) Opening up a whole new world for students with intellectual disabilities within a third level setting. *British Journal of Learning Disabilities*, 37: 285–92.

Parmenter, T. (2011) What is intellectual disability? How is it assessed and classified? *International Journal of Disability, Development and Education*, 58(3): 303–19.

Pitetti, K., Baynard, T. and Agiovlasitis, S. (2013) Children and adolescents with Down syndrome, physical fitness and physical activity. *Journal of Sport and Health Science*, 2: 47–57.

Richards, S.B., Brady, M.P. and Taylor, R.L. (2015) *Cognitive and Intellectual Disabilities. Historical Perspectives, Current Practices, and Future Directions*, 2nd edn. London: Routledge.

Ryndak, D., Taub, D., Jorgensen, C., Gonsier-Gerdon, J., Arndt, K., Sauer, J., Ruppar, A., Morningstar, M. and Allcock, H. (2014) Policy and the impact on placement, involvement, progress in general education: critical issues that require rectification. *Research and Practice for Persons with Severe Disabilities*, 39: 65–74.

Silverman, W. (2007) Down syndrome: cognitive phenotype. *Mental Retardation and Developmental Disabilities Research Reviews*, 13: 228–36.

Sipperstein, G., Parker, R., Bardon, J. and Widman, K. (2007) A national study of youth attitudes towards the inclusion students with intellectual disability. *Exceptional Children*, 73: 435–55.

Strnadová, I. and Cumming, T.M. (2014) Importance of quality transition process for students with disabilities across settings: learning from the current situation in New South Wales. *Australian Journal of Education*, 58(3): 318–36.

Thoma, C.A., Lakin, K.C., Carlson, D., Domzal, C., Austin, K. and Boyd, K. (2011) Participation in postsecondary education for students with intellectual disabilities: a review of the literature 2001–2010. *Journal of Postsecondary Education and Disability*, 24(3): 175–91.

UN General Assembly (1989) *Convention on the Rights of the Child*, 20 November 1989, United Nations, Treaty Series, Vol. 1577, p.3, available at: www.refworld.org/docid/3ae6b38f0.html [accessed 2 February 2015].

UN General Assembly (2006) *Convention on the Rights of Persons with Disabilities*, 13 December 2006, A/RES/61/106, Annex I, available at: www.refworld.org/docid/4680cd212.html [accessed 2 February 2015].

van Gameren-Oosterom, H.B.M., Fekkes, M., Buitendijk, S.E., et al. (2011) Development, problem behavior, and quality of life in a population based sample of eight-year-old children with Down syndrome. *PLoS ONE*, 6(7): e21879. DOI: 10.1371/journal.pone.0021879.

Van Hooste, A. and Maes, B. (2003) Family factors in the early development of children with Down syndrome. *Journal of Early Intervention*, 25: 296–309.

Wehman, P., Chan, F., Ditchman, N. and Kang, H. (2014) Effect of supported employment on vocational rehabilitation outcomes of transition-age youth with intellectual and development disabilities: a case control study. *Intellectual and Development Disabilities*, 52: 296–310.

Wehmeyer, M., Lawrence, M., Garner, N., Soukup, J. and Palmer, S. (2004) *Whose Future is it Anyway? A Student-Directed Transition Planning Process. Coach's Guide*, 2nd edn. Lawrence, KS: Beach Center on Disability, KUCDD University of Kansas.

Westling, D.L., Kelley, K.R., Cain, B. and Prohn, S. (2013) College students' attitudes about an inclusive postsecondary education program for individuals with intellectual disability. *Education and Training in Autism and Developmental Disabilities*, 48(3): 306–19.

Wishart, J.G. (2007) Socio-cognitive understanding: a strength or weakness in Down's syndrome? *Journal of Intellectual Disability Research*, 51(12): 996–1005.

Wishart, J.G., Cebula, K.R., Willis, D.S. and Pitcairn, T.K. (2007) Understanding of facial expressions of emotion by children with intellectual disabilities of differing etiology. *Journal of Intellectual Disability Research*, 51: 551–63.

Woodcock, S. Dixon, R. and Tanner, K. (2013) *Teaching in Inclusive School Environments*. Macksville, NSW: David Barlow Publishing.

World Health Organization (2014) *Genes and Human Disease: Genes and Chromosomal Diseases*. Downloaded from: www.who.int/genomics/public/geneticdiseases/en/index1.html.

Attention Deficit Hyperactivity Disorder (or Hyperkinetic Disorder)

14

Richard Soppitt

Learning objectives

This chapter will help readers to:

- Recognise the characteristics of Attention Deficit Hyperactivity Disorder (ADHD) and its relationship with other common developmental and mental disorders
- Understand that aetiology is usually multi-factorial involving interaction between bio-psychosocial factors
- Identify treatment interventions including educational, parenting, cognitive behavioural therapy and pharmacological
- Appreciate that ADHD remains a highly pernicious chronic condition. Effective interventions can help prevent associated social and educational exclusion

Introduction

Disorders, problems and difficulties

Mental health difficulties in childhood and early adolescence are best understood as emotions or behaviour outside the normal range for age, sex and cognitive ability, linked with an impairment of development and where the child suffers as a result. It is usually not the child who complains about the problem but rather one of the many adults involved in that child's life.

In contrast to most adult mental health disorders, ADHD is a neurodevelopmental disorder and represents a quantitative shift from normality within a developmental framework. It describes the most severe 1–3% of the childhood population in terms of hyperactivity, inattention and impulsiveness in more than one setting which is usually assessed within Community Paediatrics and CAMHS teams for pharmacotherapy. The Health and Social Care Information Centre's Adult Psychiatric Morbidity in England – 2007 survey estimated that 8% of adults in England have ADHD.

Applying a life course perspective to ADHD, we know that current diagnostic criteria require symptoms of ADHD be present before the age of seven. However, evidence shows that ADHD can be diagnosed competently in pre-schoolers and the correlates of pre-school ADHD are similar to those found in school age children and include deficits in executive functioning and delay aversion regarded as essential features of core ADHD.

The key clinical features of ADHD can be summarised into a triad from early childhood of severe:

- restlessness
- inattention
- impulsiveness

Brown (2000) has produced a helpful model of executive function seen in ADHD focusing on six areas, alongside which he listed the expected impairments:

1. Organise, prioritise and activate
2. Focus, shift and sustain attention
3. Regulate alertness, effort and processing speed
4. Manage frustration and modulate emotion
5. Working memory and accessing recall
6. Monitor and regulate action

Media myths and controversy

Media myths abound and the tabloid press is full of headlines such as 'ADHD an excuse for bad parenting'. Undoubtedly a controversial diagnosis, the issue of reliance on medication without addressing social, educational or family issues can lead to justified criticism. On the other hand, the consensus of evidence to date supports medication using stimulants (e.g. methylphenidate or ritalin) or non-stimulants (atomoxetine) as being the most effective intervention (MTA Study: www.nimh.nih.gov/funding/clinical-research/practical/mta). Without medication, many of the other sensible angles in treatment such as specialist education cannot be easily accessed by the pupil. However, with appropriately specialised teaching within small classes and high adult-to-pupil ratios, then a child with ADHD may not require medication or at least need a lower dose.

Epidemiology of ADHD

Relationship with other conditions

Multiple co-existing psychiatric conditions have been reported with childhood ADHD. Indeed, it is uncommon to have a child with merely ADHD alone. In a Swedish population sample with ADHD, the prevalence rate for another condition was 87%, whilst the prevalence rate for two or more co-morbidities was 67%. The most common co-morbid conditions reported have been antisocial disorders, especially Conduct Disorder (CD) in up to 25% and Oppositional Defiant Disorder (ODD) in up to 50%. The latest NICE guidance on CD (March 2013: www.nice.org.uk/) notes that in some groups of young people, 40% of those with conduct disorder have ADHD. The presence of co-morbid antisocial disorders could often be linked to mothers' psychiatric disorders or to negative parenting practices. A wide spectrum of developmental and learning disorders have been found to be associated with children with ADHD. These include: specific learning difficulties such as dyslexia, dysgraphia, dyscalculia and dyspraxia; Tourette's syndrome; and tic disorders. Until recently, the presence of pervasive developmental disorder, i.e. autistic spectrum disorders, was thought to rule out a diagnosis of ADHD. However, research and practice has demonstrated that the two can be diagnosed as separate conditions in the same individual. It has been shown that other syndromes on the autistic spectrum such as Asperger's syndrome can co-occur with ADHD. ADHD is associated with a five-fold increase in mental disorders such as depression. Common coexisting conditions in adults include personality disorders, bipolar disorder, obsessive–compulsive disorder and substance misuse, noted in Quality Standard 139 NICE, July 2013 (www.nice.org.uk/), which inputs into outcome frameworks published by the Department of Health.

DSM-5, the North American diagnostic system (APA, 2013) includes no exclusion criteria for people with Autism Spectrum Disorder (ASD), since symptoms of both disorders often co-occur. However, ADHD symptoms must not occur exclusively during the course of a psychotic disorder and must not be better explained by another mental disorder (e.g. dissociative/personality disorder, or substance intoxication). The previous DSM-IV criteria worked as well for adults as they did for children, but a lower threshold of symptoms (five instead of six) was sufficient for a reliable diagnosis.

Assessment and detection of ADHD

Case study

Kieran was on the go all the time from his first steps at the age of 15 months. He was into everything and did not sleep properly through the night until he was nearly five. His parents were exhausted and found that their extended family were not keen to look after him. By the start of primary school, Kieran had fractured his clavicle and elbow from jumping off trees and heights.

During infant school, Kieran struggled to sit still at circle time and was not popular with his peers. The school SENCo discussed the class teacher's concerns with the parents. He was referred by the GP to the local community paediatrics team who recommended parent training around positive reinforcement and giving him some additional support to remain on task in school at School Action Plus of the Code of Practice. Parents felt blamed as bad parents by their friends but had two other older boys with no difficulties at all.

After a six-month trial of positive behavioural management and parenting classes, his parents were less punitive and found that there had been a short-term response to praise and clear targets. However, the progress did not last and he continued to 'be all over the place' and not able to sit and watch a film all the way through without getting up and making a nuisance of himself. He had no friends at school. His morale was low and he was struggling to read.

The community paediatrician discussed medication options with the parents who initially were sceptical as they were worried about side effects and using medication in such a young child now aged seven. After careful reassurance, they decided that something needed to improve as Kieran was being excluded for disruptive behaviour and hitting his peers. He seemed to be gravitating towards all the 'problem children' at the school.

After a few months of medication, he was being invited to parties again for the very first time and his parents were in tears as they had been so worried about his social isolation.

(Continued)

(Continued)

The primary school took advice from the behaviour support specialist teacher service and instigated individualised approaches with as much one-to-one time with his teaching assistant as possible; increased computer-based learning helped his focus; egg timers were employed to help with time management and awareness. Kieran was provided with a 'tangle' which is a plastic spiral which allowed him to fiddle with his hands under the table and not distract other children near him. He sat at a table close to the teacher so that he did not have the additional distraction of people in front of him. Tactical ignoring of attention-seeking behaviour and use of visual cards to prompt him to remain on task were found to work. Target charts were used between home and school to reward him for clear goals, and immediate rewards were given wherever possible. Kieran was placed with good role models to help him with learning appropriate behaviour. Nuisance items such as rubber bands and rulers were strategically removed, whilst activity reinforcement was employed using the less desirable task before the more desirable reward task. His parents were included as partners in Kieran's success. Close home–school liaison was maintained with email and diaries, with the focus on the positives and reinforcing targets.

Exercise was found to promote Kieran's focus. He enjoyed football and could concentrate better in a team now, although would need prompting when group instructions were given. His parents joined ADDIS UK and the local ADHD support network for parents.

Careful planning for the transition to secondary school was undertaken involving both SENCos and the community paediatrician. His parents found a school which also provided nurturing for the Year 7 transition and had good links with the local community paediatrics and CAMHS team.

Kieran's medication needed to be changed to a preparation which covered the early evenings as well as during the school day and a suitable longer-acting preparation of methylphenidate was started. Kieran melatonin to help his sleep pattern at night.

Aetiology and underlying theoretical models

Biological factors

The diagnosis of ADHD does not imply a particular underlying cause. The presence of psychosocial adversity or risk factors should not exclude the diagnosis of ADHD, which involves the relationship between multiple genes and environmental factors. ADHD is viewed as a disorder with many different sub-types resulting from the interplay of different risk issues.

Genetic influences

ADHD symptoms show powerful genetic influences. Twin studies suggest that genes explain around 75% of the heritability of ADHD symptoms in the population (heritability estimate of 0.7 to 0.8). The genes affect the distribution of key ADHD symptoms across the wider population. No single gene has been identified in ADHD.

Environmental influences

A range of biological factors can negatively affect brain development during the perinatal period and early childhood is associated with an increase in the risk of ADHD or ADD. Such risk factors include maternal substance misuse during pregnancy, foetal hypoxia and very low birth weight; also brain injury, and exposure to toxins such as lead and deficiency of zinc.

Epidemiological research indicates a link between additives in the diet and levels of hyperactivity; and a small proportion of children with ADHD demonstrate individual reactions to some foods or artificial additives, and could be helped by an exclusion diet with appropriate dietetic or medical advice.

Psychosocial factors

ADHD has been associated with severe early psychosocial adversity, for instance, in children who have survived depriving institutional care (Roy et al., 2000). The mechanisms are not known but may include a failure to acquire cognitive and emotional control and the impact of early emotional neglect on brain development, as well as the probability of disrupted parenting due to familial ADHD and substance misuse by parents.

Parental–child relationships can be improved in children where ADHD symptoms have been successfully treated with stimulants. Parents themselves may also have unrecognised and untreated ADHD, which can also undermine relationships.

Dysfunctional relationships are more common in the families of young people with ADHD. Stressful family relationships may be related to the problems of living with a child with ADHD as well as a risk for the disorder itself. In ADHD, a harsh and punitive parenting style is a risk factor for developing oppositional and conduct problems.

Focus groups of children with ADHD have expressed very clear desires for better public understanding of the condition. They asked for empathy for their situations and less stigma attached to ADHD diagnoses. Experiences of stigma, such as bullying, name-calling, negative assumptions and differential treatment were distressing to children, and negatively affected their self-evaluations, self-esteem and self-confidence. Close friendships were an important protective factor against the initiation and/or continuation of fights that arose as a result of the child with ADHD being bullied. These friendships were mentioned at least as often as medication, as factors that helped children to restrain their impulse to fight and/ or to continue fighting (NICE Guidance, 2008).

Treatment interventions

Psychological therapies and parenting interventions

Parent-effectiveness training is a behaviour therapy intervention instructing parents of children with ADHD to use behaviour therapy techniques with their child. Parent training originated in the 1960s based on behavioural learning theory and play therapy. This intervention has developed further, addressing beliefs, emotions and wider social issues as well as targeting poor self-confidence, depression, social isolation and marital difficulties but further research is needed with better reporting of study process and results (Zwi et al., 2012).

The focus is primarily with the child or young person's main caregiver although some programmes add a child-directed component based on the principles of social skills training.

NICE (TA 102 2006) (www.nice.org.uk/TA102) recommended that all parent-training/ education programmes, whether group or individual-based, should:

- be structured and have a curriculum informed by principles of social-learning theory
- include relationship-enhancing strategies
- offer a sufficient number of sessions, with an optimum of 8–12, to maximise the possible benefits for participants
- enable parents to identify their own parenting objectives
- incorporate role-play during sessions, as well as homework to be undertaken between sessions, to achieve generalisation of newly rehearsed behaviours to the home situation
- be delivered by appropriately trained and skilled facilitators who are supervised, have access to necessary ongoing professional development, and are able to engage in a productive therapeutic alliance with parents
- adhere to the programme developer's manual and employ all of the necessary materials to ensure consistent implementation of the programme

Examples of programmes that demonstrate the essential characteristics listed above included the Webster–Stratton Incredible Years Programme and the Triple P – Positive Parenting Programme. Parents who might have the greatest needs could find it difficult to engage in groups.

Behaviour therapy

The chief technique involves the use of rewards or positive reinforcers that are thought likely to encourage the young person to make helpful changes in motor, impulse or attentional control. This may involve concrete rewards such as extra time for recreational and leisure activities or the means to obtain items that the young person values. 'Tokens' (such as stars, chips, marbles, and so on) may work for younger children in their own right, whereas for older children tokens will need to be exchanged for items of value to them. Social approval, such as praise or achievement certificates and self-praise, is a useful adjunct in such programmes.

Rewards are specific to an individual and what is of value to one child is not necessarily of value to another. There are also practical, financial, cultural and moral issues that make some rewards more suitable for some parents or teachers than others. Parents often argue against the use of 'blackmail' or 'bribery' when discussing similar techniques.

A further set of techniques involves punishments or negative reinforcers. This approach may have some value when a particular impulsive behaviour is offensive to others and needs to cease immediately. Verbal reprimands, which have the merit of being simple and effective, may be delivered by parents, carers and teachers. Response cost techniques involve the loss of a potential reinforcer. These can take the form of deductions either from rewards already earned or from an agreed set of rewards given in advance but from which deductions can be made for inappropriate behaviour.

The third most common technique is 'time out' from social reinforcement, and is helpful where it is felt that inappropriate behaviour is being reinforced by the attention of others.

There is no evidence yet that psychological interventions for children with ADHD have measurable positive effects on teacher ratings of either ADHD symptoms or conduct-related behaviours. Beneficial effects of psychological interventions for ADHD therefore do not appear at present to transfer to the classroom environment.

However, psychological interventions for children with ADHD taking into consideration their developmental level have moderate helpful effects according to parent ratings of ADHD symptoms and conduct problems, both for children not on medication and as an adjunct to continued routine medication for ADHD.

Combining medication with psychological interventions may be especially important in the management of older adolescents and adults with ADHD and co-morbid antisocial behaviour, and they benefit from interventions to develop pro-social skills, emotional control, problem-solving negotiation and conflict resolution.

Educational interventions

It is well established that children with ADHD fall behind their peers academically. It has been shown that this trend extends to children who are severely inattentive, hyperactive and impulsive in the classroom, even if they do not have a formal diagnosis of ADHD. Inattention is particularly related to academic underachievement. Moreover, children who had been identified by their teachers in the reception year of school as having severe ADHD symptoms were found to fall behind their peers academically and are a challenge to inclusive practice (Westwood, 2013).

Situational variation with how ADHD presents is well established in schools. There are clear differences in behaviour across secondary schools using observation and self-report measures which have been replicated.

Galloway and colleagues (1995) proposed that 'differences between teachers are substantially greater than differences between schools', and posited that the teacher was the dominant influence on behaviour in the classroom. Gray and Sime (1988) suggested that the majority of the variance in behaviour lay within schools themselves. In the Elton report (HMSO, 1989) it is stated that 'a teacher's general competence has a strong influence on his or her pupils' behaviour'.

A study set in one Local Education Authority (LEA) found that more than half the teachers had some experience of teaching a child with a diagnosis of ADHD (Sayal et al., 2006), and that a time-limited educational intervention for teachers has been found to raise awareness and improve recognition and management of children with possible ADHD (Aguiar et al., 2012).

Teacher-led educational interventions consist of managing academic activities or adapting the physical environment. A description of a wide range of educational strategies for use with children with ADHD is given by Cooper and Bilton (2013) who suggest techniques such as:

- seating the child in a place that is relatively free from distraction (for example, doors and windows) in a position where the teacher can easily intervene if the child is not attending
- having a designated quiet area for a child to work in
- providing stimulating activities
- giving concise, clear instructions
- following a defined, regular timetable
- avoiding repetitive tasks
- breaking down tasks into a series of small steps
- giving frequent positive feedback
- working in a pair rather than a group
- isolating the child from the class for a short time when they are misbehaving
- giving points or tokens as rewards to be exchanged at a later time for a favourite activity or treat
- taking away points or tokens if the child misbehaves

The provision of in-service training, peer observation and coaching by professionals can be effective, but the process takes time, and Adey and colleagues (2004) suggested that 30 hours of in-service provision are necessary to create sustained changes to teachers' classroom practice.

Teacher-led interventions, such as giving clear and effective commands, have large beneficial effects on behavioural problems of children with ADHD. Teachers who have received training about ADHD and its management should provide behavioural interventions in the classroom to help children and young people with ADHD (NICE Guidance, 1998, Key priority).

Dietary recommendations

Health professionals need to emphasise the importance of a balanced diet, good nutrition and regular exercise for those of any age with ADHD. Some have found the elimination of artificial colouring and additives from the diet to be helpful. Dietary fatty acid supplementation (e.g. Omega 3) is not recommended by NICE.

Pharmacological treatment

A helpful update on the use of stimulant treatments in ADHD is provided by Stevens et al. (2013). They make the following clinical points:

- Pharmacotherapy of ADHD with stimulants is a mainstay of evidence-based treatment for ADHD across the lifespan
- Stimulants have relatively few serious interactions with commonly prescribed medications
- Certain adverse effects of stimulants (e.g. decreased appetite, insomnia) can be anticipated by virtue of their known pharmacologic properties, whereas others (e.g. tics, mood changes) are idiosyncratic

Safety issues

In 2006, the USA FDA conducted a review on reports of sudden death in patients treated with ADHD medications using data from their *Adverse Event Reporting System*. The review concluded that the rate of sudden death with methylphenidate and atomoxetine was below background rates available.

The consensus (e.g. Stevens et al., 2013), is that sudden death is a rare event in youths with ADHD, and there are insufficient data to establish a causal link with stimulant medication used to treat this condition. Nevertheless, it would be prudent to follow the guidelines for the use of stimulants in youth (monitoring risk factors and measuring blood pressure and pulse), although obtaining an electrocardiogram is not mandatory. Pertinent questions that should be asked with regard to family history of premature sudden death under 30 and a personal history of cardiovascular symptoms need to be considered by the treating clinician. Patients answering any of these questions affirmatively should be examined and investigated more carefully by a cardiologist.

The MHRA (UK) published a drug safety update in January 2010 (www.gov.uk/drug-safety-update/methylphenidate-new-patient-information) and concluded that:

> The benefits of methylphenidate continue to outweigh the risks when used to treat ADHD in children aged 6 years or older and adolescents. The longer-term safety of methylphenidate remains under close review, and the results of ongoing studies to characterise the known or potential risks of ADHD medicines will be evaluated when available.

People with ADHD have a higher risk than the general population for running into problems with substance misuse. The risk appears to be linked with the presence of conduct disorder and social adversity. In UK clinical experience, however, the misuse of prescribed drugs by people with ADHD is very uncommon, and the slower-release preparations and non-stimulant options reduce risk. The use of illicit drugs, such as cannabis and cocaine, is probably not increased by receiving stimulants, at least in the short term:

> The follow up from MTA study found that medication for ADHD did not protect from, nor contribute to, visible risk of substance use in adolescence. There is a need to identify alternative or adjunctive adolescent-focused approaches to substance abuse prevention and treatment for boys and girls with ADHD, especially given their increased risk for use and abuse of multiple substances that is not improved with stimulant medication (Molina et al., 2013).

It is important to note that use of alcohol or cannabis is not a contraindication to stimulant prescribing but rather should raise the possibility of drug diversion and should impact upon the choice of preparation in favour of the longer-acting medicines with very low abuse potential. Concomitant cannabis and stimulant use should be closely monitored because of the theoretical risks of increased dopamine in the genesis of psychosis in some studies.

Methylphenidate at a higher dose is more likely than placebo to cause the following short-term adverse effects: insomnia, anorexia, irritability, moodiness, thirst, itching, diarrhoea, palpitations, stuttering, reddened eyes, incoherent speech and decreased bodyweight. The long-term studies of methylphenidate indicate an increased risk of side effects including an increase in systolic blood pressure and heart rate.

Methylphenidate is thought to increase intrasynaptic concentrations of the neurotransmitters dopamine and noradrenaline (norepinephrine) in the frontal cortex as well as subcortical brain regions associated with motivation and reward, and thus improve the saliency of academic tasks.

Atomoxetine is a non-stimulant drug relatively recently introduced into the UK, licensed for use in children of six years and over and young people for the treatment of ADHD as well as having a continuation license into adulthood. It is thought that it works by selectively inhibiting the pre-synaptic noradrenaline transporter, thus inhibiting noradrenaline reuptake.

Atomoxetine has less potential for misuse and does not require the same strict prescribing and storage conditions as methylphenidate and dexamfetamine as it is not a controlled drug.

Methylphenidate and atomoxetine have similar side effects profiles with respect to effects on appetite, growth, pulse and blood pressure requiring similar monitoring. Rarer harm events associated with atomoxetine include initial increased risk of suicidal thoughts and very rare hepatic damage.

Conclusions

Drug treatment is not indicated as the first-line treatment for all school-age children and young people with ADHD. It should rather be held back for those with severe symptoms, such as those with the more severe ICD-10-defined hyperkinetic disorder (1–2% of the population) and impairment, or for those who have refused non-drug interventions, or have not responded sufficiently to parent-training/education programmes or group psychological treatment. However, NICE (NICE Guidance, 2008) recommends that following treatment with a parent-training/education programme, children and young people and adults with ADHD and persisting significant impairment should be offered drug treatment. Use of medicines in the treatment for children and young people with ADHD should always form part of a comprehensive treatment plan that includes psychological, behavioural and educational advice and interventions.

It is mandatory that before starting drug treatment, children and young people with ADHD should have a full pre-treatment assessment, which should include:

- full mental health and social assessment
- full history and physical examination, including:

  o assessment of history of exercise syncope, undue breathlessness and other cardiovascular symptoms
  o heart rate and blood pressure (plotted on a centile chart)
  o height and weight (plotted on a growth chart)
  o family history of cardiac disease, sudden death under 30 and examination of the cardiovascular system

- an electrocardiogram (ECG) if there is past medical or family history of serious cardiac disease, a history of sudden death in young family members or abnormal findings on cardiac examination
- risk assessment for substance misuse and drug diversion (where the drug is passed on to others for non-prescription use)

Future directions for training and multi-agency development

Multi-agency working in relation to ADHD raises challenges as does transition into adulthood where there are limited pathways for ADHD treatment into later life or for those who need diagnosis in adulthood. The new Child and Families Act (2014) which came into force in late 2014 allows Education, Health and Care Plans to replace Statements of SEN, up until the age of 25. There is a need for youth mental health services which encompass the years 13–25 so that discontinuities do not occur at such a critical time in a young person's development (see IAYMH declaration: Coughlan et al., 2013). Different models of disability and how to respond to it are held by different agencies. Parents, young ADHD patients and carers also need to be able to be part of steering groups or have their views represented.

A number of successful multi-professional teams for ADHD are emerging with protocols for multi-professional working, including the role of GPs in monitoring aspects of care, and the 'GP with a special interest' model has proved helpful for ADHD transitional and adult clinics. There remain, however, difficulties regarding transitional arrangements between CAMHS and adult mental health services (AMHS), and a general lack of support for adults with ADHD because of the difficulties associated with getting a diagnosis and treatment (Asherson, 2013; Paul et al., 2014), which indicates the need for joined-up youth mental health services with good multi-agency links (McGorry, 2007). There has also been an Adult ADHD European Consensus Declaration which supports urgent inclusion of ADHD into adult mental health services (Kooij et al., 2010).

Summary

1. Apart from the impact on the individual, ADHD has a pernicious impact on society in the following areas (Coghill, 2006):

    a) The healthcare system: 50% increase in bike accidents, 33% increase in emergency room visits, two to four times more vehicle accidents
    b) School and occupation: 46% expelled, 35% drop out and lower occupational status
    c) Family: three to five times increase in parental divorce or separation and two to four times increase in sibling fights
    d) Employer: increase in parental absenteeism and decrease in productivity
    e) Society: twice the risk of substance misuse, with earlier onset, and individuals are less likely to quit in adulthood
    f) Children with ADHD are in the bottom 5% of children in terms of quality of life

2. Research has shown (Brassett-Grundy and Butler, 2004) that men and women who had childhood ADHD were significantly more likely than those without ADHD to face negative outcomes in adulthood, affecting various degrees of social exclusion. ADHD is as much a female problem as it is a male problem and the adult lives of those with childhood ADHD are typified by social deprivation and adversity.

3. Recommendations for cutting down the public and personal cost of ADHD include:

    a) Better screening for ADHD, perhaps in primary care
    b) Wider use of sensitively designed early interventions and individually tailored treatment plans

c) Ongoing treatment and support for those with ADHD through adolescence into adulthood. Consideration of youth mental health services (e.g. 13–25)

d) Raised awareness of ADHD amongst parents, health professionals, social care workers, educationalists and those in the criminal justice system

4. These measures will help to ease the negative impact that childhood ADHD has on the life-course, stopping young sufferers from becoming socially excluded and unproductive adults.

Discussion points

- ADHD has been seen by the media as an excuse for bad parenting, what role has the media had in terms of reducing or promoting stigma around SEN issues in recent times?
- Developmental disorders are life-long conditions but adulthood provides greater freedom and opportunity for round pegs to find round holes. Services for adults, however, lag well behind children's services; and in adults ADHD has much more of an equal gender split in terms of recognition and referral. What are the possible explanations for this?
- DSM-5 has recently changed the age cut-off for recognition of ADHD up to the age of 12 in recognition that developmental disorders may only become obvious with sufficient stress and challenge. How does this contrast with the concepts around ASD and in particular the demise of Asperger syndrome from DSM-5?

Further reading

Alban-Metcalfe, J. and Alban-Metcalfe, J. (2013) *Managing Attention Deficit/ Hyperactivity Disorder in the Inclusive Classroom: Practical Strategies*. Abingdon: Routledge.

Cooper, P. and Bilton, K.M. (2002) *Attention Deficit Hyperactivity Disorder: A Practical Guide for Teachers*. London: David Fulton Publishers.
This is a user-friendly and concise resource.

O'Regan, F. (2007) *ADHD*, 2nd edn. New York: Continuum International Publishing Group. Fintan O'Regan was head teacher of the only specialist school in the UK for teaching and managing ADHD (the Centre Academy).

(Continued)

(Continued)

Phelan, T.W. (2003) *1-2-3 MAGIC: Effective Discipline for Children: Training Your Child to Do What You Want Them to Do.* Glen Ellyn, IL: ParentMagic, Inc.
Written by the parent of an ADHD child, this book provides easy to follow steps for disciplining without yelling, arguing or smacking.

Spohrer, K.E. (2009) *Teaching Assistants' Guide to ADHD.* New York: Continuum International Publishing Group.
This book demonstrates the import of recognising and developing the abilities of all children with ADHD.

Useful websites

www.addiss.co.uk.

www.rcpsych.ac.uk/healthadvice/problemsdisorders/adhdinadults.aspx.

ADHD in adults.

www.aacap.org/aacap/Families_and_Youth/Resource_Centers/ADHD_Resource_Center/Home.aspx.

Helpful ADHD resource centre through the American Academy of Child and Adolescent Psychiatry.

References

Adey, P., Hewitt, G., Hewitt, J., et al. (2004) *The Professional Development of Teachers: Practice and Theory.* London: Kluwer.

Aguiar, A.P., Kieling, R.R., Costa, A.C., et al. (2012) Increasing teachers' knowledge about ADHD and learning disorders: an investigation on the role of a psychoeducational intervention. *Journal of Attention Disorders,* DOI: 1087054712453171.

APA (2013) *Diagnostic and Statistical Manual of Mental Disorders* (DSM-5), 5th edn. Washington, DC: American Psychiatric Association.

Asherson, P. (2013) ADHD in adults: a clinical concern. In C.B.H. Surman (ed.), *ADHD in Adults.* New York: Humana Press, pp. 1–17.

Brassett-Grundy, A. and Butler, N. (2004) *Attention-Deficit/Hyperactivity Disorder: An Overview and Review of the Literature Relating to the Correlates and Lifecourse Outcomes for Males and Females* (Bedford Group for Lifecourse and Statistical Studies, Occasional Paper No. 1). London: Institute of Education, University of London.

Brown, T. (2000) *Attention Deficit Disorders and Comorbidities in Children, Adolescents and Adults.* Washington, DC: American Psychiatric Association.

Coghill, D. (2006) Personal communication.

Cooper, P. and Bilton, K.M. (2013). *Attention Deficit Hyperactivity Disorder: A Practical Guide for Teachers*. Abingdon: Routledge.

Coughlan, H., Cannon, M., Shiers, D., et al. (2013) Towards a new paradigm of care: the international declaration on Youth Mental Health. *Early Intervention in Psychiatry*, 7(2): 103–8.

Galloway, D., Leo, E.L., Rogers, C., et al. (1995) Motivational styles in English and mathematics among children identified as having special educational needs. *British Journal of Educational Psychology*, 65: 477–87.

Gray, J. and Sime, N. (1988) A report for the committee of inquiry into discipline in schools. Part 1: Findings from the national survey of teachers in England and Wales. In *The Elton Report* (1989). Enquiry into Discipline in Schools. London: HMSO.

HMSO (1989) *The Elton Report*. Enquiry into Discipline in Schools. London: HMSO.

Kooij, S.J., Bejerot, S., Blackwell, A., et al. (2010) European consensus statement on diagnosis and treatment of adult ADHD: the European Network Adult ADHD. *BMC Psychiatry*, 10(67): 1–24.

McGorry, P.D. (2007) The specialist youth mental health model: strengthening the weakest link in the public mental health system. *Medical Journal of Australia*, 187(7): S53–S56.

Molina, B.S., Hinshaw, S.P., Eugene Arnold, L., et al. (2013) Adolescent substance use in the multimodal treatment study of attention-deficit/hyperactivity disorder (ADHD) (MTA) as a function of childhood ADHD, random assignment to childhood treatments, and subsequent medication. *Journal of the American Academy of Child and Adolescent Psychiatry*, 52(3): 250–63.

NICE Guidance (2008) www.nice.org.uk/guidance/cg72.

Paul, M., Street, C., Wheeler, N. and Singh, S.P. (2014) Transition to adult services for young people with mental health needs: a systematic review. *Clinical Child Psychology and Psychiatry*, 1–22. DOI: 10.1177/1359104514526603.

Roy, P., Rutter, M. and Pickles, A. (2000) Institutional care: risk from family background or pattern of rearing? *Journal of Child Psychology and Psychiatry*, 41: 139–49.

Sayal, K., Hornsey, H., Warren, S., et al. (2006) Identification of children at risk of attention deficit/ hyperactivity disorder: a school-based intervention. *Social Psychiatry and Psychiatric Epidemiology*, 41: 806–13.

Stevens, J.R., Wilens, T.E., and Stern, T.A. (2013) Using stimulants for attention-deficit/hyperactivity disorder: clinical approaches and challenges. *The Primary Care Companion for CNS Disorders*, 15(2): DOI: 10.4088/PCC.12f01472.

Westwood, P. (2013) *Inclusive and Adaptive Teaching: Meeting the Challenge of Diversity in the Classroom*. Abingdon: Routledge.

Zwi, M., Jones, H., Thorgaard, C., York, A., Dennis, J. (2012) Parent training interventions for Attention Deficit Hyperactivity Disorder (ADHD) in children aged 5 to 18 years. *Cochrane Database of Systematic Reviews*: 12.

Visual Impairment and Mainstream Education

15

Beyond Mere Awareness Raising

John Ravenscroft

Learning objectives

This chapter will help readers to:

- Understand the national register of severely sight impaired and sight impaired people
- Recognise the difference between clinical and functional visual assessments
- Be familiar with current research on the profile and prevalence of children with visual impairment (VI) living in the UK
- Understand the roles of the Qualified Teacher of the Visually Impaired in empowering the mainstream teacher
- Appreciate the balance between academic attainment and independent daily living skills

---

Background

Parents of a child with visual impairment often face the difficult task of deciding which school their child should attend. Parents, however, cannot fully participate in this decision process, if they have not been provided with the information and knowledge that will allow them to make informed choices as an equal member of the team that is involved in the child's education. Often parents feel unsure about what is the best way forward for their child. They may want to know more about their rights as parents; about what types of educational placement would suit their child. Parents may want to know if any special preparations will be made for their child starting school and/or be concerned about how he/she will cope once there. Parents may desire more information about the school curriculum; the level of specialist visual impairment support provided; access at the school; and extra-curricular activities. Most of all, as we have seen from a variety of studies (see Royal National Institute of Blind People, 2000, 2001a, 2001b, 2001c; Roe, 2008; Ravenscroft, 2009) children and parents may be worried about whether they or their child will 'fit in', and will have friends and enjoy school.

A theme that frequently emerges from the literature is the requirement for collaborative services to meet the needs of children with visual impairment. This is never more needed than when we consider transition from school into further or higher education or employment. The Facilitating Inclusive Education and Supporting the Transition Agenda (FIESTA) Best Practice Report (Davis et al., 2014) highlights nine important areas that professionals and parents and children should focus on through this important transition period. These nine areas are briefly summarised in Table 15.1, and show how in order for successful collaborative working to occur an inclusive and informed approach for all involved is necessary.

The lack of engagement of young people in the transition process (points 3, 4 and 5 from Table 15.1) has also been reported by Hewett et al. (2014) where 47 participants with visual impairments were interviewed as they made their transition from compulsory education into further and higher education, and employment. It appears that many students did not engage with the more formal pre-transitional preparation process of the transition review, although most participants did report that overall they felt supported and prepared. It is certainly important that whatever process of transition the child with visual impairment is entering, whether it is from the early years pre-school setting to primary, from primary to secondary, or from secondary onwards, that children are involved in the process and are considered active agents in that their comments and their wishes should be taken seriously.

In order to achieve this, it is essential that parents, educationalists and other professionals work closely together to determine the successful delivery of an appropriate, planned education that enables the child with visual impairment to thrive at school (Townsley et al., 2004). The driving force of this approach is the belief that coordination of services will avoid duplication of effort and provide children and families with better outcomes. Atkinson et al. (2007) identified several positive outcomes for those that have adopted a multi-agency approach. These outcomes include access to services not previously available to children and families, improved educational attainment for children within mainstream schools and a reduced need for more specialist services. Integrated service provision also leads to significant benefits for those staff and services that are part of a multi-agency framework (Gray, 2008).

However, in order to plan and develop successful integrated services, well-trained and competent professionals need to acquire an accurate demographic profile detailing

Table 15.1 Nine steps to support the transition process of children with visual impairment (Davis et al., 2014)

1.	*Formal transition framework*	Professionals together with parents need to develop a formal transition framework which is flexible to the individual needs of children with visual impairment and adaptable based on national policies – a framework that details pre-transition preparations and post-transition evaluation to ensure successful transition and meaningful inclusion
2.	*Holistic approach*	Recognise the educational, psychological, social and cultural contexts of a child with visual impairment and of their families, which will provide a holistic approach to learning and remove barriers for learning
3.	*Participation*	Ensure children with visual impairment and their parents are involved and are at the centre of all decisions that affect them
4.	*Tailor made*	Facilitate children with visual impairment through bespoke approaches and pedagogy tailored to their individual requirements
5.	*Information*	Provide relevant, up-to-date, timely information to children with visual impairments and their parents in an accessible manner
6.	*Key worker*	The key worker (point of contact) is an essential role for all professionals to liaise with and communicate with ensuring a clear pathway of communication for all. Formalise a key working system for children with visual impairments and their parents to support them throughout the transition process
7.	*Continuation of support*	Identify a clear pathway for the continuation of support for children with visual impairment during and subsequent to transition
8.	*Collaborative working*	Ensure professionals in education, health and social work collaborate using a proactive approach to meet the needs of children with visual impairment
9.	*Training*	Provide training and continuous professional development for professionals that centre on managing transition, adapting the curriculum, models of inclusion, disability and childhood

numbers of VI children who will require support. Yet, in the UK, there is still no accurate record of how many children and young adults there are who have a significant visual impairment. This gives policy makers and managers charged with the forward planning of integrated service provision the difficult task of delivering services based on information that may not describe the full scale or spectrum of children needing support. Perhaps a simple analogy would help to convey the concerns being issued here. Not having accurate details on the numbers (and potential numbers) of users of services such as education, health and social work, is surely like an architect planning a large public building, but not knowing how many people will go into it, or consequently what the internal and external requirements should be.

Certification and registration of people including children who are visually impaired

In the UK the current certification system is when a consultant ophthalmologist can certify that a person is either severely sight impaired (blind) or sight impaired (partially sighted) and that person is eligible to be placed on a register, usually held by either a blind welfare society or local authority social work department. Only a consultant ophthalmologist can certify that a person is either blind or partially sighted; however, there are pathways of referrals from either the eye clinic, or the optometrist directly to social services which alert them to the needs of people with visual impairments in advance of certification (Durnian et al., 2010).

There are many problems with the current registration system, the main one being under-registration. There is a growing body of evidence which suggests that data from the register(s) is unreliable (Barry and Murray, 2005) and particularly so for children (Clunies-Ross and Franklin, 1997; King et al., 2000; Ravenscroft et al., 2008). Possible explanations for this under-representation of children may include a lack of awareness by children and parents about the process of certification and registration and the people who may provide support. It is also not compulsory and some children and adults may already be in receipt of any benefits they are entitled to. There could also exist a communication gap, perceived or real, between social, educational and health care staff; for it has been claimed that there is a lack of awareness among staff in schools and local authority education/children and family departments about the process of certification and registration (Scottish Executive, 2001; Alexander et al., 2009). Despite the failings of the registration system, local authority services still refer to the register and use it as a guide to anticipate the expected number of VI children that may need support, and to initiate funding and implement strategic processes.

Clinical assessment of people with visual impairments

Before we examine the profile of children with visual impairments we need to ascertain what exactly we mean by visual impairment and how it is measured. We measure how well a person sees by measuring visual acuity. The term 'visual acuity' was introduced by Donders in 1862 to describe 'sharpness' of awareness, although nowadays it is the ability to resolve fine detail and, specifically, to read small high-contrast letters. Visual acuity is therefore the best direct vision that can be obtained, with appropriate spectacle correction if necessary, with each eye separately, or with both eyes (Thomson, 2005).

In a formal clinical setting the standard measure of visual acuity is usually assessed through the 'Snellen' notation. The 'Snellen acuity' uses letter recognition on a Snellen vision chart as shown in the left chart of Figure 15.1. If another test is used to measure acuity it will often have a Snellen equivalent since this is the most easily interpreted vision scoring method.

A Snellen vision score is derived from the number of letters correctly identified on a Snellen vision chart from a recommended testing distance of 6 metres (in the UK, or twenty feet in the USA). The Snellen score is found by recording the smallest size of letter that can be correctly identified and is recorded as a fraction. For example, if only the top letter of a standard Snellen chart is correctly identified the resultant Snellen score will be 6/60.

Snellen Chart   Bailey Lovie, LogMAR Chart

Figure 15.1   A comparison of the Snellen and LogMAR charts

The numerator (6) corresponds to the testing distance, whilst the denominator (60) equates to the size of the letter. The value 6/60 indicates that a person can correctly identify a letter at 6 metres, which a person with normal vision would be able to identify at distance of 60 metres. A 6/60 value indicates poor vision. In contrast, a score of 6/6, would denote a vision within the normal/average range since the letter is correctly identified at 6 metres.

The Snellen chart although universally accepted does have its flaws (McGraw et al., 1995). For example, the limited number of letters at the top of the chart does put people with very poor visual acuity at a disadvantage compared to those with better acuity. There is also the problem of irregular progression of letter sizes within the Snellen chart. The jump in difference between the letters representing acuities of 6/5 to 6/6 is an increase of 120% whereas the difference from 6/36 to 6/60 is 167%. As Thomson (2005: 57) states 'this is analogous to a ruler which is marked with different length graduations'.

Bailey Lovie (1976) charts, which negate some of the disadvantages of the Snellen chart are now being introduced. The Bailey Lovie charts (see Figure 15.1) convert a geometric sequence of letter sizes to a linear scale, and give a LogMAR notation of vision loss. LogMAR vision testing offers a consistent and scientific method of recording vision scores. Although LogMAR is seen as the gold standard in measuring visual acuity it is still common parlance to use the Snellen notation, and to convert it using a similar table as found in Table 15.2. However, due to the reasons just explained, these conversions are only approximate and good practice dictates that comparisons between LogMAR and Snellen should not be made.

Definition of visual impairment

We can now consider the term visual impairment and certification as it relates particularly to children and young adults. In the UK, it is the National Assistance Act 1948 that defines 'blindness' for certification. The act states that a person can be certified as severely sight impaired if they are 'so blind as to be unable to perform any work for which eye sight is

Table 15.2 LogMAR to Snellen conversion

LogMAR	Snellen equivalent
0.0	6/6
0.3	6/12
0.5	6/18
0.6	6/24
0.8	6/36
0.9	6/48
1.0	6/60
1.1	6/72
1.3	6/120
1.5	6/180
1.8	6/360

essential' (National Assistance Act Section 64(1)). In this definition, the language of certification and registration is closely related to the adult world and clearly has no relevance at all to children. Nowadays, the explanatory notes issued to consultant ophthalmologists and hospital eye clinic staff from the UK's Royal College of Ophthalmologists (Levy, 2007), are used and define three distinct levels of certification for severely sight impaired people. The first of these are for people who may be regarded as blind[1] who have an acuity score of less than 3/60 Snellen. The second group are those who have an acuity of 3/60 but are less than 6/60 Snellen.[2] The remaining severely sight impaired people are those that have a visual acuity of 6/60 or better, who would not normally be regarded as being blind, but are certified (blind) if the field of vision is considerably contracted, especially in the lower part of the visual field.

For those children and adults that are partially sighted there is no legal definition and so there are only guidelines which indicate that a person should be certified as sight impaired if they have a visual acuity of 3/60 to 6/60 Snellen and a full visual field, or up to 6/24 Snellen with a moderate contraction of the visual field, or even 6/18 Snellen if there is a gross visual field deficit. Generally, it is likely that a child will receive intervention from a qualified teacher of visual impairment (QTVI) in the UK if the child's visual acuity is less than 6/18, or if the child has very good acuity but has a significant reduction of visual field or if the child has cerebral visual impairment (CVI). The child's use of vision will be monitored by a multi-agency team if the congenital eye condition is likely to deteriorate.

---

[1] Note that some vision may still remain.

[2] This group of people will also be classed as blind if their visual field is contracted. The visual field is the portion of the individual's surroundings that can be seen at any one time (Wilson, 2005).

Function visual assessments

It is important to recognise the distinction between measurements of visual acuity for a clinical measure, which can be part of a diagnostic assessment or is enveloped within a treatment regime, and measurements of visual acuity/function within a functional assessment. Clinical measures are measures of visual function which depend on the status of ocular, refractive and ocular-motor systems as well as the visual pathway (Hansen and Fulton, 2005). The purpose of functional assessments should be to obtain information which can be used to gain an understanding of the impact of visual impairment and the use of vision in everyday activities for the individual and to observe ways in which the person's remaining vision is used or could be used in a variety of real-life environments.

Children do not develop and learn how to acquire skills and concepts in isolation, for example we do not see play, socialisation, language and cognition all developing in isolation from each other. What we do see is a complex interweaving of cognition, mobility and orientation, language, emotional and social integration skills, in which functional vision impacts. Deficit models of assessment, those that are commonly found within a medical context tend not to unwrap this complex weave, nor do isolated tests within functional assessments achieve any better results. There is a requirement therefore to move from this deficit stance if we are to move towards more appropriate assessments for the child with visual impairment; assessment that is encapsulated within a strength-based paradigm, a paradigm that sees the child holistically, and one which emphasises the capabilities or the positive aspects of the child's vision.

Functional visual assessments are therefore best achieved through a multi-agency approach, but the multi-agency team must take into account their own constructions of the child they are assessing, for we can learn from those theorists such as Woodhead and Faulkner (2000) who see concepts of childhood as being created. In other words, we need to be careful that functional assessment teams, where the assessment tools are being guided by this construction, do not measure a child's functional vision within a pre-conceived framework of that child. The framework could contain issues of class, gender, race and even parental expectations. Teams need to examine the appropriateness of the functional assessment tools they use to assess a child's vision, for it is the assessment tools that will in part shape that child's life and determine future support and need.

The profile of children with visual impairment

In the last two decades there have been various attempts at determining the numbers and profile of VI children living in the UK (see Evans, 1995; Rogers, 1996; Foster and Gilbert, 1997; Rahi and Dezateaux, 1998; Keil and Clunies-Ross, 2003; Rahi and Cable, 2003; Bodeau-Livinec et al., 2007; Ravenscroft et al., 2008). In 2003, the Royal National Institute of Blind People (RNIB) estimated that there were 23,680 children and young people known to visual impairment services across England, Wales and Scotland (Keil and Clunies-Ross, 2003). This figure can be compared with the number of children who are officially registered blind or partially sighted in 2005 across England, Wales and Scotland. This number of 11,514 clearly shows the under-registration of children on local authority registers. Nevertheless, in 2007 the RNIB commissioned another study by Morris and Smith (2008) and found, by sending questionnaires to local authorities in England, Wales and Scotland, 16,008 children were receiving support from their local authority due to their visual impairment. Morris and Smith claim their data only represents 66% of children with visual impairment educated in England, and 34% of children in Scotland and 80% of children in Wales. Consequently, Morris and Smith suggest the original figure of 16,000 (with some caveats) should be extra-polated, using data from the 2006 census, to 25,305. However, in 2014, the RNIB reported that there were an estimated 40,000 children and young people aged up to 25 years with visual impairment (VI) that required specialist support, and approximately 25,000 were under 16 years old (Royal National Institute of Blind People, 2014). So it seems that the accurate figure is still to date unknown.

One way of determining the number is perhaps not to do a 'count' of how many children there are who are visually impaired but to look at the incidence and prevalence of visual impairment. Two influential studies (Bodeau-Livinec et al., 2007; Rahi and Cable, 2003) examined the rates of VI and blind children within the UK population and reported lower results. Children with a corrected visual acuity of 6/18 to 6/60 in the better eye were defined as having visual impairment and children with corrected visual acuity in the better eye of less than 6/60 or no useful vision are defined as having severe visual impairment or as blind. Bodeau-Livinec et al. suggest that 13 in every 10,000 children born in the UK will be diag-nosed with a visual impairment by their twelfth birthday, which amounts to around 950 new cases a year (p. 1101). They also found a cumulative incidence rate of 5.8 per 10,000 at five years of age for children that were severely VI or blind, which supports Rahi and Cable's (2003) finding of 5.3 per 10,000.

Ravenscroft et al. (2008) using data from the Visual Impairment Scotland (VIS) notification database found the most common single cause of childhood visual impairment was not damage to the eyes but damage to parts of the brain that are responsible for seeing. The study claims that in over half (51%) of the 850 children notified at the time of analysis, visual impairment was due to some form of damage to the brain or visual pathways, exactly the same percentage as Bodeau-Livinec et al. (2007). There were a total of 75 different con-ditions named by eye health professionals as the primary cause of visual impairment in the children listed on the VIS database. However, on closer analysis of the children on the database 18% of all children had CVI as the most identified single primary diagnosis given by the child's ophthalmologist. Albinism (9%) was a distant second. Given damage to the brain is a major factor responsible for a child's visual impairment, it is no surprise that the study found the majority (71%) of children with visual impairment also had some additional disabilities (in addition to their visual impairment).

The majority of children on the VIS dataset, who were able to be examined, either clinically or functionally fell within the 6/18 to 6/60 visual acuity range. This highlights the fact that very severe loss of sight or blindness is of very low incidence in children, indicating the term 'blind' is in fact quite misleading, for most children with visual impairment have some vision. Again this comes back to the notion of constructions we make about children. More often than not the 'blind' child can be a seeing child and it is important mainstream classroom teachers and QTVIs utilise what vision the child has and for most cases (except those where the child has no light perception at all) support the child as a 'seeing' child rather than as a 'blind' one.

Through the following case study, issues and strategies for teaching and learning for Peter, a boy with oculocutaneous albinism[3] with low vision and nystagmus,[4] can be explored.

Case study

Peter is nine years old, and at a local mainstream primary school. As a result of his albinism, he is photophobic and dislikes the bright light. He also doesn't like to go out into the playground and needs sun glasses and a hat, but he dislikes wearing his hat as it affects his field of vision. He has no additional disability over and above his visual impairment, and is fully ambulant. He has poor vision and his distance vision has been assessed at 0.9 LogMAR, therefore he needs support in seeing things at a distance. His near vision has also been assessed at 0.6 LogMAR which indicates he will also need help with close-up work. A QTVI has identified that he likes materials presented to him in font size 24 and particularly with sans serif fonts such as Verdana or Helvetica. Peter has a hand-held magnifier, which stays in his bag until he is reminded to bring it out by his class teacher, especially at times when the class are reading story books. Peter is an average reader for his age, although as a result of his nystagmus he reads very slowly and needs extra time for assessments.

In the classroom, specific adaptations have been made in order for Peter to feel comfortable within the learning space and to access the curriculum. These adaptations include a considered seating position, lighting, high-contrast materials, slope boards, and a reduction of the glare on computer screens as well as a reduction of the amount of clutter on worksheets.

---

[3]Oculocutaneous albinism are a group of conditions that affect the pigmentation of the skin, hair and eyes and also reduce pigmentation of the iris and the retina.

[4]Nystagmus is uncontrolled movements of the eyes; in most people that have nystagmus the eyes usually move from side to side, but in others the eyes can move so that they swing up and down or even in a circular motion.

He is a shy boy, and although he does claim to have some friends, his class teacher would dispute this. He finds it difficult to maintain eye contact due to his nystagmus and does not look at people when talking to them. Peter does not do any extra-curricular activities for he sees himself as clumsy and as a result his confidence and self-esteem are low. He can on occasion get a little disorientated and does not go far beyond his own local area. Although he tries to be independent within the school environment he is lacking in some basic core mobility and daily living skills.

Discussion point

Before reading the research about how to respond to the case study: what immediate questions do you have? What approaches would you take and why?

Responses to the case study

Empowerment of the mainstream class teacher

Peter is visually impaired. The policies that are in place within his local authority mean that he has been included in the early intervention strategies since he was a few months old. Peter has routinely been included in multi-agency team assessments. A single shared report is given to him and his parents, and shared with other professionals within the team and used to constitute a significant part of the information necessary for completion of Peter's Individual Education Plan, Personal Learning Plan, Individual Transition Plan, and other planning documents. However, one of the most important issues to consider for Peter is that he is a full member of the classroom and as such he should be treated as any other member. Gale et al. (1998) suggest quite correctly that Peter 'is more similar to, than different from his sighted peers' (p. 147). They stress the importance of the classroom teacher providing a positive role model to encourage Peter's peers to accept him. The classroom teacher may require support to achieve this aim.

Support for the classroom teacher is available from many sources but one of the most fundamental sources of support will be from the QTVI. One of the main roles of the QTVI is to empower others, by collaborating and consulting with the classroom teacher and others (including Peter's peers), and to provide awareness raising that will inform them about the implications a visual impairment may have. Importantly though, the concept of empowerment goes beyond mere awareness raising in order to change the behaviour and assumptions that surround the pupil with visual impairment. Clearly stated, awareness raising, although necessary is simply not sufficient. Awareness raising for staff and pupils is a one-way process, placing little responsibility on the recipient, for they are passive receptors of the information given to them by QTVIs. Mainstream teachers need to be empowered to change their practice. As Coburn (2001) and more recently supported by Printy (2008) suggest, teachers change their practice dramatically as a result of interaction with individuals that are outwith their own 'community of practice'. If this is the case, the importance of the role of the QTVI in empowering the actions of the mainstream teacher cannot be underestimated.

The responsibility for changing behaviours must not lie only with the QTVI. Stein and Nelson (2003) argue that 'teachers must believe that serious engagement in their own learning is part and parcel of what it means to be professional and they must expect to be held accountable for continuously improving instructional practice' (p. 425). Empowerment in this context then is a two-way relationship between the QTVI and the mainstream teacher; in that the QTVI must set the right enabling conditions for empowerment to occur, through dialogue and consultation; however, the mainstream teacher, through self-agency, must take hold of these conditions and deliver change themselves.

Research tells us that having a special health care need generally is associated with being bullied (van Cleave and Davis, 2006). Sweeting and West (2001) found increased bullying was more likely 'among children who were less physically attractive, overweight, had a disability such as a sight, hearing or speech problem' (p. 225). We see in the case study a disconnect between the teacher's perception of friendship and Peter's. Pupils with visual impairment appear to use the concept of friendship to protect themselves against bullying (Buultjens et al., 2002) and professionals need to beware of the exact status and nature of friendship amongst pupils with visual impairment. Roe (2008) developing Buultjens' stance defines the issue clearly in that professionals need to create a variety of social contexts to promote social inclusion and in each of these contexts the child should not be seen as one with difficulties. Instead, there should be an examination of how each of these created contexts impacts on the child with visual impairment. Roe is almost right however; in order to have a positive impact on learning, mainstream teachers need to feel empowered to be able to create the right contexts, and empowerment again comes in part from discourse with the QTVI and other professional colleagues.

Empowerment from orientation and mobility

Empowerment for Peter is essential; however, he must develop his mobility skills so that he is able to move around confidently in his surrounding environment. Orientation and mobility skills should be delivered by qualified habilitation[5] instructors who are trained to

---

[5]Notice the term is habilitation instructors and not rehabilitation instructors. Children with visual impairment do not need to be re-habilitated, in their orientation, mobility and daily living skills.

work with children. It is not enough to have instructors who are trained to work with adults, who then suddenly find themselves working with children, this smacks of viewing the child as a 'little adult'. Nor are QTVIs qualified to plan and deliver these skills either. QTVIs do receive some training in sighted guide techniques but it is not commensurate with fully qualified orientation and mobility instructors. Students who receive mobility and orientation instruction are more likely to be employable, have higher levels of independence, and have the skills necessary to utilise a variety of transport options, that are not limited to 'getting a taxi' (Carey, 2006). However, conflict can arise within the school environment. There are issues of when the instruction is going to take place within the school timetable. Is the pupil for example expected to miss classes in core subjects to receive mobility training? Importantly, instruction also needs to take place at home, and between home and school. The rhetoric of the 'community school' is entrenched within policy and ideology, yet when it comes to orientation and mobility training for the VI child this rhetoric often gets ignored.

Discussion point

Peter's social competence, his confidence and independent skills are affecting his home and school life; however, he is obtaining average grades. If pushed Peter might be able to obtain even higher grades. As a mainstream teacher, to what degree would you focus on Peter obtaining good academic grades at the expense of his own social competence skills? Or would you focus on ensuring that when Peter leaves school he can live a full and independent life which may mean limiting his academic achievements?

Relate this case study to your own area of practice and discuss how social competence is promoted.

Independent living skills or attainment?

Related to core mobility issues is employment. One of the major problems facing professionals involved in the education of children and young people who are visually impaired is the employment/further education rates of children leaving education services. Research shows that there is a high unemployment rate for people with visual impairment and especially those with additional support need(s) (see Meager and Carta, 2008; Douglas et al., 2006; Douglas et al., 2009). Meagar and Carter (2008) report the overall employment rate for people with seeing difficulties is low, and even lower for people who are disabled by their sight problems. If they have additional disabilities or health problems the employment rate drops even lower. However, a low unemployment rate should not be automatically equated with levels of educational attainment. Cebulla and Chanfreau (2009) highlight a small education attainment gap for pupils with visual impairment if visual impairment is the pupil's only additional support need: 15% of pupils with visual impairment and an additional special educational need achieved five or more GCSEs (A*–C) – compared with 64% of pupils without any additional support need.

If pupils with visual impairment with no other additional support needs are achieving only slightly less in attainment than their sighted peers but have a higher unemployment rate, what could be causing the disparity between the two? I would like to suggest part of the problem is the delivery (or not) of the mobility and independence curriculum. If single-disability VI children are achieving near standard attainment rates, but are leaving school with very little independent living skills, then although their attainment levels may allow the student to be called for an interview with prospective employers, the employer soon recognises the poor independence and social skills that are presented, and consequently the student is less likely to be successful in obtaining employment. It is important to point out in this scenario it is not the visual impairment per se that causes the difficulty; it is the lack of mobility and independent living skills. The two are separate issues.

If VI pupils leave school but are unable to go shopping, wash their clothes or cook for themselves then I would suggest the academic attainment counts for very little. If VI people are to lead full and successful lives within a working, and day-to-day environment they must be able to do so independently.

This is not an easy problem to solve. What could be a possible solution to ensure VI children are able to access a curriculum that includes independence and daily living skills within a mainstream school? Controversially, I suggest that for some pupils, especially those who should be accessing independent living skills lessons, it may be appropriate to ignore – or if this seems too strong, to focus less on – academic attainment and concentrate mainly or even wholly on developing independent living skills. Academic attainment may be achieved later, as for many young sighted adults who attend further education colleges. If this suggestion is accepted in schools then the training in independent living skills must be supported by appropriately trained habilitation workers, employed by local education authorities, and then supported by social work habilitation workers during out-of-term time. This mixed model of delivery ensures that all aspects of daily living and mobility needs are catered for not only at school but within the community as well.

To be clear, I am not advocating that VI children are taken out of mainstream classes to be instructed in their daily living skills. This may lead to segregation and greater feelings of isolation, but it may be possible within the mainstream classroom to increase the independent living skills of children through project-based learning. Take for example the Scottish Curriculum for Excellence (Scottish Government, 2004) where it is stressed that every child and young person is entitled to develop skills for learning, skills for life and skills for work. Within the new Curriculum there will be a shared responsibility between schools and partners to take a holistic approach to ensure that children and young people are fully engaged members of society. Thus we may find that adapting to such an approach is not in conflict with the mainstream curriculum, but is in fact wholly supported by it.

To conclude, if the trend to include pupils who are visually impaired within mainstream education continues, then there is a need to think very strongly about the relationship between academic attainment and independent living skills. With the introduction of new curricula, the time may be right to readdress the balance, and to take a brave step forward and focus on ensuring that children who are blind or partially sighted can function independently, to the best of their ability, in a sighted world; and not, as at present, have some children who attain excellent grades but cannot engage with the world around them.

Educationalists should be moving towards holistic education programmes and by doing so we may find that educators and professionals are recognising differences between each child and identifying exactly each and every one's own particular needs, and consequently are best supporting that child through school and into their early adult years (Ravenscroft, 2013).

Summary

This chapter has:

- Identified a number of issues concerning the assessment, registration and education of children in mainstream schools.
- Considered the inappropriate use of the main certificate of visual impairment register as a tool for future planning of services, including education, for children with visual impairment due to the under-representation of children on the register.
- Discussed the profile and prevalence of significant visual impairment and the likelihood of a visually impaired child attending mainstream schools.
- Through the case study of a child with oculocutaneous albinism with low vision and nystagmus, stressed the importance of developing a two-way relationship between the QTVI and the mainstream class teacher, and particularly focused on the role of the QTVI in empowering the mainstream class teacher, rather than simply providing guidance or informative awareness-raising sessions.
- Discussed the interaction between academic attainment and daily living skills with an emphasis on that, perhaps for some, it is better to concentrate on developing greater social competence within the child than to achieve some degree of academic success.

Discussion points

- As we have seen, a changing profile of children who are visually impaired is occurring. More and more children who are born with VI are also born with additional disabilities. What do you think are the major issues for inclusion into mainstream schools for children with VI and co-morbidities, and does this affect the debate that surrounds inclusion?
- Imagine that you are head of a service that supports the education of children with visual impairment in your local authority. What actions do you take to ensure that you know precisely the number of children with visual impairment who are transitioning from health service responsibility (say, from birth to three years) to the responsibility of the education authority?
- You are still the head of service, except this time you are aware that there are a number of children with visual impairment, who will in a year's time transition from your education service to either full-time further or higher education, employment or move into adult service responsibility. Consider what mechanisms you would use to measure the successful impact of this transition period. In other words, how do you know that the services you have provided have successfully impacted on the lives of the children currently going through the transition period?

Further reading

Corn, A.L. and Erin, J.N. (2010) *Foundations of Low Vision: Clinical and Functional Perspectives*, 2nd edn. New York: American Foundation for the Blind Press.
An excellent second edition on how best to assess and support both children and adults with low vision and plan programmes and services.

LaVenture, S. (ed.) (2007) *A Parent's Guide to Special Education for Children with Visual Impairments*. New York: American Foundation for the Blind Press.
For the parent and training practitioner, it gives a comprehensive guide to understanding the process of educating a child with visual impairments.

Roman-Lantzy, C. (2007) *Cortical Visual Impairment: An Approach to Assessment and Intervention*. New York: American Foundation for the Blind Press.
An excellent book for the practitioner who is interested in cortical/cerebral visual impairment.

Salisbury, R (ed.) (2007) *Teaching Pupils with Visual Impairment: A Guide to Making the School Curriculum Accessible*. Abingdon: Routledge.

A book that has many practical ideas on making the curriculum accessible. Many of the chapters are written by experienced teachers of pupils with visual impairment.

The Curriculum for Excellence website: www.ltscotland.org.uk/curriculumfor excellence/index.asp.
An all-encompassing website for the Curriculum for Excellence.

Useful websites

www.educationscotland.gov.uk/parentzone/mychild/entitlements/girfec.asp.

www.fiesta-project.eu.

www.perkinselearning.org/teaching-resources.

www.ssc.education.ed.ac.uk.

www.tsbvi.edu.

References

Alexander, P., Rahi, J.S., Hingorani, M. (2009) Provision and cost of children's and young people's services in the UK: findings from a single primary care trust. *British Journal of Ophthalmology*, 93(5): 645–49.

Atkinson, M., Jones, M. and Lamont, E. (2007) *Multi-agency Working and Its Implications for Practice: A Review of the Literature*. Reading: CfBT.

Bailey, I.L. and Lovie, J.E. (1976) New design principles for visual acuity letter charts. *American Journal of Optometry and Physiological Optics*, 53: 740–45.

Barry, R.J. and Murray, P.I. (2005) Unregistered visual impairment: is registration a failing system? *British Journal of Ophthalmology*, 89: 995–8.

Bodeau-Livinec, F., Surman, G., Kaminski, M., Wilkinson, A.R., Ancel, P.Y. and Kurinczuk, J.J. (2007) Recent trends in visual impairment and blindness in the UK. *Archives of Disease in Childhood*, 92(12): 1099–104.

Buultjens, M., Stead, J. and Dallas, M. (2002) *Promoting Social Inclusion of Pupils with Visual Impairment in Mainstream Schools in Scotland*. Edinburgh: Scottish Sensory Centre.

Carey, K. (2006) Visual Impairment in a time of change: self understanding as the basis for effective living. *Key Note Address: Institute for Blind and Visually Impaired Young People and Adults in Copenhagen and Vision Centre for Children*. Retrieved 20 June 2010 from: www.humanity.org.uk/articles/blindness-visual-impairment/self-understanding-effective-living.

Cebulla, A. and Chanfreau, J. (2009) Educational attainment of blind and partially sighted pupils. National Centre for Social Research (NatCen) forRNIB. Retrieved 22 June 2010 from: www.natcen.ac.uk/pzMedia/uploads/Downloadable/f4ef4271–f81d-41d8–b758–2ff39a3deb2b.pdf

Clunies-Ross, L. and Franklin, A. (1997) Where have all the children gone? An analysis of new statistical data on visual impairment amongst children in England, Scotland and Wales. *British Journal of Visual Impairment*, 15(2): 19–20.

Coburn, C.E. (2001) Collective sensemaking about reading: how teachers mediate reading policy in their professional communities. *Educational Evaluation and Policy Analysis*, 23(2): 145–70.

Davis, J. et al. (2014) FIESTA Best Practice Report. Retrieved 18 September 2014 from: www.fiesta-project.eu/sites/default/files/BP_Fiesta_Report_2014_0.pdf.

Douglas, G., Corcoran, C. and Pavey, S. (2006) *Network 1000: Opinions and Circumstances of Visually Impaired People in Great Britain: Report Based on over 1000 Interviews.* Birmingham: Visual Impairment Centre for Teaching and Research, University of Birmingham.

Douglas, G., Pavey, S., Clements, B. and Corcoran, C. (2009) *Network 1000: Access to Employment Amongst Visually Impaired People.* Birmingham: Visual Impairment Centre for Teaching and Research, University of Birmingham.

Durnian, J.M., Cheeseman, R., Kumar, A., Raja, V., Newman, W. and Chandna, A. (2010) Childhood sight impairment: a 10–year picture. *Eye*, 24: 112–17.

Evans, J. (1995) Causes of blindness and partial sight in England and Wales 1990–1991, *Studies on Medical and Population Subjects*, 57. London: HMSO.

Foster, A. and Gilbert, C. (1997) Epidemiology of visual impairment in children. In D. Taylor (ed.), *Paediatric Ophthalmology*, 2nd edn. Oxford: Blackwell Science.

Gale, G., Kelley, P., d'Apice, P., Booty, J., Alsop, P., Bagot, N., Foreham, B., Williams, B., Pfisterer, U. and Sheik, K. (1998) Accessing the curriculum. In P. Kelly and G. Gale (eds), *Towards Excellence, Effective Education for Students with Vision Impairments.* North Rocks, NSW: Royal Institute for Deaf and Blind Students, pp. 146–76.

Gray, C. (2008) Support for children with a visual impairment in Northern Ireland: the role of the rehabilitation worker. *British Journal of Visual Impairment*, 26: 239–54.

Hansen, R.M. and Fulton, A.B. (2005) Development of the cone ERG in infants. *Investigative Ophthalmology and Visual Science*, 46(9): 3458–62.

Hewett, R, Douglas, G. and Keil, S. (2014) Post-16 transition experience of visually impaired young people in England and Wales: early findings from a longitudinal study. *British Journal of Visual Impairment*, 32: 211–22.

Keil, S. and Clunies-Ross, L. (2003) *Survey of Educational Provision for Blind and Partially Sighted Children in England, Scotland and Wales in 2002.* London: RNIB.

King, A.J.W., Reddy. A., Thompson, J.R. and Rosenthal, A.R. (2000) The rates of blindness and partial sight registration in glaucoma patients. *Eye*, 14: 613–19.

Levy, G. (2007) *Certificate of Visual Impairment.* London: Royal College of Ophthalmology. Retrieved 22 June 2010: from www.rcophth.ac.uk/standards/cvi.

McGraw, P., Winn, B. and Whitaker, D. (1995) Reliability of the Snellen chart. *British Medical Journal*, 310: 1481–82.

Meager, N. and Carta, E. (2008) *Labour Market Experiences of People with Seeing Difficulties: Secondary Analysis of LFS Data.* London: Institute for Employment Studies/RNIB.

Morris, M. and Smith, P. (2008) *Educational Provision for Blind and Partially Sighted Children and Young People in Wales.* London: NFER/RNIB.

Printy, S.M. (2008) Perspective leadership for teacher learning: a community of practice. *Educational Administration Quarterly*, 44: 187–226.

Rahi, J.S. and Cable, N. (2003) Severe visual impairment and blindness in children in the UK. *Lancet*, 25; 362(9393): 1359–65.

Rahi, J.S. and Dezateux, C. (1998) Epidemiology of visual impairment in Britain. *Archives of Disease in Childhood*, 78(4): 381–6.

Ravenscroft, J. (2009) What parents of children with vision impairment ask their child's teachers. *Journal of South Pacific Educators of Vision Impairment*, 4(1): 34–40.

Ravenscroft, J. (2013) High attainment–low employment: the how and why educational professionals are failing children with visual impairment. *International Journal of Learning*, 18(12): 135–44.

Ravenscroft, J., Blaikie, A., Macewen, C., O'Hare, A., Creswell, L. and Dutton, G.N. (2008) A novel method of notification to profile childhood visual impairment in Scotland to meet the needs of children with visual impairment. *British Journal of Visual Impairment*, 26(2): 170–89.

Roe, J. (2008) Social inclusion: meeting the socio-emotional needs of children with vision needs. *British Journal of Visual Impairment*, 26(2): 147–58.

Rogers, M. (1996) Visual impairment in Liverpool: prevalence and morbidity. *Archives of Disease in Childhood*, 74(4): 299–303.

Royal National Institute of Blind People (2000) *Shaping the Future* (summary report). London: RNIB.

Royal National Institute of Blind People (2001a) *Shaping the Future: The Educational Experiences of 5 to 16 Year-Old Blind and Partially Sighted Children and Young People*. London: RNIB.

Royal National Institute of Blind People (2001b) *Shaping the Future: The Social Life and Leisure Activities of Blind and Partially Sighted Children and Young People Aged 5 to 25*. London: RNIB.

Royal National Institute of Blind People (2001c) *Shaping the Future: The Health and Wellbeing of Blind and Partially Sighted Children and Young People Aged 5 to 25*. London: RNIB.

Royal National Institute of Blind People (2014) *Evidence Base Review: Children and Young People*. Retrieved 18 September 2014 from: www.rnib.org.uk/sites/default/files/RNIB_evidence_based_review_of_children_and_young_people.pdf.

Scottish Executive (2001) *Report of the Certification and Registration Working Group* (May 2001). Social Work Services Inspectorate, Scottish Executive.

Scottish Government (2004) *A Curriculum for Excellence – The Curriculum Review Group*. Retrieved 19 June 2010 from: www.scotland.gov.uk/Publications/2004/11/20178/45862.

Stein, M.K. and Nelson, B.S. (2003) Leadership content knowledge. *Educational Evaluation and Policy Analysis*, 25(4): 423–48.

Sweeting, H. and West, P. (2001) Being different: correlates of the experience of teasing and bullying at age 11. *Research Papers in Education*, 16(3): 225–46.

Thomson, D. (2005) VA testing in practice: The Snellen chart. *Optometry Today*, April: 57.

Townsley, R., Abbott, D. and Watson, D. (2004) *Making a Difference? Exploring the Impact of Multi-agency Working on Disabled Children with Complex Health Care Needs, Their Families and the Professionals Who Support Them*. Bristol: Policy Press.

Van Cleave, J. and Davis, M.M. (2006) Bullying and peer victimization among children with special health care needs. *Pediatrics*, 118(4): 1212–19.

Wilson, F.M. (2005) *Practical Ophthalmology*, 5th edn. San Francisco: American Academy of Ophthalmology.

Woodhead, M. and Faulkner, D. (2000) Subjects, objects or participants? Dilemmas of psychological research with children. In P. Christiansen and A. James (eds), *Research with Children: Perspectives and Practices*. London: Falmer Press, pp. 10–39.

Inclusive Education for Students who are Deaf or Hard of Hearing

16

Jill Duncan

Learning objectives

This chapter will help readers to:

- Understand important issues related to the inclusive education of students who are deaf or hard of hearing, including hearing technology, communication modality, literacy and cognition
- Appreciate the barriers to family-school engagement and the cultural diversity of families of children who are deaf or hard of hearing
- Learn practical strategies for supporting classroom teachers
- Identify specialist practitioner teaching behaviours for students who are deaf or hard of hearing

Understanding students who are deaf or hard of hearing is complex because, in addition to general education matters, the specialist practitioner must have expert knowledge of communication development, including signed language, spoken language, speech, audiology and auditory development. Furthermore, political and emotional undercurrents frequently burden the deaf education sector. These controversial issues will not be addressed here. Instead, this chapter will bring to light critical issues important for educating all students who are deaf or hard of hearing. This is an introductory chapter and the reader is encouraged to investigate the selected readings at the end of the chapter for detailed examination of pertinent issues.

Terms found in this chapter require upfront explanation. For the purpose of improved readability, the term 'children who are deaf or hard of hearing' is inclusive of children who are culturally Deaf who use signed language and children who are hearing impaired and use auditory-based spoken language to communicate. The term 'caregiver(s)' denotes the person(s) primarily responsible for the needs of the child. The term 'child' is interchangeable with 'student' and vice versa. The term 'specialist practitioner' refers to the teacher of the deaf, auditory–verbal therapist/educator, speech language pathologist or audiologist – not the classroom teacher. 'Intervention' refers to any specialist practitioner support – either direct intervention to the child/family or indirect intervention via support to the classroom teacher and other school personnel.

Population overview

More than 665,000 babies with moderate, severe or profound hearing loss are born worldwide each year (Olusanya and Newton, 2007). Because hearing loss can be either present at birth or acquired after birth, the prevalence of childhood hearing loss increases with age and nearly doubles by nine years of age (Fortnum et al., 2007; Olusanya, 2005).

Students who are deaf or hard of hearing are heterogeneous in nature for a range of factors including aetiology, family and environmental characteristics. This diversity is reflected in the range of communication abilities, literacy, cognitive and auditory skills (Duncan et al., 2014). Children who are deaf or hard of hearing are at increased risk of additional medically and educationally diagnosed disorders (McClay et al., 2008). Children with an additional disability have needs that are distinct from children who are deaf or hard of hearing as a single disability. When this occurs, specialist practitioners with expertise other than deafness are required, making collaboration among interdisciplinary team members essential (Duncan et al., 2014).

Assistive hearing technology

Assistive hearing technology includes digital programmable hearing aids, bone-anchored hearing aids, cochlear implants, hybrid cochlear implants and personal Frequency Modulation (FM) systems. The purpose of hearing technology is to make spoken language accessible and comfortable (Duncan et al., 2014; Seewald et al., 2005). Choice of hearing technology is generally based on severity of hearing, but sometimes on the child's anatomy. Most children who are deaf or hard of hearing in westernised countries use binaural amplification. In general, the earlier and more consistent the hearing aids and/or cochlear implant is used by the child, the better the functional use of the device.

Care and maintenance of the hearing technology is transferred from the specialist practitioner to the caregiver through explicit instruction and practical experience as soon after the device fitting as possible. Eventually the child becomes responsible for the hearing technology and audiological management. The goal is to have the student assume full responsibility of hearing technology and audiological management by the end of secondary school. Classroom teachers also require knowledge of hearing technology – in particular the FM. This is because children who are deaf or hard of hearing may have difficulty listening in situations characterised by background noise or reverberation such as classrooms (Duncan et al., 2014).

Communication modality

Children who are deaf or hard of hearing may use sign language, spoken language or a combination of sign and spoken language. Communication modality of children who are deaf or hard of hearing falls along a continuum. At one end of the continuum is exclusive use of visual (sign) language and at the other end is exclusive use of auditory-based spoken language, although for this population, communication is rarely auditory only. Upon diagnosis and after unbiased information has been provided to the family, caregivers choose the communication modality that best suits the child and culture of the family. Occasionally, aetiology may dictate a communication modality.

It is essential that the child and caregivers are fluent in the same communication modality – whether it is sign language or auditory-based spoken language. It is also critical that caregiver–child interaction is abundant and consistent throughout the child's life so that among other things, communication development is maximised.

Literacy

A strong spoken language foundation facilitates reading development (Duncan et al., 2014). A child who has atypical early exposure to spoken language may be at a disadvantage for developing adequate phonological representations (Dillon and Pisoni, 2006). If a spoken language gap existed in early childhood and persists, students who are deaf or hard of hearing may encounter barriers to developing fluent literacy skills. Students who use sign language can become literate adults; however, for this to occur it requires vigilant family and specialist practitioner assistance in developing key skills such as phonological awareness, decoding, fluency, comprehension and vocabulary (Duncan et al., 2014).

Literacy demands increase in complexity as the child progresses through school and as the difficulty of vocabulary and syntax increases. All students require metalinguistic skills, or the capability to talk about words, word structure and word meaning in a specific, decontextualised manner that demonstrates conscious understanding of metalinguistics, including phonological awareness and morphological awareness. Acquiring metalinguistic skills can be difficult for deaf or hard of hearing students for many reasons, but mainly because most do not have experience in incidental listening (Duncan et al., 2014). High-level literacy skills are required in order to participate in sophisticated problem-solving, and communication skills are needed in the academic and work environments.

Each reader's overall life experiences, or world knowledge, will influence the interpretation of the text. In literacy, the reader and writer do not share the same experience of time and physical environment. Ambiguity and interpretation of the text are not as open for clarification as in face-to-face communication (Duncan et al., 2014). When instructing deaf and hard of hearing students, it is important for the specialist practitioner and classroom teacher to consider the contribution of all language components to reading outcomes given the interaction of associated top-down and bottom-up processes. Early and appropriate evidence-based literacy instruction is critical for successful literacy development and if necessary, remediation (Easterbrooks and Beal-Alvarez, 2014; Mody, 2007).

Discussion point

In order to maximise the literacy development of students with profound deafness who use auditory-based spoken language to communicate, the school principal, specialist practitioner, classroom teacher and parents might consider these options. The principal might facilitate the classroom teacher's attendance at deafness-related professional learning seminars. Upon consultation with the classroom teacher, the specialist practitioner might integrate phonological awareness into direct intervention with the student while using key subject vocabulary. The classroom teacher might integrate literacy-based activities into all academic subjects. The parents might provide an abundant supply of highly motivating reading materials and opportunity for the student to practice oral reading as regularly as possible.

Cognition

Historically, children who are deaf or hard of hearing generally fall behind their hearing peers academically including in literacy and mathematics (Duncan et al., 2014; Marschark, 2003). This is due to a number of reasons including diagnosis, aetiology, language and instructional practices. Marschark (2003) in reference to children who used sign language, surmises that it is reasonably possible that children who are deaf or hard of hearing have different knowledge bases, cognitive strategies and experiences that influence literacy and academic skills.

Executive function makes up the higher order cognitive processing responsible for metacognition and behaviour regulation and is influenced by many factors. Children who are deaf or hard of hearing follow the expected milestones for executive function although its development is closely related to family and school environments and practitioner instruction (Duncan et al., 2014; Hauser et al., 2008). Executive skills are essential skills that should be explicitly monitored and if necessary taught by the specialist practitioner and classroom teacher. Executive skills include:

- response inhibition
- working memory
- emotional control
- sustained attention
- task initiation
- planning/prioritising
- organisation
- flexibility (Dawson and Guare, 2010)

It is important for the specialist practitioner and classroom teacher to maintain vigilant surveillance of executive function development for children who are deaf or hard of hearing because of its relationship to overall academic achievement.

Families

As children grow, their developmental capacities increase in both level and range, which in turn influences their relationship with caregivers and other significant people in their lives (Bronfenbrenner and Morris, 2006; Duncan, 2010; Duncan et al., 2014). Caregivers remain the primary agents of change throughout childhood, which is why it is important to consider the family ecology (Dishion and Kavanagh, 2003; Duncan, 2010). However, as the child develops, persons outside the immediate living environment, such as peers and school personnel, become increasingly important (Bronfenbrenner and Morris, 2006). It then becomes essential for the specialist practitioner to review the influence of these individuals on the developing child (Duncan, 2010).

The family is a social system and so intervention with the child who is deaf or hard of hearing will influence the entire family (Duncan et al., 2014). Therefore, it is impracticable to implement intervention with children without family involvement. Care should be taken to avoid isolated focus on the student who is deaf or hard of hearing; the specialist practitioner is encouraged to maintain a family systems' outlook.

A positive caregiver–child relationship is one in which the caregiver balances the needs of the child with the overall needs of the family (Dishion and Kavanagh, 2003). Family equilibrium can be difficult when a child has a disability. Caregivers may inadvertently allocate a disproportionate amount of time and resources to support the child who is deaf or hard of hearing.

A positive caregiver–child behaviour monitoring system is one in which the caregivers have continual developmentally appropriate surveillance of the child's behaviour (Dishion and Kavanagh, 2003). Developmentally appropriate surveillance is the suitable degree of supervision for the age and stage of the child. The caregiver, specialist practitioner and classroom teacher should take care to relinquish control to the child as the child develops into a young adult (Duncan et al., 2014).

A positive caregiver–school association is one in which the caregiver, school community and specialist practitioner regularly communicate in a proactive and productive manner. The classroom teacher and specialist practitioner offer a menu of caregiver communication options depending on the age of the child and family needs, including email, family communication journal, telephone meeting, electronic bulletin board, web-based portfolio, face-to-face meetings (Carlisle et al., 2005; Knopf and Swick, 2008; Thompson et al., 2007). This ongoing consistent communication assists in maintaining transparent and congruent child expectations.

School and classroom placement

There is a continuum of educational placement options for students who are deaf or hard of hearing, depending on support requirements. At one end of the continuum is special school placement with no or little integration with typically developing hearing peers. This placement is for those students who have the highest specialist support needs. The further along the educational placement continuum, the more the child who is deaf or hard of hearing is included into the regular school learning and social environment. This is not to say that fully included children need no specialist support. Regardless of school and classroom placement, students who are deaf or hard of hearing require special provisions including such things as specialist practitioner, hearing technology, access to curriculum in the student's first language – whether sign language or auditory-based spoken language, access to peers and/or mentors who are deaf or hard of hearing, and annual communication assessments (Duncan et al., 2014). It is critical that consistent access to learning opportunities occurs in all classroom placements.

Attendance in a mainstream school does not automatically cause inclusion (Angelides and Aravi, 2006/2007). Integration can cause children who are deaf or hard of hearing to feel isolated and may influence identity and self-esteem development. The essential elements for success are opportunities for peer and adult communication, which lead to developing healthy interpersonal skills. The *Inclusion Screener* (Table 16.1) is a quick and easy tool,

Table 16.1   Inclusion screener for students who are deaf or hard of hearing

Communication skills	Yes	No
1. Student initiates conversation with classmates		
2. Student takes conversational turns		
3. Student maintains conversation topic		
4. Student joins group conversation		
5. Student contributes to class discussions		
6. Student uses appropriate greetings with peers		
7. Student uses appropriate greetings with adults		
8. Student understands abstracts concepts		
9. Student understands classroom jokes		
10. Student understands classroom instructions		
11. Student requests assistance when required		
12. Student answers teacher's questions in class		
13. Student retells out-of-class events		
14. Student uses age-appropriate sentence structure		
15. Student uses logical written thoughts		

Social skills	Yes	No
16. Student interacts with other children in the classroom		
17. Student interacts with other children in the playground		
18. Student takes turns during classroom activities and games		
19. Student is willing to share with others		
20. Student gets along with classmates		
21. Student displays appropriate classroom behaviour		
22. Student forms friendships with other students		
23. Student joins in whole-school activities		
24. Student asks class teacher for permission when required		
25. Student assists other students when requested		

School routines skills	Yes	No
26. Student is well organised		
27. Student completes homework appropriately		
28. Student successfully uses classroom technology		
29. Student makes choices when given the opportunity		
30. Student works with teaching assistants appropriately		
31. Student follows classroom routines		
32. Student completes set work within allocated time		
33. Student enjoys being a part of the class		

Source: Adapted from Richards (2003)

which can assist classroom teachers to identify student attributes that may require specialist practitioner attention.

Change in either classroom or school placement is inevitable and occurs for many reasons, including family relocation, academic concerns and incongruent school–family expectations. A change in schooling can be a time of increased family stress. Caregivers and the student undergo a process that requires them to weigh the benefits and disadvantages of placement options (Duncan, 2009). There may not be a perfect option and families may feel they are required to settle for second best. Paramount to facilitating a positive learning environment change for the student and family is unbiased access to information and transparent knowledge of specialist service provision options.

Family–school engagement

The family–school relationship influences student self-educational expectation (Falbo et al., 2001). Caregivers are encouraged to monitor the student's educational and social life so that school routines, teachers, friends and extracurricular activities are familiar to the whole family. This facilitates open and continuous family communication. Caregivers should endeavour to consider student academic information so that progress is transparent and the student receives adequate support. Caregivers are also encouraged to facilitate a positive peer network in which the student feels comfortable. Finally, caregivers should make an effort to maximise direct school participation.

Family–school participation can occur in many formats, including communicating with the teacher or school personnel, attending school functions, volunteering in the classroom or the school, caregiver–teacher conference, caregiver organisations and school governance roles (Harvard Family Research Project, 2007). These activities are important in several ways. School involvement assists the caregiver in understanding the school community and monitoring their child's participation in it. In addition, family–school participation conveys to the student the importance of school as a function.

When caregivers are involved in schools, they are more likely to obtain support from the schools when assistance is needed (Anderson-Butcher and Ashton, 2004). There are many by-products of family–school collaboration. These include the fact that students and their families are supported, appreciated and valued, families feel empowered, caregivers gain parenting skills, school personnel and family working alliances are formed, and knowledge between parties is shared more easily (Anderson-Butcher and Ashton, 2004).

Establishing effective family–school–specialist practitioner partnerships is a process requiring honest, transparent intentions over time (Thompson et al., 2007). No isolated intervention assures positive family–school relationships (Thompson et al., 2007). Mismatches may occur when the home culture and values are at odds with those of the school or specialist practitioner.

Cultural diversity

Although the population of students in today's schools is increasingly diverse, the population of teachers is not (Carlisle et al., 2005). Teachers most often come from the majority culture (Al-Hassan and Gardner, 2002). Carlisle et al. (2005) suggest that when the family and specialist practitioner cultures differ, caregivers may not feel their family's culture is understood or appreciated. Further, some cultures may feel it is disrespectful to communicate with schools or specialist practitioners, making family participation more challenging (Carlisle et al., 2005).

Specialist practitioners need to be aware that effective caregiving takes on various roles depending on the culture of the family (Dishion and Kavanagh, 2003). The family's level of acculturation involves the extent to which caregivers have attained a social status and education level comparable to the dominant culture (Harry, 2008). Working with families requires knowledge of cultural norms regardless of whether the family is part of the minority or majority culture.

Potential barriers to participation by families with diverse needs include:

- limited language proficiency
- lack of written information in the language of the family
- specialist practitioner's unfamiliarity with the culture of the family
- unfamiliarity with common practices and legislative rights
- differing views of the importance of family educational involvement (Al-Hassan and Gardner, 2002)

An increasing number of ethnically diverse families require specialist practitioner and school personnel to have expertise on the influence of deafness in a variety of cultures. Specialist practitioners must recognise that identified strengths may vary from culture to culture (Duncan, 2007).

Pedagogy and practice

A fundamental belief within deaf education is that learning occurs within a social learning paradigm, which views the specialist practitioner as a facilitator and the student as a significant decision maker as they learn from each other (Duncan et al., 2014). Instruction is expected to be purposeful, matching students' interests and experiences. In order to maximise learning, regular assessment of students who are deaf or hard of hearing is based on authentic, real-life procedures with direct and immediate carryover into life. The specialist practitioner embraces the premise that learners construct knowledge based on their own experience and previous beliefs. Learning cannot be de-contextualised. It does not occur in isolation from the circumstance in which it occurs. The specialist practitioner encourages opportunities for meaningful and genuine exploration, engagement in activities, interactive group work and student ownership of the learning process (Snider and Roehl, 2007).

The responsibilities continuum views the classroom teacher as responsible for academics and the practitioner as responsible for those aspects of the children's development which will facilitate cognitive linguistic growths.

Underpinning all teaching strategies is the belief that no pedagogical domain is compartmentalised or considered in isolation of the other, but rather integrated (Duncan, 2006). Thus, specialist practitioners incorporate a range of suitable linguistic, auditory, cognitive, socio-emotional and speech objectives into all interactions where necessary. For example, the specialist practitioner targeting the goal of understanding non-literal language will also apply auditory and cognitive goals and if appropriate, socio-emotional and speech goals. Regardless of objectives, specialist practitioners create enjoyable and motivating environments while maintaining high, but realistic shared expectations (Duncan et al., 2014).

Within a mainstream school context, there are two primary models of specialist practitioner intervention for children who are deaf or hard of hearing – push-in and pull-out. In the 'push-in model', the specialist practitioner works within the classroom performing a variety of roles. These include team teaching with the classroom teacher, small group discussion with the child who is deaf or hard of hearing and hearing peers, and one-on-one intervention in a quiet area of the classroom. There are three primary benefits of this model. First, the student does not leave the classroom, implying continuous membership. Second, the student avoids stigmatisation as being different and needing to be taken out of the classroom for remediation. Third, the specialist practitioner has a readily available model of hearing peers that assists in benchmarking age and stage development of the student who is deaf or hard of hearing. The fundamental disadvantage of the push-in model is that the classroom is a noisy, busy environment making specialist speech, language auditory cognitive intervention difficult, if not impossible. With the pull-out support model, the specialist practitioner withdraws the student from the classroom for direct expert instruction.

Strategies for supporting school personnel

There are many opportunities for school principals and specialist practitioners to support school personnel, especially the classroom teacher, in their endeavour to maximise student learning. Here are four simple strategies. First, allow classroom teachers to gain an authentic understanding of family perspectives. Second, provide hearing-related pre-service and in-service opportunities to classroom teachers. Third, ensure teachers have appropriate planning time to communicate with the specialist practitioner. Fourth, provide a meeting place, either virtual or face-to-face, for classroom teachers to communicate and support each other.

Discussion point

In an effort to support classroom teachers who have academic responsibility for students with profound deafness who use sign language to communicate, the school principal might organise access to these three key activities: 1) sign language instruction for all school-based personnel; 2) in-service training related to deafness; and, 3) a face-to-face or online support group for classroom teachers. The specialist practitioner might provide the classroom teacher with fortnightly sessions to review student progress and re-evaluate long- and short-term goals.

Guiding principles of instruction

Working with students who are deaf or hard of hearing is complex. It requires continual surveillance of many learning domains concurrently. Duncan et al. (2014) describe guiding principles that assist novice specialist practitioners as well as classroom teachers to focus on teaching behaviours beneficial for students who are deaf or hard of hearing. These guiding principles are conceptually important to educational practice in general:

1. Use ongoing, consistent formal and informal assessment as a foundation for setting goals and objectives
2. Use predictable developmental hierarchies in all planning
3. Prioritise essential knowledge and skills with the student and their caregivers
4. Use a process-focused approach so that the learning 'how to learn' is prioritised over 'what to learn'
5. Use metacognitive strategic process knowledge with domain-specific knowledge in an effort to encourage the student to think about his or her own thinking
6. Use a fluid, dynamic process approach, continuously scaffolding learning
7. Use a responsive and needs-based approach to working with the student, family and school personnel
8. Use challenging material that is meaningful to the student
9. Recognise and promote student abilities
10. Integrate learning so that no one domain (linguistic, auditory, cognitive, speech and social skills) occurs in isolation (Duncan, 2006; Duncan et al., 2014)

Access the curriculum

The fundamental responsibility for equal access to the curriculum resides with the school personnel. The specialist practitioner and family share a supporting role in the overall process of educating students who are deaf or hard of hearing. Accessing the curriculum is dynamic and dependent on many factors including school and teacher ethos. The following case study illustrates one family's struggle to secure a learning environment that genuinely facilitated full access to the curriculum.

Case study

Paul was born into a close-knit family with both his father and mother holding postgraduate qualifications and an older brother who was developing typically. Paul's family had no previous history of childhood hearing loss. After an initial misdiagnosis by a paediatrician, he was diagnosed at 15 months with a bilateral profound hearing loss, greater than 100 dB at all frequencies. He did not have sufficient residual hearing to develop spoken language and at three-and-a-half years, Paul was the first pre-schooler in his state to receive a cochlear implant. He continued to receive habilitation support from a listening and spoken language specialist.

Paul commenced school at five years with a significant language delay. He attended a small religious school with a supportive professional and parent community. Paul received two-and-a-half hours of support from a visiting specialist practitioner per week who focused on audition, language, speech, cognition and social–emotional development in a pull-out model. There was excellent rapport between the school personnel and the specialist practitioner. The school consistently charged Paul's FM and his teachers used it effectively. The specialist practitioner provided Paul's mainstream teacher with instruction to maximise Paul's access to the curriculum. The specialist practitioner incorporated curriculum vocabulary and content into Paul's programme. Paul flourished socially and academically.

At eight years, Paul transferred to a school with a special unit, which supported students with hearing loss. The unit was staffed by teachers of the deaf who again applied a pull out model of curriculum support. There was a respectful relationship between the unit and the mainstream school, although the unit was autonomous in its support of students with hearing loss. Parents were encouraged to take a backseat and leave the education to the specialist practitioner. At this point Paul started to struggle socially. He had previously been garrulous and outgoing but rejection and bullying resulted in his gradual disaffection with and withdrawal from peer relationships. From this point through to the end of his schooling, Paul tended to be befriended by other students who were culturally marginalised. Annual standardised assessments showed that Paul was maintaining receptive and expressive language scores in the low average range.

At 13 years, Paul's parents employed the support of a specialist practitioner who was a qualified Listening and Spoken Language Auditory-Verbal Therapist who provided

(Continued)

(Continued)

out-of-school support in audition, language, speech and cognition that consistently pushed Paul out of his comfort zone. This specialist practitioner advised Paul and his parents that they would need to raise their expectations of him if he wanted the option of a university education.

Because Paul's academic performance and social inclusion was declining, when Paul turned 15 years, with the encouragement of his specialist practitioner, his parents transferred him to an independent school. Paul was fully mainstreamed apart from one hour per week of pull-out support from a visiting specialist practitioner who provided specialist audition, language, speech and cognition instruction. In high school, Paul was not a strong self-advocate and used his FM intermittently, although this was in part due to its notorious tendency to break down. Paul's parents employed a fellow student to help him develop skills in essay writing and later to help him develop independent study skills. The special education teacher at the school was supportive and facilitated a constructive relationship between the specialist practitioner, the mainstream teaching personnel and Paul's parents.

Paul achieved his matriculation and went on to gain a Bachelor's and a Master's qualification in economics, accounting and finance. At university, he matured in his study habits. Despite attending lectures with up to 400 other students, some of whom engaged in habits such as talking on their mobile phones, his only support came from fellow student note-takers. Additionally, his oral language and literacy skills improved greatly, now being well above the mean.

Factors that contributed to Paul's maximum access to the school curriculum include:

- Communication modality which was aligned with the family's culture
- Continuous pursuit of maximisation of hearing technology usage
- Active engagement of parents in the habilitation and educational processes
- Maintaining high cognitive-linguistic outcome expectations
- Enrolment in a supportive school
- Use of out-of-school specialist support and academic assistance when necessary

Specialist practitioner teaching behaviours

Despite early diagnosis, early intervention, the presence of residual hearing and the use of hearing technology, the process of learning may not be spontaneous for children who are deaf or hard of hearing (Duncan, 2006; Duncan et al., 2014; Geers et al., 2008). Irrespective of the communication system used, children who are deaf or hard of hearing have a variety of learning styles, coping strategies and attitudes toward academic situations (Duncan et al., 2014).

It may therefore be necessary to structure specific learning conditions to encourage and facilitate the learning process (Duncan, 2007).

Specialist practitioners are encouraged to use a holistic, developmental approach whereby the development of cognitive and linguistic functioning is achieved through social interaction. Emphasis is placed on the development of communication through natural social discourse including play, rhymes, songs and daily routines, as well as structured activities within and outside of a formal learning context.

There are conventional teaching behaviours that facilitate learning for children who are deaf or hard of hearing. Duncan et al. (2010) identified some such teaching behaviours. Specialist practitioners use these behaviours during intervention with young children and their caregivers or with school age children without the caregiver present. These teaching behaviours also assist novice practitioners to focus on key pedagogical practices. They are an elucidation of good teaching practice. The Duncan et al. (2010) teaching behaviours presented here are not to be used in isolation, but concurrently.

Cognitive/linguistic

Where appropriate, the specialist practitioner will endeavour to:

- Plan and implement a range of integrated cognitive, linguistic, auditory, social and speech objectives based on stages of typical development.
- Converse with the child/student slightly above his/her cognitive/linguistic level.
- Communicate with child/student and caregivers in a manner that facilitates natural social discourse.
- Use expectant pauses/wait time to encourage turn taking and auditory/cognitive processing.
- Facilitate transfer of target language to informal social discourse.
- Employ strategies to stimulate creative and independent thinking.

Auditory

Where appropriate, the specialist practitioner will endeavour to:

- Monitor hearing device function and proper use of the hearing device, and transfer responsibility for the hearing device to the caregiver/student.
- Provide specific input through audition first and last.
- Vary auditory stimuli length using word and/or sentence and/or discourse activities.
- Maximise audition in both formal and incidental context.
- Use acoustic highlighting appropriately, by proceeding from more to less.
- Maximise audition by positioning the child/student/caregiver appropriately to encourage a listening attitude/posture.
- Incorporate an auditory feedback system to facilitate the child/student's self-monitoring of speech and spoken language production.

Speech

Where appropriate, the specialist practitioner will endeavour to:

- Model and facilitate speech and spoken language with natural rate, rhythm and prosody.
- Accept or facilitate the child/student's intelligible speech production, including effectively implementing appropriate strategies for development/remediation.
- Facilitate transfer of appropriate speech production into natural social discourse.

Caregiver/student guidance

Where appropriate, the specialist practitioner will endeavour to:

- Provide opportunities for the caregiver/student to reflect and share relevant experiences.
- Describe learning objectives to the caregiver/student before beginning each activity.
- Model (demonstrate) and explain strategies and techniques clearly to the caregiver/student.
- Discuss with the caregiver/student the outcome of each activity throughout the session or at the conclusion.
- Identify with the caregiver/student goals for future planning and carryover.
- Maintain rapport with the caregiver/student through active and constructive listening techniques.
- Maintain active involvement/participation/practice of the caregiver/student through coaching in a constructive and supportive manner while creating an environment that is enjoyable and motivating.

Instructional presentation and planning

Where appropriate, the specialist practitioner will endeavour to:

- Seize 'learnable' moments through informal and incidental opportunities.
- Evaluate and review previous targets and set new targets as required, incorporating caregiver/student feedback and suggestions.
- Use diagnostic teaching techniques by incorporating ongoing informal appraisal of student performance and share results with the caregiver/student.
- Use scaffolded teaching strategies such as modelling, recasting, explaining and questioning.
- Provide encouraging and appropriate feedback to the caregiver/student.
- Maintain appropriate pacing that enables the caregiver/child/student to learn.
- Provide balance between child-led and adult-led activities, appropriate for the child's age and stage of development.
- Select and implement a variety of instructional materials, activities and/or strategies to accommodate the needs, capabilities and learning styles of the caregiver/student.

- Integrate appropriate pre-literacy/literacy activities linked to objectives.
- Employ positive behaviour management techniques and transfer skills to the caregiver/student.
- Maintain adequate record keeping that ensures appropriate monitoring of the child/student's development (Duncan et al., 2010).

Summary

Students who are deaf or hard of hearing have diverse learning needs. They, along with their families and classroom teachers, require specialist practitioner support in order to maximise learning potential and facilitate inclusive education. Appropriate choice and consistent use of hearing technology and communication modality is essential. Clearly delineated principles of instruction and specialist practitioner teaching behaviours contribute to maximising learning outcomes for students who are deaf or hard of hearing.

Further reading

Duncan, J., Rhoades, E.A. and Fitzpatrick, E. (2014) *Auditory (Re)habilitation for Adolescents with Hearing Loss: Theory and Practice*. New York: Oxford University Press.

This recent book is progressive in its investigation of students who are deaf or hard of hearing aged 11 to adulthood. Explanations include audiological management, psychosocial development and pedagogical foundations.

Marschark, M. and Spencer, P. (eds) (2011) *Oxford Handbook of Deaf Studies, Language and Education, Vol.1*. New York. Oxford University Press.

Marschark, M. and Spencer, P. (eds) (2011) *Oxford Handbook of Deaf Studies, Language and Education, Vol.2*. New York. Oxford University Press.

In this two-volume set, Marschark and Spencer draw together top experts in deaf education to explore important issues. Study of its contents is essential for any specialist practitioner serving children who are deaf or hard of hearing and their families.

Rhoades, E.A. and Duncan, J. (eds) (2010) *Auditory-Verbal Practice: Toward a Family-Centered Practice*. Springfield, IL: Charles C. Thomas Publishers.

This comprehensive book explains aspects of oral deaf education and its history, and the role of families in maximising learning outcomes for their children. Chapter authors include family therapists, auditory-verbal practitioners and academics.

(Continued)

(Continued)

Useful websites

Action Deafness: http://actiondeafness.org.uk/
Action Deafness aims to improve quality of life by promoting independence and equality of opportunity for deaf, deafened, deafblind and hard of hearing people

Deaf Education: http://deafeducation.org.uk/
Deaf Education through Listening and Talking is a voluntary association of young deaf adults, and the families and teachers of deaf children. DELTA is a national charity which supports and develops the Natural Aural Approach to the education of deaf children.

National Deaf Children's Society: www.ndcs.org.uk/
The National Deaf Children's Society is the leading charity dedicated to creating a world without barriers for deaf children and young people.

References

Al-Hassan, S. and Gardner, R. (2002) Involving immigrant parents of students with disabilities in the educational process. *Teaching Exceptional Children*, 34(5): 52–8.

Anderson-Butcher, D. and Ashton, D. (2004) Innovative models of collaboration to serve children, youths, families, and communities. *Children and Schools*, 26(1): 30–53.

Angelides, P. and Aravi, C. (2006/2007) A comparative perspective on the experiences of deaf and hard of hearing individuals as students at mainstream and special schools. *American Annals of the Deaf*, 151(5): 476–87.

Bronfenbrenner, U. and Morris, P.A. (2006) The bioecological model of human development. In W.W. Daman and R.M. Lerner (eds), *Handbook of Child Psychology, Vol 1: Theoretical models of human development*. New York: Wiley, pp. 793–828.

Carlisle, E., Stanley, L. and Kemple, K. (2005) Opening doors: understanding school and family influences on family involvement. *Early Childhood Education Journal*, 33(3): 155–62.

Dawson, P. and Guare, R. (2010) *Executive Skills in Children and Adolescents: A Practical Guide to Assessment and Intervention*, 2nd edn. New York: Guilford Press.

Dillon, C. and Pisoni, D. (2006) Nonword repetition and reading skills in children who are deaf and have cochlear implants. *Volta Review*, 106(2): 121–45.

Dishion, T. and Kavanagh, K. (2003) *Intervening in Adolescent Problem Behaviors: A Family-Centered Approach*. New York: Guilford Press.

Duncan, J. (2006) Application of the auditory-verbal methodology and pedagogy to school age children. *Journal of Educational Audiology*, 13: 39–49.

Duncan, J. (2007) Family-centred practice: concerns, barriers, controversies and challenges. *Deafness Forum Australia Newsletter*, 54: 3–4.

Duncan, J. (2009) Parental readiness for cochlear implant decision-making. *Cochlear Implants International*, 10(S1): 38–42.

Duncan, J. (2010) Circles of influence. In E.A. Rhoades and J. Duncan (eds), *Auditory–Verbal Practice: Toward a Family-centered Approach*. Springfield, IL: Charles C. Thomas Publishers, pp. 97–112.

Duncan, J., Rhoades, E.A. and Fitzpatrick, E. (2014) *Auditory (Re)habilitation for Adolescents with Hearing Loss: Theory and Practice*. New York: Oxford University Press.

Duncan, J., Kendrick, A., McGinnis, M. and Perigoe, C. (2010) Auditory (re)habilitation teaching behavior rating scale. *Journal of the Academy of Rehabilitative Audiology*, 43: 65–86.

Easterbrooks, S. and Beal-Alvarez, J. (2013) *Literacy Instruction for Students Who Are Deaf and Hard of Hearing*. New York: Oxford University Press.

Falbo, T., Lein, L. and Amador, N. (2001) Parental involvement during transition to high school. *Journal of Adolescent Research*, 16(5): 511–29.

Fortnum, H., Stacey, P., Barton, G. and Summerfield, A. (2007) National evaluation of support options for deaf and hearing-impaired children: relevance to education services. *Deafness & Education International*, 9(3): 120–30.

Geers, A., Tobey, E., Moog, J. and Brenner, C. (2008) Long-term outcomes of cochlear implantation in the preschool tears: from elementary grades to high school. *International Journal of Audiology*, 47(Suppl. 2): S21–S300.

Harry, B. (2008) Collaboration with culturally and linguistically diverse families: ideal versus reality. *Council for Exceptional Children*, 74(3): 372–88.

Harvard Family Research Project (2007) Family involvement in middle and high school student's education. *Harvard Family Project*, 3: 1–12.

Hauser, P., Lukomski, J. and Hillman, T. (2008) Development of deaf and hard-of-hearing students' executive function. In M. Marschark and P. Hauser (eds), *Deaf Cognition*. New York: Oxford University Press, pp. 286–308.

Knopf, H. and Swick, K. (2008) Using our understanding of families to strengthen family involvement. *Early Childhood Education*, 35(5): 419–27.

Marschark, M. (2003) Interactions of language and cognition in deaf learners: from research to practice. *International Journal of Audiology*, 42: S41–S48.

McClay, J.E., Booth, T.N., Parry, D.A., Johnson, R. and Roland, P. (2008) Evaluation of pediatric sensorineural hearing loss with magnetic resonance imaging. *Archives of Otolaryngology – Head and Neck Surgery*, 134(9): 945–52.

Mody, M. (2007) Neurobiological correlates of the language–literacy connection in normal and atypical development. Talk for a Lifetime Conference: Research and Application in Neurodevelopmental Research. Washington, DC: Paulander Graham Bell Association for the Deaf and Hard of Hearing.

Olusanya, B.O. (2005) Can the world's infants with hearing loss wait? *International Journal of Pediatric Otorhinolaryngology*, 69: 735–8.

Olusanya, B.O. and Newton, V.E. (2007) Global burden of childhood hearing impairment and disease control priorities for developing countries. *Lancet*, 369: 1314–17.

Richards, J. (2003) *Inclusion Rating Scale*. Perth, Western Australia: WA Institute for Deaf Education.

Seewald, R., Moodie, S., Scollie, S. and Bagatto, M. (2005) The DSL method for pediatric hearing instrument fitting: historical perspective and current issues. *Trends in Amplification*, 9(4): 145–57.

Snider, V. and Roehl, R. (2007) Teacher's beliefs about pedagogy and related issues. *Psychology in Schools*, 44(8): 873–86.

Thompson, J., Meadan, H., Fransler, K.W., Albert, S. and Balogh, P. (2007) Family assessment portfolios: a new way to jumpstart family/school collaboration. *Teaching Exceptional Children*, 39(6): 19–25.

Autistic Spectrum Disorder

17

Challenges, Issues and Responses

Gavin Reid, Sionah Lannen and Colin Lannen

Learning objectives

This chapter will help readers to:

- Understand autistic spectrum disorders (ASDs)
- Appreciate the criteria for identification and assessment
- Gain some insights into the branches of research and the implications of changes made in *Diagnostic and Statistical Manual of Mental Disorders* (DSM) 5
- Obtain an overview of intervention strategies
- Understand issues relating to co-morbidity

Background and history of autistic spectrum disorder (ASD)

The last 25 years have witnessed a significant rise in the number of children diagnosed with autism. In the UK, the figures suggest almost 40 in every 10,000 are autistic and 116 per 10,000 for the entire autistic spectrum (Baird et al., 2006). There is some debate about whether this increase represents a true increase in the prevalence of autism or whether it reflects changes in the criteria used to diagnose autism, along with an increased recognition of the disorder by professionals. Many questions, hypotheses and accompanying explanations have been put forward for this dramatic rise in autism. These range from environmental factors to better and more accurate detection, and neurobiological, chemical and emotional influences, or even misdiagnosis. Whatever the cause of this increase there is a need for teachers, parents and professionals to collaborate and work towards effective and lifelong intervention. This chapter looks at these issues and challenges and suggests some responses to them.

Historical aspects

The term 'Kanner's syndrome' was first assigned to autism following the work of Dr Leo Kanner in 1943 of the Johns Hopkins Hospital in the USA (Kanner, 1943). He studied a group of 11 children and introduced the label 'early infantile autism' into the English language. At the same time, a German scientist, Dr Hans Asperger, described a milder form of the disorder that became known as Asperger syndrome (Asperger, 1991). This latter group was characterised by Asperger for their social and communication deficits, and their obsessions and dependence on rituals and routines. Kanner's syndrome was characterised by abnormal communication, abnormal social communication, ritualistic and stereotyped behaviour and resistance to change (Howlin, 2002). This is shown in detail in the *International Classification of Diseases and Related Health Problems* (ICD-10) (WHO, 1992), which stated, for example, that 'abnormal or impaired development' needs to be in one of the areas of receptive and expressive language, social attachment and reciprocal social interaction, and functional or symbolic play, and should be evident before the age of three. ICD-10 also goes on to give specific symptoms in each of these categories (for example, in social interaction, a failure to make eye contact and inappropriate facial expression, body posture and use of gesticulation). In communication, for example this would be a delay in spoken language and a failure to sustain conversational exchange, and, in play, a preoccupation with non-functional elements of play.

Hence, these two disorders are also described in DSM IV TR (fourth edition, text revision) (APA, 1994) as two of the five pervasive developmental disorders (PDD), more often referred to today as ASD. All these disorders are characterised by varying degrees of impairment in communication skills and social interactions, and restricted, repetitive and stereotyped patterns of behaviour. The three PDDs that relate to autism are:

- autistic disorder (also called autism, classic autism and AD)
- PDD–NOS (pervasive developmental disorder – not otherwise specified)
- Asperger's disorder (also called AS, Asperger's syndrome and Asperger syndrome)

DSM-5

A number of issues rise from these three differing PDDs, and these issues have gained more attention since 2013 when DSM-5 was implemented. For example, DSM IV categorised autism as a mental health disorder, but there is some debate about whether this classification is appropriate as some may classify it as a language disorder. Additionally there still remains some confusion on whether autism and Asperger's syndrome represent different conditions. Happé (2011), a member of the neurodevelopmental disorders work group for DSM-5, indicated that it made a lot of sense to collapse some labels into the broader ASD category. She suggested that Asperger's does not work as a diagnostic label because it does not have any clear boundaries and cannot be qualitatively distinguished from autism. It can however still be used as a descriptive category. The guidance that emerged from DSM-5 is given below.

Diagnostic and Statistical Manual of Mental Disorders (DSM-5) May 2013

Autism spectrum disorder (ASD) is a new DSM-5 name that reflects a scientific consensus that four previously separate disorders are actually a single condition with different levels of symptom severity in two core domains. ASD now encompasses the previous DSM-IV autistic disorder (autism), Asperger's disorder, childhood disintegrative disorder, and pervasive developmental disorder not otherwise specified.

ASD is characterised by:

1. Deficits in social communication and social interaction
2. Restricted repetitive behaviors, interests, and activities (RRBs)

Because both components are required for diagnosis of ASD, Social Communication Disorder is diagnosed if no RRBs are present.'

F84.0 Childhood Autism

A pervasive developmental disorder defined by the presence of abnormal and/or impaired development that is manifest before the age of 3 years, and by the characteristic type of abnormal functioning in all three areas of social interaction, communication, and **restricted repetitive behaviours**.

Must meet criteria 1, 2 and 3:

1. Clinically significant, persistent deficits in social communication and interactions, as manifest by all of the following:

    a) Marked deficits in non-verbal and verbal communication used for social interaction
    b) Lack of social reciprocity
    c) Failure to develop and maintain peer relationships appropriate to developmental level

2. Restricted, repetitive patterns of behavior, interests and activities, as manifested by at least TWO of the following:

    a) Stereotyped motor or verbal behaviors, or unusual sensory behaviors
    b) Excessive adherence to routines and ritualised patterns of behavior
    c) Restricted, fixated interests

Symptoms must be present in early childhood (but may not become fully manifest until social demands exceed limited capacities) (APA, 2013)

DSM-5 sees the loss of the Asperger's label, which has always been recognised as part of the autistic spectrum. Additionally, the category PDD–NOS will no longer exists as a separate category and is subsumed into the ASD label in the same way as Asperger's.

Yet, despite this, Howlin (2002) suggests there are a number of factors that differentiate between autism and Asperger's syndrome. She suggests the prevalence rates may be higher for Asperger than for autism. She also suggests that the research indicates that there is often a significant difference in the ages at which children from the two groups are first diagnosed. In the autism group she suggests that the average age of diagnosis was 5.5 years, while in the Asperger group it was 11.3 years, and almost all (88%) of the children in the study with autism had been diagnosed before 10 years of age compared with only 45% of the Asperger group. At the same time, it can be argued that the obvious similarities between the two syndromes suggest that they lie in the same continuum or spectrum. Asperger's syndrome is often considered to be a type of 'high-functioning' autism but there is some clinical controversy about whether it is a milder form of autistic disorder or a distinct disorder. Additionally, the term 'high-functioning' can be misleading as it does not necessarily translate to lower needs. This can have considerable implications for intervention and the allocation of resources.

Characteristics of ASDs

There are a number of general characteristics of ASD. The most prevalent are as follows.

Verbal and non-verbal communication:

- *Speech and language skills*: these may begin to develop but then be lost, or they may develop very slowly or they may never develop. It has been estimated that around 40% of children with ASDs may not talk at all unless intensive early intervention is in place
- *Communication*: gestures may be used or outstretching of the arm instead of attempting to use language. It may be difficult or impossible to imitate sounds and words
- *Echolalia*: this is repeating something heard. For example, if you ask, 'Are you ready?' the response may be, 'Are you ready?' instead of answering the question. The repeated words might be said right away or much later and may be repeated over and over
- *Non-verbal communication*: there may be difficulty in using gestures, such as waving goodbye, or using facial expressions to convey meaning
- *Speech*: there is often an unusual pitch and rhythm in speech

Social interaction:

- *Attention*: some people with ASDs may prefer to be left alone, showing no interest in people at all. They may not notice when people are talking to them
- *Fitting in*: some people with ASD might be very interested in becoming part of a group, but do not know how to conduct themselves and relate to others. Difficulty 'joining in' is common in ASDs because individuals find it hard to 'read' or understand other people
- *Peer group*: children with ASD may not relate to their own age group and prefer the company of adults or older children
- *Eye contact*: some people with ASD make no eye contact or are less responsive to eye contact. Some may use peripheral vision rather than looking directly at others
- *Facial expressions*: children with ASD may have difficulty in responding to or understanding facial gestures
- *Tactile sensitivity*: children with ASD might not like to be held or cuddled, or might cuddle only on their terms. They can be sensitive in terms of touch
- *Self-control*: they may have difficulty in controlling emotion and excitement

Repeated and unusual behaviours, interests and routines:

- *Ritualistic behaviours*: people with autism may have ritualistic actions that they repeat over and over again, such as spinning, rocking, staring, finger flapping and, in some cases, hitting themselves
- *High anxiety state*: they can show intense anxiety or an unusual lack of anxiety. Anxiety, fear and confusion may result from being unable to 'make sense' of the world in the usual way

- *Gait*: they can display unusual postures, walking or movement patterns
- *Routines*: they might fiercely depend on routines and want things always to stay the same, and minor changes in the environment or in daily routines might trigger acute distress or fear

Responses to sensations:

- *Stimulation processing*: they may have difficulty in making sense of environmental stimulation. People with ASD may have both auditory and visual processing problems, and sensory input may be scrambled and/or overwhelming to them. Sensory sensitivities vary in autism from mild to severe hyper- and hypo-sensitivities
- *Sensory stimulation*: they may have unusual sensitivities to sounds, sights, touch, tastes and smells

High-functioning ASD and co-morbidity

Co-existence of disorders is the rule rather than the exception!

The correlation of co-morbidity of various Specific Learning Difficulties, including high-functioning ASD has been prevalent from the 1960s. However, for a variety of reasons few professionals have either understood its relevance or have been willing to make the 'jump' from research to practice. Fortunately, Ginny Russell and Zsuzsa Pavelka, have brought together much of the relevant research in their article 'Children who share symptoms of autism, dyslexia and attention deficit hyperactivity disorder' (Russell and Pavelka, 2013). Children with ASD have a higher risk of suffering from several other conditions including dyslexia, ADHD, dyspraxia, SLI and dyscalculia (Gillberg, 2010).

Various studies have looked for ADHD or ADHD symptoms in samples of children with ASD. Rates of ADHD have ranged from 28% to 78% of these samples (Ronald et al., 2010). Studies that look at ADHD symptoms have reported even higher numbers: for example, Sturm et al. (2004) looked at a sample of around 100 high-functioning children with ASD and found 95% had attention problems, 75% had motor difficulties, 86% had problems with regulation of activity level and 50% had impulsiveness.

Gillberg (2010) points out that clinicians have become focused on dichotomous categories of disorder and that clinics have become increasingly specialised and overlook difficulties not within their immediate jurisdiction. Gillberg has argued that co-existence of disorders is the rule rather than the exception but ASD also shows overlap with dyslexia in both cognitive and behavioural features (Reiersen and Todd, 2008; Simonoff et al., 2008). A proportion of children share symptoms of dyslexia, ADHD and ASD.

Although the cognitive/psychological theories of dyslexia and autism seem quite distinct, some research does suggest children with both ADHD and dyslexic difficulties show a distinctive deficit in rapid naming speed, so it may be that processing speed underlies the link (Bental and Tirosh, 2007).

Two conclusions can be drawn. First, co-morbidities between developmental disorders are common, and second, the causes of these overlapping difficulties are likely to be complex, multifactorial and interacting. The high overlap between symptoms of different developmental disorders has been identified in a number of studies and there is an international consensus on this overlap. Studies from Canada, the UK, the USA and Scandinavia all show how hard it is provide an unequivocal diagnosis, leading to the quote from Kaplan and her colleagues (2001) in developmental disorders '*co-morbidity is the rule, not the exception*'.

It is plausible that the same underlying genetic or neurological mechanisms may underlie co-occurrence of dyslexia, ADHD and ASD.

Snowling (2012) suggests a new dimensional classification of disorder, where deficits in different components of learning are seen as additive, impacting on the potential for remediation, rather than classing children into dichotomous 'disorder' categories. Taylor (2011) notes that for many children, it is better to think of changes in cognitive style, learning and motivation rather than symptoms. Both conclude that it is important to examine children for evidence of co-occurring disorders, and not simply continue to examine the areas which we expect to be impaired according to categorisation. The practical application of assessing children for a range of difficulties is that children will be best helped not by any all-encompassing diagnosis, but by individual analysis of their strengths and weaknesses.

Research

There is now considerable activity in the research field concerning explanations for autism and ASD and there is certainly too much to be discussed in any detail here. This chapter, however is more concerned with the issues and the challenges rather than recounting the details of research findings although, as we note, some of these issues will stem directly and indirectly from these. What is particularly staggering is the number of local initiatives taking place as well as major national and international projects. This can be noted when looking at the policy documentation of different areas of different countries. For example, in Ireland, the report of the Task Force on Autism (2001), which was one of the earliest policy initiatives in the field, laid the groundwork for local research run by teachers, psychologists and parents. It recommended that, as a matter of urgency, research be conducted into the national prevalence of autistic and Asperger disorder (p. 7). The report also suggested that formalised Department of Education and Science–university partnerships should be established to develop appropriate programmes for people with ASDs and that research should be carried out on methodologies and approaches, on the benefits of various clinical interventions and on the specific components of teacher and classroom assistant training, as well as on curricular interventions and strategies. The report suggested there needs to be a systematic evaluation of all pilot projects.

It is this connection between international and national initiatives and local pilot studies or policy studies that needs to be synchronised. If there are no local initiatives or clear policies to guide parents (and teachers), they may grasp at some sensational newspaper headline story offering new treatments and cures for autism and may opt for these, even though they may not be scientifically validated. It was interesting that the Ireland in its task-force report made considerable efforts to include parents at all stages of assessment and provision. For example, one of the recommendations was the introduction of Statutory Child and Adult Family Support Plans for those with an ASD. This multi-agency coordination was also profiled in the Additional Support Needs Act 2004 in Scotland in terms of the development of coordinated support plans. While the Act does make it clear that a child does not necessarily need to have a diagnosis or disability to be considered as having additional support needs, it is also quite clear that people with an ASD will be considered as having a disability. This means that the parents of children who have been diagnosed with an ASD will need to ensure that their child receives the additional support necessary. The implication of this is that labels in themselves, although they can be helpful, will not necessarily guarantee addition support.

In England and Wales, the Special Educational Needs Disability Act 2001 (SENDA) highlighted the need for schools to make reasonable adjustments and that failure to make reasonable adjustments so that students have equal access to admission arrangements and to education services is unlawful and this has been developed further in the more recent SENDA (2014). The reasonable adjustments duty requires schools to anticipate the barriers that disabled students, such as those with autism, may face. The National Autistic Society in the UK has provided an example of this where a boy with autism became anxious when the fire alarm sounded. There may have been reasonable adjustments the school could have made to prevent this. For example, staff at the school could have been trained about autism, about strategies to avoid difficulties and about how to overcome difficulties if they did arise. The pupil could have been given training for social situations and strategies for coping when the fire alarm is sounded. The NAS offer a range of strategies for coping with this and other similar situations at school (see www.autism.org.uk/working-with/education/professionals-in-schools/lessons-and-breaktimes/how-to-help.aspx). It is clear, therefore, that legislation, policy and training all have a major role to play in ensuring that the needs of students with ASD are met.

Theoretical perspectives

According to Pellicano (2007), the three main theories that relate to ASD are the theory of the mind (the ability to recognise one's mental states and that of others), the theory that relates to executive functioning (which involves independent and responsible thinking and dealing with new situations) and the theory of information processing (particularly relating to coherent and organised thought processes). But Pellicano also suggests that these accounts fall short of providing a full picture of ASD.

It is important to acknowledge the point made by Frith (2014) who comments that 'we know that Autism can occur at all levels of intellectual ability, including very superior levels'. Although much popular attention has been given to the higher end of the intellectual spectrum Frith points out that we need to consider that about half the children diagnosed with autism also suffer from a marked degree of intellectual disability. Jarrett (2014) debunks popular myths about ASD and attempts to provide a sense of reality about what autism is really like. He suggests that although many people with autism have islands of relative or impressive strengths – e.g. in maths he indicates that the reality is that 0.05% of the autistic population has an extreme talent or genius level gift (figure obtained from the National Autistic Society).

Singh and Elsabbagh (2014) assert that there is increasing recognition of the complexity, heterogeneity and variable impact of autism across individuals. This can make clinical research more challenging and it in fact has led to more large-scale studies which have paved a path for new scientific discovery. They cite the discovery of rare genetic underpinnings in around 20% of individuals with autism and overlapping conditions, as well as the specification of the variable rates in developmental progress along the autistic spectrum, suggesting that the condition is more broad than narrow definitions capture.

Early detection and genetic explanations

It is interesting to review data on the early detection of autism and particularly theories on causes. Roberts (2010) suggests that one of the recent achievements in this field is the possibility of identifying the neurobiological manifestations of autism as early as nine months. She suggests that between nine and 15 months infants with autism begin to withdraw and, with training and precise indicators, we could be looking at detection around that age range. This will clearly have a profound effect on the child's developing competencies. As Roberts suggests, at this age one is more likely to be able to modify the association pathways of the developing brain before they are too firmly established. Despite the clear biological case for ASD, according to Gillberg and Coleman (2001: 111), 'there are as yet no reliable and valid biological markers for autism'.

There is, however, vigorous activity in the field of genetics in relation to ASD. The Autism Genome Project (which includes 50 academic institutions from 15 countries collecting data from 8000 people and 1600 families) represents a significant breakthrough in this area. The result is, as Szatmari (2010) claims, that more progress has been made in the last five years than in the 50 years previously (see also Pinto et al., 2010). He suggests that 90% of autism arises from of genetic differences. The researchers in the project have located a considerable number of target genes which appear to play a role in how nerve cells communicate with each other. This is a current area of focus in early detection and may lead eventually to intervention and preventative work.

Identifying ASD

There are a great many issues and a great deal of controversy in the diagnosis of autism. These issues include either (or both) late diagnosis or misdiagnosis. There are examples of autism being misdiagnosed for attention deficit hyperactivity disorder (ADHD), auditory processing disorder, Rhett's syndrome, hearing difficulty, language disorders, speech delay, developmental delay and selective mutism. It is important therefore that a diagnosis should not rest on one test, or even one professional, but should be from a multidisciplinary team approach using a range of assessment methods. A good example of this is in British Columbia where the Sunny Hill Health Centre has a multidisciplinary team located at the Autism Spectrum Disorder Clinic. This team undertakes assessments for autism for children of all ages that are designed to meet individual needs, and it undertakes school planning and medical and/or behavioural management and links with the British Columbia Autism Assessment Network.

Assessment procedures

The procedures for identifying autism should be made clear to parents and they, themselves, should have an important role in this process. Ideally the process should include the following:

- An examination and evaluation of the child's sensory status (hearing, vision (including visual skills such as tracking), depth perception and auditory skills (such as source matching and auditory discrimination).
- Interviews with parents, teacher and, where appropriate, the child.
- Direct behavioural observation in multiple settings.
- Completion of checklists by or with parents or caregivers.
- Formal psychometric evaluation of the child's cognitive, social, emotional, behavioural and adaptive functioning.
- An evaluation of literacy and numeracy readiness or attainment.
- An evaluation of the skills involved in the activities of daily living.
- A functional analysis of targeted behaviours (in cases where behavioural difficulties have been identified).
- An evaluation of learning style (e.g. preference for verbal or visual).
- An observation and evaluation of instruction (for example, how the child best scans and focuses to receive visual information, attention and concentration on tasks).

- An analysis of their problem-solving approaches.
- An examination and evaluation of the child's gross and fine motor skills, of sensory integrative functioning and lateral dominance.
- An evaluation of mental-health status and possible affective disorder.
- An assessment of the child's social status with peers.

It is important to note that the characteristics of children with ASD will vary greatly in severity from individual to individual. According to the National Institute of Mental Health (NIMH) in the USA, following an assessment using observations and test results, the specialist should only make a diagnosis of autism if there is clear evidence of poor or limited social relationships; underdeveloped communication skills; and repetitive behaviours, interests and activities. People with autism will normally have some impairment within each of these categories, although the severity of each symptom may vary. The NIMH diagnostic criteria also require that these symptoms appear by the age of three.

Tests and strategies

In an interesting and forward-thinking discussion paper on autism in 1997 for Lancashire County Council in the UK, Connelly asserted that keeping the diagnosis of autism as a medical one may be helpful but it can cause confusion and:

> can cause immense problems in terms of local people prepared to take on this role. I think [one] should accept that in local circumstances … local arrangements should be made to accept diagnosis by such groups as our own. (p. 13)

This statement does capture the potential for conflict between the medical professionals and educational and psychological assessors. As the report goes on to say, however, 'with good liaison between various agencies, it is not important who makes the diagnosis'. It appears that the emerging consensus and best examples of practice in different countries are in fact in those areas that have specially trained psychologists in the field of autism working collaboratively as part of a diagnostic team with other professionals and medical personnel. A number of medical authorities have taken initiatives for diagnosing autism. For example, in Scotland the National Health Service commissioned a Scottish Intercollegiate Guidelines Network report. In their report of July 2007 (www.sign.ac.uk/pdf/sign98.pdf) SIGN advocate the benefits of the diagnostic criteria of ICD-10 and DSM-IV (see earlier in this chapter) and they quote three studies (e.g. Klin et al., 2000) that agree that using DSM-5 or ICD-10 will make the diagnostic procedure more reliable. They also suggest that the aim of specialist assessment is to formulate a multi-agency management plan 'leading to an appropriate programme of supportive intervention'.

Although there are commonly used tests for autism, it is important to reiterate that a test alone will not be sufficient to diagnose autism accurately. It is also important to contextualise the assessment for practice and that interventions should result from the assessment as well as a diagnosis – if appropriate. With the revamping of DSM some of the tests have now been redesigned with DSM-5 in mind. For example the Autistic Spectrum Rating Scale (ASRS) is now related to the DSM-5 index.

Intervention

Just as in the area of assessment the often marked difference in perspectives between the medical and educational professions can be noted in intervention. This is an ongoing issue but with increasing legislation and a task group looking at the area of autism, there now appear to be more concerted and collaborative efforts by the range of professionals who are involved in ASD. We are aware that there is no known and unequivocally accepted cure for ASD. There are, however, a vast number of therapies and interventions designed to remedy or modify specific symptoms, and these can bring about substantial improvement in many cases (see Chapter 18 by Jo Page). Ideally the most effective intervention is one that coordinates 'therapies' and 'interventions' that meets the specific needs of individual children. Most educational and healthcare professionals agree that the earlier the intervention, the more likely a desirable outcome will result.

Impact on learning

The characteristics of ASD noted earlier in this chapter do mean that children in the ASD spectrum will have considerable challenges in learning. As a result they will need specific teaching methods in a sensitive and carefully planned environment. For example, in the educational setting they may show the following:

- An inability to imitate sounds, gestures and gross or fine motor movements that are all necessary for learning, particularly in the early years.
- An inability to focus on the task at hand. Some children will have a very short attention span or concentrate only on one thing obsessively.
- Difficulty working collaboratively with others in the class.
- Difficulty with abstract ideas, such as in using items or toys to represent real objects (make-believe play and role play).
- Difficulty grasping the concept of time and the order of events.

There are, in fact, numerous learning challenges that can be experienced by children in the ASD spectrum. Howlin (2002) notes the vast range and diversity of approaches that are used with children with ASD. These include: auditory integration training; a range of different types of behavioural approaches; cranial osteopathy; dietary and vitamin treatments; facilitated communication; and Gentle Teaching (McGee, 1995; Jones and McCaughey, 1992) – a non-aversive method of reducing challenging behaviour that aims to teach bonding and independence through gentleness and respect. Other well-known methods include Holding Therapy – the aim of which is to provoke a state of distress until the child will feel a need for comfort through holding (Howlin, 2002).

Music therapy has become accepted as a useful intervention for people with autism since it was introduced to the UK in the 1950s and 1960s by such practitioners as Juliette Alvin, Paul Nordoff and Clive Robbins. Nordoff and Robbins describe significant changes in the communicative and social behaviour of individuals with autism who took part in music therapy (www.nordoff-robbins.org.uk). In November 2005, the Nordoff–Robbins Research Department hosted a research symposium entitled 'Evidence-based practice and music therapy: a further perspective', with a keynote presentation by the sociologist, Tia DeNora, on the role of music therapy. One of the many resulting publications offered stringent advice and procedures for empirical evaluations and randomised control trials of music therapy (Nordoff and Robbins, 2009). This publication has been internationally helpful in offering snapshots of current research supporting the use of music therapy.

Woodward (2004) found that music therapy can play an important role for the parents of children with autism by fostering relationships and developing positive interactions, and Gold et al. (2006) found that music therapy may help children with ASD to improve their communicative skills. This theme is advanced by DeNora (2006) from health and sociological perspectives. Other therapies that have been noted include: pet therapies; physical exercise; psychotherapy; and sensory integration therapies. Some of the key points on intervention are commented on below.

Educational/behavioural interventions

There has been a recent increase in interest in verbal behaviour therapy in particular (Barbera, 2007). This type of therapy can be controversial because it is based on a philosophy – applied behaviour analysis (ABA) – which is an intensive, one-on-one, highly structured behaviourist programme. It is usually utilised by trained therapists employing intensive skills-oriented training sessions to help children with ASD develop social and language skills. ABA is based on the work of Ivor Lovaas and is detailed in Chapter 18 by Jo-Ann Page.

Factors to consider

When selecting therapies/intervention for autism, the following factors need to be considered:

Educational:

- Provision – extent of inclusion/specialist provision
- Curriculum issues – is a full curriculum offered/extent of differentiation?

- Is the individual education plan (IEP) appropriate and are the classroom management strategies in place?
- Interventions and specialist therapies – the availability of verbal/behaviour approaches and other specialist programmes

Home:

- Challenges and issues at home
- Support available for parents and siblings
- Links with school

Social:

- Social models of disability – community support
- Concept of neurodiversity – the role of individual differences – spectrum of differences rather than disabilities

Post-school:

- Support available
- Needs of the young person – further education and the workplace
- Issues for the family

The above points raise some of the issues that can become a challenge for the young person and their school and family in relation to ASD. To discuss these here would be beyond the scope of this chapter, but we have included at the end of the chapter a list of useful websites of relevant organisations that discuss and advise on these issues. Some have been referred to throughout this chapter and their work is both current and impressive. It is this sort of endeavour and supportive advice based on sound professional principles that can provide both hope and inspiration to all involved in this field.

In view of the number of behaviours, the spectrum from mild to severe and the changes in DSM-5, which indicate that the category of Asperger's should not be used, it has been decided not to include a case study in this chapter because this may be misleading. But it is important to keep in mind the insightful and penetrating comment made by Rita Jordan (2010) when discussing intervention for children with ASD: 'treating them equally does not mean treating them the same, but treating them differently to ensure equal access.'

Summary

- The prevalence of autism has increased in recent years, but the cause of this increase is subject to debate.
- The criteria for the identification and assessment of autism have been reviewed in DSM-5, and the implications of this have been discussed.

- Autism and Asperger's syndrome are different disorders that lie somewhere on the same continuum.
- There are a range of specialised approaches that can be used for assessment, testing and intervention.

Discussion points

- When you consider the evidence for and prevalence of overlap which is discussed in this chapter, how beneficial is the use of a label?
- Comment on the benefits from your own situation of the use and application of the ASD label.
- Reflect on the DSM-5 changes relating to ASD and comment on how these impact on your professional work or as a parent.
- Reflect on the legislation in your area, e.g. SENDA (2014) in England, and discuss its implications for teachers and for parents.

Further reading

Barnett, K. (2014) *The Spark: A Mother's Story of Nurturing, Genius and Autism*. New York: Random House Publishing.

Baron-Cohen, S. et al. (2001) The autism spectrum quotient. *Journal of Autism and Developmental Disorders*, 31: 5–17.

Baron-Cohen, S. et al. (2006) *The Adult Asperger Assessment (AAA): A Diagnostic Method* (www.autismresearchcentre.com/tests/aaa_test.asp).

Gilliam, J.E. (2006) *Gilliam Autism Rating Scale*, 2nd edn (GARS-2). Upper Saddle River, NJ: Pearson Education.
GARS-2 assists teachers, parents and clinicians in identifying and diagnosing autism in individuals aged 3–22. It also helps estimate the severity of the child's disorder. The items on the GARS-2 are based on the definitions of autism adopted by the Autism Society of America and DSM IV TR. See www.autism-world.com/index.php/2007/03/27/childhood-autism-rating-scalecars for a list of rating scales used in different countries.

Grandin, T. and Panek, R. (2014) *The Autistic Brain: Helping Different Kinds of Minds Succeed*. New York: Mariner Books.

Jordan, R. (1999) *Autistic Spectrum Disorders: An Introductory Guide for Practitioners.* London: David Fulton.
This book has been reprinted a number of times and is an excellent resource. It is written for practitioners working in the field of autism and related disorders (including Asperger's syndrome), and it offers an overview of understandings of these disorders from a behavioural, biological and psychological perspective.

Le Couteur, A. (2003) *Autism Diagnostic Interview-Revised (ADI-R).* San Francisco: Western Psychological Services.
The Autism Diagnostic Interview-Revised, better known as the ADI-R, is a set of interview questions that are administered to the parents of young children with possible symptoms of autism or an ASD (autism.about.com/od/diagnosingautism/f/ADI-R.htm).

Rogers, S.J., Dawson, G. and Vismara, L.A. (2012) *An Early Start for Your Child with Autism: Using Everyday Activities to Help Kids Connect, Communicate, and Learn.* New York and London: Guildford Press.

Sara, S. et al. (2005) *Vineland Adaptive Behavior Scales*, 2nd edn. (Vineland-II; Pearson's assessment). Forms: birth–90-years-old: Survey Interview Form, Expanded Interview Form and Parent/Caregiver Rating Form; 3:0–21:11: Teacher Rating Form (www.pearsonclinical.com/psychology/products/100000668/vineland-adaptive-behavior-scales-second-edition-vineland-ii-vineland-ii.html).

University of North Carolina (UNC) School of Medicine (2014) *TEACCH Approach* (teacch.com/about-us/what-is-teacch).

Useful websites

Autism Society, USA: www.autism-society.org.

Autistic Society, Canada: www.autismsocietycanada.ca.

Checklist for Autism in Toddlers (CHAT): www.autismresearchcentre.com/tests/chat_test.asp.

Kuwait Centre for Autism: www.q8autism.com.

National Autism Association, USA: www.nationalautismassociation.org.

National Autistic Society, UK: www.nas.org.uk.

Nordoff–Robbins Music Therapy: www.nordoff-robbins.org.uk/musicTherapy/research/index.html.

(Continued)

(Continued)

Scottish Society for Autism: www.autism-in-scotland.org.uk.

TEACCH: www.teacch.com.

The US Department of Health and Human Services has a federal Interagency Autism Coordinating Committee. One of the committee's key functions is developing a strategic plan for spectrum disorder research: sacramento.bizjournals.com/sacramento/stories/2010/04/26/daily69.html.

World Autism Organisation: www.worldautismorganisation.org/en/projects.html.

References

APA (1994) *Diagnostic and Statistical Manual of Mental Disorders* (DSM IV), 4th edn. Washington, DC: American Psychiatric Association.

APA (2013) *Diagnostic and Statistical Manual of Mental Disorders* (DSM-5), 5th edn. Washington DC, American Psychiatric Association.

Asperger, H. (1991) 'Autistic psychopathy' in childhood (translated and annotated by U. Frith). In U. Frith (ed.), *Autism and Asperger Syndrome*. New York: Cambridge University Press (originally published in 1944).

Baird, G. et al. (2006) Prevalence of the disorders of the autistic spectrum in a population cohort of children in South Thames. *The Lancet*, 368: 210–15.

Barbera, M.L. (with Rasmussen, T.) (2007) *The Verbal Behaviour Approach: How to Teach Children with Autism and Related Disorders*. London: Jessica Kingsley.

Bental, B. and Tirosh, E. (2007) The relationship between attention, executive functions and reading domain abilities in attention deficit hyperactivity disorder and reading disorder: a comparative study. *Journal of Child Psychology and Psychiatry*, 48(5): 455–63.

Connelly, M. (1997) *Assessment and Diagnosis in Children with an Autistic Spectrum Disorder: A Discussion Paper*. Lancashire County Council.

DeNora, T. (2006) Evidence and effectiveness in music therapy: problems, powers, possibilities and performances in health contexts (a discussion paper). *British Journal of Music Therapy*, 20: 81–99.

Frith, U. (2014) Autism – are we any closer to explaining the enigma? *The Psychologist*, 27(10): 744–5.

Gillberg, C. (2010) The ESSENCE in child psychiatry: early symptomatic syndromes eliciting neurodevelopmental clinical examinations. *Research in Developmental Disabilities*, 31(6): 1543–51.

Gillberg, C. and Coleman, M. (2001) *The Biology of the Autistic Syndromes*, 2nd edn. Cambridge: Cambridge University Press.

Gold, C., Wigram, T. and Elefant, C. (2006) Music therapy for autistic spectrum disorder. *Cochrane Database of Systematic Reviews*, Issue 2, Art. no. CD004381; DOI: 10.1002/14651858.CD004381.pub2.

Happe (2011) Why fold Asperger syndrome into autism spectrum disorder in the DSM-5? *Spectrum*. From: https://spectrumnews.org/opinion/viewpoint/why-fold-asperger-syndrome-into-autism-spectrum-disorder-in-the-dsm-5/.

Howlin, P. (2002) *Children with Autism and Asperger Syndrome: A Guide for Practitioners and Carers*. Chichester: Wiley.

Jarrett, C. (2014) Autism: myth and reality. *The Psychologist*, 27(10): 746–9.

Jones, R.S.P. and McCaughey, R.E. (1992) Gentle teaching and applied behaviour analysis: a critical review. *Journal of Applied Behavioural Analysis*, 25: 853–67.

Jordan, R. (2010) SpLD in the context of autism. Paper presented at the Dyslexia Association of Singapore (DAS) seminar week, Perspectives on Specific Learning Difficulties, 25 November, Singapore.

Kanner, L. (1943) Autistic disturbances of affective contact. *Nervous Child*, 2: 217–50.

Kaplan, B.J., Dewey, D.M., Crawford, S.G., and Wilson, B.N. (2001) The term comorbidity is of questionable value in reference to developmental disorders: data and theory. *Journal of Learning Disabilities*, 34(6): 555–65.

Klin, A., Lang, J., Cicchetti, D.V. and Volkmar, F.R. (2000) Brief report: interrater reliability of clinical diagnosis and DSM IV criteria for autistic disorder: results of the DSM IV autism field trial. *Journal of Autism Developmental Disorders*, 30: 163–7.

McGee, J.J. (1995) Gentle teaching. *Mental Handicap in New Zealand*, 9: 13–24.

Nordoff, P. and Robbins, C. (2009) *Presenting the Evidence: A Guide for Music Therapists Responding to the Demands of Clinical Effectiveness and Evidence-based Practice*. From: www.nordoff-robbins. org.uk/sites/default/files/Presenting%20The%20Evidence_1.pdf.

Pellicano, L. (2007) Autism as a developmental disorder: tracking changes across time. *The Psychologist*, 20: 216–19.

Pinto, D. et al. (2010) Functional impact of global rare copy number variation in autism spectrum disorders. *Nature*, 466: 368–72.

Reiersen, A.M, and Todd, R.D. (2008) Co-occurrence of ADHD and autism spectrum disorders: phenomenology and treatment. *Expert Review of Neurotherapeutics*, 8(4): 657–69.

Roberts, W. (2010) Research: treatments and interventions 'babies start to withdraw as early as nine months'. *The Globe and Mail*, 1 April.

Ronald, A., Edelson, L., Asherson, P. and Saudino, K. (2010) Exploring the relationship between autistic-like traits and ADHD behaviors in early childhood: findings from a community twin study of 2–year-olds. *Journal of Abnormal Child Psychology*, 38(2): 185–96.

Russell, G. and Pavelka, Z. (2013) 'Children who share symptoms of autism, dyslexia and attention deficit hyperactivity disorder'; licensee InTech. DOI: 10.5772/54159.

Simonoff, E., Pickles, A., Charman, T., Chandler, S., Loucas, T. and Baird, G. (2008) Psychiatric disorders in children with autism spectrum disorders: prevalence, comorbidity, and associated factors in a population-derived sample. *Journal of the American Academy of Child and Adolescent Psychiatry*, 47(8): 921–9.

Singh, I. and Elsabbagh, M. (2014) Autism research beyond the bench. *Autism*, 18(7): 754–5.

Snowling, M.J. (2012) Editorial: Seeking a new characterisation of learning disorders. *Journal of Child Psychology and Psychiatry*, 53(1): 1–2.

Sturm, H., Fernell, E. and Gillberg, C. (2004) Autism spectrum disorders in children with normal intellectual levels: associated impairments and subgroups. *Developmental Medicine and Child Neurology*, 46(7): 444–7.

Szatmari, P. (2010) Genome project identifies anomaly in DNA that may enable earlier diagnosis and treatment. *The Globe and Mail*, 1 April.

Task Force on Autism (2001) *The Report*. Dublin: The Stationery Office.

Taylor, P.G. (2011) *A Beginner's Guide to Autism Spectrum Disorders*. London: Jessica Kingsley Publishers.

WHO (1992) *International Classification of Diseases* (ICD-10), 10th edn. *Diagnostic Criteria for Research*. Geneva: World Health Organization.

Woodward, A. (2004) Music therapy for autistic children and their families: a creative spectrum. *British Journal of Music Therapy*, 18: 8–14.

Autism Spectrum Disorders

Applied Behavioural Analysis (ABA) Treatment and Research

Jo-Ann Page

18

Learning objectives

This chapter will help readers to:

- Understand the background and history of Autism Spectrum Disorders (ASD)
- Recognise the available treatments for those with ASD
- Understand the key components of Applied Behavioural Analysis (ABA)

Background and history of ASD

The last 20-plus years have witnessed a significant rise in the number of children diagnosed with autism. Of that, there is absolutely no doubt. Based on European studies at the time, it has been suggested that 40 years ago, one in 2500 children were diagnosed with autism. Today the United States Centers for Disease Control and Prevention (CDC) puts the figure at one in 68 from research conducted in 2010 (CDC, 2014). This is an increase on the incidence rate found in previous studies conducted in the United States of 1 in 150 in 2002, one in 110 in 2006 and 1 in 88 in 2008. The CDC survey assigned a diagnosis of autism spectrum disorder based on results of its Autism and Developmental Disabilities Monitoring (ADDM) Network research of eight-year-olds in eleven communities throughout the United States. The CDC estimates that 5.7– 21.9 per 1000 (from almost 3 in 500 to more than 3 in 150) children have an ASD. Occurrence was 4–5 times higher with boys than girls, with 1 in 42 boys compared to 1 in 189 girls. This is more or less in line with prevalence from ten to twenty years ago.

In the UK, estimates also indicate that the prevalence of autism is high. The figures suggest almost 40 in every 10,000 are autistic and 116 per 10,000 for the entire autistic spectrum (Baird et al., 2006). There is some debate on whether this increase represents a true increase in the prevalence of autism or whether it reflects changes in the criteria used to diagnose autism, along with increased recognition of the disorder by professionals. Many questions, hypotheses and accompanying explanations have been put forward for this dramatic rise. These range from environmental factors to better and more accurate detection and neurobiological, chemical and emotional influences, or even misdiagnosis. Whatever the cause of this increase, there is a need for teachers, parents and professionals to collaborate and work towards effective and lifelong intervention.

Historical aspects

The term Kanner's Syndrome was first assigned to autism following the work of Dr Leo Kanner of the Johns Hopkins Hospital in the USA in 1943. He studied a group of 11 children and introduced the label *early infantile* autism into the English language. At the same time, a German scientist, Dr Hans Asperger described a milder form of the disorder that became known as Asperger syndrome (Asperger, 1991 [1944]). This later group was characterised by Asperger by their social and communication deficits, and their obsessions and dependence on rituals and routines. Kanner's syndrome was characterised by abnormal communication, abnormal social communication and ritualistic and stereotyped behaviour and resistance to change (Howlin, 2002). This is shown in detail in the *International Classification of Diseases and Related Health Problems* (ICD-10) (WHO, 1992) which stated for example that the, 'abnormal or impaired development' needs to be in one of the areas of receptive and expressive language, social attachment and reciprocal social interaction and functional or symbolic play and should be evident before the age of three. ICD-10 also goes on to show specific symptoms in each of these categories, for example in social interaction, failure to make eye contact, inappropriate facial expression, body posture and use of gesticulation; in communication, delay in spoken language and failure to sustain conversational exchange; and in play, for example a preoccupation with non-functional elements of play.

Thus, these two disorders are also described in the *Diagnostic and Statistical Manual of Mental Disorders-5* (DSM-5) (APA, 2013). However, DSM-5 now defines ASD to include, 'the previous DSM-IV autistic disorder (autism), Asperger's disorder, childhood disintegrative disorder, and pervasive developmental disorder not otherwise specified' (APA, 2013). Autism Spectrum Disorder is used here as, 'a new DSM-5 name that reflects a scientific consensus that four previously separate disorders are actually a single condition with different levels of symptom severity' (APA, 2013). All of these disorders are characterised by varying degrees of impairment in communication skills, social interactions and restricted, repetitive and stereotyped patterns of behaviour. The changes in DSM-5 will be discussed in more detail later in this chapter.

In 2002, Howlin had suggested that there were a number of factors that differentiated between autism and Asperger syndrome. She suggested that the prevalence rates may have been higher for Asperger than for autism. She also suggested that the research indicated that there was often a significant difference in ages when children from the two groups were first diagnosed. In the autism group she suggested that the average age of diagnosis was 5.5 years, while in the Asperger group it was 11.3 years, and almost all (88%) of the children in the study with autism had been diagnosed before 10 years of age compared to only 45% of the Asperger group.

In support of DSM-5, it can be argued that the obvious similarities between the two syndromes lie in the same continuum or spectrum and that Asperger syndrome has often been considered to be a type of 'high-functioning' autism. However, although DSM-5 (APA, 2013) claims a 'scientific consensus' that they are the same condition, there is still some clinical controversy about whether it is a milder form of autistic disorder or a distinct disorder. Additionally, the term 'high-functioning' can be misleading as it does not necessarily translate to lower needs. This can have considerable implications for intervention and the allocation of resources.

Available treatments

Today there are a myriad of therapies available which claim to be able to treat autism. Some of these are supported by wide-scale scientifically conducted research that supports their efficacy; however, with others, there is often little or no empirical evidence to support suggestions made in support of them. Each therapy should therefore, be assessed and evaluated critically and objectively before being embarked upon. These therapies can broadly be considered as belonging to one of two categories: educational, psychological and therapeutic interventions; or biomedical interventions. This section will focus on the former.

Within the category of educational, psychological and therapeutic interventions perhaps one of the best known therapies is Applied Behaviour Analysis (ABA). Its practitioners aim to improve behaviour that is socially important by using interventions that are based on principles of learning theory and that have been evaluated through experimentation using replicable and independent measurement. The United States Surgeon General concluded in 1999 that, 'Thirty years of research demonstrated the efficacy of applied behavioral methods in reducing inappropriate behavior and in increasing communication, learning and appropriate social behavior'. ABA will be covered in more detail in the fourth section of this chapter. Other therapies that may be considered to offer most benefit include Augmentative Communication (AAC), neurofeedback and video modelling.

AAC relies on alternate methods of communication that replace or enhance conventional spoken language in order to express needs, wants and feelings. These may take the form of gestures, sign language, picture exchange (including the Picture Exchange Communication System), pointing and electronic aids. Research indicates that AAC may improve communication skills with children who have limited or no verbal communication when ABA methods are used to teach it. Hourcade et al. (2004) caution however that, 'children with good verbal imitation skills demonstrate better speech production than those with poor verbal intimation skills, with or without AAC'. They further caution:

> simple signs may be a support for children learning to speak or an additional mode of communication for children who have no speech or limited speech ... it is very rare to find a child with autism who learns to sign fluently (in sentences) and flexibly.' Hourcade et al. (2004)

Video modelling is a form of observational learning that is used to develop and strengthen communication skills, academic performance, and social and self-help skills. This is achieved by watching a video of targeted desirable behaviours to be learnt and then memorising, imitating and generalising the behaviours. Video modelling has been found to lead to quicker acquisition rates and increases in generalisation when compared to live modelling (Charlop-Christy and Daneshvar, 2003). A form of video modelling that is based on Discrete Trial Training (DTT) was devised and recorded as a way to teach those who do not respond well to other therapies. Video modelling can be successful in teaching 'theory of mind' or the capability to empathise and, 'see things from another person's point of view' (Happé et al., 1996). It is also more efficient in terms of time and cost to train and implement. (Graetz et al., 2006).

Neurofeedback (NFB) measures brain waves or flow of blood to the brain in order to produce a signal to be used as brain activity feedback. This enables self-regulation of brain function to be taught. Feedback with this therapy is often in the form of audio or visual signals (video display). Positive feedback is given for desirable brain activity and negative feedback is given for undesirable brain activity. Research has claimed that NFB is helpful in the treatment of Attention Deficit Hyperactivity Disorder (ADHD) although it should be noted that the UK National Institute for Health and Care Excellence (NICE) clinical guideline no.72 (NICE, 2009) says, 'Biofeedback has been employed as a non-invasive treatment for children with ADHD since the 1970s but it is probably not used as a significant intervention in UK clinical practice'.

Other educational, psychological and therapeutic interventions that have been shown to have some or mixed support from scientific research include: Auditory Integration Training (AIT), music therapy, the Picture Exchange Communication System , the TEACCH® autism programme (Treatment and Education of Autistic and related Communication-handicapped

Children), recreational sport and exercise, Sensory Integrative Therapy (SI or SIT) and socialisation-related classes.

AIT is used as an intervention to identify sounds to which a person is believed to be either hyper- or hypo-sensitive. There are three main types of AIT which are the Tomatis, Clark and Berard methods. Dr Guy Berard, a French otolaryngologist put forward the theory that such auditory alterations may cause behavioural disturbances including autism (Berard, 1993). Berard's method uses audiograms to discern such 'abnormalities' before AIT treats such distortions by exercising the muscles of the middle ear in the same way as physiotherapy (Berard, 1993). Some small-scale studies have illustrated benefits and others have provided mixed results. However, the American Speech-Language-Hearing Association (2004) report:

> this method has not met scientific standards for efficacy and safety ... The American Academy of Audiology (1993), ASHA (1994), the American Academy of Pediatrics (1998), and the Educational Audiology Association (1997) all concur that AIT should be considered an experimental procedure.

Music therapy uses music in a therapeutic manner to address behavioural, communication, physical, psychological, sensory-motor, social and cognitive functioning. A client will be involved in listening to music, playing instruments and singing, as well as creative activities. The therapist will conduct activities in an arranged and systematic manner to effect change with target behaviours and responses. Some research indicates that music therapy may enhance functioning (Kaplan and Steele, 2005; Whipple, 2004) but further research is required with robust experimental designs to evaluate these findings.

The Picture Exchange Communication System (PECS) was developed in 1984 by Lori Frost and Andrew Bondy. PECS is a six-phase system of augmentative communication which allows children who have little or no communication capabilities, a means of communicating non-verbally. A student will use pictures and symbols to communicate by learning to exchange a picture or symbol card of an item for the actual item itself. In doing this, the child is able to initiate communication. Studies have suggested that PECS may be effective in teaching communication of single words or short phrases but further studies are required to understand whether the claim that PECS can stimulate acquisition of more complex and flexible language by building sentence structures is supported. Research published in the *American Journal of Speech Language Pathology* (Flippin et al., 2010) suggests that:

> PECS is a promising but not yet established evidence-based intervention for facilitating communication in children with ASD ages 1–11 years. Small to moderate gains in communication were demonstrated following training. Gains in speech were small to negative.

It has also been proposed that PECS may help with the development of verbal language and reduce tantrums.

The TEACCH® autism programme was developed by Eric Schopler and Robert Reichler at the University of North Carolina during the 1960s. The programme promotes, 'an array of teaching or treatment principles and strategies based on the learning characteristics of individuals with ASD, including strengths in visual information processing' (UNC, 2014). Visual skills are emphasised as they may be more advanced than verbal skills in children with autism. For this reason, instructions may be presented as pictures rather than words, and tasks may utilise visual prompts to achieve them. TEACCH claims that its services are, 'grounded in empirical research, enriched by extensive clinical expertise, and notable for flexible and individualized support of individuals' (UNC, 2014). The National Research Council (2001) found that TEACCH could be effective as a plausible intervention. Ozonoff and Cathcart (1998) found that TEACCH parent training may accelerate development of both cognitive and self-help skills in children.

Recreational sports and exercise such as gymnastics, swimming or martial arts provide opportunities for a child to develop physical abilities, participate within a group environment and interact with other children. There is strong empirical evidence that putting children with autism in settings with typically developing peers – and no other intervention – may increase their social interactions (Lord and Hopkins, 1986). Where these typical peers act as role models, this can effectively increase social interaction further (McConnell, 2002). Such activities may also reduce aggressive and repetitive behaviour in some cases (Celiberti et al., 1997; Rosenthal-Malek and Mitchell, 1997).

Ayres' theory of sensory integration describes sensory integration as the normal developmental process of the body's central nervous system to organise sensations from the external environment as well as within the body in order to make adaptive responses necessary for emotional and behavioural regulation, learning and participation in daily life (Ayres, 2005). Those who suffer from sensory integration dysfunction may experience difficulties with integrating such input through touch, smell, hearing, taste, sight, coordination and sensing where one's body is in a given space. Sensory Integration Therapy (SIT/SI) is an intervention where the participant receives sensory stimulation with the objective of improving attention and cognitive functioning and decreasing disruptive and repetitive behaviours. This can include compressing elbows and knees, swinging, spinning and brushing the body. Some children with autism may enjoy a sense of firmly applied pressure that would otherwise be considered claustrophobic, such as being squashed between mattresses. Recent studies (Fazlioglu and Baran, 2008; Pfeiffer et al., 2011; Schaaf, 2014) have suggested that children with autism who have received SIT, have shown substantial gains in social engagement and performance.

Socialisation-related classes include attending pre-school and provide an opportunity for a child to interact with other children by participating in group activities. Such classes allow enjoyable recreation and opportunities to generalise the skills that have been learnt in more formal therapy settings. As with recreational sports and exercise, there is evidence of the benefits of interaction with typically developing peers.

There are other therapies that may offer some benefit but around which more research is required. This category could include animal therapy, art therapy, Developmentally-based Individual-difference Relationship-based intervention (DIR), oral-motor training, Son-Rise and vision therapy. Beyond these there are other therapies which the current weight of academic and empirical evidence suggests are ineffective in the treatment of autism.

History of ABA

In 1913, it was proposed that behaviour is dependent upon external environmental events and that observable behaviour is the appropriate subject-matter for psychology. This stimulus-response approach to psychology founded what has become known as behaviourism. In *The Behavior of Organisms* (1938), Skinner later differentiated between what Pavlov called 'respondent conditioning' (conditioned reflexes) and 'operant conditioning' (the behaviour consequence controls future behaviour occurrences). Skinner also defined the principles of behaviour such as reinforcement, prompting, shaping and fading. These principles constitute the science of behaviour analysis in its pure sense. Generally, when we talk of applied behaviour analysis we are talking of the science in its applied sense: that is to say, the way that we apply the 'pure' principles. There are many different ways to apply this science and it is these that will be discussed here and in the next section.

From the 1960s Lovaas began to propose that at least for some children, autism could be treatable. His 1987 article 'Behavioral treatment and normal educational and intellectual functioning in young autistic children' proposed that with training some autistic children were capable of catching-up their typical peers and becoming indistinguishable from them. His work showed that children could be taught social skills that meant that they did not need to be institutionalised but could succeed in society. Prior to this, autism had been claimed to be a neurosis with children being treated (to little discernible benefit) through psychotherapy, or misdiagnosed and regarded as retarded.

Lovaas applied behaviourism, claiming that using what was known as behaviour modification or applied behaviour analysis in an individual setting could improve the child's condition. Lovaas designed a curriculum and an implementation sequence for teaching what became known as the Lovaas model. His model underlined the need for repetitive therapy and focused on its intensity with children working in excess of 35 hours each week with each session lasting five to seven hours. The Lovaas model promoted sitting still, table exercises and learning to make eye-contact, and placed an important emphasis on early intervention with children before the age of three–and-a-half.

The model itself used rewards, and originally aversive punishments, to promote or discourage appropriate and inappropriate behaviours respectively. Today, the use of aversives does not form any part of the programme and this aspect of the original model has been condemned for being overly punishing, outdated, immoral and often illegal. Only positive reinforcement like 'edibles' are used today to provide acceptable alternatives to self-stimulatory ('stimming') behaviour.

The original method involved breaking down desired behaviours and skills into manageable steps or tasks (intermittent trials). The target behaviour would first be taught alone before 'distracters' were introduced. Then another behaviour would be taught in this fashion before the two target behaviours would be randomly rotated. Each of these trials utilised a series of verbal or physical prompts to shape the child's correct response which in turn could increase the child's attention capability. A correct response would be reinforced verbally, with an edible or another desired item.

In excess of 500 articles have been written in support of the Lovaas method yet the original findings of Lovaas' work have not been able to be replicated with the same degree of success. Criticism of the method is directed at the rigour and design of the original trials. Today, the system appears to be successful for some children and not others, and despite the scale of Lovaas' work, it should not be seen as a panacea.

The effectiveness of ABA interventions generally is well known and well documented. In 1972, Hingtgen and Bryson reviewed research articles from the previous decade and found that interventions that were based on behaviour illustrated more consistent results than interventions that were not. In 1981, DeMyer et al. found, 'evidence strongly suggests that the treatment of choice for maximal expansion of the autistic child's behavioral repertoire is a systematic behavioral education program, involving as many child contact hours as possible'. Since Lovaas' 1987 article, further research has been produced to support the efficacy of a behavioural approach to treating autism. In 1996, Baglio et al. reviewed research from the previous 15 years and commented that the type of research itself was evolving to be more refined and incorporating more broad applications of ABA. Research continues to support ABA and, unlike with other 'treatments', studies have not been able to show that behavioural intervention is not effective.

ABA available today

ABA can be thought of as the application of behaviourist principles in order to effect positive changes in a person's behaviours. ABA explains behaviour in relation to external events that can be influenced, and not internal concepts that cannot. Where people refer to different types of ABA therapy, this simply refers to different styles of application of the behavioural science and not distinct sciences. In 1968, Baer et al. identified what they saw as seven fundamental attributes of ABA:

- Applied – has practical value
- Behavioral – behavior itself is targeted
- Analytical – functional relationship can be established

- Technological – methods are well-documented and replicable
- Conceptually systematic – based on sound theoretical principles
- Effective – produces socially meaningful results
- Generalised – applicable across different settings (Baer et al., 1968)

As we have seen, empirical findings have shown that ABA can be effective in helping children with ASD to improve their academic abilities, communication skills, general socialisation and simultaneously reduce inappropriate behaviours. ABA can be utilised holistically in a range of situations from the classroom to the home and broader community environments.

ABA works through a process of systematic instructions to teach broken-down steps of a desired skill. One of the procedures for this that is used in early and intensive treatments is known as Discrete Trial Training (DTT). There are generally five accepted parts to DTT:

1. Antecedent
2. Prompt
3. Response
4. Consequence for a correct and for an incorrect response
5. Inter-trial interval (Smith, 2001; Malott and Trojan-Suarez, 2006)

With DTT, a therapist will provide different learning opportunities in order to establish a child's repertoire for correctly responding to directions to obtain positive reinforcement (a reward). Initially, rewards may take the form of primary reinforcement such as food edibles, and as the child progresses these may move towards secondary reinforcement such as tangibles and social praise. By utilising a strategy of appropriate teaching and rewards, the child will be able to quickly learn new skills and behaviours. Smith (2001) claims that: 'Discrete Trial Training is one of the most important instructional methods for children with autism.'

Verbal Behaviour Therapy (VB/AVB) utilises DTT but places an additional emphasis on communication skills. This is done in accordance with Skinner's analysis of language and its functions which he described (creating the new terms 'echoics', 'intraverbals', 'mands' and 'tacts') in his 1957 book *Verbal Behavior*. As Skinner merely described these, it fell to others such as Carbone, Michael, Partington and Sundberg to apply his analysis of VB within ABA. VB suggests that a child's language facilitates their desire to obtain something from someone else and so it teaches the child to make demands ('mand'). This is different to other forms of ABA in that it is teaching the child that by communicating they can receive an instant positive reinforcement and so it can be considered less rigid than other types of ABA. VB encourages the child to take on a more active role within a session and can increase their motivation to complete trials.

In order for a child to be capable of generalising what they learn to all environments, the opportunity for generalisation should be included into the teaching from the outset.

Natural Environment Teaching (NET) sets out to achieve this without learning behaviours and skills in one setting (usually the structured classroom) and then having to adapt and learn to generalise these to other scenarios. With NET the therapist or teacher must be clear about what they want to achieve and how they can achieve it in a varied, moveable setting. In order to establish instructional control with NET the teacher must first effectively associate themselves with positive reinforcement. This is done through 'pairing'. This will begin with non-contingent reinforcement where reinforcement is offered without any demands having been placed on the child (other than his or her acceptance of the reinforcement and an absence of undesirable behaviour). Where this happens constantly, the teacher can begin to slowly introduce demands of the child. In this way the required response before reinforcement can also be increased. More opportunities of varying degrees of difficulty can then be attempted without lowering the value of the reinforcer. The teacher must be able to pair herself with robust reinforcers so that she actually becomes a reinforcer herself. From this point on the teacher becomes a conduit and everything about her – *ergo* learning – will become reinforcing. The key to NET is being inventive with teaching the desired skills and behaviours in a way that remains motivational and fun for the child.

Pivotal Response Training (PRT) was developed by Koegel and Schreibman in the 1970s. Its goals include, 'the development of communication, language and positive social behaviors and relief from disruptive self-stimulatory behaviors' (Autism Speaks, 2014) it can be used to develop generalisation of stimulus and response, reduce dependency on prompts and increase spontaneity and motivation. It is a naturalistic intervention whose motivation strategies promote natural reinforcement (Schreibman, 2000) where the reward is directly related. For example, a child demanding a toy is rewarded by being given the toy and not a more abstract reward. PRT is centred on child-instigated play. Such interventions are said to have a positive effect on the child and parents who implement PRT.

Rather than target specific behaviours, PRT targets pivotal components that affect a wide range of a child's behaviours in the areas of academic study, communication and socialisation. When pivotal behaviours are encouraged they are thought to produce improvements in other behaviours that have not been specifically targeted. These pivotal behaviours are: initiating social interaction, motivation, response to multiple cues and self-management. Koegel et al. (1999) report that an enhancement of pivotal behaviours can induce an improvement in autonomy, child learning and generalising new skills. Humphries (2003) claims that PRT is: 'an efficacious evidence-based intervention for children with ASD'.

Changes in DSM 5

The *Diagnostic and Statistical Manual of Mental Disorders* (DSM) was updated in 2013 from the fourth edition, text revision (DSM IV TR) to DSM-5 which took effect from May 2013. DSM-5 has made several important changes in the way that conditions are named and categorised. The term 'autism spectrum disorder' is itself a new term to DSM-5 and includes what was previously termed 'autistic disorder' (APA, 2013). Asperger's disorder, childhood disintegrative disorder and Pervasive Developmental Disorder Not Otherwise Specified (PDD–NOS) have also been subsumed by this new nomenclature. This new definition is said to reflect, 'scientific consensus that four previously separate disorders are actually a single condition with different levels of symptom severity' (APA, 2013). These symptoms are split into two core domains; 'Persistent deficits in social communication and social interaction across multiple contexts' (APA, 2013) and 'restricted, repetitive patterns of behavior, interests or activities' (APA, 2013). DSM-5 continues, 'Individuals who have marked deficits in social communication, but whose symptoms do not otherwise meet criteria for autism spectrum disorder, should be evaluated for social (pragmatic) communication disorder' (APA, 2013). As a consequence of these new definitions a new series of severity levels is also published in DSM-5. These range from: 'Level 1 "Requiring support"', 'Level 2 "Requiring substantial support"' to 'Level 3 "Requiring very substantial support"' (APA, 2013). This then provides for a clear categorisation of conditions and levels of support. However, in practical terms, it means that many children are now receiving an autism spectrum disorder Level 1 diagnosis, who previously would have been diagnosed as PDD–NOS. The implication of this is that this can affect the child in situations such as school admission where a label of autism may be prohibitive but one of PDD–NOS would not have been. This suggests that there is a good deal of work to be done to educate those who need to understand this new terminology as well as how it relates to previous definitions given in DSM IV.

Summary

Rates of autism have risen in successive and varied research and it can be suggested that this is likely to continue to be the case. As we have seen in this chapter, this rise has enabled many therapies which have varying degrees of efficacy in different aspects of treatment to become established, as demand for services has increased exponentially. Whilst this has undoubtedly provided parents and carers with choice, it is important to realise that a degree of assessment and individual suitability will always be required because a recommended treatment that had results for one child may be completely ineffective and inappropriate for another.

A reputable clinic offering services will always seek to meet with and interview parents to understand extant diagnoses and evaluate a child through assessment before determining appropriate services. Evaluative systems can then be used to assess whether or not a behavioural intervention has the impact that was envisioned and desired and allows for the effectiveness of the intervention to be appraised. It is used uniquely with each child due to their individualistic nature.

In this way, treatments can be effective and offer an improvement in the overall quality of life for children living with autism.

Discussion points

- From your own experience, comment on the efficacy of the various therapies outlined in this chapter.
- Paying particular attention to the 'severity levels' of DSM-5, do you believe that these will assist treatment or become prohibitive to school admissions?
- Reflect on the degree of choice available from the therapies outlined in this chapter. Is this a good thing or is regulation warranted?
- Consider the importance of an intake assessment meeting for a child and their family and discuss the implications for those involved.

Further reading

Additional information on many of the topics discussed in this chapter can be found at: www.autismspeaks.org.

APA (2013) *Diagnostic and Statistical Manual of Mental Disorders* (DSM-5), 5th edn. Washington, DC: American Psychiatric Association.

CDC (Centers for Disease Control and Prevention) (2014) *Prevalence of Autism Spectrum Disorder Among Children Aged 8 Years* – Autism and Developmental Disabilities Monitoring Network, 11 Sites, United States, 2010. *Surveillance Summaries* [online]. 63 (SS02). Available from: www.cdc.gov/mmwr/preview/mmwrhtml/ss6302a1. htm?s_cid=ss6302a1_w.

Cooper, J.O., Heron, T.E. and Heward, W.L. (2007) *Applied Behavior Analysis*, 2nd edn. Upper Saddle River, NJ: Pearson Education, Inc.

Howlin, P. (2002) *Children with Autism and Asperger Syndrome: A Guide for Practitioners and Carers*. Wiley: Chichester.

Useful websites

The National Autistic Society: www.autism.org.uk/
The leading UK charity for people on the autism spectrum (including Asperger syndrome) and their families.

The Autism Education Trust: www.autismeducationtrust.org.uk/
The Autism Education Trust is dedicated to coordinating, supporting and promoting effective education practice for all children and young people on the autism spectrum.

The Autism Alliance: www.autism-alliance.org.uk/
Dedicated to co-ordinating and improving education support for all children on the autism spectrum in England.

References

American Academy of Audiology (1993) Position statement: auditory integration training. *Audiology Today*, 5(4): 21.

American Academy of Pediatrics (1998) Auditory integration training and facilitated communication for autism. *Pediatrics*, 102(2): 431–3.

APA (2013) *Diagnostic and Statistical Manual of Mental Disorders* (DSM-V), 5th edn. Washington, DC, American Psychiatric Association.

ASHA (American Speech-Language-Hearing Association) (1994) Auditory Integration Training. *ASHA*, 36(10): 55–8.

ASHA (American Speech-Language-Hearing Association) (2004) *Auditory Integration Training: Working Group in AIT*. [N.K.]: ASHA.

Asperger, H. (1991 [1944]) 'Autistic psychopathy' in childhood. Translated and annotated by U. Frith. In U. Frith (ed.), *Autism and Asperger Syndrome*. New York: Cambridge University Press, pp. 37–92.

Autism Speaks (2014) *Pivotal Response Treatment* [online]. Available from: www.autismspeaks.org/what-autism/treatment/pivotal-response-therapy-prt (Accessed 29 November 2014).

Ayres, A.J. (2005) *Sensory Integration and the Child: Understanding Hidden Sensory Challenges* (25th anniversary edn, revised and updated by Pediatric Therapy Network; photographs by Shay McAtee). Los Angeles: WPS.

Baer, D., Wolf, M. and Risley, R. (1968) Some current dimensions of applied behavior analysis. *Journal of Applied Behavior Analysis*, 1: 91–7.

Baglio, C., Benavidiz, D., Compton, L., Matson, J. and Paclawskyj, T. (1996) Behavioral treatment of autistic persons: a review of research from 1980 to present. *Research in Developmental Disabilities*, 17: 433–65.

Baird, G., Siminoff, E., Pickles, A. et al. (2006) Prevalence of the disorders of the autistic spectrum in a population cohort of children in South Thames. *The Lancet*, 368: 210–15.

Berard, G. (1993) *Hearing Equals Behaviour*. New Canaan, CT: Keats Publishing.

Celiberti, D.A., Bobo, H.E., Kelly, K.S., Harris, S.L. and Handleman, J.L. (1997) The differential and temporal effects of antecedent exercise on the self-stimulatory behavior of a child with autism. *Research in Developmental Disabilities*, 18: 139–50.

CDC (Centers for Disease Control and Prevention) (2014) *Prevalence of Autism Spectrum Disorder Among Children Aged 8 Years* – Autism and Developmental Disabilities Monitoring Network, 11 Sites, United States, 2010. *Surveillance Summaries* [online]. 63 (SS02), pp. 1–21. Available from: www.cdc.gov/mmwr/preview/mmwrhtml/ss6302a1.htm?s_cid=ss6302a1_w (Accessed 26 November 2014).

Charlop-Christy, M.H. and Daneshvar, S. (2003) Using video modeling to teach perspective taking to children with autism. *Journal of Positive Behavior Interventions*, 5(1): 12–21.

DeMyer, M.K., Hingtgen, J. and Jackson, R. (1981) Infantile autism reviewed: a decade of research. *Schizophrenia Bulletin*, 7: 388–451.

Educational Audiology Association (1997) Auditory integration training: educational audiology association position statement. *Educational Audiology Newsletter*, 14(3): 16.

Fazlioglu, Y. and Baran, G. (2008) A sensory integration therapy program on sensory problems for children with autism. *Perceptual and Motor Skills*, 106(2): 415–22.

Flippin, M., Reszka, S. and Watson, L.R. (2010) Effectiveness of the picture exchange communication system (PECS) on communication and speech for children with autism spectrum disorders: a meta-analysis. *American Journal of Speech Language Pathology*, 19(2): 178–95.

Graetz, J., Mastropieri, M. and Scruggs, T. (2006) Show Time: using video self-modeling to decrease inappropriate behavior. *Teaching Exceptional Children*, 38: 43–8.

Happé, F., Ehlers, S., Fletcher, P., Frith, U., Johansson, M., Gillberg, C., Dolan, R., Frackowiak, R. and Frith, C.D. (1996) 'Theory of mind' in the brain: evidence from a PET scan study of Asperger syndrome. *Neuro Report*, 8: 197–201.

Hingtgen, J.N. and Bryson, C.Q. (1972) Recent developments in the study of early childhood psychoses: infantile autism, childhood schizophrenia, and related disorders. *Schizophrenia Bulletin*, 5: 8–54.

Hourcade, J., Pilotte, T.E., West, E. and Parette, P. (2004) A history of augmentative and alternative communication for individuals with severe and profound disabilities. *Focus on Autism and Other Developmental Disabilities*, 19: 235–44.

Howlin, P. (2002) *Children with Autism and Asperger Syndrome: A Guide for Practitioners and Carers*. Wiley: Chichester.

Humphries, T.L. (2003) Effectiveness of pivotal response training as a behavioral intervention for young children with autism spectrum disorders. *Bridges: Practice-Based Research Syntheses*, 2: 1–9.

Kaplan, R.S. and Steele, A.L. (2005) An analysis of music therapy program goals and outcomes for clients with diagnoses on the autism spectrum. *Journal of Music Therapy*, 42(1): 2–19.

Koegel, L.K., Koegel, R.L., Harrower, J.K. and Carter, C.M. (1999) Pivotal response intervention 1: overview of approach. *Journal of the Association for Persons with Severe Handicaps*, 24: 174–85.

Lord, C. and Hopkins, J.M. (1986) The social behavior of autistic children with younger and same-age nonhandicapped peers. *Journal of Autism and Development Disorders*, 16: 249–62.

Lovaas, I. (1987) Behavioral treatment and normal educational and intellectual functioning in young autistic children. *Journal of Consulting and Clinical Psychology*, 55(1): 3–9.

Malott, R.W. and Trojan-Suarez, E.A. (2006) *Principles of Behaviour*. Upper Saddle River, NJ: Pearson Prentice Hall.

McConnell, S. (2002) Interventions to facilitate social interaction for young children with autism: review of available research and recommendations for educational intervention and future research. *Journal of Autism and Developmental Disorders*, 32: 351–72.

National Research Council (2001) *Educating Children with Autism*. Washington, DC: National Academy Press.

NICE (2009) *Guideline No. 72 Attention Deficit Hyperactivity Disorder: Diagnosis and Management of ADHD in Children, Young People and Adults*. Leicester: British Psychological Society/National Collaborating Society for Mental Health.

Ozonoff, S. and Cathcart, K. (1998) Effectiveness of a home program intervention for young children with autism. *Journal of Autism and Developmental Disorders*, 28: 25–32.

Pfeiffer, B.A., Koenig, K., Kinnealey, M., Sheppard, M. and Henderson, L. (2011) Effectiveness of sensory integration interventions in children with autism spectrum disorders: a pilot study. *American Journal of Occupational Therapy*, 65: 76–85.

Rosenthal-Malek, A. and Mitchell, S. (1997) The effects of exercise on the self-stimulatory behaviors and positive responding of adolescents with autism. *Journal of Autism and Developmental Disorders*, 27: 193–202.

Schaaf, R.C. (2014) An intervention for sensory difficulties in children with autism: a randomized trial. *Journal of Autism and Developmental Disorders*, 44(7): 1493–506.

Schreibman, L. (2000) Intensive behavioral/psychoeducational treatments for autism: research needs and future directions. *Journal of Autism and Developmental Disorders*, 30(5): 373–8.

Skinner, B.F. (1938) *The Behavior of Organisms: An Experimental Analysis*. Cambridge, MA: B.F. Skinner Foundation.

Skinner, B.F. (1957) *Verbal Behavior*. Englewood Cliffs, NJ: Prentice-Hall.

Smith, T. (2001) Discrete trial training in the treatment of autism. *Focus on Autism and Other Developmental Disabilities*, 16: 86–92.

UNC (University of North Carolina School of Medicine) (2014) *TEACCH Approach* [online]. UNC. Available from: teacch.com/about-us/what-is-teacch (Accessed 29 November 2014).

United States Surgeon General (1999) *Mental Health: A Report of the Surgeon General*. Washington, DC: USSG.

Whipple, J. (2004) Music in intervention for children and adolescents with autism: a meta-analysis. *Journal of Music Therapy*, 41: 90–105.

WHO (1992) *International Classification of Diseases* (ICD-10), 10th edn. *Diagnostic Criteria for Research*. Geneva: World Health Organization.

Understanding Tourette Syndrome

19

Judy Barrow

Learning objectives

This chapter will help readers to:

- Understand the traits and make-up of Tourette Syndrome (TS)
- Appreciate how TS impacts on the lives of children with the condition, particularly while at school
- Understand how gaining a sound knowledge of the condition can lead to effective management
- Appreciate how, by working together, practitioners can use techniques to overcome barriers to learning
- Explore suggestions for overcoming situations that arise from the condition to alleviate exclusion or low attainment

What is TS?

TS is a tic condition that is present from birth, that usually becomes evident in early childhood and that continues for life. The prime symptom is to have repeated tics, which are motor (bodily movement) and/or vocal in nature and have been present for more than a year. A tic is a repetitive, sudden movement or sound that has no purpose and, in general, you cannot help doing – for example, blinking, throat clearing, head nodding and making involuntary sounds. These can wax and wane and can vary from minor to severe, such as from just eye blinking to complex movements of the whole body.

The syndrome is a neurological, not a mental health, condition. Minor anomalies are known to occur in the structure and working of the brain in children and adults with TS. There is known to be an anomaly with a number of the brain chemicals, such as dopamine, serotonin and noradrenalin.

TS is frequently linked to other behaviours, such as obsessive–compulsive disorder (OCD) and attention deficit hyperactive disorders (ADHD). It is sometimes associated with high-functioning autism, such as Asperger's Syndrome (AS), as many families presenting with a TS member also feature a member with AS. Therefore, a child who has TS is also likely to have one or more related conditions. The most common conditions seen with TS are as follows:

- Learning difficulties due to poor concentration on classwork (as the children are absorbed in suppressing the tics) – although the child may be of good intelligence
- Mood disorders, such as depression or anxiety
- Conduct disorders
- Autistic Spectrum Disorders (ASD)
- Self-harming behaviours, such as head banging
- OCD or Obsessive–Compulsive Behaviour (OCB)
- ADHD
- Central Auditory Processing Disorder (CAPD)
- Sensory Modulation Difficulties (SMD)

What the above conditions have in common is that the children can't always process information in the same way as others because their ears, eyes and brain don't fully coordinate while they are dealing with the tics. With CAPD, something adversely affects the way the brain recognises and interprets sounds, most notably the sounds composing speech; and the same is true for those who also have difficulty with the recognition of shapes or letters. Add to this, the pure concentration required to suppress a tic or simply to deal with the impacts of ticcing while in the classroom and it is evident that the child can have a very negative educational experience.

However, children with TS can have many types of tics, or sudden movements and noises, and the tics can be prevalent throughout their life, although they do wax and wane. Tics may change in frequency and severity over periods of time, and new tics can manifest themselves without warning. TS is very 'suggestive'. Therefore the child or young person may develop a new tic within the classroom within the space of an afternoon.

Some one in 100 children and young people in the UK are thought to have TS, although the figure is thought to be higher due to misdiagnosis in the early part of the person's life.

For example, it is recognised that some children have been thought to have had epilepsy before a later diagnosis of TS is made. Diagnosis is based on such factors as having chronic tics for more than a year, having them at night and TS being present within the family.

Much is misunderstood about TS and prejudice is widespread. Most commonly in the educational setting, a child will be scolded for being naughty or disruptive, particularly in primary education. It is crucial, therefore, that these pupils are supported and given the chance to explain their syndrome, through the teacher, peer pupils and their parents. In the early stages, if the TS is treated as a nuisance or ignored, then the child will go through their early life stigmatised and isolated.

Profile of children and young people with TS

The most notable features of TS, especially in children and young people, are multiple tics that can change and also wax and wane over time The presence of such tics can be identified as early as the age of five. Most tics become very evident by the age of eight, and by this time the child has developed a range of either motor (bodily movement) and/or vocal tics. These can be further classified as simple or complex:

- *Motor tics* include things such as blinking, head turning, head nodding, kicking, facial grimacing, touching, licking or smelling objects. Complex movements are manifested as a series of movements at one time, from head to toe
- *Vocal tics* include things such as throat clearing, coughing, sniffing, yelling or making animal sounds, mimicking and repeating whole sentences

Tics in all forms come and go – the child may change the nature of a tic simply because another tic has suggested itself and thus becomes another part of their repertoire. There are several other symptoms that occur:

- *Coprolalia*: the involuntary use of obscenities and swear words. (This only occurs in about one in 10 people with TS. If this occurs, it should be noted that the child cannot help swearing, and it is not a reflection on their moral character or upbringing)
- *Echolalia*: copying what others say, repeating their speech and phrases
- *Palilalia*: repeating your own last word or syllable after the end of a sentence
- *Non-obscene socially inappropriate (NOSI) behaviours*: such as making inappropriate or rude personal comments
- *Echopraxia*: imitation of other people's actions; copying of body movements

These children can also experience sleeplessness as part of the syndrome, as they will be ticcing at night, even during deep sleep. Ongoing research has found that sleep was significantly disturbed in people with TS as against a comparison trial of those without TS. TS tics, particularly movements, were still clearly evident during sleep and led to repeated awakenings during the night. The severity of TS during the day correlated with the number of awakenings and with the percentage of sleep deficiency. In schoolchildren this has a detrimental effect on their being able to concentrate, remain alert or relax during the school day:

> he couldn't settle to sleep at night due to constant 'ticcing', that is, having loads of involuntary tics all through the night/and going through his OCD rituals during the night. It was a nightmare, he would be crying, or wandering around the house in the small hours … he is just tired from not sleeping, he can't turn off at night, brain wasn't shutting down … he finds it hard to totally unwind enough to get to sleep at night, or stop whatever he is compulsively doing at the normal bedtime … TS keeps the stress levels at a high, in the past making it impossible to even be tired … I feel like a vampire … I can't sleep at night and then have to sleep the following day. I feel like a recluse. (Parent of a TS child)

Therefore, lack of sleep is common due to the need to tic, hyperactivity and, sometimes, OCD. Some have night terrors and sleepwalking. This often leads to trouble waking up once asleep, through sheer tiredness; many have said that the tics are very severe when waking up. This, in turn, leads to a lack of performance at school or in being able to attend school. At this point, parents and carers will be advised to find a method of inducing sleep, which could include mild medication or relaxation techniques.

In addition to this, research has shown that children with TS have a need to move about continually, to 'fidget' – whether pacing, twisting around or fiddling – and, as such, appear to be restless. This can mean that they lose calories while in the throes of the movement. It is acknowledged that children with TS have repetitive movements and generally move about more than others, as they are genetically inclined to do so – TS has involuntary movement in its portfolio of traits. These actions are called 'Non-Exercise Activity Thermogenesis', or NEAT. All this may be useful to know and bear in mind with regard to children who fidget in class.

Unique features of children and young people with TS

The tics change in nature as the young child becomes a teenager, peaking at puberty, but certain social situations, such as the supermarket, can make them worse. Between the ages of 10 and 16 years this is particularly acute and often proves a difficult time for the young person. While their behaviour might be disruptive, it is very important to recognise that these behaviours are involuntary and driven by compulsion. This is particularly true of OCD-style behaviours and rituals, which make up the whole:

> When Paul has to put his things away in the same place every day, the kids in class say that it's because he is too stupid to look for his stuff. When he walks in exactly the same places all the time, they laugh. (Parent of a TS child)

Because the tics are not consistent, it may be thought that the child is either 'putting it on' or doesn't have TS – that they are just being disruptive. This makes it more difficult for a mutual understanding to be reached, as the child will then try to suppress their tics or become unable to express themselves as having TS. Denial of having TS is common.

Unpredictability is the most predictable feature of TS. An adaptation in the classroom may work well one week and then not the next. Well-thought-out plans may need to change, sometimes frequently. Recognising this will reduce stress both for the teacher and the child, and reduce frustration when things do not appear to be going well.

Another parent says:

> The teacher didn't see anything that they recognised as Tourette syndrome, so our son wasn't being identified as having the condition. Our son was coming home from school distressed, very tired, angry or touchy, and his tics were obvious to us. He was also often refusing to go to school because he was worrying about his tics in class. This manifested itself in tummy aches and headaches. (Mother of an 11-year-old TS boy)

It is often a feature of TS that the child feels particularly stressed, anxious and insecure, leading to absences while at school and in not attending school through a fear of being seen to tic.

Underpinning research

More health and educational practitioners are introducing 'evidence-based practice' with respect to TS. This means that individuals and their families, when wishing to gain effective support for their child's education, can seek out an expert who is familiar with the condition and who can liaise with the families and educators in a 'user-friendly' way. They can work together to demonstrate workable, proven interventions using models from evidence gained elsewhere. In this way, the families, students and educators can add to the evidence base.

Most research adheres to the theory that the condition is inherited. It is generally believed that a genetic factor is responsible for most cases of TS. Genes are passed on to a child from each parent; a child is more likely to develop TS if they have a father, mother, brother or sister with the condition or related conditions. It has been said that environmental factors can exacerbate the development of the condition, but this has not been proven. In many cases, the diagnosis of the child leads to a diagnosis for older members of the family, as diagnostic methods have improved over the past decade. However, it is clear that the presence of certain factors does have an effect on the child or young person with TS. Noise, whether sudden or in the background, smells or a change in usual settings have the effect of triggering a range of tics, through an anxiety response. It is crucial to understand the compulsive side of TS – that the urges are involuntary and necessary to the child and that the syndrome is a mix of compulsions and behaviours.

In terms of SMD, this is a part of the syndrome 'mix', and teachers can play an invaluable part in understanding the child's particular sensory issues. However, there is nothing like teacher–parent collaboration to assist in identifying and supporting the child's needs – for example, significant food preferences due to hypersensitivities to taste and touch in the mouth may limit opportunities to participate in mealtimes with peers. Similarly, a fear of touching objects due to hypersensitivities may interfere with participation in school and social activities. Abnormal responsiveness to sensation may also restrict interests and activities, impacting on play behaviour. For example, peer interactions in the playground may be limited due to excessive fear of typical playground equipment, or due to hypersensitivity to noise, light or being touched.

Identifying students with TS

Vocal tics can range from coughing or throat clearing to the involuntary utterance of whole words or phrases. During a tic a person is fully aware of their actions but cannot stop, though they may be able to suppress them temporarily. People with TS are of normal or even higher intelligence but may also have educational difficulties due to trying to overcome the urge to tic – to 'suppress', which affects their concentration levels. If not given appropriate help they can become frustrated, withdrawn or do poorly at school.

The child with TS may feel unable to share their concerns or explain their condition to others. They may find ways to 'suppress' by not speaking or leaving the room suddenly and often. Children with TS do this frequently as a coping mechanism and, if they haven't explained about their TS or it is not disclosed to the educationalists, this may be seen as odd behaviour (Cavanna and Robertson, 2008).

Parents will know that their child has some traits and may be the first to seek a formal diagnosis:

> We knew our child had tics, and suspected Tourette syndrome; we learnt more about the condition and noticed that despite the fact that our son was intelligent and academically bright, there were areas he was struggling with when in school, because of his tics. After he was formally diagnosed, a plan was agreed by the school and us which was discussed at each subsequent review meeting. We also worked closely with an educational psychologist who was able to identify with our son's condition and this gave us much needed support. This support has continued to work well over the years. (Parents of a TS boy, aged 16)

Many people with TS lead normal lives, with understanding and support. Others find the condition, and people's prejudices about TS, to be an obstacle to school, to learning and in forming peer relationships:

> Growing up with TS was very difficult. I believed I was different from everyone else due to the involuntary symptoms. I often felt unloved and unwanted by family and friends and felt that I

was being a hindrance to the rest of my family. I was very self conscious about my condition especially when all I wanted to do was fit in with my peers ... I was often very paranoid at everything and everyone around me and at times felt very alone. (Davidson, 2010)

Students with TS may:

- have poor concentration in class
- have problems with organising themselves
- be slow producing their work
- have poor handwriting skills, although computer skills are very good
- become anxious with change or a different routine, especially when unexpected
- have low self-esteem through negative experiences
- have poor social skills due to isolation
- stay away from school rather than endure bullying or exclusion
- try to suppress their tics
- have unexpected absences during class

Effective interventions, support and accommodating children and young people with TS

Children will be more prone to changeable tics and outbursts when changing classes or schools, or feeling insecure in a given situation. They will be more likely to change tics or manifest vocal tics if they are nervous or afraid. A record of their TS and, more importantly, a note of the types of tics they show, updated when new tics appear, would assist in the educationalist's role of accommodating the needs of the TS child. When asked, many teenagers with TS will say that the worst part of their syndrome while at high school is bullying or mimicking.

The child should have a support mechanism around them that allows for communication, support and mentoring in regard to bullying or feelings of isolation. A useful approach is to provide a time when the child or young person can explain their condition to their peers – in a safe and sociable setting, such as in a personal and social development class. Reviewing this approach with the child will be helpful, making adaptations that are flexible to the situation as it stands – as TS can vary and change in constancy, the approach will need to take into account the person's current condition. Many such classroom adaptations will benefit the entire class. Be creative and implement awareness discussions about TS for all students, which will create less stress in the end. For example, giving the child the option of flexible outlines and due dates will help them plan their work and give them structure during a particularly 'ticcy' time. A consistent dialogue with carers/parents will help the child to adapt to school schedules and can help keep constancy in attendance, thus helping the child to feel confident.

Strategies such as allowing the child to leave the classroom – even to deliver a note or go on an errand – will help distract them and give them a reason to be absent during a time when it is evident that they would prefer to leave the room. Otherwise, giving the child 'time out' and the ability to leave the room when they need to will help lessen the stress they might otherwise feel during a ticcing session. Some personal favourites for reducing anxiety include sitting the child next to a door in the classroom so they feel they can easily leave the room if the tics become too severe, or sitting them by a window where they may feel less restricted.

Children tend to acquire strategies to adapt to school life: 'I often sit tapping my fingers and tapping my foot which for me helps to alleviate the tics and gives me something to concentrate on', says one child. The child will respond well to being left alone to tic or being allowed to leave the place they are in with minimum fuss: 'My self-confidence goes up and down like a yo-yo and tends to be increased when I have good friends and lots of support around me', says a young person with motor and vocal tics. 'Having constant reassurance helps tremendously and, of course, being given lots of positive feedback about achievements,' explains another.

It is clear that, with the understanding of classmates and tutors, a young person with TS will feel encouraged to tell their peers about their condition and explain its symptoms, causes and how they can help. In many such cases, the child then tics less in the classroom because their anxieties are lessened, in terms of being less lonely and isolated, and in terms of being allowed to tic, in the knowledge that they will not be punished: 'I find having somewhere quiet to go and gather myself is very helpful'.

The best and most effective coping mechanism that has been identified by youngsters with TS is having the understanding of and being shown patience from others around you, whether that is a tutor or a peer. Having an open and honest dialogue about how the child may feel in different situations helps others to understand what they are going through and therefore encourages them and gives them reassurance.

Pre-planning, letting the child know about any future changes in the school day, and encouraging other pupils to ignore tics can assist the child in dealing with their TS when in class. Differences from the home setting, where life is fairly static and the child feels safe, often show in the performance given by the child in terms of work done in school. Homework may be excellent but classwork may not demonstrate the same level of concentration or intellect. However, the opposite may also be true in some cases: 'I often find that I can't concentrate on homework when I get home as I am so tired at the end of the school day.'

Youngsters can often feel overwhelmed with either the list of instructions they need to follow, because of their concentrating on suppressing a tic, or indeed with the difficulty of processing information adequately. Some youngsters can then appear to be either disorganised or demotivated, or may be obsessive about having everything organised 'just so' – but this can be counterproductive because of the time that obsession may take. Help, such as written instructions/sheets being made available to the child, can assist greatly with this. If the member of staff ensures that the child has understood all that is required, this is also very useful: 'I wish the teacher would slow down as I can't take in everything he says and I miss what I am supposed to do.'

If writing or reading is slow, poor or erratic, then access to a computer, AlphaSmart keyboarding device and a reader/scribe has proved exceptionally beneficial: 'I knew what I wanted to say in my English exam but I was worried about writing it down without making a mess, then I would get stressed and tic, which just made things worse.' Exams and tests can be challenging for anyone, but for someone with TS they are even more stressful. Apart from the symptoms they have that may interfere with their performance, they also worry about how they may disturb their peers. It is important to establish how best to deal with this and have prior discussions as to what suits all. It may be necessary for someone to have their own room for an exam or a base with fewer people there. It is also important that extra time is allowed for tests or exams.

Some interventions which have worked include the following:

- Allowing for the movement and noise of tics/compulsions
- Ignoring the tics (remember, not all tics are visible or audible)
- Using distraction tactics, a reason for the child to be able to leave the room – and giving 'time out'
- Identifying their strengths and weaknesses to instil confidence and address problems
- Using written instructions to help with organisational skills and technology aids where necessary
- Being clear about the expectations of both the teacher and the child; allow for flexibility
- Being patient. Try not to take inappropriate vocal tics personally, and keep a sense of humour

And, finally, ensure that all teachers, especially substitute teachers, teaching assistants and outside trainers, are continually aware of the condition and are well acquainted with the child in question.

It is important to understand that the transition to school, and also between lessons, can be very difficult for the student with TS. The creation of a safe atmosphere and patient perseverance from the teacher will pay dividends.

As the child progresses through school their teachers are always changing and, in some cases, information is not always fully conveyed from teacher to teacher. It may then be up to the child or their parents to ensure that this is done. Often assumptions are made that the child's condition is known to all. Some cases have become acute by the time it is discovered that the child's condition has been the root of their behaviour, by which time there has been distress to the child, the parent and within the classroom setting itself. This is where full knowledge of the condition and how it manifests in a particular child will make for a supportive, nurturing approach. Regular reviews and communication should include parents and guardians. Some have used 'personal passports' to profile the progress of the child, which are regularly updated by mutual agreement.

Current issues

Raising awareness about TS is a key to assisting practitioners in understanding the condition and making appropriate support available, and in allowing for the person with TS and their families to be able to explain the condition to others. The ability to explain and allow for the condition varies from school to school, and particularly at primary-school level, where disruptive behaviour has more of an impact. Some schools prefer to leave it to the parents to resolve what they see as 'problems' with TS. Yet, practice shows that the school is the best place to explain the condition so that teachers and pupils can work out a way forward. A view that all experiences should be positive also makes that approach a truthful one.

Therefore, rather than respond to the behaviours with a set of standard approaches, the school and those who support children with different needs could help by taking the approach that the TS is there to stay and should be managed rather than punished or ignored – that the condition is involuntary, and the child is not able to react in a different manner, nor was their intention to be disruptive. Assuring a policy of openness and honesty, sharing and constant review will create a climate in which the child will feel safe.

John Davidson (2010) has explained that, when he was a lonely 16-year-old boy with severe TS, he was too scared to venture outside and face people. His uncontrollable outbursts and violent body jerks denied him a normal life during his school and college years:

> A BBC documentary about me when I was 16 changed my life tremendously due to the public awareness it created.
>
> I felt that people now believe I'm not just a nutter and that I was a decent kid who unfortunately has this misunderstood condition. I then had the confidence to walk down the street without feeling I was being watched and laughed at.
>
> Most importantly it put TS out there and has encouraged other people to go get a diagnosis and has allowed me to make many friends over the years.

While attention difficulties are a challenge for teachers, tics are the most overwhelming element of TS in a classroom. If this is labelled as antisocial behaviour and there are incidents between the student, peers and the teacher, the culmination of this could be exclusion and a negative experience for all. The most negative experience felt by the person with TS – disruption and being singled out – will make them more anxious and less likely to do well in class.

The most common issues are that a child is not believed when they explain that they have TS, and a parent has to intervene. In some cases, the parent has been held to blame for the perceived bad behaviours of their child, which negates any effort by the parent and child to gain understanding and support for the condition. Some families have reached a review meeting stage with no agreement on either side, and the child has become more isolated as a result.

An issue arises when substitute or probationary teachers are in place. If they are not aware of the condition or of the child having the condition, the 'status quo' which may have worked well enough can be disrupted. We have cases of children being excluded by such teachers working in strange situations, and the child being confused at what was a safe haven becoming an unknown quantity. A recent case showed that a probationary teacher thought that TS was one tic, and that being for life. They did not believe the child with TS and exclusion was threatened. Once the usual teacher was alerted, all was resolved. A lack of accurate and wide knowledge and understanding about the syndrome has been identified as the main cause of concern for children in school (www.schoolbehavior.com/disorders/tourettes-syndrome).

Practice, provision and policy

Many young people with TS have tried relaxation exercises at home, have attended cognitive therapy and take medication to alleviate the tics and the OCD. However, it is clear that this does not 'cure' TS, which is inherent in the person who has the condition. The honest, truthful approach in explaining the condition to those around the child, and to help the child to manage their learning despite the need to tic, has worked well in many cases. Where the child has been scolded, excluded or the school does not acknowledge the existence of the condition, many problems have arisen, which exacerbates the anxiety for the teacher, parents and other children in the class.

Where the school has taken the approach to treat the child as they would a 'naughty' child, the situation arises where neither the child nor or their teacher benefits from any exchanges arising from what are regarded as incidents rather than a consequence of TS. In order that a resolution is reached, parents and teaching staff should share their knowledge of how the TS manifests in their children and pupils, and share that with the class and with other practitioners.

It is known that such knowledge works well although, in some instances when the knowledge or understanding is not shared or passed on during changes in the schooling, the situation can reverse and the child can be excluded through no fault of their own. A constant approach, building on the facts about the condition and the child who has it, and working with the family and the child's cohorts to gain support and understanding, will allow the child to flourish in the classroom. This is very important in the early years, as the child will then become confident about school, which should help them in their further schooling and higher education.

Understanding TS in schools and colleges is of paramount importance if children and young people are to feel integrated and safe. Many institutions have instigated a policy on the treatment of children with TS and have recognised that, due to its nature and complexity (manifesting a range of behaviours), 'record keeping with respect to children with TS is critical to a uniform approach' (Woods et al., 2008).

It is also crucial that teachers recognise that the behaviours shown by children and young people with TS are involuntary and that they are usually concentrating hard on trying to suppress or mask their tics, and that review meetings begin at an early stage. Many parents are already traumatised by the impact of TS on their children's lives and may have other siblings in the spectrum. A sympathetic approach at review meetings will address any rift in understanding and set the scene for mutual acceptance. It is particularly critical that substitute teachers or teachers who are new to the child are given a full briefing and speak to the child, their carers and families before making any assumptions about the child's behaviour.

One parent said:

> Once we had spoken to the head and the teaching staff about their having training on Tourette syndrome in the school, they went ahead with a programme of awareness raising and it brought a lot more support and understanding for our son.

Including the facts about TS in the training for in-service days and raising awareness of the condition will assist in the management of the condition and in an appreciation of what the child has to endure. Creating the right environment and engendering understanding from all who encounter the child while at school are essential to help them attain a good education and to do well in their future life.

Case study

Connor, aged 11, was missing school because he was unhappy with the classroom setting. He couldn't concentrate and his teacher was excluding him for 'disruptive behaviour'. Connor's mother knew his TS traits and had explained his condition to his peers and his teachers, so was mystified when he suddenly stopped going to school. It transpired that, as Connor moved up a class, his new teacher didn't comprehend his condition and had been punishing Connor for bad behaviour. Connor and his mother, fearing long-term exclusion, asked to meet with all his teachers to come up with a management plan. It was evident from this that Connor's TS was of a complexity that wasn't within the knowledge base of the school at that time. After this was recognised it was noted that his OCD and his sensory deprivation were major triggers for his main tics. He was moved near the door in class and allowed 'time out' if his tics built up. A safe place was made for him to go to. All his teachers were made aware, and he was asked to do a special class about his TS traits. He started back at school and, feeling safer, he ticced less during class because he didn't have to think about constantly suppressing his urge to tic and, consequently, his concentration levels went up.

Discussion points

In response to children whose behaviour is attributable to TS traits, the practitioner might seek out the support and help of self-help organisations, such as Tourette Scotland, Tourette Support Ireland or Tourettes Action (UK). They can provide skills sets, toolkits and up-to-date research, plus some management techniques. The practitioner could use their knowledge of the family, who are acutely aware of what the condition is like for their child at all times, to devise a joint plan that suits all.

Summary

- This chapter has identified the traits that make up the condition of TS, which can be more complex and integrated with other spectrum conditions than may be evident to those who have not come across the condition previously.
- Discussions with the person living with the condition and their carers can give an insight into how it feels to live with the condition.
- Children, in particular, are at risk of low attainment, exclusion and isolation at a time when they need to be given better chances.
- The interventions described here are known to be effective and can be developed further by the practitioner.

Further reading

Carroll, A. and Robertson, M. (2000) *Tourette Syndrome – A Practical Guide for Teachers, Parents and Carers*. London: David Fulton.

Cavanna, A. and Robertson, M. (2008) *Tourette Syndrome: The Facts*. New York: Oxford University Press.

Cohen, B. and Wysocky, L. (2005) *Front of the Class – How Tourette Syndrome Made Me the Teacher I Never Had*. Acton, MA: VanderWyk and Burnham.

Fabulous Films (1989) *John's Not Mad* (DVD, www.fabulousfilms.co.uk): A documentary on John Davidson and his experience of growing up with TS.

Kutscher, M.L. et al. (2005) *Kids in the Syndrome: Mix of ADHD, LD, Asperger's, Tourette's, Bipolar, and More! The One Stop Guide for Parents, Teachers, and Other Professionals*. London: Jessica Kingsley.

McKinlay, B.D. (2007) *Nix the Tics*. Calgary: Freelance Communications.

Woods, D. et al. (2008a) *Managing Tourette Syndrome: A Behavioral Intervention for Children and Adults (Therapist Guide)*. New York: Oxford University Press.

Woods, D. et al. (2008b) *Managing Tourette Syndrome: A Parent's Guide*. New York: Oxford University Press.

Recent publications

Buffolano, S. (2012) *Coping with Tourette Syndrome: A Workbook for Kids with Tic Disorders*. Oakland, CA: New Harbinger.
This professional edition includes both the *Instant Help* book and a companion CD that offers the complete book and printable worksheets for your clients. Tics are a fact of life for kids with TS and related disorders. And for most kids, the symptoms of their disorder aren't even the most frustrating part – others' reactions can make children feel anxious and extremely self-conscious. This practical workbook includes 40 activities to help kids with TS, OCD, or ADHD understand, prepare for and mask their tics. Kids will also learn how to best explain their tics to friends and curious strangers using humour, games, or brief scripts they have prepared. The activities in *Coping with Tourette Syndrome* address managing TS and related disorders in specific situations, such as at school, at the movies, when out to dinner, on special occasions, when visiting friends for sleepovers or parties, when taking tests, and in places of worship. After completing these exercises, kids with TS will have all the tools they need to handle their tics with confidence and grace in any situation.

Walkup, J.T., Mink, J.W. and McNaught, K. (2012) *A Family's Guide to Tourette Syndrome*. Bloomington, IN: iUniverse.
Providing authoritative and up-to-date medical and scientific information about TS, *A Family's Guide to Tourette Syndrome* speaks to patients, families, care providers, academic institutions, and medical centres in easy-to-understand language about this neurodevelopmental disorder that affects children, adolescents, and adults worldwide. Each chapter is authored by leading neurologists, psychiatrists, psychologists, scientists, and others with expertise and research interests in TS.

Howard, T. (2015) *The Keeper*. London: Harper Collins.
In this inspiring, down-to-earth memoir, the revered goalkeeper and American icon idolised by millions worldwide for his dependability, daring and humility recounts his rise to stardom at the 2014 World Cup, the psychological and professional challenges he has faced, and the enduring faith that has sustained him.

In *The Keeper*, the man who electrified the world with his amazing performance in Brazil does something he would never do on a soccer field: he drops his guard. As fiercely protective about his privacy as he is guarding the goal on the field, Howard

(Continued)

(Continued)

opens up for the first time about how a hyperactive kid from New Jersey with Tourette's syndrome defied the odds to become one of the world's premier goalkeepers.

The Keeper recalls his childhood, being raised by a single mother who instilled in him a love of sports and a devout Christian faith that helped him cope when he was diagnosed with Tourette's in the fifth grade. He looks back over his fifteen-year professional career – from becoming the youngest player to win Major League Soccer Goalkeeper of the Year to his storied move to the English Premier League with Manchester United and his current team, Liverpool's Everton, to becoming an overnight star after his record-making performance with the United States Men's National Team. He also talks about the things closest to his heart – the importance of family and the Christian beliefs that guide him.

Told in his thoughtful and articulate voice, *The Keeper* is an illuminating look at a remarkable man who is an inspirational role model for all of us. *The Keeper* is illustrated with two eight-page colour photo inserts.

Williams, M.E. (ed.) (2012) *Tourette Syndrome*. Detroit and London: Greenhaven Press and Cengage Gale.
This edited book can also provide a good introduction to TS.

Useful websites

www.goodschoolsguide.co.uk/special-educational-needs.

www.nhs.uk/conditions/Tourette-syndrome.

www.patient.co.uk.

www.tourettes-action.org.uk.

www.tourettescotland.org.

References

Cavanna, A. and Robertson, M. (2008) *Tourette Syndrome: The Facts*. New York: Oxford University Press.

Davidson, J. (2010) 'The Boy Can't Help It': BBC Films and Tourette Scotland web interview. From: www.tourettescotland.org/information/johninterview.aspx (Accessed 5 May 2015).

Woods, D. et al. (2008) *Managing Tourette Syndrome: A Behavioral Intervention for Children and Adults (Therapist Guide)*. New York: Oxford University Press.

PART IV
Working Together

The Role and Perspectives of Practitioner Educational Psychologists

20

Kevin Woods

Learning objectives

This chapter will help readers to:

- Understand the origins and development of the role of the practitioner Educational Psychologist (EP)[1] in relation to Special Educational Needs (SEN)
- Appreciate current contributions by EPs to the education, development and well-being of children and young people with SEN across different settings
- Consider issues shaping the future development of the EP's role

---

[1]The term 'practitioner educational psychologist' indicates those professionals statutorily registered with the UK Health and Care Professions Council as 'practitioner psychologists' in the 'educational' division and thereby being the sole persons eligible to identify themselves to members of the public as practitioner educational psychologists. The term is comparable to that of 'school psychologist' within the USA, where the term 'educational psychologist' most commonly refers to an academic psychologist who researches within the field of education and pedagogy (Jimerson and Oakland, 2007).

Origins and development of the practitioner educational psychologist role

It has often been acknowledged that what an EP does may not be entirely clear to those who have not worked within, or closely alongside, the profession (Frederickson and Miller, 2008; Fallon et al., 2010). Possible reasons for this lack of clarity are returned to in the final section of this chapter, but the imperative here is to outline what EPs do and how that role has developed. Squires and Farrell (2007) identify two public concerns which prompted the appointment of the first EP by London County Council in 1913. First, the need to place children appropriately within the available educational provision, which then included newly emerging special schools; this task was previously carried out by medical officers lacking in the necessary psychological and educational knowledge. Second, the need to address concerns from school teachers about children showing social, emotional or behavioural difficulties, who were not achieving their academic potential. By the early 1920s, several other local authorities had also employed EPs to assist with these two functions, with further appointments supported by the proliferation of 'child guidance clinics' which were established to help understand and prevent juvenile misbehaviour (Wooldridge, 1994). Further stimulation to the growth of the profession of educational psychology arose from:

- The 1944 Education Act's stipulation that local education authorities[2] provide suitable education for children who were deemed 'subnormal', 'maladjusted' or 'physically handi-capped', which required expansion of capacity to understand the needs of children who appeared to be developing differently
- The 1968 Department for Education and Science (DfES) Summerfield Report which recommended that there should be a publicly appointed EP for every 10,000 school-age children
- The 1981 and 1996 Education Acts, which laid down responsibilities of local education authorities for the processes of assessment and monitoring of children's SEN. These Acts necessitated increases in local authority capacity to support school staff in their provision for SEN and required local authorities to seek in complex cases formal advice on a child's SEN from an EP

Most recent data show that there are 3946 registered EPs in the UK (HPC, 2011).

Although the historical background may seem remote from the detail and context of present-day descriptions of the EP's role (cf. Norwich, 2000a, 2000b; SEED, 2002; Stobie, 2002a, 2002b; Farrell et al., 2006), it can be seen that the historical overview on the

[2]In England and Wales, the terms 'local education authority', 'local authority' or 'Children's Services' encompasses the state mandated and funded education service (at county, borough, district or city level).

functional development of the role provides a clear and relevant insight into *what* EPs fundamentally do (i.e. their broad institutional function, cf. Rowan and Miskel, 1999) which is:

- provide, more or less formally, expert assessment of children's and young people's needs and link this to patterns of educational provision and placement (summative function/ role)
- actively support the development of provisions for children and young people that are appropriate to their needs and which improve outcomes for them (formative function/role)

The historical view also locates the origins of practitioner educational psychology within areas currently identified with SEN (i.e. learning difficulties; physical difficulties; social, emotional and behavioural difficulties), though the role has now expanded to include a wide range of groups of vulnerable or marginalised children and young people who may receive input from Children's Services (Farrell et al., 2006; Woods, 2014a). Notably, Frederickson and Miller (2008) highlight the relevance of the historical perspective on the EP's role by identifying similarities between the role of the first appointed EP and the role as defined by local authority educational psychology services in the twenty-first century.

More recently, administration in England relating to children and young people's SEN and disabilities has come under the governance of the Children and Families Act 2014 (HMG, 2014), the ramifications of which for the work of EPs remain to be seen. Anecdotal evidence, however, suggests an initial increase in demand for the services of EPs as a result of these legal changes: first, as a result of administrative requirements to review previous statements of SEN and to convert where appropriate to Education, Care and Health (ECH) plans; second, following from the local authority requirement to plan for young peoples' special educational provision up to the age of 25.

With the core institutional functions of the EP role identified, it is interesting to consider why, in particular, it is a professional *psychologist* that is employed to fulfil these institutional functions; indeed, the distinctive contribution of the EP has been frequently debated (Norwich, 2000b; Ashton and Roberts, 2006; Cameron, 2006; Farrell et al., 2006). However, arguing that the issue of distinctive contribution is a judgement more for the service user (e.g. local authority) rather than the service provider, Fallon et al. (2010) provide a useful elaboration upon the EP's role with the following definition:

> what EPs actually do appears to have been reasonably clearly articulated: EPs are fundamentally scientist practitioners who utilise, for the benefit of children and young people, psychological skills, knowledge and understanding through the functions of consultation, assessment, intervention, research and training, at organisational, group and individual level across educational, care and community settings, with a variety of role partners. (p. 4)

The notion of scientist practitioners drawing upon and applying knowledge and skills from the discipline of psychology has developed as a central and remarkably simple response to current conceptualisations of the EP's role and contribution (Lane and Corrie, 2006; Frederickson and Miller, 2008). From this perspective it can be seen how, one could, in the same terms, query the distinctive contribution of a professional teacher to education, of a professional social worker to safeguarding children, or of a medic to health care, since the functions of all of these professionals could be replaced, *to some degree*, by a worker not qualified in the particular applied discipline.

Table 20.1 Summary of undergraduate curriculum for training as a practitioner educational psychologist

Biological psychology	*Individual differences*
to include:	to include:
• biological bases of behaviour	• psychological testing
• hormones and behaviour	• personality
• behavioural genetics	• intelligence
• neuro-imaging	• cognitive style
• neuropsychology	• emotion
• socio-biology	• motivation
• evolutionary psychology	• mood
	• mental health (including social, biological and cognitive processes)
Cognitive psychology	• gender and ethnicity
to include:	
• attention, learning	*Social psychology*
• perception	to include:
• memory	• social cognition
• thinking	• attribution
• language	• attitudes
• consciousness	• group processes and intergroup relations
• cognitive neuropsychology	• close relationships
	• social constructionism
Developmental psychology	
to include:	*Conceptual and historical issues in psychology*
• childhood	to include:
• adolescence	• psychology as a science
• life-span development	• social and cultural construction of psychology
• development of attachment	• conceptual and historical paradigms and models
• social relations	• political and ethical issues
• cognitive and language development	
• social and cultural contexts of development	*Research methods*
	to include:
	• qualitative and quantitative methods
	• research design
	• statistical analyses
	• an empirical project

Source: BPS (2010)

Table 20.2 Summary of postgraduate curriculum for training as a practitioner educational psychologist

Core professional skills

to include how to:

- assess, formulate and intervene psychologically
- apply knowledge to different settings and situations
- demonstrate self-awareness as a reflective psychological practitioner
- think critically and be able to evaluate
- exercise duty of care to safeguard children
- maintain effective working relationships with role partners
- engage young people and their carers as active participants
- apply research evidence to practice
- self-organise effectively
- communicate psychological insights effectively
- have effective interpersonal, reporting and recording skills.

Practice of applied educational psychologists

to include how to:

- practise within psychological models and frameworks
- formulate interventions applying psychological knowledge and skills
- support national and local initiatives
- work at levels of the individual, family, organisation, local authority
- interpret assessment with respect to client needs and intervention possibilities
- apply therapeutic skills
- apply evidence-based practice including monitoring and review of outcomes
- act preventively to support psychological well-being
- work consultatively and within multidisciplinary groups.

Personal and professional standards and values

to include understanding how to:

- adhere to the British Psychological Society Code of Ethics and Conduct
- take account of differences and diversity upon life opportunities
- engage proactively and reflectively with continuing professional development and professional supervision
- work with autonomy within an awareness of the limits of one's own competence
- develop strategies to deal with the emotional and physical impact of the work

Application of evaluation, research and enquiry

to include skills to:

- plan and conduct high quality and ethical research, which is both critical and self-critical
- understand different philosophies of knowledge
- evaluate the effectiveness of interventions to inform evidence-based practice
- work with others in research activities and support local authorities in conducting high quality research

Source: BPS (2014a)

Interestingly, the route to developing the EP's professional skills set has changed relatively recently. Up until 2006, all EPs were psychology graduates, trained and experienced as teachers who had also completed a one-year master's programme in training in applied educational psychology. From 2007, the requirement for work as a schoolteacher was changed to experience of direct work with children and young people within educational, care or community settings, and the masters' programmes replaced by three-year full-time doctorate programmes in applied educational and child psychology (BPS, 2014a). This restructuring of initial professional training reflects a broadening of the EP's role beyond the education sector, towards service delivery across integrated Children's Services/Trusts, including social care or primary health care settings (Farrell et al., 2006; Fallon et al., 2010). Currently, the British Psychological Society (BPS) specifies the curricula for both undergraduate (Bachelors) and professional training (Doctorate) degrees undertaken by those who train to work as EPs (BPS, 2010, 2014a), which are summarised in Tables 20.1 and 20.2, respectively.

The respective curricula show a marked and complementary shift from 'pure' psychological knowledge and skills at the undergraduate level, to applied/contextualised psychological skills and understanding at the postgraduate level. In addition, the postgraduate training programme, which statutorily must be approved by the Health and Care Professions Council (HCPC), incorporates approximately 300 days of fieldwork practice, which is structured by specialist university-based academic/professional EPs, and supervised by trained fieldwork supervisor EPs within frontline psychological services. Commonly, entrants to postgraduate practitioner educational psychology training have at least two years' work experience in roles such as school teachers, teaching assistants, learning support assistants, assistant educational psychologists, assistant clinical psychologists or residential social workers. This combination of requirements for further/higher level study and targeted work experience means that even the most direct route to training as an EP would span eight years. Making comparisons to the much shorter initial professional training routes for other professional groups such as social workers and teachers, the question might be asked whether the EP's role requires this extent of initial training, and whether other models (e.g. apprenticeship) might be more economically feasible or attractive to potential entrants to the profession. As it stands however, the breadth and depth of training does provide to employers, schools and families, a very flexible, expert resource, which may ultimately be more cost efficient. For example, following a period of contraction within Children's Services since 2010, a range of specialist services might need to be rationalised. A single EP, who is trained to provide services across learning, behavioural, communication and physical/sensory domains of child development, can work at levels of individual child, whole school or a whole organisation, and in relation to both statutory and non-statutory functions (Farrell et al., 2006). From an organisational perspective, then, the EP can cover a range of work that might otherwise require several other specialist professionals (e.g. positive behaviour manager, learning support teacher, assessment officer), in much the same way as might a medical general practitioner within a health centre, and so the extensive initial professional training of an EP could be seen to represent relatively good value for money.

Having summarised what EPs do, and how they are prepared for that role, the next section of this chapter gives examples of how they carry out their work at different levels and in different settings.

EPs' contributions to the education, development and well-being of children and young people with SEN

Reviews of the role of the EP have identified the wide range of their professional activities at individual, group and organisational levels, which contribute to the education, development or well-being of children and young people (SEED, 2002; Farrell et al., 2006); each level is considered in the next sub-sections of this chapter. Notably, Woods et al. (2011) identify two further dimensions to the work of EPs:

- The reactive/preventive dimension
- The focus dimension, to indicate whether the work is aimed at universal, targeted or specialised levels[3] (cf. also Fallon et al., 2010)

Given the focus here upon SEN, work by EPs at targeted and specialised levels will be considered.

EP SEN work at individual level

Farrell et al. (2006) report the majority of EP work with SEN to be focused at the individual level, with almost half of this relating to children/young people's social, emotional or behavioural needs. Within the case examples cited, Farrell et al. (2006) clearly identify both the EP's summative and formative core functions:

> One educational psychologist provided a detailed account of the contribution she made to the assessment of a preschool child with complex learning difficulties and of how her key role in this process helped the child transfer to an appropriate school.

> The headteacher of a nursery school stated that the educational psychologist provides support to the staff in ensuring that the needs of the child are met. (p. 27)

In respect of the EP's supportive (formative) role, Ewing et al. (2014) report an action research evaluation project aimed at improving behavioural and emotional well-being. The intervention involved the use of non-directive play by school-based play workers with individual children and young people ranging in age from three to 14 years. Non-directive play therapy (sometimes known as child-centred play therapy) assumes that play is the core transactional medium for children and is therefore amenable to surfacing and working

---

[3]Service work at 'Universal level' aims to benefit all children without additional needs; work at 'Targeted level' aims to benefit children with additional needs; work at 'Specialised level' aims to benefit children with complex additional needs. Universal, Targeted and Specialised levels of intervention in the UK correspond to Core, Supplemental and Individual levels of intervention in the US.

through underlying issues and themes which may be relevant to emotional and behavioural development. During play, the therapist helps the child to externalise their perceptions of their experiences, themselves, others and the world using toys, helping the child to 'cognitively restructure' any thoughts, feelings and beliefs deemed to be unhelpful to the child. The educational psychology service in the project provided extensive non-directive play therapy training for several play workers whose main professional roles in school included teacher, nursery nurse, (higher level) teaching assistant, learning mentor and family liaison officer. Children exhibiting difficult behaviours or emotional problems, as identified by teacher ratings on a structured ratings scale, were referred by the school's SENCo for non-directive play intervention by the school-based trained professional. Using a structured evaluation questionnaire with teachers, parents and children, Ewing et al. (2014) found that the intervention was generally successful in improving children's prosocial behaviour and in reducing hyperactivity/inattention, emotional symptoms, conduct problems and peer problems. They identify the benefits of training school-based workers for this kind of effective individual intervention as it potentially reduces the time a child may wait for intervention, where there is a reliance upon resource-limited external agencies such as the Child and Adolescent Mental Health Service (CAMHS). In turn, timely intervention could reduce the possibility that a child's difficulties would intensify, as well as enabling CAMHS to focus on those clients with the greatest need.

Contrastingly, Nuttall and Woods (2013) responded to a local authority context where cases of entrenched school non-attendance had become problematic, by providing a retrospective investigation of two successful, highly specialised individual interventions with school-refusing adolescents. They identify factors underlying school refusal which may be considered as either 'pushing' children away from school, or 'pulling' them towards home, including bullying, separation anxiety, coping difficulties and difficulties with peer or teacher relationships. A range of possible intervention approaches have been indicated including cognitive behaviour therapy (CBT), pharmacotherapy and behavioural approaches, but, in the absence of conclusive evidence on which approach works best, there was a need to understand how such approaches might be successfully integrated within the context of a particular school and home environment. The authors gathered in-depth information from eight participants in each of the successful cases of school-refusal intervention including, the young person, the parent, teachers and other professionals such as an attendance officer or parent support advisor. They identified in each case the specific details of psychological support, family support and the role of professionals in bringing about improved school attendance. Psychologically, it was found that issues of safety, belonging, confidence, preparedness for learning and aspiration, needed to be addressed by providing positive experiences for the young person, positive feedback from school about the student's contribution to school, support for social interaction and development of self-awareness, and an active interest in the young person as a whole, not just as a 'school refusal problem'. For the family, it was important to provide easily available, positively perceived, regular contact with school and other professionals, even changing personnel where these requisites cannot be established. A positive and skilled key-worker relationship facilitated engagement with the network of professionals and the development of parenting skills and a whole family plan to support re-integration to school. Within the professional network for each child, early identification of need, intervention planning and review, celebrations of progress and communication between professionals were identified as important to the success of the intervention. Within the school setting, consistency of approach at different phases of the re-integration was highlighted, and across all aspects of intervention, persistence and resilience of the professionals was seen as a critical success factor since planned strategies did not always work first time and would need to be adapted. Providing direct information about legal sanctions for school non-attendance was viewed with some ambivalence, though some professionals see it as being useful at specific points where disengagement might have occurred. Nuttall and Woods (2013) draw together the detail of their findings into an 'ecological' model for school re-integration which offers multiple strategies at the levels of home, school and community to develop a child's sense of security, self-worth and aspiration as a basis for engagement with the re-integration process. They propose that such models, when based upon explanatory case studies, provide practice-based evidence from which other practitioners can understand the mechanism and context of successful intervention (Bower and Gilbody, 2010).

In respect of their summative role, EPs have had a central role in providing psychological advice for local authority statutory assessments of SEN for children and young people, as well as the related activities of reviews of local authority statements of SEN and SEN Tribunals in respect of individual children/young people (Woods, 2014a). Though the process of commissioning and involvement for EPs may change, this role will continue under new legislation which introduces EHC plans as the means of identifying and securing provisions for long-term and complex SEN (DfE/DoH, 2014; AEP, 2014). The Association of Educational Psychologists (AEP, 2009) provides guidance on the EP's role in preparing statutory advice to Children's Services authorities. In this guidance, the AEP (2009) outlines the inter-related purposes, nature, principles and core components of the EP's advice on a child's SEN (see summary in Table 20.3)

In addition, the AEP (2009) emphasises the EP's paramount duty of care to the child when making recommendations or giving advice to overcome barriers to learning. The child is the psychologist's client, whereas the local authority, as commissioner of the child assessment, is the psychologist's 'customer'. This duty of care to the child is placed above the EP's responsibilities to the local authority employer, and the psychologist's advice should therefore not be influenced by considerations such as local authority financial, or other, constraints. An important theme throughout the AEP (2009) guidance on psychological assessment is the adoption of an 'interactionist' paradigm, which runs counter to enduring positivist philosophies that assume the psychologist's assessment would aim to 'diagnose' what is 'wrong with' the child and recommend an appropriate 'treatment' plan (cf. Bronfenbrenner and Morris, 2006; Frederickson and Miller, 2008):

Table 20.3 Purpose, nature, principles and core components of the educational psychologist's statutory advice to Children's Services authorities

Purpose

- Define the educational and psychological barriers to learning faced by the child
- Advise the local authority about strategies that might help to overcome such barriers
- Ensure effective progression towards appropriate outcomes

Nature

- Find solutions to barriers or problems through hypothesis testing
- Determine the current state of affairs
- Formulate specific desired outcomes
- Generate possible intervention strategies
- Test out one or more intervention strategies through the proposed intervention
- Close links between assessment data and intervention

Principles

- Child's view gathered directly by the educational psychologist
- Communication and consultation with people who have frequent direct contact with the child
- Direct observation carried out by the educational psychologist
- Individual assessment carried out by the educational psychologist
- Discussion and collaboration with other professionals, e.g. speech therapists, paediatrician
- Evidence from intervention over a period of time

Core components

- Background to the case to include significant developmental, family or cultural factors and sources of information used in the assessment by the psychologist
- Description of the child to include physical, sensory, medical, cognitive, social, emotional, language functioning; child's feelings and attitudes; educational and psychological barriers faced by the child; outcomes of previous interventions
- Summary of objectives of future provision and the required strategies to include methods and approaches, organisational arrangements, support of professional groups, monitoring arrangements

Source: AEP (2009)

The focus of concern (the functioning of the child) should not be separated from the analysis of the interactions between the child and the context or environment (family, peers, teachers, classroom setting or community). (AEP, 2009: 5)

The Division of Educational and Child Psychology (DECP) of the British Psychological Society (BPS, 1999) also provides general guidelines on psychological assessment and extends the interactionist perspective towards social constructionist considerations of ethics, politics, personal values and equality of opportunity:

The purpose of the [psychological] assessment is to generate understanding of what is happening, who is concerned, why it is a problem and what can be done to make a difference to the situation. (p. 2)

Alongside the summative role assumed in local authority statutory SEN assessments, EPs often act as expert advisors to the courts, tribunals, other agencies, or groups, carrying out assessments of children/young people and sometimes their parents or carers (e.g. Carter Brown, 2015). In these assessments, which often involve children with some social, emotional, behavioural or learning needs, the EP receives a set of very specific questions ('instructions') with respect to the case of a particular child or children, and is required to form a psychological opinion on those questions to assist the court in reaching decisions on the issues under consideration (e.g. whether residential education placement is appropriate, whether developmental delay is likely to have been caused by parenting). This area of work is highly specialised, requiring additional training and supervision in legal processes and the presentation of psychological evidence in court.

EP SEN work at group level

Farrell et al. (2006) identified a wide range of EPs' successful work with groups of children, school staff and parents, including:

- Training for parents in the management of children's behaviour difficulties, autistic spectrum disorder, procedures and provision for SEN
- Training for school staff in the use of specialist techniques such as social stories, precision teaching, learning styles, challenging behaviour
- Groupwork with children/young people on anger management or cognitive behavioural problem solving
- Research in relation to targeted groups in school such as those with social and emotional learning needs or those who are looked after by the local authority

More recently, the Children's Workforce Development Council (CWDC, 2010) provides several examples of EPs' innovative and successful work with groups of children and professionals including:

- A project providing booster classes and support at home for targeted groups of nursery aged children who were finding it difficult to cope with the demands of nursery
- A support group for parents of children with autistic spectrum conditions

In addition, group-level work is also reported by EPs themselves (Burton, 2006; Apter et al., 2010; Ubha and Cahill, 2014). For example, Apter et al. (2010) sampled behavioural difficulties in class groups across the UK and found a positive correlation between student on-task behaviour and teacher verbal approval for desired social behaviour, suggesting that this teacher behaviour may to some extent mitigate social and behavioural difficulties. Ubha and Cahill (2014) report upon a 10-week school-based intervention with a group of five school children aged between seven and nine years, each identified as having insecure attachment styles. The intervention – known as the 'secure friendship group' – drew upon nurture group and therapeutic story writing techniques to provide a consistent session structure, facilitated by the psychologist and school learning support assistant. Post-intervention and follow-up evaluations showed some improvements in standardised measures of behavioural adjustment and self-esteem, whilst child interview and observational data suggested significant improvements in positive interaction and sense of belonging. Ubha and Cahill (2014) highlight the relevance of attachment theory as a basis for intervention to support children's learning and interaction, as well as the benefits of EPs working directly alongside school staff to plan, deliver and monitor group interventions.

Group Consultation

Ground Rules and Process

> The purpose of this group is to provide a supportive, non-judgemental forum where school staff and psychologists can discuss concerns and generate solutions.

These are our ground rules:

Confidentiality will be clarified and agreed at the beginning of each meeting
We are all responsible for the effective running of this group
We talk to and about people with compassion and respect
Everyone's contribution is equally valued
We all try to contribute creative ideas
We aim to be positive and encouraging
We all listen when someone is talking
We are mindful of time constraints

Mobile phones off please!

These are the Steps in Our Group Consultation Process:

	Person with Concern	Group	Time needed
Step1 The description	Outline concerns; say what you want from session	Listen and reflect Do not comment/ ask questions yet	6 mins
Step 2 The reflection	Listen and reflect	Ask questions, clarify, encourage, reflect	6 mins
Step 3 The key concern	Summarise main priorities	Listen and reflect	1–2 mins
Step 4 The brainstorm	Listen and reflect	Generate creative, supportive, positive solutions; share experiences	6 mins
Step 5 The preferred solution	Select preferred solutions and ask for clarity/support	Listen, reflect and clarify	2–4 mins
Step 6 The first steps	Tell us what first step you will take (within 3 days)	Listen, reflect and encourage	2–4 mins

Figure 20.1   Group consultation poster: ground rules and process. *Source*: Nugent et al. (2014)

Working with groups of teachers, including principals, class teachers and special resource teachers, Nugent et al. (2014) established consultation groups, in order to provide support for school-referred problems, 80% of which related to individual children, most commonly with emotional and behavioural difficulties, including some autistic spectrum disorders. The teacher consultation groups were set up in order to afford economies of scale, particularly where small schools were spread across large geographical areas. Following extensive academic and practice research, and a pilot project, the psychologists devised the group consultation session structure shown in Figure 20.1.

The psychologists provided training in the group consultation process for groups of teachers. Across 75 schools, between 10 and 12 school cluster groups were formed, each meeting approximately once per term, with evaluations showing strong indications for the capacity of the groups to: devise a feasible plan for the referred problem; offer opportunities to benefit from colleagues' experience and knowledge; contribute own professional knowledge; benefit from the expertise of the psychologist facilitating each group. Strategies suggested in relation to the range of referred concerns were very varied and included ideas for promoting parental involvement, social skills, social stories, praise and planned ignoring. The continued expansion of the psychologist-facilitated teacher consultation groups, which has occurred without any additional staff resourcing, is perhaps the strongest testimony to its perceived effectiveness and utility. The authors highlight considerations about the best timings for the group sessions as most teacher participants need to travel from other schools to the group meeting venue; group size is also a factor affecting the balance of opportunity to bring cases with the opportunity to contribute to possible strategies.

EP SEN work at organisational level

Work at an organisational level requires an understanding of organisational processes (Argyris, 1999; Stoker, 2000; Weick, 2001), and there are numerous examples of EPs working across organisations to improve outcomes for children and young people with SEN (e.g. Farrell et al., 2006; Hayes, et al., 2007; Woods et al., 2011; CWDC, 2010; Woods et al., 2013). For example, Woods et al. (2011) report four case studies of EPs who have developed provision for child protection and safeguarding across whole local authorities with particular reference to children with social and communication difficulties and those with significant disabilities. In each case, a specialist EP coordinated developments in policy, practice and training spanning several years. Features associated with the success of these organisational developments included the EP's knowledge of normal and different child development, understanding of the educational context and professional roles within it, and the ability to manage different groups of professionals and processes over a period of time. Farrell et al. (2006) made similar observations in relation to EPs' work at organisational level:

Typically EPs have a detailed knowledge of the range of resources that exists in and outside the local authority, the procedures that are needed in order for pupils to access these, and of the role and function of other professional groups who work in the local authority ... This knowledge is used to help agencies work together and to 'oil the wheels' of joint working and decision making. It also places EPs in an excellent position to work with others in identifying gaps in services for children and in the planning and evaluation of new initiatives. (p. 101)

Woods et al. (2013) draw upon and evaluate organisational theory in the process of developing and launching a local authority policy for dyslexia, gathering data from the policy project group, SENCos and the EP who led the project. This highlighted not only group facilitation skills, but also leadership and project management skills, of the lead psychologist. Closely monitoring the 'roll out' of the new dyslexia policy, the lead psychologist identified a gap in current pre-requisite knowledge and so a package of school-level training on professional practice for dyslexia was developed in order to support policy implementation. Woods et al. (2013) concluded that policy implementation needs to be closely balanced with an understanding of current knowledge and skills within the relevant practice context. If the policy is dissimilar to local practice, the balance between them cannot be struck and the policy will not significantly affect or develop practice. Consequently, policy implementation is necessarily a developmental process, one which requires monitoring and adjustment, and one which may require a different approach for different schools/ teachers at different points in time.

Having considered examples of EPs' SEN-related work at individual, group and organisational levels, the final section of this chapter briefly considers current issues within the future development of the EP role.

Future role of EPs in relation to SEN

Though the focus of the present chapter is upon EPs' roles in relation to children, young people and young adults with SEN, there is recognition of the considerable evidence of their contribution to education at universal level, leading to benefits across the school-age population (cf. Farrell et al., 2006; Cline, 2008; Miller, 2008b). For example, CWDC (2010) cites the example of an EP who ran meditation sessions in a primary school which were seen to have significant benefits to children's abilities to concentrate and learn. Similarly, Burton et al. (2010) report upon a participatory project in which classes of children from different schools were trained in research skills and then supported to develop research projects across their schools. Nonetheless, Farrell et al. (2006) acknowledge EPs' work to promote achievement and inclusion of children with SEN as being central to their role past and present. The passing of the Children and Families Act 2014 (HMG, 2014) and associated inception of EHC plans (DfE/DoH, 2014), will bring the challenge of responding to an extended client age range up to 25 years. Whilst a few educational psychology services have developed some services within the further and higher education sectors (e.g. Henry and Thatcher, 1994; EGS, 2014), the need and opportunity to extend a full range of services to the 16–25 age range is currently a source of intense debate and development within the profession for individual practitioners, services and training providers (UCL, 2014).

The profession of educational psychology continues to expand; in 2014 there was a 10% increase in central government funding to support training of new entrants to the profession and post vacancy levels in 2014 are high. It is surprising then that there have been perennial challenges in communicating the value and distinctive contribution of the EP's role within SEN (Farrell et al., 2006; Frederickson and Miller, 2008; Fallon et al., 2010). Baxter and Frederickson (2005) offer some insight to this problem by explaining that EPs work within a 'service business model', in which, they most often work for the benefit of children and young people through assessment, consultation and intervention planning, alongside or through other professionals or adults. Within the EP's service business model, Baxter and Frederickson (2005) highlight the challenge to EPs to evaluate clearly the effectiveness of their work in improving outcomes for children and young people, lest their contribution be obscured, or, worse still, negated. Though the issue of evaluating impact may be similarly challenging to other professional groups (e.g. health visitors, social workers), the evaluation of the impact of the EP's work may also be particularly crucial since the EP's work often necessarily involves 'soft' skills of interpersonal facilitation and empowerment, including the use of challenge, which build upon the capacities of the team around the child, but which may seem relatively invisible, intangible or counter-intuitive to others working on behalf of the child (Wood, 1998; Farrell et al., 2006; Frederickson and Miller, 2008; AEP/BPSDECP/NAPEP, 2009; Fallon et al., 2010). Accountability for the outcomes of EPs' work for children and young people became particularly significant since the beginning of an era of service 'commissioning', underpinned by a principle of providing 'value for money' (Fallon et al., 2010). However, with the acceleration of 'trading' of psychological services both from within and without local authority establishments, Woods (2014b, 2014c) observes the clear success of many psychological services, social enterprises and sole traders, in establishing flourishing customer bases in schools (e.g. EGS, 2014; OneEducation, 2014; Acorn, 2014; Catalyst Psychology, 2014). Though the reasons for this apparent paradox may be somewhat complex and inconspicuous, Woods (2014b) suggests that the 'need' for educational psychology services, vis-à-vis the functions they fulfil, may be clearer in direct experience of the circumstances that lead to it, rather than through retrospective or external evaluation.

Notably, such changes in the way in which psychological services are commissioned, has led to the development of highly distinctive, specialist services (e.g. assessments for special provisions, mediation services, work with children in care, training for social and emotional well-being), which in turn are more 'marketable' and less susceptible to being under-cut by a better/better-value provider (Fallon et al., 2010). It has also been noted that directly linking EPs to several individual commissioners, possibly for individual pieces of work, throws into sharp focus the EP's strong ethical responsibilities, including the aforementioned paramount duty of care to the child (BPS, 2014b; AEP, 2009). The conduct, ethics and performance of all EPs are statutorily regulated by the Health and Care Professions Council (HCPC, 2012) and EPs' initial professional training includes development of understanding about ethics within professional practice (see Table 20.2). Fourteen 'standards' set by the Health and Care Professions Council (HCPC, 2012) include the requirements to act 'in the best interests of service users' and 'with honesty and integrity'. Such standards are fundamental in those inevitable circumstances where there may be challenge to, or dissonance with, commissioners' views or expectations: for example, where a teacher's request for a specific assessment approach as part of commissioned work with a young person is deemed inappropriate by the EP; or where an EP's research to evaluate a commissioner's favoured intervention suggests that the intervention is relatively ineffective.

Furthermore, whilst EPs will act honestly and in the best interests of the service user, accepting that this could sometimes possibly affect the likelihood of future commissions of work, there may also be an issue relating to equality of access to EP services for children and young people, as some schools or settings might choose not to 'buy in' EP services which challenge preferred ways of working. It is suggested that although this may be challenging to some EP practitioners' notions of a public service ethic of equality of opportunity, this issue is essentially a political and personal one, rather than one relating to ethical professional practice (Wilson, 1994; BPS, 1999, 2014b).

Summary

EPs have two core institutional roles: a formative role in which they actively support the development of provisions for children and young people; and a summative role in which they link specialised assessments of children and young people to available provisions. Though EPs do work at a universal level, and with other groups of potentially vulnerable or marginalised children, work with children with SEN continues to be a significant part of their role.

EPs have completed extensive postgraduate training in applied psychological knowledge, understanding and skills, which complement their undergraduate psychology studies. Once qualified, EPs engage in a wide variety of work with, and on behalf of, children and young people with SEN at individual, group and organisational levels.

Challenges for the future development of the EP role are the development of a full range of services extending to children and young people aged up to 25, and the management of the possible transition to an increased variety of commissioners of their work.

Discussion points

- How does educational psychology assessment of special educational needs bring any additional value to that of good teacher assessment?
- To what extent can educational psychologists be viewed as 'experts' across a wide range of ages and types of special educational needs?
- With a broadening of the range of work for educational psychologists, how is their role different to that of clinical psychologists who work with children or younger adults?
- What dilemmas might arise for educational psychologists in advocating for the needs of the child within the demanding contexts within which schools operate? How might such dilemmas be approached?
- What specific challenges and opportunities might be presented to educational psychologists in developing their work with young adults in the 20–25 age range?

Further reading

Farrell, P., Woods, K., Lewis, S., Rooney, S., Squires, G. and O'Conner, M. (2006) *Function and Contribution of Educational Psychologists in Light of the 'Every Child Matters: Change for Children' Agenda*. London: DfES.

Based upon a comprehensive national survey of practice in 2006, this report remains a touchstone document for anyone wishing to learn more about the breadth of the educational psychologist's role, its core processes and how it is embedded within local authority Children's Services.

Useful websites

Association of Educational Psychologists: www.aep.org.uk.

The AEP represents over 90% of practising educational psychologists in the UK and its website provides an indication of the issues that currently concern educational psychologists

British Psychological Society: www.bps.org.uk.

Through its register of chartered psychologists, the BPS quality-assures educational psychologists and their training. Its website highlights the most relevant publications

(Continued)

(Continued)

and events in different areas of applied and academic psychology, as well as giving information on careers in psychology.

Health and Care Professions Council: www.hcpc-uk.org.

The HCPC is the organisation with statutory responsibility for overseeing the performance, conduct and ethics of all practitioner educational psychologists, as well as their initial and continuing professional development. Its website outlines all of the standards that educational psychologists are expected to develop and maintain, which educational psychologists are currently registered to practise, and how a client may make a complaint about an educational psychologist.

References

Acorn (2014) *Psychology and Support Services*. Available from: www.acornpsychology.co.uk (Accessed 31 October, 2014).

AEP (Association of Educational Psychologists) (2009) *Guidance to Educational Psychologists in Preparing Statutory Advice to Children's Services Authorities*. Durham: AEP.

AEP (Association of Educational Psychologists) (2014) *Implementation of New SEND Procedures*. From: www.aep.org.uk/members-home/latest-news-members/implementation-of-new-send-procedures-request-for-information-pl (Accessed 27 October 2014).

AEP/BPSDECP/NAPEP (Association of Educational Psychologists, British Psychological Society Division of Educational and Child Psychology and National Association of Principal Educational Psychologists) (2009) *The Evaluation of Educational Psychology Services in the Light of Outcomes for Children: A Report from a Joint Working Group*. Durham: AEP.

Apter, B., Arnold, C. and Swinson, J. (2010) A mass observation study of student and teacher behavior in British primary classrooms. *Educational Psychology in Practice*, 26(2): 151–72.

Argyris, C. (1999) *On Organisational Learning*. 2nd edn. Oxford: Blackwell Publishing.

Ashton, R. and Roberts, E. (2006) What is valuable and unique about the educational psychologist? *Educational Psychology in Practice*, 22(2): 111–24.

Baxter, J. and Frederickson, N. (2005) 'Every Child Matters': Can educational psychology contribute to radical reform? *Educational Psychology in Practice*, 21(2): 87–102.

Bower, P. and Gilbody, S. (2010) The current view of evidence-based practice. In M. Barkham, G. Hardy and J. Mellor-Clark (eds), *Developing and Delivering Practice-Based Evidence: A Guide for the Psychological Therapies*. London: John Wiley & Sons.

BPS (British Psychological Society, Division of Educational and Child Psychology (DECP) (1999) *Framework for Psychological Assessment and Intervention*. Leicester: British Psychological Society (DECP).

BPS (British Psychological Society) (2010) *Guidance for Undergraduate and Conversion Degree Programmes*. Leicester: British Psychological Society.

BPS (British Psychological Society) (2014a) *Standards for the Accreditation of Masters and Doctoral Programmes in Educational Psychology*. Leicester: British Psychological Society.

BPS (British Psychological Society) (2014b) *Ethical Trading: Guidelines for Educational Psychologists.* Leicester: British Psychological Society.

Brofenbrenner, U. and Morris, P.A. (2006) The bio-ecological model of human development. In R.M. Learner and W. Damon (eds), *Handbook of Child Psychology*, 6th edition, Volume 1: *Theoretical Models of Human Development.* Hoboken NJ: John Wiley, pp. 793–828.

Burton, D., Smith, M. and Woods, K. (2006) Working with teachers to promote children's participation through pupil-led research. *Educational Psychology in Practice*, 26(2): 91–104.

Burton, S. (2006) 'Over to you': Group work to help student avoid school exclusion, *Educational Psychology in Practice*, 22(3): 215–36.

Cameron, R.J. (2006) Educational psychology: the distinctive contribution. *Educational Psychology in Practice*, 22(4): 289–304.

Carter Brown Associates (2015) *The Expert Service.* Available from: www.carterbrownexperts.co.uk (Accessed 5 August, 2015).

Catalyst Psychology (2014) *Catalyst Psychology Social Enterprise.* Available from: www.catalystpsychology.co.uk (Accessed 31 October, 2014).

Cline, T. (2008) Effective communication in school: do teachers and students talk the same language? In N. Frederickson, A. Miller and T. Cline, *Educational Psychology.* London: Hodder Education.

CWDC (Children's Workforce Development Council) (2010) *Leading Change: Educational Psychologists Showcase Their Innovative Work.* Leeds: CWDC.

DfE/DoH (Department for Education/Department of Health) (2014) *Special Educational Needs and Disability Code of Practice: 0 to 25 Years.* London: DfE.

EGS (Educational Guidance Service) (2014) *The Educational Guidance Service.* Available from: www.egs.org.uk (Accessed 27 October, 2014).

Ewing, D.L., Monsen, J.J. and Kwoka, M. (2014) Behavioural and emotional well-being of children following non-directive play with school staff. *Educational Psychology in Practice*, 30(2): 192–203.

Fallon, K., Woods, K. and Rooney, S. (2010) A discussion of the developing role of educational psychologists within Children's Services. *Educational Psychology in Practice*, 26(1): 1–24.

Farrell, P., Woods, K., Lewis, S., Rooney, S., Squires, G. and O'Conner, M. (2006) *Function and Contribution of Educational Psychologists in light of the 'Every Child Matters: Change for Children' Agenda.* London: DfES.

Frederickson, N. and Miller, A. (2008) What do educational psychologists do? In N. Frederickson, A. Miller and T. Cline, *Educational Psychology.* London: Hodder Education.

Hayes, B., Hindle, S. and Withington, P. (2007) Strategies for developing positive behavior management: teacher behavior outcomes and attitudes to the change process. *Educational Psychology in Practice*, 23(2): 161–75.

HCPC (Health and Care Professions Council) (2012) *Standards of Conduct, Performance and Ethics.* London: Health Professions Council.

Henry, C. and Thatcher, J. (1994) Psychological service support for colleges of further and higher education. *Educational Psychology in Practice*, 9(4), 227–33.

HMG (2014) *Children and Families Act 2014.* London: HMSO.

HPC (Health Professions Council) (2011) *Profession and Modality Data – Practitioner Psychologists.* Personal email communication to the author, 23 February 2011. London: Health Professions Council.

Jimmerson, S.R. and Oakland, T. (2007) School psychology in the United States and England. In S.R. Jimmerson, T.D. Oakland and P.T. Farrell (eds), *The Handbook of International School Psychology*. London: Sage Publications.

Lane, D.A. and Corrie, S. (2006) *The Modern Scientist Practitioner: A Guide to Practice in Psychology*. Hove: Routledge.

Miller, A. (2008) Raising educational achievement: what can instructional psychology contribute? In N. Frederickson, A. Miller and T. Cline, *Educational Psychology*. London: Hodder Education.

Norwich, B. (2000a) *Education and Psychology in Interaction: Working with Uncertainty in Interconnected Fields*. London: Routledge.

Norwich, B. (2000b) Educational psychology and special educational needs: how they relate and where is the relationship going? *Educational and Child Psychology*, 17(2): 3–12.

Nugent, M., Jones, V., McElroy, D., Peelo, M., Thornton, T. and Tierney, T. (2014) Consulting with groups of teachers: evaluation of a pilot project in Ireland. *Educational Psychology in Practice*, 30(3): 255–71.

Nuttall, C. and Woods, K. (2013) Effective intervention for school refusal behaviour. *Educational Psychology in Practice*, 29(4): 347–66.

OneEducation (2014) *Educational Psychology Service*. Available from: www.oneeducation.co.uk/index.php/our-services/specialist-pupil-services/educational-psychology (Accessed 31 October 2014).

Rowan, B. and Miskel, C.G. (1999) Institutional theory and the study of educational organizations. In J. Murphy and K.S. Louis (eds), *Handbook of Research on Educational Administration*, 2nd edn. San Francisco: Jossey-Bass.

SEED (Scottish Executive Education Department) (2002) *Review of Provision of Educational Psychology Services in Scotland*. Edinburgh: SEED.

Squires, G. and Farrell, P. (2007) Educational psychology in England and Wales. In S.R. Jimmerson, T.D. Oakland and P.T. Farrell (eds), *The Handbook of International School Psychology*. London: Sage Publications.

Stobie, I. (2002a) Processes of change and continuity in educational psychology – Part 1. *Educational Psychology in Practice*, 18(3): 203–12.

Stobie, I. (2002b) Processes of change and continuity in educational psychology – Part 2. *Educational Psychology in Practice*, 18(3): 213–37.

Stoker, R. (2000) The sixth discipline of the learning organization – understanding the psychology of individual constructs and the organization (or PICTO). *Educational and Child Psychology*, 17(1): 76–85.

Ubha, N. and Cahill, S. (2014) Building secure attachments for primary school children: a mixed methods study. *Educational Psychology in Practice*, 30(3): 272–92.

UCL (University College London) (2014) Educational psychologists working for 16–25 year olds: what are the possibilities? Available from: www.ucl.ac.uk/educational-psychology/resources/leday_flyer_apr14.pdf (Accessed 27 October 2014).

Weick, K.E. (2001) *Making Sense of the Organisation*. Oxford: Blackwell Publishing.

Wilson, J.E. (1994) Is there a difference between professional and personal development for a practising psychologist? *Educational and Child Psychology*, 11(3): 70–83.

Wooldridge, A. (1994) *Measuring the Mind: Education and Psychology in England c.1860–c.1990*. Cambridge: Cambridge University Press.

Wood, A. (1998) OK then: what do EPs do? *Special Children*, May: 11–13.

Woods, K. (2014a) The preparation of practitioner educational psychologists in England. *International Journal of School and Educational Psychology*, 2(3): 198–204.

Woods, K. (2014b) The contribution of educational psychology to the rights of the child. Sarah Fielden Lecture, Manchester Institute of Education, University of Manchester, 26 November. Available at: www.seed.manchester.ac.uk/subjects/education/research/fielden-seminar-series/kevin-woods (Accessed 27 November 2014).

Woods, K. (2014c) 'In this together': Developing university–workplace partnerships in initial professional training for practitioner educational psychologists. In O. McNamara, J. Murray and M. Jones (eds), *Teacher Learning in the Workplace: Widening Perspectives on Practice and Policy. Part 2: Insights from Practice across Professions and Nations.* London: Springer, pp. 87–102.

Woods, K., Stothard, J., Lydon, J. and Reason, R. (2013) Developing policy and practice for dyslexia across a local authority: a case study of educational psychology practice at organisational level. *Educational Psychology in Practice*, 29(2): 180–96.

Woods, K., Bond, C., Tyldesley, K., Farrell, P. and Humphrey, N. (2011) The role of school psychology in child protection and safeguarding within the UK. *School Psychology International*, 32(4): 361–76.

Expert Evidence

21

Changes in the Law

John Friel

Learning objectives

This chapter will help readers to:

- Appreciate the legal context in relation to Special Educational Needs and Disabilities (SENDs)
- Understand the legal definitions of a learning difficulty and the appropriate provision, the rights of appeal and tribunals, and the implications of the Equality Act 2010, the Children and Families Act 2014 and case law
- Understand the role of the psychologist, definitions of independent expert witness and the rules of tribunals

The Children and Families Bill became law, on the 13 March 2014, bringing into force, the Special Educational Needs Provisions of the Children and Families Act as it has now become. It introduced, in place of a Statement of Special Educational Needs an Education

Health and Care plan, which is far more complex. In addition, statutory definition of Special Educational Provision has changed and is now much wider as a result of Section 21(5) of the 2014 Act.

Some new legal considerations now apply to the role of an expert psychologist. This is because the 2014 Children and Families Act is now law, as from September 2014.

The new system, which came into force in September 2014, involves phased introduction, until 2018. For older young persons, the new system has commenced. The 2014 Act applies to England. The Welsh Assembly is consulting on a similar system, but has not rushed to introduce it, quite sensibly. The law in Scotland and Ireland is separate. However, the issues for experts, particularly considering, child special educational needs and/or Equality Act issues remain essentially the same.

The 2014 Children and Families Act, includes changes to the law on Adoption, Youth Justice, and finally in relation to the law concerning children and young persons with special educational needs and disabilities. The new approach is that there should be a Health, Education and Care (EHC) plan, although in essence, the legal rights and duties, changed to a degree only, by certain amendments in Parliament, remain virtually exactly the same. There is one major change, namely extending the new EHC plan for young persons with special educational needs, up to the age of 25.

The idea of an EHC plan is not a bad idea, save for the fact that the law still places all the duty on education as before. It still places very little statutory responsibility on health and social care. The new Care Act 2014 may provide a greater incentive to care. The appeal rights which are set out below, are the same as before. There are no major changes in the appeal system. The Tribunal will still have jurisdiction over the education issues only. It is not possible to give clear guidance as to how far this will go forward, as all is new. The legal definition of educational provision has however increased somewhat.

1996 Act and all that

The earlier current legislation in relation to special educational needs can be found in the Education Act 1996 as amended. Until 2014, the most recent amendments were made in the Education and Inspection Acts 2006, which included in Section 13A a duty to promote high standards and the fulfilment of potential and includes:

* The duty on the local education authority to promote the fulfilment of every child concerned in its area, to his educational potential

The coalition Government initially produced a Green Paper in 2011. As a result, it set up a number of pilot schemes with local authorities. However, having issued the Green Paper, a White Paper was issued in September 2012, at the same time as the responsible Minister was dropped from the Government. The pilot schemes were in fact ignored. The White

Paper was then referred to the Education Select Committee. A number of concessions had been made in relation to this White Paper, before the report of the Select Committee, which advised, among other issues, the system should continue to preserve parental rights. The new law will affect the likely contents of a report by an educational psychologist, whether working for the local authority or in the independent sector.

A psychologist, in practical terms, is more likely to deal with children and young persons who for whatever reason, come to the attention of psychologists at about school age, or after entering school. For those who have disabilities which are significant or special educational needs which are plainly apparent at an early age, they are likely to be identified. This is because under the new education health plan system, there are increased responsibilities on children's services and local authorities, to identify these children as early as possible, and make provision for them. Thus, the intention of the EHC plan is for there to be joint intervention from health, education and social care, which for those with significant disabilities apparent from birth or picked up soon after, will mean they enter this system at a much earlier age than other children.

For those children whose problems are not so apparent at an early age, the new Code of Practice, July 2014, deals with identifying needs in school and replaces the old Code of Practice.

Under the old system and the new system, there remain two categories of children; they are:

1. First, those children who have special educational needs or a disability, who do not have an EHC plan
2. Second, children with an EHC plan

It is clear from the Department of Education guidance, Transitional and Saving provisions, published June 2014, that the law now is exactly the same as before as to entitlement to an EHC plan. This is also apparent from the statutory provisions. The Department's June 2014 guidance is very helpful on this issue.

The July 2014 Code of Practice provides an assessment process that requires the child's school to:

1. Assess
2. Plan
3. Do (i.e. take action and put in place provision)
4. Review the effectiveness of the intervention

The Code requires the class teacher working with the special educational needs coordinator to establish a clear analysis of the pupil's needs and advises that parental concern should be taken seriously. The assessment of the child should be regularly reviewed.

It is quite likely that psychologists, whether working for local authorities or independently for parents, will be asked to advise at the point when there is no statutory assessment for an EHC plan, in order to consider whether in fact the child's needs have been identified, whether the intervention is appropriate to meet needs and what should be done.

The Code of Practice and the Act itself make it clear that anyone can bring a child or young person who they believe have special educational needs, to the attention of a local authority. This includes early years providers, schools and colleges, together with health authorities, parents and any other interested person. It is therefore important for a psychologist to be aware of this fact. It is not relevant that the local authority has not in fact triggered the assessment, the key issue is whether the assessment is in hand or should be requested and carried out. The question will be, has the school to date identified the child's needs? The task looks at the effectiveness of the intervention, and should come to clear conclusions as to whether all the needs have been identified and whether the intervention is in fact effective.

The previous Code was far more helpful in looking at the issue of adequate progress.

Adequate progress

Currently the Code, July 2014, provides that adequate progress:

- Is similar to that of peers starting from the same baseline
- Matches or betters the child's previous rate of progress
- Closes the attainment gap between the child and their peers
- Prevents the attainment gap growing wider

However, the previous Code of Practice was basically very much better when advising as to the criteria to measure adequate progress. The fact that the current Code is less clear on the issue of adequate progress, means that a psychologist looking at a child's progress and whether it is adequate, would be well advised to keep in mind the earlier criteria. Although those criteria are no longer contained in the Code, they are still practical factual issues which should always be borne in mind and are as follows:

1. Adequate progress should ensure access to the full curriculum
2. Adequate progress should demonstrate an improvement in self-help or personal skills
3. Adequate progress should be likely to lead to appropriate accreditation
4. Adequate progress should be likely to lead to participation in further education and training and/or employment

The code itself has been revised already in 2015, although not in relation to adequate progress. There are a number of additional concerns about the content of the code, and these matters are being taken up with the Department of Education, currently. It remains to be seen whether the code will be further revised.

The test for an EHC plan

As this chapter is concerned not with a detailed analysis of law, but with the role of the psychologist, it is important not to get lost in a detailed discussion of case law. The test both in the 1996 Act and under Section 36(3) of the 2014 Act, is whether first of all, a statutory assessment is necessary; and secondly, whether after the assessment, it is necessary to make an EHC plan. The statutory provisions are in exactly the same form as before.

Case law, for a long period of time, made it clear that 'necessary' effectively means, really needed. It comes from the approach of Lord Keith in *Re An Enquiry under the Company Securities Act (Insider Dealing) Act 1985*, where necessary was defined as really needed. Most recently, the Upper Tribunal has considered the test. The Upper Tribunal replaced the High Court in education appeal cases. In *Buckinghamshire County Council v HW (SEN)* 2013 UKUT 0470 (ACC), the Upper Tribunal held that the test of necessity fell between the words 'really useful' and 'essential'.

It is also clear from earlier case law, see *R v Secretary of State Ex Parte E* 1997 2 FLR pg.377 Court of Appeal, firstly that the statutory provisions look at the whole child, and secondly, if the school without external advice, can meet the child or young person's needs, then a statement and now an EHC plan, is not necessary. However, it follows from the case law that if the school is not meeting and cannot meet such needs, then the EHC plan would be necessary.

Educational provision

Psychologists will normally be familiar with what is education and what is not. The courts have made the point that educational provision, and indeed the definition of education, is very much wider than simply teaching in a school.

However, Section 21(5) of the 2014 Act, provides as follows, and extends the definition of special educational provision:

> Health Care provision or Social Care provision which educates or trains a child or young person is to be treated as special educational provision (instead of health care provision or social care provision).

Thus, the area of what may be necessary to determine special educational provision, has undoubtedly been expanded. Under the previous case law, solely social care provision was not included, see *G v Wakefield* 1998 96 LGR 69 (QBD).

There can be and has been considerable debate as to what is educational provision. The Court of Appeal in *Bromley v The SENT* 1999 Education Law Reports pg.260 accepted that it could include many needs, some of which may be considered to be medical or practical care needs, which covers a wide spectrum of potential areas, but still fell within the definition of education. In *W v Leeds* 2005 ELR pg.617, the Court of Appeal pointed out that there was a general duty to approach these cases not as a separate department, but looking at the child's overall needs, whether or not they were classified as educational or purely social needs. In a later case, overall cost, i.e. health, education and care, was held to be relevant, *O v Lewisham* 2007 EWHC Admin.

It is relevant to refer to the case of *K v The London Borough of Hillingdon* 2011 UKUT 71 (ACC), the Upper Tribunal Judge Pearl made it clear that the duty on the local authority and the Tribunal in its place, was to look at the whole picture, i.e. consider overall, in complex cases of need, what was being done for the child and look at its effectiveness as well.

The 2014 Act and the 1996 Act presuppose that children with special needs but without a Statement will be educated in a mainstream school, and provide that parents of a child with an EHC plan can insist on a mainstream school unless the placement of a child in a mainstream school interferes with the provision of efficient education for other children. The law does not take into account the efficient use of resources in such circumstances.

Section 33 of the 2014 Act requires that a local authority must secure, where a child has an EHC plan, that the child or young person is educated in a mainstream school or a mainstream post-16 institution, unless that is incompatible with:

(a) The wishes of the child or young person's parent; or
(b) The provision of efficient education for others.

There was considerable case law previously under Section 316 and 316A of the Education Act 1996 in relation to the right to insist on a mainstream school. Without considering the legal points in detail, the cases reported by the Courts have looked at instances where all the professional advice has been that the child needed to be in a special school and should not be in a mainstream school. Even if that is so, unless the child breaches the incapability test, namely the provision of efficient education for others within the school, irrespective of two factors, costs and meeting the needs, the child must be educated if the parents so request, in a mainstream school.

The statutory right to effectively veto special schools or alternative provision other than a mainstream school, undoubtedly will cause educational psychologists both professional concern and difficulty.

Psychologists need to remember that they should operate under their professional codes, and in considering their professional advice and opinion, they need to be frank and fair. A psychologist faced with such a situation will clearly have to consider whether the child's education will interfere with the education of other children within the whole school environment, not simply the classroom. But a psychologist will need to advise on the alternatives, namely the right professional option, which would probably be a special school in such a case, and what can be done to make a mainstream school as compatible as possible, where a mainstream school is insisted upon.

In the case of *Harrow Council v AM* 2013 UKUT 0157 (ACC), Judge Mark indicated that a statutory intent was that the local authority could not say (he was looking at complicated statutory provision) that – *It will educate a child in a mainstream school without providing for it.*

Thus, it looks pretty clear that the issue of those who strongly support integration, remains embedded or enshrined in the statutory provisions, so doing this does match advice and obligations created internationally, but it causes obvious practical difficulties, which will have to be borne in mind.

EHC plans

As already indicated, the test as to whether an EHC plan is necessary remains the same. Section 42 governs the duty to deliver special educational provision and health provision in accordance with EHC plans and provides in particular that the local authority must secure the special educational provision for a child or young person.

EHC plans must still specify the special educational provision and now other provisions, as did statements of special educational needs before them. There is a clear duty of continuing to be specific, see *L v Clarke & Somerset County Council* 1998 ELR pg.129. The form and content of an EHC plan are now contained in the 2014 Special Educational Needs and Disability Regulations, Statutory Instrument No. 1350. Regulation 12 requires the plan to include the following:

(A) The views interests and aspirations of the child or young person;
(B) The child or young person's special educational needs (Section B of the plan, no change);
(C) The child or young person's health (this is new and if it is an educational need, it needs to also go into Sections A, B and C);
(D) The child or young person's social care needs which relate to their special educational needs and disability (Section D, this is new);
(E) The outcome sought for him and her (Section E, no change here, as currently there are objectives);
(F) The special educational provision required by the child or young person (Section F, no change, but experts need to be aware of the expansion of the definition of special educational provision which now covers some health care (it did so previously, but has been extended) and some social care (this is an extension);
(G) Any health care provision reasonably required by the learning difficulty and disabilities which result in a child or young person having special educational needs (Section G, this is new);
(H) This is the social care provision and is divided into two sections, H1 and H2;

(I) The school, maintained school or post-16 institution or type of school or institution; and

(J) Direct payments if applicable (Section J is new).

Major change

The most major change, apart from the introduction of EHC plans, is the definition of special educational provision in Section 21(5). Basically special educational provision includes:

- Health care provision, which educates or trains, or social care provision, which educates and trains. This should be borne in mind for the purposes of all expert reports

The new definition needs to be considered.

Rights of appeal

Parents have a continued right of appeal to the Tribunal under the statutory provisions as set out above where:

- the council refuses to assess a child's needs
- the council refuses to make an EHC plan following an assessment
- against the contents of a plan
- where the parents seeks a change of a particular type of school
- in relation to the decision to cease to maintain a plan
- following an annual review of a plan

As a result of the President's Practice Direction given in 1994, the Tribunal looks at the child's needs at the date of the hearing, whether they have improved, or not, and on the basis of the information available to the Tribunal at the date of the hearing, not at an earlier date.

Equality Act

This area is not affected by the new law. The Disability Discrimination Act 1995, now, as a result of amendments made in 2001, has entered the area of education. The Equality Act 2010 has extended that duty. It imposes a duty on the responsible body not to discriminate against the disabled person:

- in arrangements made for determining admission to a school as a pupil
- in the terms on which a pupil is admitted
- by refusing to accept an application
- in a very important provision generally, namely the provision of education or associated services offered to or provided to a pupil
- as an additional duty to ensure that pupils are not substantially disadvantaged
- in the duty to make reasonable adjustments for disabled pupils

The responsible body is normally the school or institution but can, where there are residential duties or joint responsibility, be the local education authority.

As the earlier Code of Practice on Disability Discrimination points out, children with special educational needs will often be disabled, but won't necessarily be disabled as defined under the Act. However, a recent decision by the Employment Appeal Tribunal, which has the equivalent status to the High Court, has certainly widened the prospective scope of what is thought to be a disability, where it found that a senior police officer who required concessions in exams, fell within the definition of disability. The Equality Act now increases the duties on schools and local authorities.

The twin concepts of disability and disabled persons are central to the operation of disability discrimination law. This remains an issue under the Equality Act. Someone who can satisfy the definition of a disabled person within the meaning of the Act can enjoy the protection of its framework. The disabled person is defined as a person who has a disability. The person has a disability if he or she has a physical or mental impairment which has a substantial and long-term adverse effect on his or her ability to carry out normal day-to-day activities, see Schedule 1 to the Act. These provisions are supplemented in some areas by regulations.

The apparent intention of the Act was to create a commonsense definition of disability and avoid vagueness. In general, issues that arise under the Equality Act 2010 in Disability Discrimination fall to be determined eventually by a Tribunal or an employer or an institution in education as follows:

- Does the claimant have an impairment?
- Does the impairment have an adverse effect on the ability to carry out normal day-to-day activities?
- Is the adverse effect substantial?
- Is the adverse effect long term?

(Where somebody is overcoming a disability, they are also protected for a certain period under the Act).

The issue of Disability was more rigidly defined but has been amended by the Equality Act 2010. In 2005, it was earlier amended to be less rigid and not dependent on for example,

World Health Organisation definitions or alternatively ICD-10 criteria. It should be remembered the World Health Organisation in its 1980 clarification of impairment, disability and handicap, defined impairment as *any loss or abnormality of psychological, physiological or anatomical structure or function.*

In relation to the Act, it gives guidance on carrying out day-to-day activities, it refers to impairments in the following:

* Mobility
* Manual dexterity
* Physical coordination
* Continence
* Ability to lift, carry or otherwise move everyday objects
* Speech hearing or eyesight
* Memory or ability to concentrate, learn or understand
* Perception of the risk of physical danger

However, a disability which includes a tendency to commit criminal actions or similar conduct is excluded. This covers the excluded criminal act but may not cover a manifestation of a disability which is associated with the criminal act.

It is also clear that it is the effect on the particular person and not people generally, that matters. In *Goodwin v The Patent Office* 1999 IRLR pg.4, the Employment Appeal Tribunal pointed out that the Act was concerned with an impairment on a person's ability to carry out activities. The fact that that person could carry out such activities does not mean that his ability to carry them out has not been impaired. It is not the doing of the act which is the focus of attention, but the ability to do it or not do the act. The focus of the act is on what cannot be done or what can only be done with difficulty rather than what can generally be done by the person.

In *Paterson v The Commissioner of the Police for the Metropolis* Employment Appeal Tribunal, in dealing with the definition of disability, the Employment Appeal Tribunal made it much clearer as to what was a disability. The court applied the European court case of *Chacon Navas v Eurest* 2007 All ER (EC) 59, the decision of the European Court. In essence, although Mr Paterson's disability was described as mild, even by the psychologist, whose evidence was accepted, it was decided that he was clearly disabled. Carrying out an assessment or an examination was properly to be described as a normal day-to-day activity. The court pointed out that moreover, the act of reading and comprehension was itself a normal day–to=day activity. That gave meaning to day-to-day activities by also encompassing those which were relevant to participation in professional life. As the effect of a disability such as dyslexia might adversely affect promotion prospects, it hindered professional life. A proper basis for establishing a disadvantage was to compare the effect on the individual of the disability in how they carried out an activity with somebody who carried out the activity not suffering from the impairment. If the difference was more than the kind of difference one might expect, taking a cross-section of the population, then it would be substantial whether or not it was described as mild or medium, etc. Concessions in exams were enough.

It is a defence to show:

- That it was not known the person was disabled.
- That the responsible body could not reasonably be expected to know the person was disabled.
- That the failure to take a step was attributable to the lack of knowledge.
- That the actions taken were justified.
- That the act itself complained of is excluded. This will be a rare defence.

Reference should be made to the Codes of Practice issued by the General Human Rights Commission.

Involvement of psychologists

In relation to special educational needs or Equality Act cases, psychologists or education experts working for local authorities or other similar bodies will generally be involved in:

- Providing reports prior to or on the initial assessment or at some later stage when the case is being re-assessed for the purpose of deciding whether a Statement should be made or not.
- Following up on such reports and advising the school generally by regular visits where appropriate.
- When an appeal is taking place providing an initial report, or colleagues having left and not been involved, looking at the case overall, and the state of the case generally once an appeal has been lodged and all information exchanged after the Case Statement period – see below.
- Providing independent reports for an appeal which is being contemplated by parents, looking at the child's needs, progress and the effectiveness of provision and advising on the aspects of the case.
- Looking at, from either side, the proposed schools and the frame of the proposed provision, i.e. special units and some other provision away from the school.
- Providing reports on the above (all or some of).
- Sometimes commenting on evidence used as part of an appeal which has produced a new view or a new light on the case.
- Sometimes EPs and not clinical psychologists give evidence in Family Law cases.

Those providing reports in pure education cases and giving evidence should remember that the statutory test is generally what is appropriate and to be added to that is probably (although the courts have not yet worked this out), what is appropriate to the child's potential? Thus, the fact that the parents do not agree with the support in place, is not on its own a reason why the EHC plan or support and the provision proposed or used is not working. There must be hard evidence as to why a particular Statement or a particular provision is not effective.

Issues for psychologist's expert evidence

In an article by Professor Ireland (2008), she outlines the whole situation from the point of view of a psychologist in an extremely cogent manner.

Local authority psychologists will be asked principally to provide reports, which may be used in the Special Educational Needs and Disability Tribunal, but more rarely in the Family Court. The Special Educational Needs and Disability Tribunal (SENDIST) is now part of an overall tribunal service. This has been a reform affecting all tribunals in England and Wales in particular, and makes them much more formal than they were before.

As a result, the Tribunal requires the same approach as an expert witness is required to use in other jurisdictions. And in those circumstances, whether the expert witness is acting as an independent expert or is acting as defined, at least initially, by Ireland as a professional witness (i.e. a witness employed by a particular party) the Tribunal will expect the same standard of competence as shown and required in the Civil Procedure Rules.

The Civil Procedure Rules are now in essence adopted in the Tribunal, as its rules and practice direction are very similar. The recent practice direction for experts is on the same footing. In a Family Court, expert evidence is more restricted. It should be noted that Legal Aid is now very restricted. In the SENDIST there is limited Legal Aid in certain cases. The idea of a single expert or an imposed expert in that sense, has been dropped in the Tribunal, due to the fact it is only the local authority that can be guaranteed to have employed psychologists and has access to other experts, and that will mean that the process is one-sided and therefore technically unfair. Thus, the SENDIST process remains less court-like and will remain less court-like.

An important issue, not in fact referred to by Jane Ireland, is that the expert witness, as required by the Civil Procedure Rules, should at the end of the report, set out a short statement signed by the expert, demonstrating they appreciate that they owe a duty to the court or the Tribunal in this case, and they understand that that is their duty. In other words, their report is not one-sided and slanted (see Civil Procedure Rules).

In particular, Jane Ireland's warning that experts should stay within their area of expertise and defer to other professionals if needed, is an important part of her advice.

The difference between an independent expert witness and a professional witness is not so clear in the Special Needs and Disability Tribunal which normally treats them the same.

The main distinction of a professional witness whose from an expert witness is to the fact that they are employed by a represented party and are therefore not independently instructed.

In court proceedings, professional witnesses are technically there to give factual evidence but this does not apply in the SENDIST.

Further, the SENDIST proceedings are far less formal than the court. There is not the same emphasis on examination in chief and cross-examination as explained by Jane Ireland. However, the formality of such proceedings varies enormously. These Tribunal proceedings are informal, but some can appear more like a court. Nevertheless, the Tribunal itself is expert, and can and does ask a number of very searching questions indeed. The fact that it is not a court does not mean that the competence and expertise of the Tribunal and those before it should be under-estimated.

Tribunal procedure rules – the system – further assessments/further reports

The system contains rules which mean that the Tribunal can order the assessment of a child. This is because they consider one party can be given adequate access to the child or that some exceptional reason arises.

The Tribunal and its practice directions do use the Family Court considerations which are different. The case law in the Family Court, and the rules, only allow the examination of a child in certain circumstances. There must be a specific reason to do so, rather than simply somebody hasn't seen the child, and somebody has left the employment of the authority.

However, children who are competent and old enough to make a decision, can themselves object and refuse. And if they are competent to make a decision, they can also choose to limit experts' access or testing. It is therefore not quite so simple as the Tribunal making an order. Further, there can be detailed legal argument on this issue.

If there is a specific reason to request a further assessment, it should be clearly defined and set out, and what is intended to be done, outlined. It should also be remembered, that the fact that the particular party to the proceedings wants an assessment, and a psychologist agrees to carry it out, may not comply with the professional duties of the psychologist as recognised by the Health Professionals Council. Once orders are made to impose assessments, and the assessment is carried out in a manner that the parents object to, this could result in complaints.

The parents can be put under pressure and may raise professional issues. They may consider the imposed assessment of their child, without as they see it, any good reason or to assist an authority to do something against which they object, is likely to result in the professional themselves facing professional difficulties due to a complaint. Obviously this will depend on the commitment of the parents and their own feelings and reactions, but this is a new rule, and it hasn't been thought out nor has its effects been thought out.

Issues for all experts

1. All experts will need to consider the new system of assessment within the school and whether there has been adequate progress.
2. There is no reason why the old definition of adequate progress should be ignored and it may well come back in the final version of the Code of Practice. It remains good guidance.
3. All experts will have to consider the extended definition of special educational provision.
4. All experts will also have to consider wider issues particularly when advising waking day/extended day issues.
5. All experts will have to consider the format of the EHC plan, if a plan exists; if it does not exist and there is a need for an assessment, the requirements are the same as now, but it becomes even more important with the new complex form of EHC plan, to be clear about what is and what is not educational provision.

As a result of the amendment to Section 21(5) certain issues, such as having a specialist epilepsy nurse on site would now no longer be medical, but could now very probably be education or training related. There seems to be absolutely no reason why a consistency of approach in care, which is put forward as an alternative to a waking day curriculum, is now no longer social care, but is also educational. Very careful attention will therefore have to be given to any proposals about a consistency of approach. The general format of consistency of approach in caretoday is to make general statements rather than specific individual provision by social care to support the family. If consistency of approach can be established as an educational provision within the new definition, it therefore becomes something that must be specific, and quantified, and not just theoretically available.

The Tribunal system

The Tribunal system is only explained in very brief detail here, as this is not a legal textbook:

1. There is a rapid appeal; it must normally be made within two months.
2. It expects but does not require, expert evidence to be given on behalf of the parties.
3. It will expect the authority to justify its position and explain it, both in a written response and before the Tribunal.
4. The Tribunal will manage the case, which will include giving directions. Those directions may include suggestions that children are assessed. However, it may not be thought to be a good idea by either one or both parties, and directions proposed should be subject to serious consideration and thought.
5. The Tribunal will expect some form of case statement and a working document to be produced and worked on by both parties. The case statement will be individual to the parties; the working document will be required in good time, namely two weeks before the hearing, at least.
6. Hearings are possibly more complex, as more witnesses are available to give evidence, than under the previous system, which limited the witnesses.

Mediation

The only difference between the old appeal system and the new system is the requirement for mediation or to obtain a certificate within three days from the mediator, stating that the parents or young person do not wish mediation. It is basically completely unbelievable that such a certificate will be supplied within three days of the request. However, the regulations governing Tribunal practice and procedure contain a regulation which allows the appeal to progress in circumstances where the Tribunal on a case management hearing, has given permission for the case to progress. Mediation could, of course, be very relevant where the appeal is not about education, but is about solely social care or solely health. Mediation may be of relevance and help there.

Firstly, mediation is highly unlikely to resolve very costly re-placements, indeed most local authorities at present will simply not agree to such a placement in any cases. Secondly, mediation will not resolve a case which involves a legal issue. Mediators are not there to determine the law. Thirdly, mediation is not likely to be effective where local authorities are known not to be prepared to agree or settle cases.

Mediation therefore may be very limited and it should be remembered by experts advising parents that mediation itself may create another level of appeal, and another level of expense. Experts would not be expected to actually be attending or involved in mediation, and in a case where an expert does need to give evidence, basically it is wholly inappropriate.

Equality Act cases

Disability discrimination cases, under the Equality Act, although going to the Special Educational Needs and Disability Tribunal, often involve the questions:

1. Is there a disability?
2. Does it meet the requirements set out above for impairment or not?
3. What adjustments should be made or were made?
4. Was there justification for an action?

The psychologist giving evidence in such cases, may then be asked to consider whether the actions taken in a particular case are reasonable, in accordance with the teaching standards, or other professional standards affecting psychologists at the time. That issue is plainly raised by the Code of Practice on discrimination, the fact that you claim you don't know of the disability, if you should know, is not a defence. Thus, a psychologist may not be solely there to answer the question: is the child/young person disabled?

Further, the extent of questions in Equality Act disability discrimination cases is much more like an employment tribunal, and is likely to be more aggressive and more hands-on and less likely to be similar to a special educational needs case. If a psychologist is examining interventions, to consider whether they have been reasonable and professionally competent, this could well involve examining quite a substantial amount of records as well as witness statements. Where any report is provided, it will need to be a fairly carefully considered report.

CPR Statement of Truth

This is required for all experts, except local authority psychologists. The statement of truth reads as follows and is relevant both to cases in the Family Court, and other courts and tribunals.

Statement of Truth

I confirm that insofar as the facts stated in my report are within my own knowledge, I have made it clear which they are and I believe them to be true and the opinions I have expressed represent my true and complete professional opinion.

(Continued)

(Continued)

1. I believe the facts I have stated in this report are true and that the opinions I have expressed are correct.
2. I understand that my duty in providing written reports and in giving evidence, is to assist the Tribunal. This duty overrides any obligations to the party who has instructed or engaged me. I have complied with my duty.
3. I have done my best in preparing this report, to be accurate and complete. I have mentioned all matters which are required relevant to the opinions I have expressed.
4. I have drawn the attention of the Tribunal to all matters of which I am aware, which might adversely affect my opinion. Moreover, when I have had no personal knowledge, I have indicated a source of factual information.
5. I have not included anything in this report which has been suggested to me by anyone, including lawyers instructing me, without forming my own independent view of the matter.

At the time of signing the report, I consider it to be complete and accurate. I will notify those instructing me if, for any reason, I subsequently consider that the report requires any correction or qualification.

Signed

As will be noticed therefore, the requirements by the courts and tribunals, have significantly tightened up as regards expert evidence. Those working for local authorities do not normally provide a Statement of Truth. However, even now tribunals are currently ordering Statements of Truth for local authority employed psychologists. If evidence is given in the Family Court, then a Statement of Truth is most definitely required unless the psychologist gives evidence as a witness of fact.

Family Court/other proceedings

In relation to the Family Court or other proceedings, the Civil Procedure Rules plainly apply, and unless the particular case involves giving evidence solely about factual history and factual events, it will involve expert opinion and will require a Statement of Truth. In the Family Court, proceedings obviously involve cross-examination and examination in chief, and are far more formal.

Summary

Overall, educational psychologists are now far more likely to be involved on rare occasions in Family Court proceedings either for child protection or in relation to issues such as access to a child or residence orders. The most frequent involvement will be in relation to special educational needs and disability cases, or Equality Act cases.

Discussion points

- What do you think are the key differences between the 1996 Education Act and the 2014 Children and Families Act, and what implications does this have for children and young people with special needs?
- What problems arise from the definition of 'adequate progress' contained within the 2014 Code of Practice?
- How does a child's statutory right to be educated within a mainstream school affect the role of an education psychologist?

Further reading

Friel, J., Nettleton, M. and Friel, C. (2015) *Special Needs and Legal Entitlement*. London: Jessica Kingsley Publishers, p. 352.

Helping parents to understand the legal entitlements of their child, this book explains the new Education, Health and Care plans which have replaced the Statements of Special Educational Needs. It explains what an Education, Health and Care plan is, how assessments are carried out, and how annual reviews, amendments, rights of appeal and tribunals work in practice. It also includes help with 25 of the most common problems encountered, a discussion of relevant cases, extracts from the official published guidance issued, and a draft Reasons for Appeal.

Useful websites

www.justice.gov.uk/tribunals/send/rules-and-legislation.

Department of Education website for current Code of Practice: www.legislation.gov.uk/UKSI/2014/1530/made.

Bibliography

Friel, J (1995) *Children with Special Needs, Assessment Law and Practice*, 2nd edn. London: Jessica Kingsley.

Friel, J. and Hay, D. (1996) *Special Educational Needs and the Law*. London: Sweet & Maxwell.

Friel, J. and Nettleton, M. (2015) *Special Needs and Legal Entitlement*. London: Jessica Kingsley.

Ireland, J. (2008) Psychologist's witnesses: background and good practice in the delivery of evidence. *Education Psychologist in Practice*, 24(2): 115–27.

Ministry of Justice (2015) *The Civil Procedure Rules*. From: www.justice.gov.uk/courts/procedure-rules/civil.

Tribunals and Enquiries England and Wales (2008) The Tribunal Procedure (First-Tier Tribunal), (Health, Education and Social Care Chamber) Rules 2008.

Special Educational Needs

22

Parents' Perspectives

Gavin Reid, Lindsay Peer, Susan Strachan and Jo-Ann Page

Introduction by Gavin Reid

The field of Special Educational Needs (SEN) with the customary cycle of government legislation and new legislation can be confusing for professionals and at the same time it can induce a situation of high anxiety for parents. The contributors to this chapter are parents each with experiences in SEN with the accompanying challenges and anxieties to ensure that their child(ren) can do well at school and that their social, emotional and educational needs are met. This is not always easy and for different categories of special needs different challenges are evident. This of course means that although the strategies may have to be different, there are some common experiences and 'tips' that parents can pass on to others. The purpose of this chapter is to achieve that. The challenges some parents have experienced and how these have been dealt with can provide hope and encouragement to all parents. Many years ago, Gill Thomson (MBE), a leading force at the time representing the Dyslexia Association in Edinburgh and South-East Scotland, always told parents at meetings that being 'forewarned is being forearmed'. This was almost like a trademark comment for her and one that was always appreciated by the parents in the audience. Parents associations can be an excellent source of support – they are initiated by parents for parents and can be invaluable. In my experiences in speaking to and working with parents associations I have found this to be the case. Gill Thomson and I many years ago wrote and presented a paper at the British Dyslexia Association conference entitled from 'Pain to Power'. This characterised the journey the association had taken from its inception to one where they had the ear of parliament and were consulted on education matters. In many ways this laid the foundation for the position of strength and respect the organisation Dyslexia in Scotland enjoys today. The journey of the British Dyslexia Association is very similar and they today hold a very influential position in the UK in relation to education matters and are regularly consulted by government for advice.

The story has been very similar in other areas of special needs – such as in autistic spectrum disorders and Down syndrome. As a parent of a young man with autism I can appreciate the range of support that is currently available. Although such support was not readily available when my son was of school age it is reassuring to know that there is now a greater awareness of autism than ever before and that interventions are more thoroughly researched and promoted, and that much is being done to ensure that young people with autism now are rightly placed alongside their peer group in an inclusive educational and social environment (see Chapters 17 and 18). This of course takes a considerable commitment and a great deal of courage from parents to put their trust in the education system and to work collaboratively with others in the hope that their child will benefit both in the short and in the long run.

The long-term considerations are always uppermost in parents' minds and it is important that they obtain some reassurance on this as early as possible in their child's school career. It was reassuring as a parent to read in the January/February 2015 edition of *Scientific American Mind* an article by Jennifer Richler on new programmes which are helping to ease the transition to adulthood for people on the autistic spectrum (pp. 37–41). These programmes highlight key aspects such as self-awareness, different forms of communication, social skills and stress management to reduce any forms of anxiety these young adults may experience. It is heartening to read that calming strategies such as meditation, yoga and exercise routines are very much part of these programme as well as work experience.

The stories below provide examples of how parents have had to consider all angles in their child's education and social and emotional development. It is remarkable to consider that few choose to have a child with special needs, few have previous training in the area but *all* in a short time become experts in the area because of the need to ensure that their child's needs are met. It is important that all children and adults with special needs achieve their potential and become fulfilled and fulfilling adults, and can fully and actively participate in work and life in the community. Parents too need to share their experiences, and that is exactly the purpose of this chapter.

The examples commence with Lindsay Peer, (*most importantly*) *parent* of dyslexic children, formerly a teacher, a SENCo and the Education Director of the British Dyslexia Association; now an educational psychologist. She is passionate about early identification and provision, alongside the need to believe in the capabilities of our children and students, using their interests to help them achieve. Her children, now grown up, have allowed her to share, with their approval, their current situations in life. She describes this as going from frustration, and at times despair, to tremendous success. As a grandparent, she now waits to see …

Susan Strachan writes about her own family experiences with both her children. Like quite a number of parents Susan is also a professional very much involved in the field of special educational needs and this clearly brings additional insights to the situation, and this in turn helps others in the same situation who may not have the professional insights shared by Susan. Many of course turn their hand to working in this field when they realise the challenges faced by their child and also realise that they have gathered experiences that can prove invaluable in a professional as well as a parental capacity. I for one was in that situation and it was my experiences as a father of an autistic boy that motivated me to embark on a career within this field.

Susan's account is followed by a heart-warming story from Jo-Ann Page (see also Chapter 19) who writes about her own education and how her experiences have equipped her, and her husband, to provide a socially, emotionally and educationally rich environment for her children who are both dyslexic (one of whom also has dyscalculia). They have emphasised the positive as well as ensuring sound home–school links. This in itself is excellent guidance for all parents.

Dyslexia, glue ear and hyper-reactivity – a parent's perspective by Lindsay Peer

We give birth to our children, never dreaming that such bright, happy, smiling bundles of joy may grow up to experience difficulties in learning to such a degree that, despite love and support from home, they may develop low self-esteem, demotivation and lack of confidence, which, if not handled appropriately, may affect them for life. My 'children', now adults, some with children of their own, were all born with dyslexia to varying degrees – from mild to severe (Statemented) and all had 'glue ear' to the extent that they needed grommets surgically inserted. One became, as I have described in the literature, a child with 'hyper-reactivity'.

What is hyper-reactivity?

'Hyper-reactivity' is a term I have cultivated and used for some years now. It describes children who display hyperactive-type behaviours at school and yet are not hyperactive.

Medication (e.g. Ritalin) does not appear to work for them. Often parents of hyper-reactive children inform me that their children's behaviour is vastly improved during the school holidays. Their children are calmer, they sleep better and they are more confident; they are more likely to display their strengths rather than focus upon their weaknesses. As soon as the holidays draw to a close, however, tension increases and the hyperactive-type behaviours return.

It is undoubtedly the case that there are many children whose behaviour deteriorates when faced with significant challenges at school; this often worsens at secondary school when faced with large classes, changing rooms, numerous teachers and varying and increasing academic demands. While there are some who become passive and withdraw, there are others who 'act out' and become the class clown or become aggressive, angry and/or oversensitive. In time they often develop low self-esteem and become demotivated.

I have seen many hyper-reactive children whose hyperactivity disappears once they are placed at an appropriate school in small classes, with specialist teachers and, when needed, therapists. I am not suggesting that all children need to be placed in specialist schools; many do well in mainstream schooling. However, it is indeed the case that for those SEN children learning within an inclusive environment, their teachers need to be trained and well-resourced if the children are to have a chance of success at school – and ultimately in life. Provision is often sitting a child with a non-trained, kindly teaching assistant; this for many is insufficient.

Children with hyper-reactive behaviours are often highly aware of what is going on around them. They cannot keep up in class, find following instructions challenging and often struggle with their homework; many of them tell me that their teachers talk too fast for them to follow and then they get into trouble for not listening. They recognise that they are constantly in trouble and underachieving academically. They see that their peers who can, for example, handwrite neater or spell better than them, are gaining higher marks than they are – even though they may well have more knowledge; this is indeed very frustrating for them. It is important that their anxieties and frustrations are recognised for what they are, and that they receive the support and appropriate teaching that they require so that they make progress academically, socially and emotionally.

What is glue ear?

Many children are born with 'glue ear' (i.e. otitis media) which is an inflammation of the middle ear. In a healthy child, an area in the middle ear is filled with air allowing for the flow of sound; when a child has glue ear, it is partially or completely filled with a sticky fluid reducing the transmission of sound and resulting in fluctuating hearing. Due to the loss of good hearing at a young age, in some children it may result in a delay in the emergence of receptive or expressive language or both. Problems with processing the good-quality sounds necessary for auditory perception and speed of processing are common. It may also become a contributing factor to poor language and literacy development, listening comprehension, academic achievement, attention and concentration, and behavioural difficulties and/or other learning difficulties. It adversely affects the development of phonological awareness as is so common in dyslexia; it may also cause difficulties with balance, including problems such as travel sickness.

Identification of glue ear and/or dyslexia with their overlapping difficulties should be carried out as early as possible to ensure that language and learning are not hindered. A medical diagnosis when young may be seen as indicating a likelihood of language and/or learning difficulties, particularly if family members have difficulties in areas of reading, spelling, writing, speaking or mathematics. The prerequisites for learning (e.g. phonological, language, listening, memory and motor skills development) should be put in place to develop early learning skills as soon as possible. Schools should be informed whenever the child is experiencing fluctuating hearing loss so that they can take the necessary steps (Peer, 2005). For a small number of these children, the usual phonological-based literacy programmes do not work well as they cannot hear the sounds; for them, a morphological approach, such as that developed and used at Maple Hayes School in Lichfield is far more likely to be an effective way forward.

My children

I was informed by various professionals on several occasions not to expect too much from my children – which as a parent and a teacher at the time was totally unacceptable to me. I felt and still feel that there is no way that any child should do any less well than that of which they are capable, or become any less of a person than they can be. All children need the opportunity to grow and become successful, happy and secure young people; if at all possible, they need to have the chances in life to become independent and successful adults. As parents and teachers, we need to believe in them and help instil a passion for their interests. My children were the catalyst for my journey into the world of dyslexia; I am very proud of them all and will never forget their struggles along the way. So where are they now?

M – is a qualified dyslexia practitioner and Teacher of English as a Foreign Language to primary-aged children at a school in Germany; she is particularly interested in the development of language and communication. She is currently working towards her master's degree. In the return to studies she relived the fear of failure – particularly in written work and examinations. She has found it 'fun' finding strategies and skills to overcome this, which has both helped herself and her students. She is very passionate about the needs of children with specific learning difficulties; she has also worked with adults and children with severe learning disabilities. She works hard on building the self-esteem of learners whom she sees struggling. She has the ability to observe children's needs quickly and works closely with them and their parents. She offers effective guidance to teachers.

Y – the child I was once told would never learn to read and write – is now an architect and a Fellow of the Royal Society of Arts. He has the dyslexic gift of visualisation, art and design. He worked successfully with the world-renowned Czech architect, Jan Kaplicky, until his untimely death. He is currently an associate at Exploration Architecture collaborating with Michael Pawlyn, leading the field of biomimicry and its application in the architecture and design field. He has worked on a number of high-profile projects and is a passionate speaker in the field. As a volunteer, he has worked with cancer patients; he has raised money for the rebuilding of a town in Peru post-earthquake as well as for medical conditions.

D – achieved her first degree in psychology and her master's degree in animal welfare. With a passion for the care and welfare of animals, she wants to change the hearts and minds of those working with, researching on and designing policy on behalf of animals – who by definition cannot speak and legislate for themselves. She worked for World Animal Protection (formerly WSPA) within education, research and external relations for several years. She organised an e-petition on the Downing Street website to campaign against the fur trade and live skinning in particular. She has organised collections for the homeless, refugees and the poor. She is currently travelling and observing attitudes and behaviour towards animal and human welfare issues overseas, as she appreciates the connection between the two.

A – became Head Boy of a specialist dyslexia school. He has been a teacher of autistic children for several years; he has run a small party business for children. He is passionate about education and engaging children in learning that is meaningful to each individual. He has successfully taken the skills and strategies he learnt as a schoolboy into his work. He is a behaviour specialist and feels that his own experiences and frustrations in the academic process help him to relate to children who find education challenging.

Dyslexia – a parent's perspective by Susan Strachan

'I'm sorry Mum, but you know what my brain's like?!' Even at the age of six years, Zoe and myself (fortunate enough to be a health professional as well as her mother) knew that her brain didn't quite work in the way that it should. It was not so much her literacy abilities in those days, but her memory, frustration levels and attention that were the main problems. Having had severely disordered language as a child (where Zoe had difficulty producing correct sounds in sequence), there was always that worry that school might never be straightforward for her. In my career as an Additional Support Needs (ASN) practitioner I supported families of children with ASN and had insight into the challenges parents faced, but was amazed at just how hard many parents of kids with ASN, including myself, have to fight to get appropriate support for their child.

In Zoe's case, this meant not just moving primary school, but local authority to ensure that her learning issues were acknowledged and appropriately supported. This was following a learning support teacher from her first school, trying to explain that Zoe could not have dyslexia, as she had demonstrated some good, almost appropriate levels in some test areas. I appreciate that we have moved away from using discrepancies in learning abilities and avoid using one-off tests to definitively identify dyslexia, but there was no credit given to the fact that this young girl was bright and so could demonstrate appropriate levels but still have dyslexia. She had spent the first five years of her life fighting to make herself understood (due to her disordered language) and like so many young people with dyslexia, had developed quite effective coping strategies. For example, the first time a speech and language therapist came to the house to 'listen' to her language at two years, Zoe disappeared and promptly returned with a clock and saying 'bye bye'.

Similar to many ASNs, parental concerns can be disregarded, particularly if your child presents very differently between home and school or does not show any obvious behavioural signs of not coping. How many parents have I, as a young naïve professional, initially considered over-anxious, too sensitive or neurotic? Fate perhaps has an ironic way of teaching you life's lessons. Here I am now with both my children affected by the 'hidden disability' of dyslexia, with my son Adam's learning being affected more severely than my daughter's learning. The existence of dyslexia is still debated among professionals, possibly because using the term can still be frequently avoided. However, I would urge anyone who doubts the existence of dyslexia, a complex processing disorder, to come and spend some time in my home!

Sometimes the pathway to recognition of need for families can seem lengthy, the process of 'gathering' information from various sources before developing a comprehensive profile can feel protracted. Luckily for us, the dyslexic issues of both our children were identified early on, unlike some whose dyslexic issues may go unnoticed until exam time or when studying in further education institutions. These differences in identification of dyslexic issues highlight firstly how contextual dyslexia can be in relation to the demand of skills required and secondly the inconsistent identification processes and conflicting perceptions of dyslexia.

Like so many ASNs, diagnosis or identification of need often still relies on professional judgement and locally agreed interpretations. Several initiatives have been developed in Scotland to assist this potential postcode lottery. These include, the Scottish Government's agreed working definition, Education Scotland's Report (2014) recommendations and Dyslexia Learning Trail, the Addressing Dyslexia Toolkit now also aimed at supporting individuals and families as well as professionals, local-authority produced guidelines for dyslexia, and several other national legislative documents. Hopefully, they help to highlight that all good ASN practice includes involving parents, making good, consistent provision for individuals' needs, and teaching in a dyslexia-friendly way. Luckily, the schools our children attended have on the whole acknowledged the need for targeted, specific teaching and utilisation of their individual learning preferences to optimise their learning experiences.

Despite this I have heard of many families' fights to gain recognition of their children's needs, to have the term 'dyslexia' openly used and to gain access to already stretched support services. It is perhaps then no wonder that so many families of dyslexic children feel the need to seek privately funded assessments. We sought private assessment for our son, not because Adam's dyslexia had not been identified, but to both confirm his intellectual abilities and ensure that his school's staff had detailed information and advice from a dyslexia expert about his significant complexities. Perhaps when there is more global appreciation of 'dyslexia as a difference and not a disability' (Mackay, 2005; Eide, 2011) there will be more freedom to discuss the hidden aptitudes, personal strengths and perception of dyslexia more positively.

Acceptance in families of any ASN can be difficult and it is often extended family members (not experiencing it daily) who perhaps do not fully appreciate the continuum of issues and often frustrating presentation of dyslexia. It was only after showing my parents a video created by our dyslexia youth group (XdysleX), that they finally began to appreciate that our son's volatile emotions, poor memory and explosive outbursts were all part of this term dyslexia and that he was not a deliberately unruly seven-year-old. They now understand both our kids better and even though Zoe and Adam's dyslexic issues are quite different, my parents try to focus activities around each of their strengths and avidly praise their successes. A good friend who knows both our kids very well, commented (at the end of a joint family holiday) that she hadn't realised, even in a non-academic environment, just how challenging our life can still be, on a daily basis. She also admitted to not fully appreciating the extent that dyslexia affects their abilities to regulate their emotions, cope with stress and sometimes with social situations.

For my husband and I, it can sometimes be like 'walking on eggshells' to avoid moment-to-moment conflicts or reactive angry outbursts from our children. Using a stern voice can be perceived as shouting, highlighting forgotten items or enforcing boundaries can end in tears, and following up on homework can end in complete meltdowns. Obviously these presentations may be indicative of their age and do not necessarily reflect a universal presentation of dyslexia, but it does highlight the influence that dyslexic issues can have on an individual's personality. I know of many children and indeed adults who would cite experiences of problems 'fitting in', coping with relationships and the existence of other overlapping conditions such as attention deficit disorder, autism and several others mentioned in this book.

When faced with identification of dyslexia, it is often an immediate reaction to assume that professionals have all the answers and know how to deal with each individual with dyslexia. But as parents we often don't realise how much essential information and expertise we have – 'knowing' the child, not just the common clinical presentation of dyslexia. Unfortunately, this can often be an oversight of educational professionals, who do not utilise family knowledge of personal 'quirks', motivational interests and behavioural techniques used successfully at home.

Being a professional in an associated field does not provide you with *all* the answers either. Over the years, I have been concerned about not having the natural skills to teach my kids phonics, spelling rules and other learning techniques. As Gavin says, working in the field can give you additional professional insights and the motivation to develop your career in a certain direction, but it does not make you immune to uncertainty and the common feeling of sometimes not 'being able to see the wood for the trees'. Parents pushed to their toleration limits in trying to ensure their child's needs are being met, often have to 'grow' the confidence to take control, use legislation, fight for collaborative working and provide much of the detailed information to explain who their child is, highlighting their strengths, motivators and potential. Again we are perhaps more lucky than most, having had a proactive, supportive primary school that listens and accommodates for their issues. Our home–school communication was invaluable to assist joint planning and consistent working, which relies on a constant process of discussion, monitoring and joint decision-making.

Secondary school can be quite different though, often there are not the same systematic opportunities to regularly communicate with teaching staff (even with an 'open door' policy), and there are differences in teaching styles and that constant worry about your kids' processing abilities and whether appropriate support is available to help them keep up with increasingly challenging coursework. As they grow up, letting go and allowing them to learn by their choices and mistakes continues to be difficult to accept. Finding and accessing further education and career opportunities can bring additional complications and stressors for dyslexic young people. But like all parents we have the powerful advantage of unlimited motivation to ensure everything can be done to help our offspring's lives be as happy as they can be!

Our kids know that they are different, just like Zoe at six, Adam too has often commented on how he 'just can't help it!' (although we have to be careful that it's never used as an excuse for not trying!). Often they are reminded just how different they are by their peers as well. Both have had brief experiences of bullying first hand, resulting in detrimental effects on their confidence and self-worth. But for them it had more to do with 'feeling' different; where they struggled with keeping up in class, were reluctant to use a laptop in class, or to accept help from classroom support staff. Both our kids have always known that they have dyslexia, it has given them a 'reason' for having the learning issues and meant that they don't feel stupid – because they can blame it on their brain, wiring, genetics, whatever … ultimately it means it's not their fault.

In our family and regularly at our dyslexia youth club, we reinforce that being dyslexic is an integral part of who they are, just like the colour of their eyes, but go on to explain that it is not a static condition like some physical characteristics, but an ever-changing process, a way their brain prefers to learn, which can make some things tricky, but also results in strengths and other positives. This can definitely include unorthodox or creative thinking and 'out the box' problem solving. Both our kids are very creative and visual learners; resulting in Zoe's striking use of colours in her art and Adam's intrinsic desire to build things that interest him from any old junk! Accepting the term itself also gives them and many youths an identity; and with an awareness of famous dyslexics and their successful lives, they can also begin to feel positive about their own learning differences and potential!

It's taken our family a long time to consider dyslexia as having positives, particularly as it has resulted in severe learning barriers for our children. We have been through the 'trying to fix or cure it' stage (at a substantial cost!), realising that a cure doesn't exist. It has helped to see how successful many people with dyslexia can be, given the correct tools and self-confidence. Getting our kids adequate support, accommodation and safely through the education system relatively unscathed is always a worry. But it's encouraging to see that there are more organisations like oil companies, designers, engineers, etc., deliberately seeking to employ dyslexics for their natural creativity and atypical 'outside the box' thinking for employment.

Being a parent of dyslexic kids and the interaction I have had with many other families, has taught me more about working with families than any course or years of professional experience. Commonly, I have found that families go through a process, not just of emotional and psychological acceptance of their child's issues, but often a difficult road: identification/acknowledgment of needs, educational provision and accommodation, and last but certainly not least, ensuring they have adequate emotional support and confidence.

Points to consider as a parent:

- empower yourself with knowledge (about dyslexia and legislation) as it's the most powerful tool a parent can utilise
- develop effective communication/relationships with involved education staff and teach your son or daughter how to ask for/utilise help available, an empowering skill needed throughout life
- promote confidence, and emotional and psychological well-being; focus on your children's interests and strengths and, most importantly for them, believe in their own potential

It is only now, with my children growing into young adults, that I am realising how important it is for me as a parent to continue reinforcing that each day can be a challenge, there are ways to see the positives about their differences and dyslexic perspective on life, to find ways around potential learning barriers and, fundamentally, to help them have confidence and faith in who they are as individuals.

Dyslexia – Jo-Ann Page

My history

I often think back to my school days and recall the level of stress and anxiety that I felt associated with school. I think of the over-riding sense of frustration at trying very hard but not achieving what my peers could, and not being able to effectively advocate for myself with my teachers. Back then, learning disabilities such as dyslexia and dyscalculia were not widely recognised and children would often be labelled as 'dim' and 'lazy'. I regularly heard that I was a sweet girl but generally, 'just didn't get it'. My reading was slow and I had absolutely no idea what was being taught – in the maths class in particular – as I hadn't been able to learn many of the fundamental prerequisites.

I knew that I was struggling on my very first day at primary school when I found it difficult to recall anything that the teacher had said. The level of difficulty particularly hit me in secondary school: I remember struggling to stay focused and trying keeping my eyes open during class as waves of overwhelming tiredness would hit me when I was required to pay attention for long periods of time. I recall my geography teacher talking to me slowly and loudly but I was too scared to tell him that I wasn't deaf and that his approach wasn't helping me to understand the lesson. In German class the only words I learned were, 'Was is daß?' because all the teacher ever said to me was 'What is that?'. Needless to say, I left school without much of a formal education.

Many years later, I grasped the nettle and went to night school to try again to achieve a basic level of education. On my first day my literacy teacher asked me if I had been tested for dyslexia and my maths teacher asked me if I had been tested for dyscalculia. At the time I did not know what these were and I hadn't been tested for either, but as I went away and read up on them, it was like an epiphany as I realised that I had many of the symptoms that were described.

By my mid-twenties I had the realisation that I almost certainly had learning disabilities but it was not until I was in my forties that I was formerly diagnosed with both dyslexia and dyscalculia. When I re-read my school reports from primary and secondary school, with hindsight, there were many obvious signs from the teachers' comments in the reports that I had learning disabilities:

> Jo-Ann has worked hard, but as her exam result shows, she needs to organise her thoughts before she writes, and to punctuate her work carefully. She should learn spellings … Keep trying.

I was making at least as much effort as my peers and trying very hard but, in this example exhibited signs of disorganisation and inconsistent spelling which today may serve as triggers to an underlying, and undiagnosed, problem.

The following comments from my school report of 30 years ago should also today be red flags that there is something fundamental that is causing such an outcome:

> Jo-Ann finds the subject very difficult. Her presentation needs improving … always tries hard, but she has difficulty understanding the concepts involved. She must revise her work more thoroughly.

The additional comment, 'She also has to put extra effort in if she is to improve her standards. She needs to take more time and care over the presentation of her work' would simply serve to demotivate, demoralise and perhaps emotionally bruise a child who may well be working many times harder than their peers just to maintain their current level of performance.

'She is a very quiet girl and lacks confidence in oral work … She is a polite and pleasant girl' should also beg the question in everyone's mind – why? It seems almost negligent to simply write such comments in an end-of-year report and present this to a child's parents without any prior attempt at understanding the underlying reasons for this or attempting to do anything about it. Quite simply, this is admitting that nothing has been done and that the child has been failed: it is too late by the time it comes to parents' evening!

From my research back in my twenties, I also understood that with many learning disabilities one has a 50% chance of passing these disabilities onto one's children. Today I have two children of my own, both of whom have learning difficulties.

My children's histories

When my son was around two years old, I noticed unusual things about him, such as he would only move one arm when he was running and he would keep his other arm straight. By the time that he was three years old, he could not sit still for very long and this was particularly noticeable when he took part in a school assembly and he constantly performed 'roly-polies' on the stage while the other children were sitting and being attentive. During the last few weeks of foundation stage when he was five years old the teacher called me for a meeting to talk about the fact that my child couldn't recall phonic sounds or write his name like the other children. I quickly booked a test for him and he was subsequently diagnosed with dyslexia and dysgraphia. My husband and I have continued to have him tested every two years and now at 10 years old he has also just been additionally diagnosed as having dyscalculia.

I first noticed my daughter was having social difficulties at around four years old but at that time she was managing at school with no negative feedback from the teacher. However, when she was nine years old she began to fall behind in maths and science. My husband and I had her assessed and she received a diagnosis of dyslexia, dyscalculia and difficulties with auditory and visual processing.

Focus on the positive

I feel that it's very important for parents and teachers to focus on the positive things that the children can do well and to play to their strengths as this really builds their confidence and self-esteem. My son has become very accomplished with computer technology to the point where the teacher comments that he teaches her things. My daughter has been recognised as being gifted in music and theatre. It's also really important that the children themselves are aware of their strengths, as it is easy for a child at any age to feel different and isolated because of disabilities.

From a parental point of view, the first step begins with listening to your child and – crucially – advocating for them in school. I have heard my own children say many distressing things over the years, such as, 'another child marked my work and then made fun of my mistakes' or 'I was made to stand up today and tell the class my spelling score and explain why it was so low' or 'I was made to sit outside during maths for not paying attention'. I have literally hundreds of such anecdotes that emerge simply through a lack of understanding from the teaching staff.

Building teacher relationships

Whether a child is diagnosed or not, it is incredibly important to build a relationship with the teacher supporting them in school. At times this can be difficult – particularly in secondary school – where often more than 10 teachers are involved in the process of a single child's education. In this case it is most efficient to have a regular meeting with a key contact in learning support who can effectively coordinate and cascade information to other teachers and advocate for the child within the school.

Teachers themselves need to feel that they are supported in order to be able to support a child in the classroom. I now work very closely with teaching staff in schools in my professional capacity, and during teacher training very little is covered in terms of special education and behaviour.

Once a child has been diagnosed, the next step is to ensure that that they have an Individual Education Plan (IEP) put into effect; that regular meetings are held to discuss this and that you are invited to and attend these meetings. During such meetings it is important to ensure that the recommendations from the psychology report (diagnosis) are included in the IEP. It is vital that the IEP is not simply put together in order to tick an administrative box, but to ensure that it is appropriate, has support and buy-in, is adhered to and used as a working document within the classrooms.

It is also important to attend parent meetings as these can be used to address other areas of difficulty that your child might have or other behaviours that may arise.

Homework

There is a high level of need to keep homework achievable. When a child has to complete homework that they don't fully understand, then it effectively sets them up for failure. In addition to this, detention or being kept in at break if homework is not completed can add to a child's distress, embarrassment and anxiety. Homework needs to be set on *pre-mastered topics* to ensure the child has a high success rate in order to reinforce their learning and encourage their achievement.

Behaviour

Often children with learning difficulties will engage in some level of behaviour. If you are dealing with behaviour it is always advisable to have a school observation to be able to establish the function before any intervention is put in place.

Escape behaviour is common as children with learning difficulties often feel over-whelmed by the level, length and difficulty of a task. Escape behaviour can be very subtle, such as the need to continually sharpen a pencil or trips to the toilet or nurse. This is a sure sign that the child is not comfortable with the task in hand. In order to reduce escape behaviour it is important to reduce the level of the task, which reduces the need for escape behaviour to occur.

Anxiety

It is also important for teaching staff to build a level of trust with the child so that they know they are not going to be put into a position that increases their adrenaline and anxiety. Some of the causes of anxiety are, reading out loud to the class, reading in a group, spelling tests, other children marking their work, substitute teachers, presenting their work to the class, being asked on-the-spot questions when the child does not have their hand up, shouting, the teacher showing frustration when they have to re-explain tasks, memorising times tables, copying from the board and time pressure, amongst others.

Children may often yawn a lot in lessons and find it hard to stay focused. This is not due to a lack of sleep but rather the fact that their brains can be working considerably harder than other children's. As I have outlined above, school can cause anxiety and so a child will often be experiencing highs of adrenaline followed by a sudden 'crash' which can cause fluctuations in their energy levels.

Things to do to support

Teachers must be prepared to explain something a number of times before a child with learning disabilities may understand it. A lesson may need to be explained as a whole and then broken down into steps – rather than the other way around. General classroom instructions may need to be repeated if the child appears lost. The child should be encouraged to choose a suitable position to sit in, such as close to the front if they are a visual learner or from where they can hear if they are an auditory learner, and be given a hand-out rather than have to copy from a board. Substitute teachers should be made aware in advance of the children in the class who have disabilities. Technology, such as calculators, laptops and tablets should be used if there is a recommendation for this from a psychologist. The teacher should make themselves very approachable, in order to establish an understanding relationship so that a child will find it easy and not embarrassing to say when they do not understand a task.

Summary by Jo-Ann Page

Over the years, I have heard many quotes from children, not just my own; quotes such as, 'The teacher shouted at me and said I wasn't listening' or 'The teacher said I had to do it, but I told her that I didn't understand and she said I had to do it anyway.' My first response to comments such as these is that the teacher may not know why that would not be the correct approach.

Through working with children with special educational needs I have come across many situations like these. However, usually, once the teacher themselves has been supported these situations do not re-occur. It is fundamental to establish and build a relationship with your child's teacher and ensure that both the child and the teacher have the necessary support to enable a child to reach their full potential.

It should also be recognised that it is not easy to teach large numbers of children in a class and to ensure that every child's individual needs are met, especially when trying to distinguish between those with learning difficulties and those who exhibit similar behaviour for different reasons. Ultimately, most teachers are passionate and teach because they care and want to develop young minds.

Further reading

The Scottish Government agreed working definition (2009):

> Dyslexia can be described as a continuum of difficulties in learning to read, write and/or spell, which persist despite the provision of appropriate learning opportunities. These difficulties often do not reflect an individual's cognitive abilities and may not be typical of performance in other areas.

> The impact of dyslexia as a barrier to learning varies in degree according to the learning and teaching environment, as there are often associated difficulties such as:

- auditory and /or visual processing of language-based information
- phonological awareness
- oral language skills and reading fluency
- short-term and working memory
- sequencing and directionality
- number skills
- organisational ability

Motor skills and coordination may also be affected

www.scotland.gov.uk/Topics/Education/Schools/welfare/ASL/dyslexia

Addressing Dyslexia Toolkit: Government-funded website for professionals and people interested in dyslexia – www.addressingdyslexia.org.

For an introduction to dyslexia

Dyslexia Scotland (2011) *Dyslexia and Us: A Collection of Personal Stories*. Edinburgh: Edinburgh City Libraries.

Dyslexia Scotland information guides: www.dyslexiascotland.org.uk/links-and-resources.

Eide, B. and Eide, F. (2011) *The Dyslexic Advantage: Unlocking the Potential of the Dyslexic Brain*. New York: Hudson Street Press.

Moodie, S. (2004) *Dyslexia: A Teenager's Guide*. London: Ebury Press.

Reid, G. (2011) *Dyslexia: A Complete Guide for Parents and Those Who Help Them*. Chichester: Wiley.

The Big Picture: Rethinking Dyslexia (DVD, 2012), available from Amazon.

Video clips about dyslexia: www.dystalk.com/topics/1-dyslexia.

Xdyslex: The Dyslexia Experience (DVD, 2012), available from Dyslexia Scotland, Stirling.

For explaining dyslexia to young people

Dyslexia Scotland's list of famous dyslexics: www.dyslexiascotland.org.uk/sites/default/files/page_content/Famous%20People%20with%20Dyslexia_2.pdf.

Hultquist, A.M. (2008) *What is Dyslexia? A Book Explaining Dyslexia for Kids and Adults to Use Together*. London: Jessica Kingsley.

For strategies to support learners with dyslexia:

Mackay, N. (2006) *Removing Dyslexia as a Barrier to Achievement: The Dyslexia Friendly Schools Toolkit*. Wakefield: SEN Marketing.

Mackay, N. (2011) *Taking the Hell out of Homework: Tips and Techniques for Parents and Home Educators*. Wakefield: SEN Marketing.

Ostler, C. and Ward, F. (2012) *Advanced Study Skills: A Student's Survival Guide*. Wakefield: SEN Marketing.

Practical parent support: www.bdadyslexia.org.uk/parent/homework-tips.

Reid, G. and Green S. (2011) *100 Ideas for Supporting Pupils with Dyslexia*, 2nd edn. London: Continuum.

Teaching and secondary subject guides: www.supportingdyslexicpupils.org.uk.

Assessment arrangements

Exams:

- Joint Council for Qualifications: www.jcq.org.uk/exams-office/access-arrangements-and-special-consideration.
- www.sqa.org.uk/files_ccc/AA_AssessmentArrangementsExplained.pdf (Scotland).

Driving test: www.bdadyslexia.org.uk/dyslexic/learning-to-drive.

For training online:

- Parents and professionals – www.icepe.co.uk.
- Professionals) – www.cpdbytes.com.

(Continued)

(Continued)

For guides to legislation

Additional support needs: www.enquire.org.uk.

Education Scotland Report (2014): www.educationscotland.gov.uk/Images/Dyslexia ReportWeb_tcm4-837927.pdf.

Equality Act (2010): www.gov.uk/equality-act-2010-guidance.

Getting It Right for Every Child – GIRFEC (2012): www.scotland.gov.uk/Resource/ 0045/00458341.pdf.

Special Education Needs and Disability Code of Practice (2014): www.gov.uk/government/ publications/send-code-of-practice-0-to-25.

References

Education Scotland Report (2014) *Making Sense: Education for Children and Young People with Dyslexia in Scotland*. From: www.educationscotland.gov.uk/Images/DyslexiaReportWeb_tcm4-837927.pdf.

Eide, B. and Eide, F. (2011) *The Dyslexic Advantage: Unlocking the Potential of the Dyslexic Brain*. New York: Hudson Street Press.

Mackay, N. (2006) *Removing Dyslexia as a Barrier to Achievement: The Dyslexia Friendly Schools Toolkit*. Wakefield: SEN Marketing.

Peer, L. (2005) *Glue Ear*. London: David Fulton Publishers.

Richler, J. (2015) Autism grows up. *Scientific American Mind,* 26(1). From: www.scientificamerican.com/magazine/mind/2015/01-01/.

Glossary

Accommodation   Also referred to as focussing, this is the change in shape of the crystalline lens in the eye to become more convex and thus better able to bring a close object clearly into focus on the retina of the eye. It is considered at its most flexible in childhood and teens, most people in their mid to late forties notice a natural change over time, but in fact many children have reduced accommodation, too.

Assistive hearing technology   Equipment used to make spoken language accessible and comfortable for students with hearing loss. It includes digital programmable hearing aids, bone-anchored hearing aids, cochlear implants, hybrid cochlear implants and personal FM systems.

Convergence   The effort required to bring the two eyes more closely together in order that a near object is seen singly. If one holds a finger up in front of one's eyes while looking into the distance, it initially appears double until the correct degree of convergence is exerted.

Coprolalia   The involuntary use of obscenities and swear words. This only occurs in about 1 in 10 people with Tourette syndrome. Note: if this occurs, the person cannot help swearing, and it is not a reflection on their moral character or upbringing.

Disability   A personal attribute or trait that impairs normal everyday function.

Down syndrome   A genetic condition. John Langdon Down, medical superintendent at the Royal Earlswood Asylum in London, first described a group of persons sharing a common set of characteristics.

Echophenomena   Copying what others say and do.

Engram   Memorised motor patterns used to perform a movement or skills, which are stored in the motor area of the brain.

Evidence-based practice   Practices that have been shown through a number of high-quality research studies to have a positive impact on student learning outcomes.

Executive function   Makes up the higher-order cognitive processing responsible for metacognition and behaviour regulation and is closely related to family and school environments and practitioner instruction.

Graphophonic   Based on symbol (letter)/sound correspondences that help readers decode and understand text. Combination of phonic and graphic knowledge used in decoding text.

Near point stress   A term describing the mismatch between focusing and convergence when they are not easily and accurately working together at the target being looked at, most commonly a book or screen. It can cause eyestrain, fatigue, blurred vision and loss of concentration on the task.

Non-obscene socially inappropriate (NOSI) behaviours   Such as making inappropriate or rude personal comments.

Palilalia   Repeating your own last word or syllable after the end of a sentence.

Psycholinguistic   Relating to the psychology of language.

Pull-out support model   Specialist practitioner withdraws the student from the classroom for direct expert instruction purposes.

Push-in support model   Specialist practitioner working within the classroom performing a variety of roles, including team teaching with the classroom teacher, small group discussion with the child with hearing loss and hearing peers, and one-on-one intervention in a quiet area of the classroom.

Scaffolding   Refers to the idea that specialised instructional supports need to be in place in order to best facilitate learning when students are first introduced to a new subject. Scaffolding techniques can include displaying graphics, activating prior knowledge, modelling an activity beforehand, and introducing motivational techniques to stimulate student interest.

Screening   In education, this can indicate that difficulties are present and that specific help or intervention is required. It is not the same as assessment. Screening can often be done with groups rather than individually.

Socially constructed disability   Impairment of an individual's everyday function that stems more from barriers within the social environment than from that individual's personal attributes or traits.

Tracking   This term is commonly used to describe both the pursuit, or following eye movements employed when following a moving target, e.g. a ball flying through the air, as well as the saccadic or jump eye moments made as one reads across a line of text with a fixation on each word, or part of a word, and the saccadic movement in between. A fixation can be considered an eye movement in itself, but one of zero velocity, since it requires the complex balance between all six extra ocular muscles in each eye to keep the eyes looking at the same target together.

Transition   In relation to education, transition usually means moving from one stage, school or environment to another; and is most commonly used in relation to transition from primary to secondary school, and from secondary school to post-schooling options.

Trisomy 21   Approximately 95% of persons diagnosed with Down syndrome have an additional chromosome on chromosome 21.

Index

Page numbers are annotated as follows: 'f' figure; 'g' glossary entry; 't' table; 'n' note.